W9-BMQ-487

BY
HONOR
AND
RIGHT

Officer in the Uniform of a Captain of Artillery.
Used by permission of Michael Haynes, mhaynesart.com.

BY
HONOR
AND
RIGHT

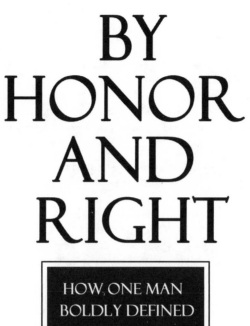

HOW, ONE MAN
BOLDLY DEFINED
THE DESTINY
OF A NATION

JOHN C. JACKSON

 **Prometheus Books**

59 John Glenn Drive
Amherst, New York 14228–2119

Published 2010 by Prometheus Books

By Honor and Right: How One Man Boldly Defined the Destiny of a Nation. Copyright © 2010 by John C. Jackson. All rights reserved. No part of this publication may be reproduced, stored in a retrieval system, or transmitted in any form or by any means, digital, electronic, mechanical, photocopying, recording, or otherwise, or conveyed via the Internet or a Web site without prior written permission of the publisher, except in the case of brief quotations embodied in critical articles and reviews.

Inquiries should be addressed to
Prometheus Books
59 John Glenn Drive
Amherst, New York 14228–2119
VOICE: 716–691–0133
FAX: 716–691–0137
WWW.PROMETHEUSBOOKS.COM

14 13 12 11 10   5 4 3 2 1

Library of Congress Cataloging-in-Publication Data

Jackson, John C., 1931–
    By honor and right : how one man boldly defined the destiny of a nation / by John C. Jackson.
        p. cm.
    Includes bibliographical references and index.
    ISBN 978–1–61614–219–3 (cloth : acid-free paper)
    1. McClallen, John, 1772–1808. 2. Explorers—West (U.S.)—Biography. 3. West (U.S.)—Discovery and exploration. 4. Northwest, Pacific—Discovery and exploration. 5. Overland journeys to the Pacific. 6. Soldiers—United States—Biography. 7. Businessmen—West (U.S.)—Biography. 8. Northwest, Pacific—Commerce—History—19th century. 9. Santa Fe (N.M.)—Commerce—History—19th century. I. Title.

F592.M33 J33 2010
978'.02092—dc22

2010022913

Printed in the United States of America on acid-free paper

CONTENTS

CONTENTS

FOREWORD

Prior to the publication of this book, John McClallen was little known and seldom mentioned. His fate remained a mystery even to members of his own family, and avid history buffs steeped in the lore of the American West likely had heard of him only in passing. John C. Jackson's meticulous research has rescued this obscure soldier, merchant, and adventurer from the shadows and placed him at center stage in the unfolding narrative of America's attempts to stake its claim to the North American continent's far western expanses. His gripping biography serves as a reminder that little-noticed individuals and their untold stories have the power to enrich the historical narrative and augment our understanding of the past.

In truth, McClallen's captivating story is of greater import than its subject. Circumstances not entirely of his own making doomed his ambitious plans, and his failings outnumbered his successes. Captain McClallen was a minor player in a grand drama, and it is that drama that makes this book so compelling. The twists and turns in McClallen's checkered career put him in contact with a host of nineteenth-century western luminaries including James Wilkinson, Meriwether Lewis, William Clark, Zebulon Pike, and David Thompson. The audacious American soldier turned entrepreneur attempted unsuccessfully to enter the Santa Fe trade, became the first US military officer to follow Lewis and Clark across the continental divide, tested William Clark's early geographical speculations, entered the Pacific Northwest via a more practical route, and sought to discourage British trading activity in the region. This is the stuff of high adventure, but sadly his actions went unnoticed and likely would have remained so had it not been for Jackson's determined historical sleuthing.

FOREWORD

By Honor and Right is important for the new details it discloses about early nineteenth-century machinations to control the far West and McClallen's interactions with various western historical icons. His relationship with Gen. James Wilkinson was especially significant, and Jackson's thoroughly researched account reveals for the first time the intent of their mysterious dealings and provides new clues about the controversial general's larger schemes and designs. Many will question if Wilkinson's motives were as benign as Jackson suggests, but they will welcome his careful explication of the links between Zebulon Pike's southwestern expedition and McClallen's failed attempt to open trade with Santa Fe. Equally significant are Jackson's confirmation that McClallen authored the mysterious 1807 letter signed by Zackary Perch and his suggestion that the specious document may have played some part in the resolution of the border dispute between Britain and the United States in 1846. Those findings alone are worth the price of admission and are sure to make this fine piece of historical detection a winner with aficionados of the American West.

William E. Foley

PREFACE

The cork came out of the inkbottle on July 10, 1807. After hunching over his field writing desk for hours and scribbling with a steel nib, the travel-worn writer leaned back, flexed his cramping hand, and considered what he had written. Years of dealing with the correspondence of an officer of artillery helped him formulate the document in the style and authority that it required. He had written a list of regulations to govern how business was to be conducted in the outer limits of the Louisiana Territory.

Composing ten regulations to govern the conduct of the Indian trade tested the author's understanding of an unfamiliar business and how the United States expected to exercise its authority over it. The first nine paragraphs were boilerplate, whatever was necessary to be convincing to intrusive foreigners. Sensing that was not enough, he added a tenth paragraph that opened a more expansive view. The author put the Montreal fur traders and by implication the British Empire on notice that the United States held indisputable right of discovery and occupation to the two great rivers of the interior continent, and all the lands where they drained. Using the rather all-inclusive address, "Fort Lewis, Yellow River, Columbia," he dated the document, "July 10th, 1807," and signed himself "Zackary Perch, Captain and Commanding Officer."

This was a declaration of the extension of United States sovereignty, not just to the bounds of Upper Louisiana Territory but across the Rocky Mountains to the Pacific slope. Less than a year after the return of the Corps of Discovery, it declared what Captain Lewis and Lieutenant Clark never dared to proclaim in their official capacity, or even President Thomas Jefferson. It was an audacious vision of a continental nation.

The challenge formulated by Captain Perch would be ephemeral. Private American trading adventures on the upper Missouri or lower Columbia River failed to take hold and allowed British traders to inherit the Pacific slope by default.

The United States claim relied on the discovery of the Columbia River by a Boston ship captain and the later exploration by Lewis and Clark. British pretensions depended on the scientific description of the lower river by Captain Vancouver, and the sources of the upper Columbia as filled in by the surveyor David Thompson. Sandwiched between the pages of an old post journal was a copy of the inconvenient document written by the enigmatic Captain Perch.

After 1818, the boundary dividing the northern plains along the 49th parallel of latitude stopped at the continental crest, and the disputed territory west of the mountains became known as the Oregon Country. Beginning in 1840, tides of defiantly pugnacious overland immigrants overwhelmed the British fur traders. With American politicians calling for a boundary set as far north as 54 degrees 40 minutes north latitude, British negotiators realized that it was past time to conclude a reasonable partition. Evidence to prove it took on new significance.

In 1845 the former surveyor and British trader David Thompson was an impoverished old man still devising a fanciful version of his crossing of the northern Rocky Mountains. Thompson's claim might have been advantageous to British diplomats until contradictory evidence resurfaced when Hudson's Bay Company clerks, scrambling to assemble evidence that British negotiators could use to support the imperial position, exhumed the long-forgotten Captain Perch.

The ghost that rose from the pages of an old writing book gathering dust on the shelves of Beaver House in London was the almost forgotten circular letter. A copy started up the chain of authority to the Crown's negotiators. Questions concerning the Oregon boundary were complex, and one letter was not going to tip the balance. But the document eroded diplomatic convictions and nudged a compromise forward. On June 15, 1846, the international boundary along 49 degrees north latitude was extended to the Pacific shore.

After that brief emergence, the fatal document slept for another 132 years until an American scholar, Robert Carlton Clark, went to

London to sort out the history of the boundary settlement. Clark came across documents in the Foreign Office referring to the confrontation between Thompson and the American officer. In 1927, when Clark published his finding in an appendix to his *History of the Willamette Valley Oregon*, he set off a history storm.

Western historians spent the next ten years trying to resolve the questions this enigmatic document raised. Those included the unquenchable curiosity of a gentle Episcopal clergyman named J. Neilson Barry, who spent a good part of his life trying to unravel the mystery of an unknown soldier's bearing on the earliest history of the Pacific slope. Barry published his version in the *Oregon Historical Quarterly*, which was answered in the next number by the Canadian surveyor J. B. Tyrrell. An admirer of his cartographic predecessor, Tyrrell had published David Thompson's *Narrative* in 1916. But Thompson made no reference to a confrontation with an American officer in his memoir.

Although the suggestion that someone blocked Thompson's expansion to the Pacific slope was decidedly inconvenient, Tyrrell obtained a copy of Captain Perch's trading regulations from the Hudson's Bay Company archives and published them in the December 1937 issue of the *Oregon Historical Quarterly*. But the identity of the author continued to torture historians.[1]

The record of western exploration and fur trade development seemed nailed by two indisputable documents written by a man who deliberately disguised his accomplishments. Two letters, preserved in British archives, were documentary fact, but what was it that brought the author to a unique place in western history? Reconstruction of the career and activities of John McClallen require seeking out and consulting many kinds of direct or peripheral sources. Providing a coherent picture of his life and adventures required pulling many disparate pieces together from many diverse and sometime oblique sources and weaving them into a comprehensible narrative. That story weaves through the lives of other people; personal agendas; corporate and mercantile objects; local, regional, national, and international politics—with all the aspirations and intrigues that a good detective story and murder mystery embraces.

Most of the great western adventures, real or fictional, involve a journey. Reconstructing the life of and astonishing audacity of the first United States officer to follow the Lewis and Clark Expedition has been a voyage of recovery. He undertook to open the Santa Fe Trail, and failing that, tested William Clark's geographical speculations about the continental interior. Twice deflected by circumstances beyond his control, the enigmatic traveler entered the Pacific Northwest, proved a practicable route across the continent, and for a brief moment, blocked British expansion of trade on the upper Columbia River. It is an accomplishment that deserves more than being brushed aside because of the lack of easy-to-find documents. What emerges is an image of a destiny-ridden man whose beau geste came at the ultimate personal cost.

CHAPTER ONE

A GUNNER OF THE REPUBLIC

O n September 17, 1806, the United States Corps of Discovery was descending the Missouri River on the last leg of their twenty-eight-month trip to the mouth of the Columbia River. They were pleased to meet the boat party of a brother officer whom Meriwether Lewis had known since 1801 when he recommended his retention in the United States Army. Their relationship was unusual because Lewis was a Virginia planter with Republican ideals and John McClallen was the product of northern mercantilism with Federalist views. What they shared was an overriding sense of duty.

After telling the explorers that they had been given up for dead, the recently resigned captain of artillery explained that he was taking an outfit of fine merchandize to open an overland trade to Santa Fe. Instead of drinking at the mythic fountain of continental waters, the place in the mountains from which all western rivers flowed, which William Clark believed they had discovered, McClallen's thirst appeared to be for the silver of New Mexico. That night, as Lewis and Clark drank the fledgling trader's liquor, they expanded on what they had seen and done. And perhaps they questioned McClallen about what brought him to undertake a risky mercantile adventure. When the two parties separated the next morning, that question was not resolved and was already destined to become an enigma of America's western development.

The activities of revolutionary France and the high-handed maritime policy of England raised concerns about the new nation's undefended coastline, and in May 1794 these concerns led to the creation of a Corps of Artillerists and Engineers to man new forts defending important seaports.[1] Lt. John McClallen was among the first officers commissioned, but after nine years of undemanding garrison duty, his military career, like Lewis's, began to change. About the time that Captain Lewis began organizing his expedition in 1803, Captain McClallen learned that he would soon be transferred to the western frontier of the newly acquired Louisiana Territory. McClallen would have preferred to stay at a comfortable Baltimore posting, but when a Baltimore friend suggested the intriguing possibility that a transfer to St. Louis might open business opportunities in the new territory, the idea appealed to someone raised in the mercantile tradition of upstate New York.

During the French and Indian War, McClallen's great uncle Robert Henry had done well supplying the British army as it moved toward the conquest of the large area of North America to the north and west of the original British colonies in the area known as New France. The Henry and McClallen families came from Maghera, Londonderry, in Northern Ireland, to frontier Massachusetts in 1742 and 1749. At the end of the French and Indian War, Henry's widowed sister sent her twelve-year-old son, Robert McClallen, to his namesake uncle Robert Henry in Albany, New York.[2]

In the summer of 1760 Robert Henry outfitted a young New Jersey army supplier, coincidently named Alexander Henry but not related, to follow the British forces descending the St. Lawrence River. After the end of hostilities between the British and the French, Alexander Henry went on to pioneer the British Indian trade.[3] The brief, bloody interior Indian rebellion that followed failed to deter the Albany firm of Henry, Farrell & Abbott from sending a consignment of illegal liquor to the inland trade depot at Michilimackinac on the narrow strait between lakes Huron and Michigan, where the resulting scandal helped sink the career of the war hero Major Robert Rogers.[4] Attempts to recover the losses of the embarrassed capitalists Henry, Farrell & Abbott found no recourse in British courts.[5] That cautionary family memory was in the background as Capt. John McClallen considered the offer of his Baltimore friend.

Young Robert McClallen matured as a store clerk during those years and married an Albany girl named Jane Williams. Their first son, John, was born January 29, 1772, when political unrest was maturing toward the rebellion of the American colonies. Uncle Robert Henry became an early Son of Liberty and his nephew Robert McClallen was an active member of the Albany committee of correspondence. Soon after British forces were penned in Boston, ragtag rebel forces marched through Albany with the intention of claiming Quebec as the fourteenth state.[6]

At the age of three, John McClallen was too young to remember the winter of 1775/76 when his father and Robert Henry followed the invasion to Montreal. For £15,000 in real money and credit, they bought blankets and other goods initially imported for the western Indian trade but critically useful to the rebel forces in the field. That stock of goods, essential to the war effort, was hauled on sleds over frozen Lake Champlain to Albany and resold.[7] Despite their patriotic intention, the devaluation of continental currency represented a considerable loss to the merchants who engaged the downstate lawyer, Alexander Hamilton, to draw up a petition asking compensation for the loss due to their acceptance of devalued congress paper. That led to further disillusionment when the politically astute Mr. Hamilton advised the New York Assembly against setting a dangerously expensive precedent. Robert McClallen never forgave that betrayal.

After the peace at the end of the American Revolution, the house of Henry, McClallen & Henry stood solidly at Number 10 State Street and the corner of Green in Albany, selling a "formitable array of goods," some still imported from England. During the war years and after, John McClallen grew up with cousins about his age, a tight little Scotch-Irish gang in an Old Dutch community, clattering over the cobblestones and finding minor mischief around the docks or the surrounding countryside. When he was old enough to be useful, he was taken to his father's store and set to sweeping, stocking, and selling superfine, second and course clothes, cloth like satinettes, half-thicks and coatings and 2, 2½ and 3 point size blankets. The young clerk sold men's small clothes, women's shawls, handkerchiefs, castor (beaver) hats, shoe and knee buckles as well as powder, bar lead, duck and pigeon shot, London pewter and Dutch tea pots. His father advertised a constant supply of liquors and groceries.[8] Few young men of that age had as broad an education in what their Presbyterian minister might have termed "worldly possessions."

On August 8, 1788, sixteen-year-old John closed up his father's store when Albany turned out to celebrate New York's ratification of America's new constitution. It was grand seeing the horse troop leading and old General Schuyler riding behind to display the document. Among the tradesmen and mechanics who marched, the brewers' dray was most impressive with Mr. Van Rensselaer astride a cask of beer as Bacchus. A team of grays pulled a Mohawk riverboat on a carriage with the proper number of rowers waving their oars, paddles, and setting poles. But the great event did not override the growing sense of unreconciled political differences because anti-Federalists pelted the marchers with debris, even pointed a cannon at them.[9]

Despite lawyer Hamilton's betrayal, Robert McClallen continued to support the Federalist view of how the new nation should be organized.[10] While Mr. Hamilton was inventing the principles of the Bank of the United States, in February 1792, Robert McClallen walked over to Robert Lewis's tavern at the corner of State and South Pearl to help incorporate the Bank of Albany.[11]

After Uncle Robert Henry and his son died, the family business was continued by Robert McClallen. As the oldest of the family of five girls and three boys, the merchant's twenty-two-year-old son should have continued helping run the store. But an attractive opportunity arose in September 1793 when the family of Alexander Hamilton appeared in Albany, fleeing the terrible yellow fever epidemic that was torturing Philadelphia. During his stay in Albany, Mr. Hamilton could hardly have avoided encountering his former client and doing something for the son of a loyal Federalist.

The Congressional Act of May 9, 1794, authorized the creation of a Corps of Artillerists and Engineers of four battalions of four companies each, and a promising young man might go far in a favored regiment intended for coastal defense.[12] On June 2, 1794, John McClallen was commissioned a lieutenant in that elite and scientific arm, and at the end of 1794 Lt. John McClallen topped the list of sixteen new subalterns in the Corps of Artillerists and Engineers.[13]

When Lieutenant McClallen joined his company at West Point, there was no school for a new officer totally green about the soldierly formalities of commanding men. McClallen's company commander was Capt. Frederick Frye, a Massachusetts soldier who had fought at

Bunker Hill and later returned to service in 1794.[14] A cantankerous old campaigner with firm convictions about military formalities, Frye's was the first of the ten new companies designated for training at West Point.

When recruits began arriving in August, it was apparent that the unit was incomplete. Frye sent Lieutenant McClallen home on recruiting duty.[15] Before he had much experience as an officer, the former store clerk faced the challenge of convincing other young men to enlist in a still-forming service. He must have been convincing because on November 2, he shipped the first twenty recruits down the Hudson River and continued shipping men downriver through April 1795.[16] Three-fourths of the recruits from Albany were just callow boys. With only a year of military experience under his red sash, Lieutenant McClallen stood rigidly on a parade ground crowded with shouting subalterns and red-faced captains. After a day of drill and exasperation, he joined the other newly minted lieutenants who drank at the notorious North's tavern, grousing that their hopeless gunners would probably blow everyone to eternity before they grasped that the wiping stick came before the ramming rod. If the dripping swab failed to quench a lingering spark, the next load could go off prematurely. One-armed gunners were a grim joke. Those old wheeled canons jumped with a whomp that a cannoneer felt in his gut, and McClallen came to love the acrid smoke and the sense of being capable of dealing death at long distance.

Much of what was won in the defeat of the western Indians at the Battle of Fallen Timbers was signed away when United States negotiators agreed to such disgraceful terms that the Senate had to consider them in closed session. For the United States to finally gain possession of the British forts on the Great Lakes frontier, treaty commissioner John Jay of New York agreed that British traders could continue to have access to the tribes in United States territory. The "old northwest," which included territory as far west as the Mississippi River, was left to the competitive mercies of foreign Indian traders spreading poison among the tribes.

After training at West Point, most of the companies returned to their regular posts, but because he wrote a fine storekeeper's hand, Lieutenant McClallen was retained at West Point as deputy quartermaster, helping to assemble supplies necessary for the takeover of the line of Great Lakes forts. In late May 1796, when he received clothing, hand tools, and hardware forwarded from the public stores at Philadelphia, McClallen became acquainted with quartermaster general Colonel James O'Hara.[17] An experienced western trader and military supplier, the Paris-educated Irishman decided in July 1796 to end his service as quartermaster general and go into private business, contracting to supply the troops and provide goods to the Indians.

In midsummer, units of the Regiment of Artillerists were ordered to proceed up the Hudson River and take over the posts that the British were finally surrendering. The company of Capt. James Bruff traveled four hundred miles by large rowboats known as bateaux on the Mohawk River to Lake Oneida in western New York, where they left a detachment at Fort Oswego on August 3. Fifty men of Captain Frye's company continued along the south shore of Lake Ontario for another one hundred and fifty miles to the strategically located Fort Niagara, where Captain Bruff assumed command.[18] The Niagara River was the connecting link between lakes Ontario and Erie, and the fort commanded it. West along the lakes' border, Capt. Moses Porter's company occupied Detroit on July 11, but it was early October before Maj. Henry Burbeck took over the important fur trade depot of Michilimackinac. United States forces now commanded the nation's border as far west as Lake Michigan, although the provisions of Jay's Treaty, as it came to be known, allowed British traders to penetrate it at will.

The national flag fluttered bravely over the extensive outworks that encompassed about five acres of land with British guns just six hundred yards away, across the Niagara River, commanding those works. Old Fort Niagara was large enough to accommodate five hundred men. Captain Frye's ragtag detachment of fifty gunners rattled around in it like dried peas in a barrel. The soldiers were housed in the big stone barracks, reeking of history, where French soldiers slept before the British conquest of New France and the redcoats thereafter. Fortifications designed to defend against attack from the south now faced the wrong way, and Lieutenant McClallen helped re-site four small field pieces to defend the most critical portage linking the Great Lakes.

Because Lieutenant McClallen had performed the duty at West

Point, Captain Bruff appointed him post quartermaster at Fort Niagara. On August 21, 1796, the forward-minded young officer dated a letter to an Albany friend named Colin McGregor concerning a conversation they had the previous winter at Albany.

> I arrived here a few days since with the advanced Guard of American Troops to take possession of this post, which we had the pleasure of doing the 10th instant. The British Officers are very polite, and we live on a friendly footing with them. I have now a Station which I consider in some measure permanent.
>
> When I had the pleasure of seeing you last winter in Albany, you hinted that should I be stationed in this part of the country something might be done for our mutual advantage. I shall be happy to receive from you any information or proposal, by which my situation in this Country can be beneficial to both. Col. O'Hara, late Q'Master Genl, now Contractor for Genl. Wayne's Army is desirous of forming a connection with some Gentleman either in Albany or N. York with this plan. The Company not to exceed, six in number.
>
> He, or his agent at Detroit, myself at this place, to procure proper persons to explore the lands contiguous, belonging to this Country or in his Brittanic Majesty's territory. He is willing to advance 10,000 doll. on the above plan or any other similar to it.
>
> I informed him that I should write you on the subject, and forward your reply as soon as it came to hand. Should the above meet with your approbation, (or any other you may conceive now advantageous) I will thank you to communicate it to me.
>
> With great respect I have the honor to be Sir, Your obedient Servant,
>
> John McClallen[19]

O'Hara had in mind stringing six forward-looking associates along the line of the Great Lakes military posts where they could forward goods and trade. Midway between Detroit and Albany, Niagara was the keystone and an agent there would be in a uniquely advantageous position to forward a potentially profitable business. During the winter of 1796/97, Lieutenant McClallen assessed what that could mean. As a consequence of the US takeover, British merchants like James McGregor transferred their business across the Detroit River to British territory but could still operate in United States territory under the terms of Jay's Treaty. According to the Canadian fur trade historian Harold Innis,

> ...after 1796 trade with the American posts continued and actually increased. In 1796 goods passing the Niagara Portage from Montreal included 43,668 gallons of liquor, 1,344 minots of salt and merchandise valued at £55,220 and furs (5,826 packs, 2,616 from Detroit, 3,210 from Michilimackinac) valued at £87,390 were sent in return. Packs from Detroit increased from 1,910 in 1796 to 2,616 in 1797 and to 2,704 in 1798.[20]

James O'Hara offered McClallen an opportunity to make a fortune. A young man who had been raised in a mercantile family surely realized the opportunity for personal improvement. His duties as post quartermaster acquainted him with private suppliers or military contractors. He knew that both Albany merchants and Montreal outfitters were eager to get back into the Indian trade and the Niagara portage was a key link in the southern lakes route.

While McClallen was considering the opportunity and seeking his father's advice, international politics impacted his thinking. Concessions to the British in Jay's Treaty gave the revolutionary government of France an excuse to take exception to the favorable treatment of an enemy nation. Opportunistic French diplomats demanded a bribe of a quarter million dollars to open negotiations with the United States. When this was publicly revealed, the nation was outraged.

On April 9, 1797, the US Congress responded to Secretary of War James McHenry's call to arms by authorizing an army of twelve thousand men.[21] The Corps of Artillerists and Engineers would be increased by four new battalions with a captain required for each of sixteen new companies. On the 1797 list of officers of the army, the commission of the youngest captain was dated July 19, 1796, and Lieutenant McClallen's prospects for promotion were almost certain.[22] It would be unpatriotic to leave the army at this critical moment.

When the secretary of war organized a second regiment of artillerists and engineers, Inspector General Hamilton became concerned that "artful or seditious" officers might contaminate the new army. Leaving no doubt that the politics of the new army were meant to be Federalist, he wrote, "we are very attentive to the importance of appointing friends of the Govern to military stations."[23]

In early 1798 Secretary of War McHenry ordered a general court-martial to try Ensign Samuel Parmele of the 3rd Regiment of Infantry on charges of defrauding the United States in connection with the enlistment and discharge of soldiers. The members of the court included Lieutenant McClallen, who had returned from Niagara by May 19, 1798. He allowed the opportunity to make a fortune at Fort Niagara slip away. Inspector General Hamilton and the Fifth Congress willing, he preferred to continue to serve the nation.

John McClallen was a young man with the world before him. The army commission had allowed him to escape the mercantile career that his father had followed since he was a boy and which he refused at Niagara. His uniform gave him a sense of status and, more important, an opportunity to do something significant.

Chapter Two

CAPT. JOHN McCLALLEN

The reorganization of the army provided opportunities for advancement. Ensign Meriwether Lewis was four years in that rank until he was promoted a lieutenant in the First Regiment of Infantry on January 1, 1799, and was sent to Detroit as regimental paymaster. It was not a promising career until March 2, 1801, when he was promoted to captain and eight days later accepted a post as the private secretary to President Thomas Jefferson.

Lt. John McClallen returned from Fort Niagara and rejoined Captain Frye's company, which was stationed on Governor's Island in New York Harbor. Certification of payments made to the detachment of artillerists and engineers stationed at Fort Mifflin included Captain Frye, lieutenants McClallen and William Wilson, as well as Surgeon's Mate Samuel Osburn, noncoms, and privates. The sum for August amounted to $647.96 for all, so no one was getting rich from national service.

The formative experiences of a young officer ranged from mundane duties of the Governor's Island garrison, such as supply and transport to the politics of the republic. On the northern frontier McClallen had been thrust into the simmering national resentment of an overbearing British imperial neighbor that had a bloody record of using Indians to fight its wars. What may have caused him to refuse the opportunity to resign his commission and seek potential fortune in the Great Lakes and western commerce may have been the advice of his father or his great uncle Henry to steer clear of a chancy business. Or was it patriotism?

McClallen had an opportunity to meet Inspector General Alexander Hamilton at Trenton, New Jersey, and on July 24, 1798, he was commissioned a captain, "vice [replacing] Pierce, deceased."[1]

Lacking a company to command, Captain McClallen remained posted at Fort Jay on Governor's Island through the rest of the year.[2]

It was his second posting to a place essential to the defense of the nation. The Albany boy was impressed by the sailing ships that crowded New York Harbor, so much larger than the Hudson River sloops that brought imported goods to his father's store or to West Point. When invasion by a French fleet seemed imminent in 1797, Congress appropriated funds to improve the fortifications. The situation seemed so threatening that patriotic students from Columbia College ferried over to help throw up earthworks. When Lieutenant McClallen arrived in May of the next year, the sod bastions had been faced with brick and a two-story blockhouse served as headquarters with barracks for the garrison of one artillery company.[3]

The critical post was a major's command and early in 1799 Captain McClallen applied to Major Adam Hoops for permission to go home to Albany "and arrange some business in which [he and] his family are materially interested."[4] While he was upstate the new captain saw an opportunity to recruit in the surrounding countryside.[5] Sent back to Albany on February 22, 1799, Captain McClallen enjoyed the confidence of Inspector General Hamilton, although it was not until March 2 that Congress passed the act authorizing the increase of the military establishment.[6] The new captain was about to get a lesson in the political implications of service to the nation.

Financing military expansion made no friends among taxpayers. The "whiskey rebellion" in western Pennsylvania previously demonstrated that taxing specific commodities was a risky source of federal revenue.[7] Now the expensive mobilization of the "new army" would be paid by a direct tax on land and houses. Riots soon erupted in Milford Township, Bucks County, Pennsylvania, causing Secretary of War James McHenry to urge President John Adams to make a firm response. Three days after that proclamation on March 12, 1799, artillery companies marched from Philadelphia, Carlisle, New York City, and West Point to rendezvous at Reading and Newtown, Pennsylvania, under command of Militia General William McPhearson.

When the old patriot Captain Frye expressed his opinion against calling out the troops to stifle civilian protest, Major Hoops ordered a court-martial and called Captain McClallen back from Albany.[8] The court-martial ran from March 17, 1800, to the first of April.[9] Afterward Major Hoops recommended Captain McClallen as a proper officer to act as Brigade Major for General McPhearson. Jumping at the opportunity, McClallen was already in Philadelphia three days later when it dawned upon him that Inspector General Hamilton might take exception to his initiative. He wrote begging him to overlook any appearance of misconduct, but a promising young captain who wore the Federalist black cockade was not discouraged in the politicized army.[10]

General McPhearson's suppression of the tax rebellion was emphatic. With a ruthless attention to duty, the troops scoured the Pennsylvania counties, making themselves obnoxious to the Pennsylvanians by wrecking newspaper presses and humiliating editors critical of taxation until resistance collapsed.[11]

At the end of June, Captain McClallen returned to Albany to resume recruiting his company. He had handbills printed and wrote a circular letter to friends in several nearby Rensselaer County towns. Militia Major Fleming provided him with a hundred blank paper cartridges for a four-pound cannon that was fired to attract attention, and Captain Ingersol loaned him a drummer to stir a crowd. Recruiters sometimes resorted to the use of liquor to fire patriotic fervor in addled minds.

Joining the army was not the promise of an easy life because regulations still referred to artillerists as sappers and miners, which didn't leave much question why fatigue uniforms were part of their kit. Ignorant of the world beyond the gatepost, most of those clod-hoppers were trading father's plow for ill-paid, voluntary servitude. At the end of July, McClallen informed General Hamilton that he was much embarrassed for the want of officers because one candidate for lieutenant was incapable of performing any kind of military duty and another had not signified his acceptance of a commission. But the Albanian William Hosack would be a promising cadet until a commission as lieutenant came through.[12]

There were also family matters distracting him. When his married sister Elizabeth died in October, John McClallen was nearby to console the family. Since the first of March 1798, his father had entered a new level of public life with the appointment as state treasurer. That he received 57 of the 94 votes cast in a slate of a dozen candidates was a clear indication of his standing, not only in Albany, but in the state.[13]

Two days before Christmas, Albany church bells rang. It had taken over a week for the news to travel north that the United States had lost its central figure with the death of George Washington. Albany mourned for almost three weeks while an appropriate funeral procession was being organized. Like other public men of the town, Captain McClallen wore black crepe on the bitter dawn of January 9, 1800, when he ordered the firing in rapid succession of sixteen guns, for the sixteen states. After that, one gun was fired every half hour until three signaled that it was time to form the procession. Militia Major Solomon van Rensselaer was the designated parade marshal, but it was Captain McClallen, as officer of the day, who saw to the details. As the solemn parade moved through the streets, Robert McClallen walked with the other public men of Albany while his son tried to keep the local militia and recruits from looking too ragged.[14]

After debating the disbanding of the new army, Congress had passed a bill on February 20, 1800, to halt recruiting. McClallen's efforts dragged on until the end of March 1800, when responses from headquarters to the captain's reports and expense accounts grew chilly.[15] Republican attacks on the military buildup during the Sixth Congress made completing McClallen's company difficult. A good deal of Republican cant spewed from a young Virginia congressman, John Randolph, who condemned loungers living on the public trough as "the most abject and worthless men of their community."[16]

At the end of April a Republican victory in the New York elections cast a shadow upon Federalist domination, and the Senate voted to suspend the appointment of any more officers. A House amendment set June 15 as the target date for the disestablishment of the new army, but for the moment, two regiments of artillery were retained.[17]

Captain McClallen marched his recruits down the Hudson River and through Pennsylvania to the year-old federal armory and arsenal at Harper's Ferry, Virginia.[18] In June McClallen's democratically minded soldiers embarrassed him by writing a letter of complaint about their quarters, supplies, and pay to Inspector General Hamilton. Nevertheless, the captain was attentive to the smallest details concerning the welfare of his men. Guessing that they might be assigned to a southern post, he suggested that white flannel rather than the usual linen would be better shirts for his soldiers. It was more durable and comfortable in a climate where men were exposed to heavy dews.

In the orders drawn on October 7, 1800, Captain McClallen was "Arranged" to the 2nd Battalion and ordered to assume the command of the late Captain Frye's company in South Carolina.[19] When McClallen arrived at Charleston, he found that he ranked Lt. George Ross by only two years and Lt. Samuel Fowle was a stranger to him, an unknown quantity. Some of the fifty men were those McClallen recruited five years earlier. Their enlistments were running out.

Castle Pinckney turned out to be a sorry battery of sand and palmetto logs planted on a large, marshy island known locally as Shutes Folly. McClallen's likely headquarters were on Sullivan's Island on the north shore of Charleston Harbor, where McClallen and his men felt as marooned as Crusoes. The fort had been heroically defended during the Revolution, but both forts were built of soft palmetto logs shoring up ten-foot-wide walls of sand.

When a well-read newspaper came to him, McClallen followed the developing national dilemma. After a hot election, the Electoral College was deadlocked in a tie for the presidency between two leading Republicans. It was mid-February 1801 before that body finally resolved the embarrassing tie between Mr. Thomas Jefferson and Mr. Aaron Burr.

President Jefferson had already named Henry Dearborn as his secretary of war, and within a week of his inauguration he asked a Virginian captain of infantry and present military paymaster to become his private secretary.[20] It was rumored that newly promoted Capt. Meriwether Lewis was brought in on account of his "knolege of the Western country, of the army & it's situation might sometimes aid us with information of interest, which we may not otherwise possess."[21] Gossip was soon circulating between officers that the personal secretary, aide-de-camp really, was drawing up a list of officers for the president's reevaluation. The enlarged army was, in President Jefferson's Republican mind, too Federalist. Reducing the organization included the elimination of officers, and with a bit of selectivity, most of those would be Federalists.[22]

In June 1801 the War Department sent Mr. Jefferson a comprehensive list of army officers. The president set Captain Lewis, who had spent most of his service in the West or recruiting around his home town, Charlottesville, to grading his fellow officers according to their abilities and performance of duty, as well as their loyalty to the republican government. The evaluation that was completed by July 14 resulted in the retirement of many of the Federalist officers who Alexander Hamilton appointed during the buildup.[23] From his headquarters at Fort Adams on the Mississippi River, south of present Natchez, Mississippi, Maj. Gen. James Wilkinson became concerned about morale and cautioned his officers, "If we are to exist as a military body much longer, a general reform in manners, principles & habit must take place."[24]

Although Captain Lewis may not have been personally acquainted with Captain McClallen, he found him to be of "the first class, so esteemed from a superiority of genius & Military proficiency," but unfortunately "more decisively opposed to the administration."[25] Because the evaluation was secret, McClallen was never aware of his good standing.

It did not help McClallen's state of mind that he had inherited Lt. Samuel Fowle, a Massachusetts man with an impossible sense of self-righteousness but flexible principle.[26] Problems with Lieutenant Fowle began when the ship *Argus* wrecked in Charleston Harbor, setting a cargo of exotic wood adrift. The consignees published notice that they would allow anyone who secured salvaged wood one-third of its value when sold at auction. Although obliged to set an example in observing the law, Fowle appropriated a mahogany log and gave two gunners extra rations of public rum to cut plank and build furniture for his quarters. He also misappropriated powder from the magazine to amuse himself bird shooting.

When called to account, Fowle made a scene at the evening parade, speaking in a "seditious" manner to the commanding officer and later embarrassing his fellow Lieutenant Ross by countermanding his orders to the mess waiter. Leaving Fort Moultrie in Charleston Harbor without permission was the last straw. Captain McClallen called for a court-martial.[27]

Unfortunately, the court was postponed and the damn fellow continued being incorrigible and disorderly in garrison. Fowle insulted the sergeant of the guard in the presence of the men, and he insulted his captain in the presence of another officer. It was disappointing when the court gave Fowle a mere slap, three months' suspension without pay, after which his sword was to be returned. Meanwhile, Meriwether Lewis was sitting at the president's elbow, compiling impressions of fellow officers who could not keep their houses in order. Rumors now held that a third of the officer corps might be eliminated.

After March 16, 1802, it was understood that the artillery was being reduced from two regiments to one. In the Military Peace Establishment of 1802 a company would consist (on paper at least) of a captain, one first and one second lieutenant, two cadets, four sergeants, four corporals, eight artificers, and fifty-six privates.[28] Four musicians were authorized in order to provide the colonel with a regimental band.

As the Republican scythe mowed a swath through the Federalist officers, more than seventy of the command class was removed from service. The dismissal of McClallen's French artillery mentor, Lt. Col. Louis Toussard, was unjust treatment for a brave officer who had lost an arm during the Revolution.

This was not the time for someone to rock McClallen's boat. Less than a month after Mr. Jefferson signed the Military Peace Establishment Act into law, Captain McClallen found himself facing a general court-martial for his conduct in trying Lieutenant Fowle. Determined to get revenge, Fowle was obliged to substantiate his charges. His demand to bring in additional witnesses was fielded by Adjutant Thomas Cushing, who curtly told him that it was up to the court to decide whether to bring witnesses from a great distance. Opinions in lieu of facts were not what the court needed for a fair and impartial investigation of the conduct of Captain McClallen. Nine days after the charges were presented at Fort Mifflin on May 10, the chagrined lieutenant watched the court exonerate McClallen.[29]

After the trial, Captain McClallen was reassigned to the command of Fort McHenry, the fortress defending Baltimore and, due to its proximity to the national capital, a conspicuous posting. Had a morning report at Fort McHenry survived it would have shown that most of the men were away on detached duty and only a few were available to man the guns. Forty-five privates, due to be discharged, were already checking off the remaining days of their enlistments. After eight years of service, McClallen had recruited two, maybe three, units, only to see them dispersed.

Before McClallen left Charleston, a friend he had made there, William Calhoun, gave him a letter of introduction to his well-placed Baltimore family.[30] The Scotch-Irish patriarch James Calhoun came from Carlisle, Pennsylvania, to Baltimore during the Revolution and stayed on to become a successful businessman. When the growing city was recently incorporated, Calhoun became Baltimore's first mayor. Pleased that Captain McClallen shared a similar background in the mercantile tradition and a latent dedication to business, Calhoun introduced him to the gentlemanly network of postwar mercantile business.[31]

It was just a three-mile ride from Fort McHenry to the graces of a cosmopolitan city and what it meant to be a Baltimore gentleman.[32] Ships from distant places were tied up in the harbor, worldly sea captains frequented the taverns, and the seamen who roistered on the wharf gave dockside a sense of bawdy excitement. Because Mr. Calhoun's sons were married, John McClallen discovered other aspects of Baltimore nightlife on his own.

When duty permitted, McClallen spent a pleasant hour in a dockside coffee shop, listening to the conversations of men about matters far from the inbred concerns of the regiment of artillerists. Because the public resented soldiers in peacetime, he kept his Federalist views to himself. He listened to frustrated shipmasters and drunken sailors bellowing outrage at British insults on the high seas and the impressments of free seamen. They told of one of their own, Boston ship captain Robert Gray, discovering the Columbia River in May 1792 after a British squadron blindly sailed past the mouth. Even before Gray's discovery, Yankee maritime traders were making fortunes on the Pacific coast by trading for sea otter skins and carrying the cargo to China.[33]

⇥⇤

There were nights when Captain McClallen rode back to Fort McHenry outraged by penny-pinchers who failed to realize what they asked of a career officer. Repeated cycles of buildups and reductions had devastated military morale and cut the heart out of the surviving cadre. What did he have to show for it? All that Captain McClallen knew was how to place a battery, to sight the guns, and to try to hold the gunners to their posts if destruction focused on them. The rest of it was just housekeeping and writing reports.

A captain's meager pay meant that he had to depend on the generosity and hospitality of friends. Forty dollars a month made it almost impossible to maintain the illusion of an officer and a gentleman. Even keeping a waiter was an extravagance.[34] Without hope of marriage or a family, John kept distant from the fairer sex. His former posts in Charleston Harbor had been sandy, sweltering prisons where a lonely soldier looked across the water to lamps glowing on distant verandas and imagined the charming ladies gliding in the moonlight. Baltimore flirts trolling for husbands could be quite charming and knew private places in the garden, but intimacy must have been beyond him.

On one of those winter nights when the stars seemed close in a cold, clear sky and a rime of frost was already forming on the great guns, Capt. John McClallen drew his greatcoat over his shoulders and strolled out to ponder what the new year had in store for him. Hanging over Whetstone Point, the moon reflected in the still water of the harbor. Loosening the stiff collar that came up under his ears, he lighted a seegar and leaned on the cold stone parapet.

Beyond the glow of the battle lanterns was a dangerous political beating ground where Federalists and Republicans contended for power. Great things were happening, but where would an impoverished soldier fit in a widely scattered army? Congress had even embarrassed the commanding General of the Army, and what could a captain with no connections expect?

The smoke had burned down to a soggy stub, and after ensuring that the guard was properly posted, Captain McClallen cast the glowing butt out into the darkness and went in to his lonely cot.

CHAPTER THREE

GEN. JAMES WILKINSON

In the first months of 1803, John McClallen was shocked to learn that his family had fallen into a financial disaster. Serving as state treasurer, Robert McClallen neglected his business and had to sell Albany town lots to maintain a respectable position in the community.[1] There is proof that he was not profiting from his position. In February 1803, John's father was found in default to the state for the appalling amount of thirty-three thousand dollars.[2] All that the respectable citizen put forward as an excuse was his old complaint "that he was a loser in a very heavy amount by the state, in the war of the Revolution, in consequence of having outlayed money in clothing and stores for the army imported from Canada, and that he had been embarrassed by those operations ever since."[3] The debt accumulated over four years from money owed to the state that the treasurer was unable to recover.

John's family was disgraced. By the time the harpies were through picking the bones, they were likely to be destitute. As the shock wore off into reality, they knew they had to raise money. The McClallen home had to be converted into a boarding house to help meet expenses.[4]

Robert McClallen had been a member of the "Ineffable and Sublime Grand Lodge of Perfection" for twenty years or more, and his humiliation appalled the 344 present Masons. His father's bondsmen—General McCarthy, Peter W. Yates, and Charles R. Webster—also stood to lose all until Solomon Southwick, the editor of the democratic paper, and Mr. Shurtleff, a representative from Schenectady, went to bat for them. They claimed that the state should have known of the defalcation and had failed to use the necessary precautions to prevent it. As the circle of neglected responsibility widened, the legislature released the bondsmen and swept the embarrassment under a rug.[5]

As the eldest son, John McClallen felt he had to do something to help his father make up the debt. But what could he do to ease the burden for his parents, for his sisters still at home, and for three younger brothers? A captain's pay was barely enough to support the social position his rank implied.[6]

As the weather and humidity of the summer of 1803 closed in, McClallen was exasperated when the tight-minded Secretary of War Henry Dearborn decided to look for economy in a beer barrel. In July McClallen was ordered to try a three-month-long experiment at Fort McHenry, substituting beer for the soldier's daily ration of a gill (¼ pint) of rum, brandy, or whiskey.[7] The cost-cutting came at a time when the enlistments of forty-five of McClallen's company would soon expire. If many of them refused to re-enlist, the captain faced a serious recruiting problem.

But other more international matters were transpiring outside McClallen's family woes and problems retaining his company. Since the beginning of the year rumors were circulating about a mysterious secret treaty between the United States and France. Almost half a century before, the defeated French empire in North America had ceded its claims west of the Mississippi River to Spain. That was a problem because Spanish authorities at the port of New Orleans could close it on a whim. Since the end of the American Revolution, France entertained the idea of recovering Louisiana. Recently, Napoleon Bonaparte salvaged his faltering European conquests by secretly forcing Spain into a retrocession of Louisiana with the idea of reestablishing French influence in North America. But the army that Bonaparte sent to the Caribbean to establish a staging base for taking over Louisiana expired in a Haitian cloud of yellow fever.

The threat of a foreign adventure against New Orleans, a vital link to the world, led President Jefferson to initiate inquiries concerning the acquisition of the port of New Orleans. In January 1803, while he waited for a response from the French, the president asked Congress to authorize funds for the exploration of an overland route to the Pacific shore. The Indian trade was a promising source of income, and Mr. Jefferson suggested that the Mississippi–Missouri River might turn out to be a better transport route than the present torturous passage that British traders used to get to the greater Northwest.[8]

In July it was made public that negotiations had been completed, not only to buy the island of New Orleans, but the whole of Louisiana west of the Mississippi River. Although the editor of the Baltimore *Gazette* had planned to forego an issue on July 4, he felt compelled to issue an extra edition discussing the ongoing threat of Great Britain and the purchase of Louisiana. Captain McClallen was probably included among the gentlemen of Fell's Point near Baltimore who gathered at Peck's Hotel to celebrate the Fourth. They drank toasts to "1. American Independence, 2. Those Who Fell on the Altar of Liberty, 3. Thomas Jefferson, The Keystone of our Federal Superstructure, 4. The Vice President [Aaron Burr], O! Fling Away Ambition, by that Sin Fell the Angels [followed by the Rogue's March], and a somewhat tardy 7th, The Memory That Suggested and the Policy that Directed the Purchase of Louisiana—Millions for Purchase, not a Cent for Conquest [followed by three playings of Yankee Doodle]."[9]

The spoon that President Jefferson had used to keep the army stirred up and the officer corps in uncertainty was put to better use when the president's secretary, Capt. Meriwether Lewis, began assembling equipment and ordering boats at Pittsburgh for an exploration. In July Captain of Artillery Amos Stoddard was ordered to put his previous orders for the location of a post on the east side of the Mississippi River on hold and wait at Kaskaskia, south of St. Louis, with Capt. Russell Biddle until it became necessary to occupy the west bank.[10] Gen. James Wilkinson remained lower on the Mississippi at Fort Adams, devising further strategic deployments until he could march south to take possession of New Orleans.[11]

During the years of McClallen's military service the commanding General of the Army was a distant authority whose headquarters seemed to be in the saddle. There was gossip of suspect relations with the Spanish, and older officers had not forgotten rumored disloyalty to Gen. Anthony Wayne during the Indian campaigns. He had raised himself from a river merchant and downstream trader and married well to a daughter of the prestigious Biddle family. Officers and gentlemen confined their speculations about a superior most had never met to stories about a fat man's elaborate uniform and expensive tastes. Still, General Wilkinson looked after his army.

The acquisition of Louisiana was a dramatic development, and Captain McClallen could not have imagined how General Wilkinson had fixed his authority on the haircut of an aging relic of the Revolution. Old Colonel Thomas Butler of the 2nd Infantry was the last holdout against Wilkinson's order requiring soldiers to wear their hair shorter.[12] Because the obstinate old man's unshorn queue dangled as a challenge to the chain of command, Wilkinson ordered a court-martial.

On May 25, 1803, orders were written at Fort Adams directing adjutant and inspector Lt. Col. Thomas H. Cushing , Lt. Col. Constant Freeman of the Regiment of Artillery, Lt. Col. Jonathan Williams of the Corps of Engineers, Maj. George Ingersol, Capts. Richard Blackburn, James Bruff, Abimael Nicoll, Nehemiah Freeman, James Stille, George Izard, Lloyd Beale, and John McClallen, all of the artillery regiment, to assemble at Fredericktown, Maryland, on September 10 to try a matter of direct disobedience.[13]

Calling that court brought most of the officers of the Regiment of Artillery together at a critical moment in history. Usually, those officers and gentlemen of the military family were scattered at widely separated posts without opportunities to get together. When the court finally assembled on November 21, they had a reunion and a rare opportunity to compare notes.

Like masters of ships at sea accustomed to a broad responsibility and independent action, half of the eight captains of artillery were veterans of the Revolution who were sympathetic to an aging comrade in arms. Younger officers like McClallen came into service in later build-ups and matured in the new organization. General Wilkinson was the only leader they had known, but in the nine years that he had been in uniform, Captain McClallen had never met the commanding general.

Officers understood the obligations of command but they could be as gossipy as a clutch of old maids when it came to service affairs. Theirs was a closed society that did not put much credence in civilian rants. Of course old Butler should have known better than to challenge the chain of command and resist discipline, but to convene a court-martial over a haircut was ridiculous.

Some of the general's other activities over the years were questionable. After lackluster service during the Revolution, James Wilkinson ended up in the role of clothier general, a job that James Calhoun of Baltimore or the former Albany merchant's son could appreciate. Returning to civilian life as an Ohio River merchant/trader, Wilkinson offended less imaginative rivals by gaining the confidence of Spanish authorities who controlled access to world trade at the port of New Orleans. Rumors held that the monopoly on export that he gained was achieved by disloyalty. Those rumors were prevalent and not forgotten when he returned to the army during the Ohio Indian Wars, which were finally concluded with the humiliation of British arms after the Battle of Fallen Timbers. Upon the death of Gen. Anthony Wayne, Wilkinson became General of the Army, the only general officer McClallen served under.

After an ungrateful Congress wounded Brig. Gen. James Wilkinson's pride, even rank was no sinecure.[14] The officers felt threatened by one of their own when Mr. Jefferson allowed a cocksure junior captain to decide their fate. According to Tom Cushing, Capt. Meriwether Lewis would not be a problem for a while. Clearing Pittsburgh at the end of August, he was on his way west to discover what Mr. Jefferson bought along with New Orleans.

⏤⧓⧔⏤

During September at Fredericktown the captains pumped Adjutant Cushing about future prospects, or slipped in sly queries about who was getting the more generous resupply of clothing. Everyone groused about having so many of their men sent off on detached duties. Fathers of half a hundred or more unruly boys had few opportunities to unwind, and this detached duty freed them from maintaining the stern example. An obstinate colonel's refusal to yield up his hair gave them a chance to let theirs down.

There must have been nights when the solemn judges reeled back to quarters, singing the old songs from times when they were raw subalterns without any real responsibility and the illusion that the republic really needed them. They stumbled along calling themselves the ass's behinds and making raucous observations about the pigtail wagging the donkey.

After a long two weeks the court-martial failed to find that Colonel Butler had been all that disobedient. A mild rebuke was not what the general expected of them and he was, to put it mildly, "displeased." The matter was not over and they still dangled in the wind on an old fool's pigtail.[15] Theirs was the dull peacetime service that produces Captain Queegs and few Mr. Roberts. For McClallen, the disparity between the rewards of private life and the poverty of public service was compounded by the financial dilemma that his father now faced.

After the haircut court adjourned on December 6, 1803, Captain McClallen remained on detached duty at Fredericktown.[16] When he finally rejoined his company at the end of the year, Louisiana was looming ever larger. On December 20, 1803, Gen. James Wilkinson and Mississippi Territory Governor William C. C. Claiborne marched four hundred regulars and about a hundred Mississippi militiamen into New Orleans to receive the turnover of the city and the transfer of a territory that the president thought might amount to 500 million acres.

⚬

That was going to require some changes in the disposition of the troops. In January 1804, Captain McClallen had an intimation of his reassignment when Regimental Adjutant Thomas Cushing suggested that the five-year enlistee John Bulow was an excellent cook, "just the one you need to manage the necessary housekeeping," who had previously served another officer in the West. In February when McClallen was ordered to Carlisle, Pennsylvania, to set up a recruiting rendezvous, his protest brought the adjutant's stern response—"You are to proceed to Carlisle with a Segt & musicians...money and clothing to be sent to you..." Cushing added, "Probably that remnant of your Company [left at Fort McHenry] may soon follow you to Carlisle, and that you may be ordered to the Mississippi as soon as your Company is complete."[17]

In mid-February McClallen lost Lt. Clarence Mulford, who was ordered west with a sergeant, a musician, and seventeen privates to join Captain Amos Stoddard's company at Kaskaskia on the Mississippi.

They would beef up the force that Stoddard was waiting to take into St. Louis to receive the transfer of Louisiana and to replace the men that Stoddard assigned to Captain Lewis's expedition for the exploration of the Missouri River.[18] In Mulford's place Captain McClallen got Lt. George Peter, not entirely a fair exchange.

The government had purchased the old barracks at Carlisle, Pennsylvania, for use as a recruiting rendezvous and training depot. McClallen had to come up with forty-five new recruits and Adjutant General Cushing optimistically provided fifty blank enlistment forms. In letters dated April 29, May 1, and in mid-May, Captain McClallen risked getting on the wrong side of Secretary of War Dearborn by trying to return to Baltimore. Dearborn was adamant that he remain until the recruiting was completed.

At Carlisle, Captain McClallen supervised the construction of gun carriages suitable for western operations. Those heavy wooden carriages were for twenty-four-pound howitzers, big guns going to New Orleans to resist potential Spanish or British naval attack, but far too heavy for maneuvering on the western plains. The artillery stationed at St. Louis would have to defend the middle Mississippi River in case a British force descended from the north. The three- and six-pound field pieces he would take to St. Louis would not be much of a threat to a well-organized invasion, but they might be useful to impress Indians.[19]

Headquarters sent a recently promoted second lieutenant and one of the first products of the new military school at West Point from Fredericktown on July 15, confirming "that the company was ordered to be in readiness for command on the Mississippi as soon as the summer heats have ceased."[20]

Pierre Chouteau, a St. Louis Indian trader who had been appointed United States agent for the tribes of the District of Upper Louisiana, brought an Osage delegation to the capital to meet the president and see the power of their new father. After touring eastern cities, they needed an escort to return home. The secretary of war ordered Lt. Moses Hooke at Pittsburgh to provide a noncommissioned officer and six sober soldiers to handle their boat. If Hooke was unable to spare men, he was authorized to call on Captain McClallen at Carlisle.[21] The gunners were being sent west piecemeal.

Army gossip held that Capt. Meriwether Lewis owed his appointment as an explorer to the favor of President Jefferson. Reviewing his own prospects, McClallen thought he owed his being stuck in a rut to a commanding officer he had never met. Gen. James Wilkinson spent his time in the West negotiating Indian treaties and attending to frontier defense along the east side of the lower Mississippi. His orders were written at Fort Adams, thirty-eight miles south of Natchez, and dispatched to other military posts. What Captain McClallen knew about his distant superior came through orders and secondhand military gossip. And there was a great deal more that a mere captain of artillery had no way of knowing.

That began to change after May 21, 1804, when the ship *Louisiana* from New Orleans tied up in New York. General Wilkinson, who loved a show, had missed the Grand National Salute and celebration of the first anniversary of the purchase of Louisiana.[22] After several days in New York, General Wilkinson went on to Washington, where he impressed his admirers by riding into the capital mounted on a splendid horse with a silver-trimmed saddle cinched upon a spectacular leopard skin. Acclaim that met him may have been too much, as on June 11, Wilkinson was feeling unwell and was unable to attend a dinner with the president. As the muggy summer of 1804 set in, the general declared humid Washington unendurable and withdrew to army headquarters at Fredericktown, leaving others to swelter in the details of national defense and warm beer. At the end of July he was also feeling the heat at Fredericktown and prepared to move to a more comfortable place at Sulphur Springs.[23]

Concerned about the state of the water level in the Ohio River, the sometime doctor Wilkinson realized that it would be too damn hot to have men baking on flatboats floating on a stagnant current. The transfer of Captain McClallen's company could wait until fall rains raised the water.

It must have been at Fredericktown that Captain McClallen finally met the commanding general. In their personal exchanges he observed that James Wilkinson was pompous, verbose, and tending to run on when in his cups, not at all the attributes the captain found in the Baltimore gentlemen with whom he socialized. At some point during this period Captain McClallen appears to have explained his personal problem to General Wilkinson. Recognizing the captain's concern about his father's predicament, the sympathetic general allowed him an opportunity to attend to critical details before the company embarked. It was agreed that Captain McClallen could have a furlough as soon as Lieutenant Gates completed the recruiting.

In early October General Wilkinson's plan to have McClallen's company "put in motion about the 20th...was prevented by the Epidemic of the Season which prostrated almost every individual of it—I have given orders for the party to be held in readiness to March on the shortest notice & if you have no other disposition for it, will put it under March for Pittsburgh."[24]

By the "epidemic of the season," General Wilkinson meant malaria. John McClallen's concern about being transferred to the western frontier went beyond the loss of a pleasant duty station at Fort McHenry. Those who ventured into the potentially fatal miasmas of the Mississippi Valley risked what was commonly known as "the ague." This debilitating condition struck Maj. James Bruff, who had participated in the haircut court-martial, soon after he was transferred to St. Louis. Bruff wrote:

> The indisposition of officers and men far exceeds my calculation. I have not had a well day since my arrival, yet am not confined except now and then with the ague (I write this with one on)...our sick report today is 23 out of 51...present...I have not yet strength, nor dare expose to the sun....[25]

The major treated himself with the concoction of Peruvian bark, an early form of quinine, but the tea brewed from it was so bitter that it required cutting it with wine. Two years before, as late as November, McClallen had experienced a similar bout of chills and fever and wanted no more of that torture. Unfortunately for McClallen and anyone else whose duty called them to the rivers of the West, malaria was a universal burden.[26]

There was a great deal that John McClallen could not guess from his superficial reaction to the man who determined his future. Others documented their opinions of Wilkinson. For instance, after Wilkinson helped sink the filibustering plans of George Rogers Clark and the Yazoo Company speculator James O'Fallon, the frustrated promoter O'Fallon rendered a telling opinion of the general.

> ... his conduct with the British, with St. Clair, with Congress, with the Spaniards and with the Company (as I have discovered beyond doubt) is too mysterious, intriguing, circuitous & meandering —, that I dare not trust him ... he cannot move but in Zig-zaggs ..., had he practiced Phsysic (altho' a man of no education at all) he would make money. As a Politician & Spy, he will never be worth a Shilling.[27]

Those such as Clark and O'Fallon who wished to stir up trouble in the Spanish-held territories in order to gain control were known as *filibusters*.

In addition to guaranteeing the free navigation of the Mississippi River, the Treaty of San Lorenzo mooted Wilkinson's lucrative monopoly to export through the Spanish-held port. Not long after Wilkinson succeeded to command of the army in 1796, his protégé, a Belfast lad named Philip Nolan, began making wild horse capturing expeditions into Texas. Then vice president Thomas Jefferson asked Nolan's views on what he had observed and Alexander Hamilton summoned Wilkinson to Philadelphia, where they discussed what might be necessary to launch a conquest of the Spanish provinces.[28]

Nolan's fixation with the Spanish Southwest continued when he left Natchez at the end of October 1800 on another horse-capturing expedition. By then the good relations that he cultivated with the Comanche Indians had alarmed Spanish administrators, who forbade him from entering Texas. They tracked down Nolan's well-armed party and killed him in the resulting fight.[29] Nolan's death was an extreme example of how James Wilkinson drew young men into his convoluted schemes.

In January 1803, while President Jefferson sent diplomats to negotiate the purchase of the city and seaport of New Orleans, Secretary of War Dearborn advised General Wilkinson to be prepared for "a different state of things." The general reported in July that he had troops sufficient to accomplish a *coup de main* if necessary.[30]

On December 20, 1803, Wilkinson and William C. C. Claiborne, the governor of Mississippi Territory, had rode into the Place d'Armes at New Orleans to receive the delivery of the island of New Orleans, and as an almost incidental by-product, the vast, nebulously defined territory of Louisiana.

Simmering in the background were the former Spanish officers whom Wilkinson had known for sometime, and a new, heavily titled player, Brigadier of the Royal Army Sebastian Nicolas de Bari Calvo de la Puerta, Marques de Casa Calvo, His Spanish Majesty's commissioner for establishing the border and limits of the province of Louisiana. For the next three months Wilkinson was available for discussions with Casa Calvo and the less imposingly titled Don Vizente Folch, the governor of adjacent West Florida.

In considering how to react to the suddenly ominous, still-undefined border between the Spanish Interior Provinces and America's Louisiana Territory, those officers looked to the general as a useful source of inside advice. He had previously received a pension (as it was termed) for services to the Spanish Administration. Since 1796 Wilkinson's secret pension had fallen in arrears and he may have seen a way to get paid by exploiting Spanish concern, for a price.[31]

The "Reflections on Louisiana" that General Wilkinson delivered to Casa Calvo and Folch after March 12, 1804, failed to contain much that the Spanish did not already know or could puzzle out for themselves.[32] But coming from the commanding general of the United States Army gave the information considerable weight.[33]

The reflections began with a statement of the phenomenal growth of the population of the United States and a prediction that in the next twenty years a million Americans would be settling west of the Mississippi River. Wilkinson warned that Louisiana might become the overland gateway to the Spanish Interior Provinces, or more precisely, Mexico, which was vulnerable to invasion by "hardened armies and adventurous desperadoes who, like the ancient Goths and Vandals, would precipitate themselves upon the weak defenses of Mexico and overturn everything in their path"[34] Wilkinson recommended posting fifteen hundred Spanish troops along the Sabine River, west of New Orleans, to protect that border from filibusters descending on them.

A paragraph commented on the intentions of Congress, as shown by the president's commission of "his astronomer," Capt. Meriwether Lewis, to determine the source of the Missouri River. The plan was that the exploratory force would proceed to the Pacific Ocean, where Wilkinson predicted the United States would have a seaport in five years. If that suspect party breeched the geographical veil, the security of the Spanish Interior Provinces might be compromised. However, the Spanish had known about the planned expedition since the end of January 1803 and recently had confirmation from St. Louis.

Wilkinson continued that Spain should work to retain the affection of the southern Indian tribes, such as the Pawnee, the Osage, and the Comanche, as a barrier to expansion west of the Sabine River. An Indian barrier would discourage those "adventurous desperados," who could threaten Mexico, or even Peru. In August 1804 Spanish officers convinced the experienced plainsman Pedro Vial to persuade the strategically located Pawnee to turn back or even attack American parties.

The plan to stop the Corps of Discovery had already occurred to the Spanish in New Orleans before Wilkinson suggested the interception and arrest of "Captain Merry Weather and his party."[35] By the end of March Spanish officers in New Orleans, Chihuahua, and Mexico City moved on that recommendation. But the distance that orders had to travel meant that nothing could be implemented until summer, and by then Lewis and Clark would have passed beyond interception.[36]

With France out of the picture, Spain and the fledgling republic were left to define what belonged to each of them. What Spain really needed to do was recover the right bank of the Mississippi River. East and West Florida might be useful as bargaining chips to trade for the return of Louisiana, an arrangement that might include funds to gradually extinguish the United States national debt for the purchase of Louisiana from France.

Wilkinson's presumption recognized that militants in the present administration thought that the territory purchased from France might have been taken more cheaply by force. But that was unlikely because the acquisition of Louisiana had extended the army's responsibilities without increasing the number of soldiers needed to do it.

The scenario implied in the "Reflections on Louisiana" did not survive in the papers of General Wilkinson. For many years, the only copy was attributed to Florida governor Don Vizente Folch. Historians have generally overlooked this important document, and there is a question whether Wilkinson actually wrote it or worked it out in a joint effort with Folch, whose name appeared on the translation.[37]

The suggestion that money was annually required for his secret services, lest they lose a man of great talent and national influence, was pure Wilkinson. In order for Spain to win over the American cabinet, he suggested that they "must make use of men who enjoy confidence, intelligence, character and influence in the government of the United States." Of course he meant himself.

On March 12, 1804, three days after Captain Amos Stoddard received the keys to St. Louis, Wilkinson submitted his convoluted "Reflections on Louisiana" with an important reservation. "My name and whatever I shall write ought not to be disclosed, except to the first Minister of State [Godoy]; to Your Excellency [Casa Calvo], to Colonel Don Vinzente Folch, Governor of West Florida, and in case of death or absence to Don Gilberto Leonard, late Comptroller of Louisiana, to Don Andres Armesto, Secretary of the Boundary Commission...my name or condition shall never be written, and always shall be designated by the number 13."[38] On March 30 Casa Calvo forwarded the observations and letter to the Spanish foreign minister at Madrid. There was no way that a response could travel there and return within a month. Ironically, Number 13 was operating in good faith.

Was Wilkinson manipulating those Spanish officers? While the rest of the country was still dazzled by the transfer of Louisiana, General Wilkinson had plotted out his version of the new relationship between the United States and the Spanish empire in North America. In March Wilkinson wrote Alexander Hamilton that he "would give a *Spanish Province* for an interview with you." He described the merits of this "Interesting portal to worlds known or unexplored which was already attracting to it men of all nations, ages, professions, Character & Complexions, and *women* to[o]."[39]

After getting troops settled in New Orleans, General Wilkinson took ship for Washington to scrounge additional forces for duty on that immense new frontier. If the Spanish made that difficult, or if the British made a play to take control of the Mississippi (as they had threatened to do in the past), the small standing army of the nation was dangerously dependent on unreliable militia.

Was it possible that General Wilkinson was trying to write himself out of looming military problems with what amounted to a strategic stall? In case of a war he would be the commanding general with insufficient forces. What he did in the "Reflections" would not be known for many years and by then other matters overshadowed his reputation. It was his previous relationship with the Spanish and his later association with Aaron Burr that has given historians a too-easy target.

How Wilkinson's actions would later affect McClallen begins by retracing the general's trip to the East Coast.

Finally sailing from New Orleans on April 25 or 27, 1804, General Wilkinson spent not quite a month out of touch with what was going on in eastern politics.[40] Upon landing in New York on May 21, 1804, Wilkinson spent two days attending to the landing and disposal of the cargo of sugar he had financed with $9,046.35 in Spanish silver.[41]

On May 23 the general sent a note to Vice President Burr at his Richmond Hill home. "To save time, of which I need much and have little ... I propose to take a bed with you this Night, if it may be done without observation or intrusion."[42] Three days later he was still in New York when he sent another note to Mr. Burr, written in French, inviting him to "call upon me at one o'clock and see my maps. General Mason, M. Dawson and six particular friends would also be present." The maps included sketches of southwest Texas obtained in 1801 by Philip Nolan at considerable cost. His life.

In that time before celebrity, some Americans like Stephen Decatur, Reuben James, or United States consul John Easton and eight marines found heroic possibilities fighting the notorious Barbary pirates and showing the world what the new nation was made of. James Wilkinson and Aaron Burr were once daring young officers like that, but the heroic moment was fleeting and in the years that followed, self-interest and political cynicism had overtaken them.[43]

By mid-June Wilkinson was experiencing a heart and breast condition and excused himself from the president's invitation to dine because he had been bleeding himself and felt too weak to socialize. That was unfortunate because the guest list included the noted scientist and explorer Friedrich Heinrich Alexander, the Baron von Humboldt. Because the noted traveler would be leaving soon, the ailing Wilkinson asked if he would provide information on the people and other details of the Spanish territories he had visited and mapped. Later, in a nefarious way, Wilkinson obtained a copy of Humboldt's map of Spanish possessions.[44]

Unless the heart condition actually represented an anxiety attack, those activities do not suggest the momentum of a double-agent about to launch a self-fulfilling prophecy. If General Wilkinson had previously been serious about considering an invasion of Spanish possessions, he should have turned to Alexander Hamilton with whom he had discussed that very idea five years before. Instead, he turned to Hamilton's political enemy, Vice President Burr.

After losing a hotly contested race for governor of New York, Mr. Burr found an excuse to blame the great Federalist Alexander Hamilton. On July 11, 1804, they met on the ledge of honor in New Jersey where Burr killed Hamilton. After the duel Burr fled to the Philadelphia home of his friend Charles Biddle, a cousin of Mrs. Wilkinson. Dueling was illegal but warrants for his arrest were limited to New Jersey. Burr was therefore still free to move about in other states. Although General Wilkinson was ailing in July, he still found opportunities to confer with Mr. Burr. Despite ongoing speculation by historians, there is no direct evidence of what they discussed. One clue is an August 6 report from British minister Anthony Merry to the British secretary of state for foreign affairs.

I have just received an offer from Mr. Burr, the actual Vice President of the United States (which situation he is about to resign), to lend his assistance to his Majesty's Government in any Manner in which they may think it fit to employ him, particularly in an endeavoring to effect a Separation of the Western Part of the United States from that which lies between the Atlantick and the Mountains, in its whole Extent.[45]

President Jefferson was still at Monticello on August 30 when he approved the appointments of four civil commandants for Louisiana, but he made no mention of an office for General Wilkinson.[46] His administration was straining to deal with the upper part of Louisiana. Compared to populated New Orleans, St. Louis seemed at the edge of the world. The most impressive display that the United States had been able to muster to receive the town was a mere captain of artillery who had been stationed across the river in 1803 to stop British infiltration by way of the upper Mississippi. His duty was to control the trade in Indian peltry from being diverted to Canada.[47]

Mr. Jefferson sent maps over to Secretary of War Dearborn to be copied, which Dearborn surely shared with Wilkinson because he was charged with conducting western military operations. The appointment as governor came later. The general was also informed that Mr. Jefferson was planning another exploration, this time of the Southwest, exactly what Number 13 had warned his Spanish friends to fear. Although a Southwest expedition introduced complexities, the general became an enthusiastic informant of the president's plans for exploration in letters dated June 19, July 13, and November 10, 1804.[48]

On September 29, 1804, General Wilkinson received a long letter from Maj. James Bruff, who was stationed in St. Louis as military commandant and was suggesting some strategic possibilities.

> Suffer me to suggest that if a Military Post was established on the Missouri at the mouth of the river Platt between whose waters and those of the del nord there is but a short carrying place; where Traders from Santa Fe meet ours as is absolutely the case at this moment or should that be thought too high up, and the mouth of the Cansas or even the Osage be prefer'd with another up the Mississippi, at or near the mouth of the Ouisconsing they might check; if not prevent; the depredations of Indians give them a higher opinion of our power to chastise them should they misbehave; protect our Traders and prevent smuggling from Canada &c.[49]

Wilkinson took the suggestion as presumptuous when the present force in St. Louis amounted to only fifty-three artillerymen, but he forwarded Bruff's letter to Dearborn and opened a discussion between them concerning measures necessary to control as well as protect the Upper Louisiana Territory. For the present, the concept of the mouth of the Platte River as a central strategic point was left to simmer.

Meanwhile, Aaron Burr was traveling through the south to assess the situation concerning East and West Florida. When he returned to Washington in November to endure his trying last months as vice president, there were opportunities for Burr and others to visit with General Wilkinson and restudy his intriguing maps, which now included Wilkinson's copy of the Baron von Humboldt's recent map of Mexico. There might be political opportunities there for an individual willing to risk it.

⚹

Commerce rather than conquest interested most western businessmen. Soon after the departure of the Corps of Discovery, the Kaskaskia merchant William Morrison launched a small trading adventure to Santa Fe.[50] On December 10, 1804, merchants Andrew and R. Steele of Shelbyville, Kentucky, petitioned their senator, John Beckenridge, to obtain the permission of the Spanish minister to extend their business to Santa Fe.[51] Andrew Steele may have been one of those enterprising neighbors whom John Adair, the registrar of the Kentucky land office, described to General Wilkinson when he wrote, "Mexico glitters in our Eyes." In January 1805, Wilkinson wrote to James Bruff for information concerning the route to "St. Afee." There is no indication whether that had to do with President Jefferson's plans for exploration, for a possible invasion of the interior provinces, or for private mercantile adventure.

Quite likely General Wilkinson saw himself being appointed governor of New Orleans, where he could control the interior drainage of the continent and the commerce floating on it, just what he tried to do eighteen years before. It was all the more desirable now that his Spanish friends had promised him the monopoly of shipping grain to Cuba. But Wilkinson's entrepreneurial expectations were dashed on March 3, 1805, when the Act for the Government of Louisiana partitioned the new country into the Territory of Orleans and Louisiana Territory. On March 11 President Jefferson notified the secretary of state that James Wilkinson of Maryland was to be governor of the Territory of Louisiana from and "after the 3rd of July next for the term of 3 years then next ensuing, unless sooner etc. Joseph Browne of N. York, Secretary of ditto from and after etc."[52] Wilkinson's appointment governing the northern part of the territory spelled disaster for his plans in the south.

Coincidentally, from distant St. Louis Major Bruff wrote that a French hunter and others who worked up the Missouri River had heard from Indians that the Spanish were sending messages to them "not to suffer us to spread further westward...," exactly what Number 13 had advised Casa Calvo and Folch to do. When Bruff's letter was received, sometime in April 1805, James Wilkinson realized that wearing more than one pair of boots was beginning to pinch.

CHAPTER FOUR

FLOATING INTO THE WEST

Although for John McClallen November 1804 was free of distractions in Baltimore, it was not because of a "pleasant
acquaintance" with a special lady of that place. No matter how glam-
orous his threadbare uniform, an officer living on forty dollars a month,
plus the two-dollar bounty for every man he enlisted, was far from a
catch. No respectable girl accustomed to the refinements of the city
would agree to accompany a husband to some raw frontier. McClallen's
concern had to do with his father's debt and the reputation of his family.

McClallen awaited orders to head for Pittsburgh, heeding
Wilkinson's concerns that they would be beset by the heat or ague if
they didn't wait.

In a demonstration of confidence, on December 25, General
Wilkinson relied on credentials of good conduct from Captain
McClallen to recommend Second Lieutenant Porter Hanks for recruiting duty. An assignment like that tested a young officer's capacity to
ingest the raw liquor he would have to swill with likely prospects. The
first months of 1805 brought another complaint that a soldier had been
enlisted "in a state of brutal intoxication" and a sharp letter from Secretary Dearborn ordering the fellow discharged. Lt. Samuel Gates, who
was under orders to move to St. Louis, was obliged to pay the costs of
the enlistment, which probably meant a bar bill.[1]

After the turn of the year 1805, McClallen sent First Lieutenant
George Peter, whose family home was in Georgetown, to root new gunners out of the patriotic beehive of muddy Washington City. It was a
subaltern's obligation to report to the commanding general, where the
impressionable young officer had the honor of being introduced to Vice
President Aaron Burr. Peter recalled that, despite the scandal following

the fatal duel with Hamilton, Mr. Burr appeared to be quite intimate with Wilkinson. It was not Burr's notorious reputation or his relationship with the general that concerned McClallen as much as being reassigned to a distant frontier.[2]

Still unreconciled to a transfer, Captain McClallen took his frustration to his friend the Baltimore merchant James Calhoun Jr. According to Calhoun's later testimony concerning General Wilkinson's travel expenses, his friend complained that he had just received orders transferring him to the western frontier.

> ... it was his hard fate as an officer in the army, who being ordered to the command of a post, and forming a pleasant acquaintance, was liable to be ordered away at every moment, to another command among strangers, of habits and manners so different, that it made his profession a very unpleasant one: and that he had formed such attachments in Baltimore that were he not so dependent, he would be highly gratified at a prospect of making it his future residence.[3]

The sympathetic Calhoun was also a businessman who had recognized the promise of breaking into western business, and his Baltimore firm had already arranged for its first consignment of peltry from New Orleans.[4] Calhoun smoothly pointed out that McClallen's transfer could be turned into an advantage.[5] As long as he was going to a new country favorable to commerce, Captain McClallen might as well take along a small assortment of goods to test that market. After disposing of those goods, he could evaluate the potential, and if there was promise, it might be to his advantage to consider leaving the army and entering business.[6]

McClallen was embarrassed to admit that he lacked the funds for even a modest mercantile undertaking. Considering the problems of his Albany connections, he had little expectation of obtaining venture capital. Calhoun replied that his firm was so interested in knowing more about the western business that they were willing to advance the goods.

Based on their agreement, McClallen began visiting other shops and warehouses, picking items that he thought might be salable. How the mercantile-minded army officer selected what to take and to sell customers unknown to him depended on instinct. Few suppliers in Baltimore were acquainted with the western trade. When he reached St.

Louis, McClallen could not expect to travel further to tribal markets, but he might wholesale his stock to someone who could. When the arrangements in Baltimore were complete, the outfit amounted to eight bundles of assorted goods weighing about twenty-four hundred to twenty-five hundred pounds with a value of $2,488.28.[7] McClallen's share of the profit would not resolve his father's debt of $33,000, but it could be a start.

About that time, McClallen's relationship with General Wilkinson started to tangle. He had known for almost a year that his company was being sent west and only the general's concern for the health of the troops and the state of the water in the Ohio River delayed it until the spring of 1805. Fortunately that allowed McClallen time to complete arrangements with Calhoun, but the opportunity involved more that just shipping a ton of salable goods to St. Louis. Getting it there required a degree of cooperation that could come from only General Wilkinson.

After a quarter century of experience in western business, Wilkinson was familiar with the mercantile opportunities.[8] An understanding was worked out that would allow McClallen to take his private cargo down the Ohio on government transport. Wilkinson allowed McClallen to carry it under the "right of transport" officer's privilege of shipping personal property to a new duty station by government boat.[9]

Captain McClallen cleaned up the last details of salvage and accounting at Fort McHenry, which defended Baltimore. He reported the condition of the works and arranged for the sale of scrap iron from old or damaged cannons. On April 12, he delivered a note for $492.60 for the salvage weight of those guns. Although the men remaining at the fort hoped to be transferred to Captain Reid's company, it appeared that they would be going west with the new recruits.

Captain McClallen turned the command of Fort McHenry over to Lt. Samuel Dyson and attended to the challenge of getting the company, its baggage, and more than a ton of private baggage over the old Forbes road to Pittsburgh. The duty of acting as military agent fell upon Lieutenant Peter, who was responsible for the expenses as far as the shipping place. Although the lieutenant was sent ahead, the captain caught up with him at Bedford, Pennsylvania, where they were joined by Lt. Samuel Gates, who was bringing detachments from Carlisle and Philadelphia to bring the company up to strength.

According to the "Return of Troops destined to St. Louis," McClallen's company of artillery was supposed to consist of First Lieutenant Peter, Second Lieutenant Gates, two unnamed cadets, and McClallen himself. The duty of riding herd on the fifty privates, mostly raw recruits, was handled by four sergeants who were assisted by four corporals. Eight artificers attended the guns and muskets, and there were two drummers and two fifers, which made a total of seventy men and five officers. As the aggregate party was eighty-one, the additional travelers were six washerwomen, some of whom may have been wives of the gunners.[10]

After nine years McClallen understood how to move men and heavy equipment. Still, getting men, guns, horses, baggage, and hangers-on across the mountains without losing those having second thoughts about desertion was no small accomplishment. Assisting the captain was second-in-command Lieutenant Peter, who seemed to be developing a bad case of simmering resentment. To make matters worse, they were soon under the critical eye of the commanding general and his staff.

When General Wilkinson caught up with them at Bedford on the road to Pittsburgh, he inquired after Mr. Burr and was told that the gentleman had passed by their party a few days previously. When they arrived at Pittsburgh, the general was disappointed to find that the vice president had already departed down the Ohio River. If the artillery officers were curious about the general's interests, that was none of their business.[11] The military party was joined by the newly appointed Territorial Secretary Joseph Browne and Territorial Justice Rufus Easton.

McClallen's company was still incomplete when it reached Pittsburgh, and the general ordered it to be brought up to the establishment by taking in the recruits and supplying the balance by lot from other units.[12] Lieutenant Peter approved and paid $135 for bringing the men and their gear from Baltimore and an additional $60 for moving Lieutenant Gates's detachment to Bedford. The total cost of moving the combined company to Pittsburgh amounted to $184.

But the lieutenant balked at paying two charges for the transport of General Wilkinson's personal property. Wagoneer John Frush carried seven hundred pounds from Baltimore for $31.50. John Phillips hauled thirteen hundred pounds for $58.50. That ton of goods represented the household goods necessary to set up the Wilkinson family in St. Louis. When Peter refused to authorize payment, the Pittsburgh military agent Lt. Moses Hooke had to step forward and assume the responsibility.[13]

Undoubtedly feeling a bit singed by the reaction to his obstinacy, the recalcitrant Lieutenant Peter began noting times when the general showed perhaps undue concern for private property, including that of his captain.[14] The eight packages of merchandise that Captain McClallen brought along were about the same weight as the general's property, but those had been carried by another wagon driver named James M'Nutty. McClallen paid his own bill.[15]

No one was enthusiastic about going to Louisiana. An unhealthy climate and river fevers made the Mississippi Valley a notorious if not fatal duty station.[16] In order to uphold discipline, McClallen had the unpleasant duty of presiding at the court-martials of men who tried to desert. That dreary charade assigned deserters or other malfeasants the lash; fifty on the bare back or sometimes a hundred charitably spread out between healing in sets of twenty-five. When Thomas McCoy of McClallen's company was sentenced to receive fifty lashes on his bare back, the general approved the sentence but "from his repugnance to disgrace a soldier...and his youth," he remitted the punishment. Private James Jefferson was not as lucky after being convicted of being drunk at post. Fifty lashes. What a way to treat men.[17]

In March the secretary of war had ordered Lieutenant Hooke to have four barges built that were capable of carrying twenty-five to thirty men and three or four tons of equipment. As an experiment he also ordered half a dozen Albany batteaux, which were thirty-two feet long by five and a half feet wide and could be rowed by six or eight oars. Captain McClallen supervised getting the eight field pieces aboard the barges and the distribution of the baggage of the company. Crammed on board flatboats and barges were the eighty-one individuals of the company and presumably some horses.[18] Somehow the captain found places for the men among the gun carriages and baggage, but having laundresses along was a nuisance.

The fifteen heavy twenty-four-pound howitzer carriages that Captain McClallen built at Carlisle were destined for New Orleans and would follow later. The flotilla transported four brass field pieces and four iron guns, which would be remounted on carriages at St. Louis. Ammunition included 528 52-pound shells, 59 rounds of canister, and 24 rounds of grapeshot. The guns were not uniform, as 1,206 round shot, 22 rounds of canister, and 24 fixed rounds for six-pound guns and 478 unfixed rounds for three-pound guns were also noted. There were 40-pound barrels of powder plus cartridge paper, and the many other articles of equipment necessary for artillery. Captain McClallen had to plan carefully in order to take his company into the field.

In addition to that responsibility, McClallen also loaded his experiment in the western trade, eight packages of trade goods that might very well decide his future. If there were an accident, it would be an investment that a captain could never hope to repay. Finding room for his goods on the government transport was only a matter of taking up some space. What difference did eight bundles of trade goods make? Officer's privilege.[19]

After drawing thirty days' provisions from the government contractor, Captain McClallen embarked his company on May 23. The fleet of barges and batteaux floating away from Pittsburgh represented the tide of the United States flooding toward a continental destiny. Such departures were not unusual because pioneers bent on taking over Kentucky or the American Bottoms along the Mississippi had been launching on those waters for almost half a century.

General Wilkinson's elegant sixty-foot-long barge accommodated his family, Secretary Browne, and others. The official entourage included his son Lt. James Wilkinson, acting as adjutant of the detachment, and Cadet Nicholas Biddle, a relative of the general's wife.[20] A nephew, Benjamin Wilkinson, was also along to look for opportunities in the new country.[21]

An idyllic float down the beautiful Ohio River was trying for women. The general's lady, Ann Biddle, was a military wife accustomed to all that meant, but Catharine Browne was accustomed to the refinements of New York and far from a frontier woman. Her family included a daughter of marriageable age and seven rambunctious boys. Personal discretion was difficult. Just above present Parkersburg, West Virginia, they passed the place where the ague and the bilious fevers were reputed to begin later in that deadly season.

Making the best of tiresome days, John McClallen and his lieutenants found excuses to row over to the barge of the official party. As a former resident of Albany, John reminded Mr. Browne of Browne's 1782 marriage there, in a dual ceremony when Theodosia Prevost, Mrs. Browne's sister, married the young lawyer Aaron Burr. Floating down the lazy Ohio, the officers tried to amuse the perspiring gentlemen, glowing ladies, and particularly Miss Browne.

⊷≒≓⊷

Those lazy days gave McClallen insights into the new administration of Upper Louisiana. During the Revolution, British-born Territorial Secretary Browne had served in the Pennsylvania line. At the turn of the century he was known to every Republican in the state of New York. After the visionary Manhattan Company water project, Browne's former brother-in-law, Burr, recommended him for the post of minister (secretary) of the navy. That appointment failed to develop, but in return Browne supported Burr in his disappointing run for governor of New York. Although the candidate carried the city, he had been beaten upstate in Federalist territory.

A week after Vice President Burr delivered his farewell address to Congress, Browne was appointed secretary of the Louisiana Territory. Now Mr. Burr was somewhere ahead, touring the West to broaden his base of political support and shadowed by rumors that he intended to break off a western nation, or create a new one through a filibuster against Spanish possessions. If that subject came up on the general's barge, discussion stopped because Wilkinson's disappointment in failing to catch up with Mr. Burr at Cincinnati was obvious.

Anticipating the impression that he needed to make at St. Louis, the general observed that Captain McClallen's company was looking a bit ragged. At Cincinnati the former clothier general of the Revolution ordered the appropriation from government stocks of proper uniforms for the artillery recruits.[22] Drifting past the Blue River in Kentucky on May 29, the general, mindful of the health of the troops, forbid them to sleep in the sun and ordered shades rigged on the boats.

At Louisville, Kentucky, General Wilkinson's barge moored on the Clarksville side apart from the troop convoy. During the evening Captain McClallen and Lieutenant Peter crossed the river to ask permission to precede with the troop boats. They found several gentlemen with the general who were planning a mutual business adventure, the financing of a canal around the nearby falls. One of them was Gen. Benjamin Hovey, of whose reputation John McClallen knew in New York.[23] At the risk of unsolicited advice, he cautioned his commander that Hovey was untrustworthy. High on great expectations, Wilkinson laughed and promised to keep a sharp eye on the corporate purse.[24]

The flotilla drifted through the unrolling panorama of a developing frontier. In the third phase of pioneer development, the primitive log cabins of the settlers were being enlarged, rebuilt, or covered with more pretentious clapboards. Where cattle and hogs once roamed at large, rail fences now outlined real fields replacing the primitive corn patches. Farther on the flotilla caught up with the advancing frontier. Stumps rotting in the fields yielded to dead standing trees, girdled to kill them, but still too formidable to be felled and burned.

The bored soldiers lolling at the rail were eastern boys unaccustomed to the rawness of a new country. They exchanged waves with the isolated families who came to the riverbank to see the boat parade. McClallen thought those ragged, barefoot children, gaunt, hollow-eyed women, and bearded men seemed like dream walkers in a daze of loneliness, overwhelmed by the impossible task of grubbing a place for themselves from unyielding, endless woods. In past wars, soldiers served with the expectation of being paid off with public land and what the gunners saw was an example of that reward. The insatiable greed for land was a terrible master.

In early June 1805 the flotilla reached Fort Massac near present Paducah, Kentucky, but on the Illinois side of the Ohio, where the general ordered the baggage and public stores, artillery, gun carriages, ammunition, provisions, and every other article unloaded. When the military equipment was secured under tents and tarpaulins, McClallen was also provided with a tent for storing the private merchandise.[25] Three days later, assisted by lieutenants Peter and Kimball, he examined the state of the provisions received at Pittsburgh and ordered what was no longer fit to eat destroyed.

General Wilkinson finally caught up with Burr. The two spent four days together. No one could say what had passed between them, but when the former vice president departed, his handsome barge was manned by a squad of ten soldiers commanded by a sergeant.[26] The boat also carried the officers being sent to New Orleans for the second court-martial of the obstinate Colonel Butler. The general's fixation on a mutinous pigtail was nothing to inspire confidence. Captain McClallen loyally believed that this was more than a personal dispute because one old obstinate officer could not be allowed to infect the troops.[27]

Another member of the first court-martial board, Maj. James Bruff, already commanded military forces at St. Louis.[28] Because officers of the territorial government were required to be property owners, in early April General Wilkinson wrote Bruff asking him to find a place of about a thousand acres within five or six miles of St. Louis that he might buy.[29]

When the first reports came back to St. Louis from the Corps of Discovery, Capt. Amos Stoddard provided Corp. Richard Warfington with a public horse and ordered him to carry the dispatches and a red box of items to William Clark's brother Jonathan at Louisville. Warfington also carried a letter dated May 22 from Pierre Chouteau to Indiana governor Harrison at Vincennes. After that, the corporal would return to Captain Campbell's company at South West Point, Tennessee. At Louisville Corporal Warfington learned that his company had been transferred to the Mississippi, and he turned back to catch up with the general's flotilla at Fort Massac. In addition to his information about the upper Missouri, Warfington delivered a letter from Governor Harrison warning that Major Bruff had created difficulties in Upper Louisiana by presuming to set up a government, drawing laws, and making appointments.[30]

Although General Wilkinson claimed that he had no particulars about the expedition, someone did, as the Frankfort *Palladium* of June 8 reported "A gentleman of respectability who resides in the neighborhood of this town has politely handed us the following interesting information." Frankfort was about fifty miles from Louisville and the source of the information must have been William Clark's brother Jonathan Clark. The news item continued:

> Letters have been received from captains Lewis and Clark by express sent by them to the commandant at St. Louis, with dispatches for the President of the United States. Our travelers have procured an animal which is called the wild dog of the prairies...also two magpies. The dog, magpies, and remarkable horn are in possession of a Captain M'Clellan, who has undertaken to carry them to the city of Washington to the president with the dispatches.[31]

The same statement was carried another eighty miles, where a fuller version was published in the Lexington *Gazette* on June 18.[32] The newspaper accounts were presumptuous since Captain McClallen was committed to conducting his company, the guns, and private goods to St. Louis. General Wilkinson was not about to send off a company-grade officer whom he needed as a dispatch rider for some oddities of no consequence.

The keelboat that returned from the Lewis and Clark expedition in the spring was sent on to Fort Massac to assist another military detachment coming from Vincennes. Two of the six soldiers who wintered at the Mandan villages on the upper Missouri River were aboard as well as Captain Amos Stoddard, who came to meet the general and fill him in on difficulties between authorities in St. Louis.[33] He told the general that another delegation of Indians was in St. Louis waiting to be sent on to meet the president. Arranging that led to a conflict of authority and confrontation between Major Bruff, Indian agent Pierre Chouteau, and Captain Stoddard, who was handling downstream matters for Captain Lewis. Major Bruff had allowed himself to be drawn into a piddling squabble, and generals were not obliged to suffer fools.

On June 10, Captain McClallen was ordered to proceed from Fort Massac and take quarters in the garrison at St. Louis. Facing an upstream pull from the mouth of the Ohio, the large keelboat was assigned to carry his men, stores, baggage, clothing, and public property.[34] Lieutenant Peter would bring along the freight boat with powder, military stores, tools, and implements as well as another small keel with provisions.[35]

Forecasts of a strong current were all too true. After nine days the flotilla was only about a league above the mouth of the Ohio. In order to make headway against the Mississippi current, it was apparent that the boats would have to be lightened and some baggage discharged. Lieutenant Kimball was left to look after the sick and Lieutenant Pike to command the stragglers.

The general's barge, Captain McClallen in the large keel, the paymaster, and the lightened boats reached St. Louis by July 2. The capital of Louisiana was not all that impressive, a couple of long streets of curiously constructed houses strung out facing the river. According to an eastern newspaper, a delegation of citizens did their best to make the arrival impressive by riding out to meet the general and escorting him to his quarters. As many of Stoddard's sickly fifty regulars who could get on their feet were drawn with their officers to salute the commanding officer. The three hundred tribesmen who discharged their guns in greeting constituted the largest assembly of Indians that McClallen had ever seen. After addresses were exchanged, everyone withdrew to the hill overlooking the river where a three-hundred-foot-long table was loaded with the delicacies of the season. At nine o'clock an elegant ball opened where "beauty sparkled before the enchanted eye" as the ladies of Louisiana claimed partners.[36]

Still attentive to McClallen's baggage, the general made a point of ordering a horseman's tent for him and Lt. William P. Clyma, as well as another for the "present protection of his clothing."[37] Placed to the right of Capt. James Richmond's infantry, McClallen's company of artillerists enjoyed a common tent for every six men.[38]

As the orders for July 3 put it, they had arrived just in time to salute "our political sabbath." The site for the Fourth of July celebration was near a bower on the hill facing the river. When the troops in complete uniform and under arms formed in the evening at six o'clock, gunners fired thirteen rounds of blank cartridges from one of the six pounders.[39] Parading the troops gave the citizens of St. Louis the opportunity to view the power of the new regime. It was not quite an army of conquest to give Spanish America cause to tremble.

After three weeks, the companies of captains McClallen, Lewis, and Campbell were ordered to march to a new encampment.[40] General Wilkinson had selected a site for the new military post and the adjoining Indian trade factory on the Missouri River, twelve miles northwest of St. Louis. That was far enough away to insulate the troops from the vile attractions of river men's hangouts along the waterfront. While their baggage went the longer way around by water, the men marched overland. The parade of McClallen's artillery recruits through St. Louis was not that impressive to locals accustomed to the polished pomposities of Spanish troops.

The place that the general had staked out as their new home was nice enough for a summer picnic, but if the troops were to spend the winter they needed something less airy than wedge tents. Through August the sappers and miners of McClallen's company applied themselves to the construction of Cantonment Belle Fontaine.[41] After a day of hard labor building their barracks and the Indian trade factory, the gunners were unlikely to get into much trouble.

As the senior engineer, Major Bruff made the important decisions and left the bothersome details of construction to the company commanders. John's fellow officers were captains Benjamin Lockwood, John Richmond, and John Campbell.[42] McClallen had to supervise the project in person because Lieutenant Peter was sent off on detached duty. Then Lieutenant Gates claimed ill health and was permitted to resign his commission. His ailment was serious, and he died in October 1806. The Mississippi Valley was almost as deadly to American arms as the fevers of the West Indies had been to Napoleon's army.

As his military duties proceeded, McClallen had to find the time to decide how to dispose of those bales of Indian trade goods. He was beginning to feel that he was living a double life. The certainties of military service were becoming obscured by misty, private concerns.

CHAPTER FIVE

THE OFFICERS AND GENTLEMEN OF ST. LOUIS

After fifty days on the rivers, the welcome given General Wilkinson, now Governor Wilkinson, and the celebration of the Fourth of July made St. Louis a less-forbidding duty station. Captain McClallen realized that the observance of Independence Day must have seemed odd to an old community subject to the flags of three nations in the last year. The hospitality came from French residents and former Americans who moved across the Mississippi to get in on Spanish land grants and were not all that certain how their claims would hold up under a new regime.

Although just a company-grade officer, over the past year Captain McClallen had developed an intimacy with the commanding general that only a few others enjoyed. Wilkinson's entourage was a tight capsule of family, aides, and trusted noncoms whose duty was insulating military headquarters from distractions of territorial government. Governor Wilkinson soon found that what needed to be done required unaccustomed forbearance in dealing with what he dismissed as "a mongrel community." St. Louis and the satellite communities roiled in uncertainty about a new regime that was less authoritarian than the previous Spanish government but more assertive about imposing a new "democratic" order.

Beginning his administration like a military command, the general immediately secured a perimeter on the edge of a vast, largely unknown jurisdiction. Detachments were placed where they could command the Mississippi and Missouri rivers, and parties launched up the Mississippi and Osage rivers. Orders were posted concerning the conduct of the Indian trade. An old western hand, Wilkinson was one of the few Americans who knew something about the new territory.

And he was about to expand that knowledge with the forces he had at hand.

⚊⚊

At Fort Massac, Wilkinson had already decided to start three or four expeditions.[1] Anticipating Secretary Dearborn's reaction, and Secretary Madison's caution about expenses, the general rationalized that those expeditions would be kept small and led by "intelligent subalterns" at little cost beyond the payment of interpreters and guides.[2]

The first expedition ordered Lt. Zebulon Pike of the First Infantry Regiment to start up the Mississippi River with a seventy-foot-long keelboat and party of nineteen noncoms and privates. He was to scout locations for military posts below Prairie du Chien, near the mouth of the Ouisconsin, Rivere St. Pierre, and the Falls of St. Anthony. Locating a company-strength garrison on the Wisconsin River should "regulate our commerce with Canada."[3] Pike's party got under way on August 10.

Because it was uncertain how the administration of the Spanish Interior Provinces was going to react to the as-yet-undefined southwestern boundary, New Mexico also came to mind. When the general, his adjutant, the younger Lt. Wilkinson, or his aide-de-camp, Cadet Biddle, set the parole (the watchword) for July 22, it was "St. Afee,"[4] an indication that headquarters was already thinking of next steps. On the same day that Lieutenant Pike started north, Wilkinson instructed the trader/Indian agent Pierre Chouteau to proceed without delay to the Osage towns and gain their permission for the establishment of a military post. He would also acquire information "relative to the route and distances from the Osages, to the Settlements of New Mexico, and particularly St. Afee."[5]

Lt. George Peter was ordered to take a confidential sergeant, a corporal, and eight good boatmen supplied with fifteen days' rations and accompany the agent to the Osage Nation to confirm permission from the Osage for a military post in their territory.

The Jefferson administration had already created a problem by saddling Upper Louisiana with four congressionally appointed district commandants. Three had already arrived and set up petty governments at St. Charles, Ste. Genevieve, and Cape Girardeau, imbibing a sense of authority that they were reluctant to give up. Former congressman Samuel Hammond, the designated commandant for St. Louis, was still on his way west, but conflicts of authority were inevitable. The new governor had been saddled with a second layer of authority that had a head start on his administration.

Wilkinson was sent to govern a vast, still-undefined territory that would have international implications north and south. Number 13 had a better handle on relationships with Spanish authorities than the Jefferson administration suspected, and he was already formulating plans for dealing with those interior provinces. But until Captain Lewis provided better geographical information, the northern bounds of the Louisiana Territory were undetermined and subject to British intrusion. All Wilkinson had to go on was the data that Lewis sent back after wintering at the Mandan villages on the upper Missouri and sixteen pages of speculative hogwash concocted by a presumptuous British fur trader named Alexander Mackenzie, who laid out in his book the British concept of how North America should be divided.[6]

Not long after he arrived in St. Louis in late 1804 as interim military commandant, Maj. James Bruff spent $2.50 for a copy of Mackenzie's *Voyages from Montreal through the Continent of North America.*[7] The British fur trader called for the consolidation of imperial interests in order to force a northern boundary at 45 degrees, or the very least, 48 degrees north latitude, which would take up most of the present states of Minnesota, North and South Dakota, Montana, Idaho, and Washington.[8] By then Mackenzie knew that the astronomer David Thompson's 1798 survey of the old line of 49 degrees north latitude fell short of the Missouri River.

Bruff's copy of Mackenzie's *Voyages* was passed around among the officers settling in at Cantonment Belle Fontaine. They must have marveled at what Canadian merchants were willing to endure in pursuit of beaver skins. Veterans, who remembered the bloody excesses promoted by British traders before the defeat of the Ohio Indians, bristled at Mackenzie's suggestion of a boundary set so deeply into Louisiana that it might cut off the upper Mississippi and Missouri rivers. Two weeks after purchasing the book, Major Bruff wrote to Wilkinson to raise the question of the defense of the southern boundary with Spain.

Suffer me now to suggest, that if a Military Post was established on the Missouri at the mouth of the river Platt between whose waters and those of the del nort [Rio Grande] there is but a short carrying place; where Traders from Santa Fe meet ours as is absolutely the case at this moment.[9]

Major Bruff suggested that a military post at the mouth of the Osage, Kansas, or Platte rivers was essential to check Indian depredations and "give them a higher opinion of our power to chastise them should they misbehave; protect our Traders and prevent smuggling from Canada &c." From the beginning, Governor Wilkinson had serious concerns on two fronts and would have to rely on his officers to address them.

In May 1805, when the Corps of Discovery keelboat returned from Fort Mandan, Major Bruff and Captain Stoddard scanned the reports and questioned the soldiers who brought the boat down. After interviewing the four men from his company who returned with Corporal Warfington, Captain Stoddard had additional data. When Major Bruff sent the keelboat up the Ohio, not to meet the general as supposed but to assist Captain Richmond, who was moving his company from Vincennes, Stoddard went along and filled the general in on the reports from the explorers.[10]

Although Wilkinson complained to Secretary Dearborn that he could "learn no particulars of [Capt. Lewis's] voyage," he located the Mandan towns at 47 degrees north latitude, which suggests that he had access to the maps or observations of Captain Lewis and to the military recommendations written by Second Lieutenant William Clark. To assert control of the Missouri River, the subaltern suggested a string of military outposts that required a total of 880 soldiers of the republic, a practical fantasy for an army with an authorized strength of not much more than three thousand.[11] Already short of men, the commander of the western army had a pressing obligation to reinforce the critical port of New Orleans.

Under the authority of the Act of March 20, 1802, to regulate trade and intercourse, Governor Wilkinson wasted no time in closing the Missouri to all trade. His first proclamation prohibited all persons from ascending the Missouri into Indian country or infiltrating the western tributaries from the upper Mississippi. The governor laid out his reasoning when he wrote Dearborn from Fort Massac that alcohol had not been previously introduced to the Missouri Indians "but now our own cupidity & the sinister enterprises of the British, are introducing this destructive Liquor into every Nation & town."[12] British traders contracted for the delivery of large amounts of Kentucky whiskey to Prairie du Chien or St. Louis. Although Indiana governor Harrison licensed a cargo of sixteen hundred gallons of whiskey from Kentucky, the general intended to prevent it from passing up the Missouri, and, if Harrison cooperated, the upper Mississippi as well. Wilkinson suggested that the British minister should warn "the Merchants of Canada, that they will not, nor their goods & merchandise, be permitted to pass the Mississippi after next autumn."[13] This was the first of several steps to gain control of Louisiana Territory for the United States.

On July 10 Governor Wilkinson prohibited persons from ascending the Missouri into the Indian country or crossing from the Mississippi to trade with the Indians but "by the permission of my hand. Having issued the proclamation I demand attested copies of the Invoices of every cargo destined to the Missouri, before I take a bond or grant a license."[14]

In August, as was the habit for the past fifteen or more years, trading outfits from Prairie du Chien came down the Mississippi River. The general complained that "this Town is now almost filled, not only with merchants, Agents, clerks and engages, all British subjects, who are here for the express purpose of carrying their enterprises into a river, where they have no right and which they never before visited."[15]

After a gesture of polling the other two members of the territorial legislature in mid-August, the governor advised Secretary of State Madison that he would "prohibit the entrance of British merchandise into the Missouri."[16] Based on his interpretation, the recent acquisition of Louisiana was outside the prior guarantees of Jay's Treaty, and the governor issued a declaration prohibiting British traders from operating among the Indian dependents of the United States.[17] Further, boats going upstream had to be manned by American boatmen, not Canadians. Although the governor anticipated that "the measure will draw upon me a load of obloquy," his "somewhat extra-judicial" decree was certainly in the national interest.[18] Given a one-month or six-week lag between the time a letter was written and when it could be expected to arrive in Washington, Wilkinson had to act on his own initiative, even if that challenged an existing treaty with Britain.

That bombshell exploded in the faces of British traders who were then arriving from the upper Mississippi with cargoes. Lieutenant Pike encountered the supplier Myer Michaels bringing three boats from Michilimackinac with a cargo for the Osage trader Manuel Lisa or his associate James Clamorgan. Two weeks later, James Aird, a trader for the struggling Robert Dickson & Company, arrived with three boats and thirty men from Prairie du Chien going to the Missouri River trade. Aird found his outfit grounded by the new regulation until October, when the wily British trader convinced the governor that he had always been a US citizen, just never bothered to declare it.[19] Rounding up a crew of newly minted American boatmen to replace prohibited Canadian voyageurs, Aird headed back to the Sioux trade.[20]

⊷≡≡⊶

Army officers standing on the rise near Cantonment Belle Fontaine watched the Indian trade rowing against the Missouri current. Captain McClallen's arrangement with Calhoun & Company included examining the Missouri River Indian trade as a business opportunity. He soon learned that previous Spanish governments never managed to check British intrusion from the upper Mississippi, Red and Assiniboine rivers, and now those intruders expected to gain access to the Missouri and continue operating under the terms of Jay's Treaty, which up until now permitted British traders to deal with Indian wards of the United States. Until the effect of the governor's regulation was known, it would be unwise for McClallen to venture his small assortment of goods in competition with experienced traders. Dealing with Indian tribes and highly competitive established traders was no place for an amateur. McClallen also learned that an adventure in the fur trade could take as long as two years to recover the investment, too long to answer his obligation to Calhoun & Company or to relieve his father's debt. McClallen decided that he could not recommend an investment in the business to his suppliers.[21]

Through July and August Captain McClallen appears to have been an interested bystander whose duties usually kept him at Cantonment Belle Fontaine. Some of the officers who shared the bachelor's mess were in transit to other duty stations, but captains Stoddard and Biddle had been near St. Louis for the past two years, and Major Bruff was military commandant for a year. At table they shared the events of the day and expectations of their futures. Unacquainted with the demands of frontier service, particularly when the western limits were uncertain, it was subalterns like Pike, Peter, or young Wilkinson who were learning how to challenge the vast unknown. But that wasn't enough, and in early September Wilkinson started a private adventure of his own.

> I have equipt a Peroque out of my Small private means, not with any view of Self interest, to ascend the missouri and enter the River Piere jaune, or yellow Stone, called by the natives Unicorn River [Big Horn tributary of the Yellowstone],[22] the same by which Capt. Lewis I since find expects to return and which my informants tell me is filled with wonders, this Party will not get back before the Summer 1807— They are natives of this Town, and are just able to give us course and distance, with the names and population of the Indian nations and to bring back with them Specimens of the natural products.[23]

It was unlikely that Aird's crawling batteaux would be able to catch up to that pirogue, and those words were all that Wilkinson ever wrote about a party that could have been as large as eight voyageurs. Only three were later mentioned. Foremost was the experienced boatman François Rivet, who had accompanied the Corps of Discovery keelboat as far as the Mandan villages and returned in the spring of 1805. An upper river trapper, Joseph Grenier, had joined Rivet at the Indian villages and returned to St. Louis with him. Except for a nameless young man mentioned later, the others are unknown. The party was under way before September 8, but they would have to drive hard to reach the upper river before it froze.

By early September, Wilkinson was also planning another private adventure to test the mercantile possibilities in the Southwest, a scheme that may have included those eight bales of goods that Captain McClallen shepherded down the Ohio and on to St. Louis. A dutiful officer was in no position to try retailing the goods, and McClallen rode to St. Louis to arrange their disposal. The former Spanish lieutenant governor had noticed that "this post abounds in dry goods of all sorts and many of the finest," which may have made disposal difficult.[24]

⚬

St. Louis was a small community where most men of any standing knew each other. Four decades of Spanish administration had not made Louisiana any less French in its soul. Captain Stoddard told McClallen that the Chouteau brothers had been very kind to him, as well as to Captain Lewis and Lieutenant Clark. As a fledgling entrepreneur with stock to dispose, and an apparent intimate of the general, Captain McClallen would have been pleased to receive an invitation to dine with the family of M. René Auguste Chouteau.[25]

Writers of the time described St. Louis in a grander style than the actuality of *poste en terre* (posts set in the ground) buildings justified. There were about one hundred and eighty houses built in the Canadian style, and the general's lady had to accommodate her family and that ton of household goods in a 22-by-30-foot place made of logs set upright directly in the earth. She would not be doing much in the way of entertaining.

At least the homes of St. Louis nabobs were comparable to the white colonial mansions of Charleston or the brick elegance of Albany or Baltimore. The large house of M. Auguste Chouteau fronted la Rue Royale with the houses of his mother, Madame Chouteau, and his brother-in-law Charles Gratiot nearby. Since February those examples of wealth and influence were missing a link because the house of Pierre Chouteau became the pyre of the old regime. Still, there was no doubt that in the fascinating mix of private and public St. Louis business, the self-interested Chouteau brothers figured large.

Stepping across the polished black oak floor of the Chouteau mansion, American officers soon realized that M. Chouteau, his half-brother Pierre, and their brother-in-law Gratiot thought of St. Louis as their town. Although the last Spanish administration betrayed him by allowing that cursed Spaniard Manuel Lisa to cut in on the Osage trade, Pierre Chouteau considered it his right to exude a certain level of control and dominance. Now that the Spanish were gone, the brothers expected to recover that privilege. When Pierre returned from the Osages, he would have the power of the United States behind him.

An evening of whist at the Chouteau game table produced interesting insights.[26] The brothers were regional merchants, but it was the expanding Indian trade that provided their market. Most of that on the lower Missouri River was in deer skins, small furs, and Indian-conditioned buffalo robes. Heavy packs of skins and robes were generally drifted downstream to New Orleans.

Given the risk of spoilage from passing through a warm climate, lucrative beaver pelts followed a cooler northern road to Canadian markets. In the Chouteau warehouse, those valuable skins were sorted, moths beaten out, and the packs were sent north through Prairie du Chien and Michilimackinac to Montreal.[27] That may seem a bit disloyal nowadays, but the exchange brought back the British manufactured goods that the tribes preferred.[28] Fine pelts north, gross robes south, that was how it was done.[29]

Auguste Chouteau recalled that as a younger man he had traveled fifteen hundred miles up the Missouri River to personally inspect the places of the inland business.[30] Now he let agents like Henri Delaurier carry his business to the middle river customers. Regimes come and go, business goes on.

In the past, British traders blatantly imposed on ineffective Spanish governors. Scanning an unpromising hand of cards, Auguste Chouteau sighed that previous attempts to oust those intruders had been a joke. Ten years earlier that bumbling old *imbecile* Jacques Clamorgan induced eight innocents to join him in forming the Company of Explorers of the Upper Missouri. But it was soon apparent that the main supplier was a British trader, Andrew Todd, who operated from the east side of the upper Mississippi. Todd smoothly switched his allegiance to Spain by promising to conduct his operations through New Orleans. He died there and Auguste helped settle the estate in the interests of the New Orleans supplier, Daniel Clark. Lately, poor old Clamorgan was reduced to dealing with the likes of that rascal Manuel Lisa. *Le bon Dieu* might forgive Lisa, but the Chouteau brothers never would.

Previously old Jacques Clamorgan's Company of Explorers of the Upper Missouri sent a point man to confront British traders on the upper river. James Mackay had been a North West Company clerk before he came to St. Louis, and his grasp of the competitive tactics of his former associates led him to stop among the Mahas (Omaha Indians). Mackay sent an innocent clerk named John Evans on to eject intruders from the Mandan villages and then go on to discover the western ocean.[31] When it came up that Evans was looking for a lost tribe of Welsh Indians, Captain McClallen amused the table by suggesting that he was misdirected. When the captain served in the south, it was believed that the Welsh Indians lived in Georgia. Laughter all around.

During the winter of 1803/04, when the Corps of Discovery was across the Mississippi at Riviere à Dubois, Auguste and Pierre Chouteau were pleased to be helpful. Pierre even loaned Captain Stoddard six hundred dollars to stage a modest gala celebrating the exchange of flags. After Lisa failed to keep his promise to find boatmen, Auguste provided eight trustworthy voyageurs. Before the expedition left, Captain Lewis made Pierre the de facto Indian agent for the lower river, and if the captain was called away, M. Charles Gratiot would exercise Lewis's power of attorney. For an established French family, becoming *americaine* was a generally pleasant transition.

Le general's acceptance of Chouteau hospitality was taken as a demonstration of his sympathy to the old inhabitants, and presumably, the sanctity of their holdings as American opportunists. Yankees often overran St. Louis in their ruthless scramble for fortune. Wilkinson's appointment was taken as an intention to bridle those ambitions. Order was prized by all.

Would it be presumptive to inquire about the governor's relationship with Mr. Burr? Kentucky newspapers printed rumors that the former vice president was trying to raise an army. Some thought that the general's appointments in readjusting the civil government created a potential cadre for a filibuster. It was rumored that even Secretary of

War Dearborn considered the possibility of an invasion of New Mexico. If his host was fishing for information, McClallen did not raise to the bait.

◄═ ═►

After a pleasant late summer afternoon in a French household, McClallen felt more at ease with the commercial establishment of St. Louis, whose mercantile concerns were not that much different from those he had known in Albany, or lately gathered from the Baltimore friends. He came away with a sense that this was the moment when new businesses could be founded. But why, when the West seemed to be tottering on the verge of a war with the Spanish, was the general so interested in pursuing a mercantile adventure to "St. Afee"?[32]

Heady from the wine and insights, the captain had time to muse on those questions during the twelve-mile ride back to Belle Fontaine. His career? What had he done in ten years but shuffle papers and account for government property? The most responsible duty he ever performed was helping a Federalist administration squelch the complaints of over-taxed citizens. No wonder they failed to respect the uniform he wore. Men of real wealth and power merely amused themselves by indulging impoverished officers. If McClallen was to contribute anything to relieve his father's horrendous debt, he could not do it on a soldier's pay, or by being another petty transporter between Pittsburgh and St. Louis. Despite his decision to abandon a mercantile career in order to serve the nation, the dutiful son was being forced into business. And that impetus was coming from his commanding officer.

CHAPTER SIX

WESTERN HORIZONS

John McClallen found himself in St. Louis while his world seemed to be changing before his eyes. As General Wilkinson moved to seize control of Louisiana and impose a United States presence, the obligation of reporting to the president and two members of his cabinet gave his administration a schizophrenic split. He was obliged to keep the secretary of war informed on military matters and Indian supervision, and the secretary of state on government and international affairs. The scientifically minded president got the specimen rocks, bones, and feathers.[1]

One of the first problems was the uncertain relationship with Spain. That old colonial power might dispute the location of the southern bounds of Louisiana Territory. Thinking about approaches to Spanish territory began in February 1805, before Wilkinson left for the West. Secretary of War Dearborn had ordered a secret survey of the still-undetermined Spanish frontier "relative to any contemplated military operation." To avoid threatening military activity, he advised that operations might be conducted by "Individuals, in the character of hunters and traders, [who] may be employed with secrecy and success."[2]

It was not that the way to Santa Fe was unknown. Wilkinson's map portfolio already included a sketch tracing the overland road to Santa Fe. Recognizing the strategic importance of the shallow Platte River as a jumping-off place for adventures toward Santa Fe, Maj. James Bruff had extracted data from two Pawnee traders, Jose Tibeau (Joseph Thibault) and Polite Cardinal, whose brother, Jean Marie Cardinalle, had a Pawnee wife. About nine years previously, in 1797, the three made a trip to Santa Fe and were able to provide the major with a sketch map showing that it was just a twenty-five-day trip for Indians or adventuresome Frenchmen.[3]

The sketch map showed that the route from the Pawnee towns on the Platte to Santa Fe was six hundred and ninety miles.[4]

In 1803 and 1804, the accomplished plainsman Joseph Gervais accompanied parties of Pawnee to the Spanish lands where they concluded treaties and received gifts.[5] An Oto trader told the outward-bound Lewis and Clark at Council Bluffs on the Missouri River (near present Atchison, Kansas) that it was a twenty-five-day journey to the pass overlooking Santa Fe.[6] Traveling from Regis Loisel's post among the Teton Sioux, James Purcell, Dioniso Lacroix, and Andre Terien reached Santa Fe in June 1805. The upper Missouri trader Jacques d'Eglise and Laurent Durocher were also believed to have gone to Santa Fe.[7]

An attempt to open trade with New Mexico had already been undertaken, with Captain Stoddard's permission, by associates of a Kaskaskia merchant.

A trader, called (William) Morrison, equipt a young french adventurer with a small Cargo destined to St. Afee, who proceeded to these [Panis] towns by water, where he had formerly traded, there he procured pack Horses, loaded his goods & commenced his March, with a party of the Natives, since which he has not been heard of. — this happened last spring.[8]

Those adventures were undependable rumors, as most of the visitors never returned to report what they had seen. But the sketch map could be confirmed because Wilkinson was able to compare it to a copy he had made of the Baron Alexander von Humboldt's map of the interior provinces of New Spain.[9]

There was also the problem of how the tribes of the interior would accept travelers. Not long after arriving in St. Louis, Wilkinson reported on "the Subject of Indian affairs in this New World":

...our relations to Spain & Britain on our Southern, Western & Northern unexplored frontiers Suggest the expediency of attaching to us, all the Nations who drink the waters which fall into the Gulph of Mexico: the Ya-i-tans or more properly, Commanches, who resort to the tract of Country between the Osages and St. Afee during the temperate Seasons, merit particular attention, because they constitute the most powerful Nation of Savages on the Continent, and have it in their power to facilitate or impede our march to New Mexico, should such movement ever become necessary.[10]

Officers at headquarters could also consult an interesting "savage delineation on a Buffalo Pelt" drawn by the Arikara chief who came down last spring with the Corps of Discovery keelboat. The Arikara's name, *pi'a hiitu* (hereafter Piahito), could be translated as "Eagle Feather," but he was also mistakenly known by the title for a village chief, *Ankedoucharo*.[11] Although Wilkinson was not initially impressed, the man did not fit the stereotype of a savage. Piahito and his people shared an intertribal trade network that stretched south to the Spanish provinces and west as far as the Pacific Ocean. They regularly dealt with British traders who came overland from the Assiniboine River with mercantile connections to distant Montreal or the shores of Hudson's Bay.

Piahito's accomplishments as a warrior were something that a military officer respected. Although he spoke eleven Indian dialects plus hand signs, his linguistic accomplishments failed to penetrate unfamiliar English and he was therefore accompanied by a French-speaking interpreter, Joseph Gravelines.

Piahito's grasp of geography was extensive.[12] While kneeling on a buffalo robe he drew the rivers Missouri and Platte. He traced what the French knew as Riviere Pierre Jaune (the Yellowstone) but the branch they called Le Grosse Horne became confused with the antelope that ranged along it. In Wilkinson's understanding, it became the Lycorne and then Unicorn River.

Captain McClallen was fascinated. The Indians that he knew as a boy in Albany, or as an officer in the south, were mostly basket weavers and trinket makers, tribal survivors living on the fringe of a world that had overwhelmed them. When he found an excuse to visit the general's headquarters in St. Louis, he was privileged to see a growing collection of maps of the territory. Wilkinson saw as his "duty, to acquire every information topographical and political, which might...become interesting to Our Country," and after arriving at St. Louis sent back a memorial on Louisiana and the West that included manuscript maps of Texas, New Mexico, and the Spanish Interior Provinces.[13]

By early August the homesick Arikara chief had seen enough of the white man's world and Wilkinson wrote the secretary of war that he intended to send Piahito home with a military escort. The party would remain at the mouth of the Platte River while a small escort of two soldiers and the interpreter Gravelines would conduct the chief the rest of the way. However, there were larger implications when he added, "I would recommend a Position on the River plate, of one Company & a small party of Artillerists, at the Panis Towns on the right bank of the said River fifty leagues (french computation) from its confluence with the Missouri, and thirteen Days moderate walk, from the Settlements of Mexico."[14] That was what Major Bruff had suggested previously. The possibility that a detachment might be stationed so far inland as the mouth of the Platte River certainly led to discussions at the Belle Fontaine officer's mess. Over meals, it was discussed as a reasonable action in the interest of military preparedness, or as Wilkinson rationalized, it would provide safe reception for the returning Corps of Discovery.[15]

On September 8 Wilkinson wrote to Dearborn, expressing his concern that the Spanish might attack New Orleans if the British fleet could be kept at bay.[16] But now that he was on the frontier, his focus was overland.

> I recollect having once disagreed with you, as to the Practicability of carrying an expedition from this point into New Mexico, and my objections were founded on the length of the March, and the difficulty of Subsisting the Troops but these Obstacles have vanished, before the information I have obtained since my arrival here.[17]

There was a perceived danger that Spain might try to recover access to the Mississippi. After outlining the strategic arrangements for an overland invasion, Wilkinson reported that the United States Army was prepared to take military action against the Spanish Interior Provinces if that became necessary.

In addition to the official report that the general sent to the secretary of war, Wilkinson also wrote a second, private letter to Dearborn on September 8.

Should We be involved in a War (which Heaven Avert) and it should be judged exped'ient to take possession of New Mexico.... I recollect having once disagreed with you, as to the Practicability of carrying an expedition from this point into New Mexico, and my objections were founded on the length of the March, and the difficulty of subsisting the Troops but these Obstacles have vanished, before the information I have obtained since my arrival here; for I find we may derive abundant supplies of meat from the fields and Forests, through which the route takes its direction, and that the practicable distance does not exceed 900 miles, over a surface in general Smooth, with the intervention on one mountain only, and that neither Steep nor broad.[18]

Although he previously disagreed with Dearborn about the "Practicability of carrying an expedition from [St. Louis] into New Mexico" because of the distance and difficulty of subsisting troops, Wilkinson had changed his mind. Since coming to St. Louis he discussed the details of an expedition that could follow the right branch of the Osage River with boating support from the Arkansas River. But before any movement, the Comanche would have to be reconciled, "which may best be accomplished through the Panis."[19]

⋘ ⋙

Plans were already under way in September for getting a secret agent into, or at least near, Santa Fe. In another letter on the same date, Wilkinson revealed that "I have also engaged a bold adventurer, who served under me during the late Indian War, and is now a Pensioner of the U. S." to look at "St. Afee" in person pending the winter, "he will take his departure from the Panis Towns on the River Plate."[20] Although this was presented as a privately financed commercial adventure, it smelled strongly of a disguised military reconnaissance.

The spy he had in mind was Robert McClellan, a former Indian scout during the last of the Ohio country wars who excelled in undercover assignments. The general's assumption was premature. McClellan, who his friends knew as Bob, refused because he was trying to break into the Omaha Indian trade, where he had previously lost heavily in competition with British traders. Perhaps the veteran frontiersman saw that the Spanish adventure could be less of a business opportunity than the spark for a war.[21]

On September 12, three days after Wilkinson described his plans to garrison the Platte and infiltrate New Mexico, Mr. Aaron Burr returned from his visit to New Orleans. After a ramble in the western country testing support, Burr bunked in with his former brother-in-law, Secretary Browne. During the following week, observers noticed several interesting guests making calls on the former vice president. Rumors were soon circulating that Mr. Burr's ideas were, to put it mildly, revolutionary. Innuendo around St. Louis during the week became thicker than the water of the Missouri.

In a time when newspapers were less disposable, well-read rags were widely circulated. The papers received in St. Louis might be two months old, and those published west of the mountains were unreliable. Before Wilkinson had arrived in St. Louis, Major Bruff read rumors in a Kentucky paper hinting that General Wilkinson was suspiciously involved with Burr. During Burr's visit, Wilkinson and David Delaunay took the former vice president over to Cantonment Belle Fontaine. Captain McClallen's gunners were looking a bit worn from their construction duties, but he had been warned to expect a dignitary, and the company washerwomen had rubbed their hands bare getting uniforms washed up.

Burr refrained from approaching the regular officers who were under the general's command, and there is no indication that John McClallen had any communication beyond the polite exchanges expected after an introduction. Later testimony suggested that restraint did not extend to militia officers like Maj. Timothy Kirby, whose testimony only emerged when Wilkinson's enemies were attacking him over this brief association with Burr. After inspecting operations, the touring party crossed the river to St. Charles and looped back through Portage des Sioux as they returned to St. Louis. Feeling out adherents for some as-yet-undefined scheme, Burr conferred with several St. Louis notables and left the impression that potential leaders were being interviewed for a filibuster against the Spanish possessions.[22] After a week, Burr went on. All that the general did for an honored guest was send him on to Governor William Henry Harrison with a recommendation for his appointment as Indiana territorial representative to Congress.[23]

Not long after Burr left, Wilkinson received letters that he did not share, even with intimates. The first was from his longtime New Orleans connection, Daniel Clark, who goaded that "You are spoken of as [Burr's] righthand man...the tale is a horrid one, if well told. Kentucky, Tennessee, the state of Ohio, with part of Georgia and part of Carolina, are to be bribed with the plunder of the Spanish Countries west of us to separate from the Union."[24]

Around the same time a letter written by Secretary of War Dearborn on August 24 finally arrived. This warned the general that he was too intimate with Mr. Burr and "ought to keep every suspicious person at arms length, and be as wise as a serpent and as harmless as a dove."[25] It was a check that Wilkinson could not, and did not intend to, ignore. Instead of a direct response to Dearborn, the general wrote to Robert Smith, the secretary of the navy and brother of his strong supporter Senator Samuel Smith, that "Burr is about something, but whether internal or external I cannot discover."[26] Wilkinson already had another plan in mind.

In keeping with the secretary of war's suggestion to send a secret agent disguised as a trader or merchant into foreign territory, Wilkinson moved ahead with a plan for a private adventure. But the arrangement that Wilkinson described on September 8 fell through when Robert McClellan saw his future in the Maha trade.

The general then fixed on Dr. Andrew Steele, whom he described as a St. Louis physician and sometime divine.[27] The previous year the Shelbyville, Kentucky, merchants A. and R. Steele asked Senator John Breckenridge to approach the Spanish minister about opening business to Santa Fe.[28] Nothing developed, but since then Dr. Steele had moved to St. Louis, and he wasted no time ingratiating himself with the new governor.[29]

Over the summer the remarkable Arikara Piahito and an Oto chief had become fever-ridden, homesick men in ill-fitting white men's clothes. As Wilkinson made plans for their return, he realized that this would provide him with an excuse to make an establishment at the Oto and Pawnee towns near the mouth of the Platte River "to prevent the machinations of the Spaniards & the sinister intrigues of the traders, and to confirm & secure the friendly disposition of those Nations to our Government."[30]

During the last week of September, Cantonment Belle Fontaine was knee-deep in the Indian delegates waiting to be taken to meet the president. The freewheeling agent Pierre Chouteau added to the bill by returning with another gang of Osages and seven representatives of the Pawnee Republic. But when Captain Stoddard finally got the delegation going by October 22, the Arikara chief was not included in the party.

In early October Wilkinson wrote that two subalterns and thirty men "properly Equipt & provided, were to accompany the returning Chiefs." After obtaining local consent "they would take post on the Platte River, about fifteen Leagues from its Mouth, under such Instructions as may secure a sound discretion should an Interview ensue with the Spaniards, of which I have no expectation."[31]

Wilkinson explained that a civilian volunteered to accompany the small military party as far as the Platte River. In return for serving as surgeon without pay, all that Doctor Andrew Steele asked was the privilege of transporting a small trading outfit, "not enough to encumber a boat," to the mouth of the Platte. From there he intended to make his way overland to Santa Fe.

That was daring because no one knew what had become of the Kaskaskia merchant William Morrison's two-thousand-dollar gamble of a trading outfit sent overland with the adventurer Baptiste LaLande, and there was a strong possibility that the trader was a victim of Mexican xenophobia. Wilkinson's risky arrangement depended on the cooperation of the tribes and the cynical seduction of New Mexican officers, just what Number 13 warned Spanish officials against.[32] If the New Mexicans mistreated Steele, could it be taken as a reason to start a war?

Wilkinson was curiously unconcerned about a Spanish reaction because the plan to send a secret agent toward the Southwest had been conceived in Washington before he started west as the new governor. Perhaps he saw a business venture as an unobtrusive way of marking out the bounds of Louisiana without perpetrating hostilities. There was no rule that profit and espionage could not be combined, and the man had a habit of sending surrogates into danger. Dr. Steele would be undertaking an adventure as risky as that which got Wilkinson's protégé, Philip Nolan, killed.

The convoluted plan had grown into a two-phase operation with an advance man who would prepare the way and soften up suspicious Spanish authorities, to be followed by a larger trading outfit anticipating a friendly entry into Santa Fe. Although the combination of public duty, international espionage, and private enterprise was just what might be expected from James Wilkinson, it does not appear to have been connected to whatever former vice president Burr was doing and had been under consideration for some time before the former vice president appeared in St. Louis. Wilkinson did not expect it to be dangerous because the command of the small military party fell to an "Intelligent Subaltern," Lt. James Biddle Wilkinson.

Upon reaching the mouth of the Platte, the lieutenant would detach two soldiers and an interpreter to escort the Arikara chief home. That round trip of about eighteen hundred miles would take some time, giving the rest of the twenty-five-man detachment time to build a temporary outpost while they waited.[33] The presence of a military party in relative proximity should gain cooperation from the Pawnee and allow Dr. Steele to make whatever arrangements were necessary to complete his trip to Santa Fe.

Tying an outwardly legitimate mercantile enterprise to undercover activities was sophisticated espionage. It would have been remarkable foresight if Dr. Steele brought the necessary stock of trade goods from Shelbyville. In order to obtain items appropriate to a New Mexican market from the east would have taken until next spring. Was it a coincidence that Captain McClallen readily disposed of the assortment of goods that he brought from Baltimore and earned enough to repay his creditors and gain a small capital to reinvest?

As long as British intruders on the upper Missouri dominated the Indian trade, the Mandan business was best left to experts. But Santa Fe was another matter, a cash market where desirable goods could be sold for Mexican silver. McClallen needed to return east and order a larger stock of goods that would be attractive to the New Mexicans. He would have to move fast in order to have another outfit ready to go by the next summer. When he returned Dr. Steele would have confirmed the road and softened up reluctant Santa Fe officials to receive an American trader.

But a mercantile adventure into Spanish territory could not be undertaken by someone wearing a United States uniform. In order to seize this opportunity, the captain would have to resign his commission. That was not a large problem because an epaulet could always be reinstated. As long as Calhoun & Company supplied the venture capital, what did the captain have to lose? McClallen heard a powerful argument, coming as it did from a respected superior.[34]

⚬⚬⚬

On October 20 Lt. Wilkinson's detachment left Cantonment Belle Fontaine to return the Indian chiefs and take station at the Platte. The party was already under way when the secretary of war in distant Washington cautioned against dispersing the troops, but he added "I am more fully convinced by your communication of the practicability, if necessary, of a military movement either by the Platt, the Osage or the Arkansas, to the Eastern part of Mexico; and I am not sure that a project of that kind may not become necessary."[35]

In October the map on a hide went to Washington with Captain Stoddard and the Indian delegation. Before they left, Wilkinson wrote,

> The Bearer hereof … has charge of a few natural productions of this Territory, to amuse a leisure Moment, and also a Savage delineation on a Buffaloe Pelt, of the Missouri & its South Western Branches, including the Rivers plate & Lycorne or Pierre jaune; This rude Sketch without Scale or Compass "et remplie de Fantaisies ridicules" is not destitute of Interests, as it exposes the location of several important Objects, & may point the way to useful enquiry.[36]

When Captain Stoddard left with the Indian delegation on October 22, 1805, for Washington, he also carried General Wilkinson's dispatches to the secretary of war. Those included the notice, "[Captain] McClellan [*sic*] has asked leave to resign and after eleven years service, I have indulged his request to return his Commission to the City of Washington where he is immediately to offer it at the end of the year."[37] After just five months in the West, and with only secondhand information about what lay on the Missouri above Cantonment Belle Fontaine, John McClallen had made an important career decision.

Lt. George Peter returned from the expedition to the Osages on

October 28, allowing General Wilkinson to reassure Dearborn on November 26 that New Mexico could be conquered in one campaign.[38] "I have a letter from Lt. Wilkinson dated at Grand River the 13th inst, his crew in health and the Arikara chief so far well pleased." But it was now in doubt that they would reach the Platte before winter and the military escort might have to stay somewhere and proceed in the spring. The general also enclosed a commission from the governor of New Mexico to a Pawnee chief of the Republican tribes that proved how the Spanish were trying to get the Indians to join them.[39]

An inventory of company property usually reflected a command turnover. On the first of December Lieutenant Peter signed a receipt for clothing received and the returns of Captain McClallen's company.[40] He would be in command until a new company commander arrived.

McClallen was starting east confident that Lt. Wilkinson would establish a military outpost at the mouth of the Platte and Dr. Steele would proceed from there to Santa Fe, guided by plains-knowledgeable Pawnee. By the time he returned with a trading outfit, a road would have been laid out to that market and the Mexicans prepared to open business.[41]

The Ohio Valley in winter was no place to tarry. Depending on the weather and the depth of the rivers to be crossed, the one-hundred-sixty-mile ride from Kaskaskia to Vincennes went through soggy bottoms and snowy woods with few comforts for a traveler. A few years before when the post route was being established, the postmaster general thought tavern bills would be minimal because there were few regular accommodations along the way. It usually took over a month for letters to go east by post rider.

When he stopped in Lexington, Kentucky, McClallen heard talk of what Mr. Burr was up to, and how the general was involved. If a war with Spain developed, would he lead an invasion? Sometime in December a quarrel developed at Lexington, exposing the enmity of the anti-Wilkinson faction that had developed in St. Louis. McClallen took exception to the criticism, though his defense of the general was not the attitude of a disillusioned subordinate contemplating the end of an unpromising career.

Two witnesses scurried back to Louisiana Territory and reported

McClallen's reaction to William C. Carr, a twenty-two-year-old lawyer and rabid enemy of the governor. After admitting that he had only met Captain McClallen once, Carr disparaged him as a mere satellite of the general.[42]

The captain rode on across winter-bound eastern Kentucky where stark trees loomed over the frosty trail. Long hours in the saddle tried McClallen's resolution and he realized how deeply he had drifted into a compromising relationship with his commanding officer. The general was willing to release him at a time when experienced officers might be needed for a war. But penetrating the Spanish barrier could be a greater service to the nation, and a dramatic cast of the dice could answer his financial problems.

CHAPTER SEVEN

VICTIMS OF CIRCUMSTANCE

As Captain McClallen rode east to put the Santa Fe business plan into operation, he heard rumors of increasing tensions with Spain. In the wayside inns where he stopped, gossip repeated news stories about President Jefferson's recent message to Congress. When the second session of the Eighth Congress assembled on December 3, the president sent his secretary, Mr. Cole, to read a long message laying out the problems facing the nation. Along with increasingly difficult foreign relations, the fatal impact of epidemics and the latest on tribal territorial cessions, Mr. Jefferson warned that Spanish patrols had advanced into what was considered Orleans Territory. In the future troops would be ready to "repell by arms any similar aggressions." All Cole read about exploration was "a state of our progress in exploring the principal rivers of the country and the information respecting them hitherto obtained will be communicated as soon as we shall receive some further relations which we have reason shortly to expect."[1]

On the same day that the president's message was being read, in distant St. Louis General Wilkinson forwarded a number of enclosures including an early report on Lt. Zebulon Pike's exploration of the upper Mississippi.[2] He had previously assured the secretary of war that "I shall ascertain every devious as well as direct route" for an invasion. In late November the secretary of war ordered General Wilkinson to "begin reconnaissance and intelligence collection throughout the region" through the agency of "individuals in the character of hunters and traders."[3]

Ever the warrior, Wilkinson wrote on December 3, "I am always ready for orders, with preference to a direct march to St. Affee if rendered necessary." Letters to headquarters usually took a month or more for delivery, and it is possible that the packet given to the War Department on January 4, 1806, a remarkably fast trip, came with Captain McClallen.

Captain McClallen was in Baltimore on January 20, 1806, when he met Senator Samuel Smith, a good friend of the general and of the president. Because there was another individual named John McClallen in Baltimore, Smith identified him as "of the artillery," suggesting that they became acquainted when McClallen commanded Fort McHenry.[4] In addition to delivering Wilkinson's letter to Smith, the captain refuted charges made by Wilkinson's enemies that the governor had conspired to pack a St. Louis jury.[5] The meeting in Baltimore was not a coincidence because what McClallen was planning certainly interested a Baltimore businessman.

Before he committed to a resignation, McClallen had to confirm the support of Calhoun & Lamot. After settling the initial loan, he delivered a negative evaluation of the Missouri Indian trade. As long as British traders continued to monopolize the upper Missouri or infiltrated the Sioux trade from the St. Peters River, American merchants could not compete with their preferred goods or price advantage. It would be another year before the governor's strong measures to limit illicit intrusions became effective.[6]

McClallen's analysis of the Southwest trade was promising. New Mexico was a landlocked market where buyers would make purchases with newly minted silver. The business plan was already in operation and the advance agent, Dr. Steele, was already traveling to Santa Fe. By the time that McClallen returned to St. Louis with suitable goods, Steele should have arranged for the favorable reception of a larger outfit and worked out arrangements with Indian packers for overland transport. McClallen & Company would be a team: supplier, transporter, and overland trader. All that was needed was the capital to exploit a unique opportunity, and the courage.

Instead of being directly submitted to the secretary of war, Captain McClallen's letter of resignation was dated at Baltimore on January 28, 1806.[7] In just three days that irretrievable act saw McClallen's company reassigned to Lt. John Baptiste de Barth Walbach, who had been General Wilkinson's aide-de-camp in the past. He was immediately promoted to captain. The general considered the former German hussar particularly suited to the command of cavalry, an indication that the army in the West was going mobile.[8] The promotion created a situation that the War Department would regret because Lt. George Peter of McClallen's company was sixth on the promotion list for a captaincy and Walbach seventeenth.[9]

Convinced that he had made a correct career decision, past captain McClallen proceeded to buy goods for the Santa Fe business. He was shocked to read a story in the February 18 issue of the *Republican Star* of Easton, Maryland, reprinted from the January 16 issue of the Frankfort *Palladium* of Kentucky.

> We have nothing worth communicating except that young Mr. Wilkinson (who went up the Missouri, as the public have been some time since informed) has just returned to St. Louis on account of a quarrel with some Indians, who killed one of his (Wilkinson's) party: upon which, the party killed one of the Indians. Since the foregoing was received the Editor has conversed with a gentleman immediately from St. Louis who informed him that the object of lieut. Wilkinson's journey up the Missouri was to establish a fort at the mouth of the river Platta; and that the party was fired upon about 300 miles up the Missouri. It was suspected that several Spaniards were with the Indians, as some white men were discovered. No information of any attack having been made on major Lewis's party, had reached St. Louis at the time our informant left it; he apprehends the report must have originated from the attack on lieut. Wilkinson.[10]

Just ten days after McClallen resigned, the bad news about Lt. Wilkinson's expedition to the mouth of the Platte was delivered to the War Department. As Wilkinson explained,

> The body of Canzes after their first, very rude and unfriendly interview in which both Parties took arms, marched up the River and took Post at a difficult and narrow pass, where they decoyed two American hunters on shore who were descending the River, one of whom they killed, and the other after shooting an Indian made his escape, but unfortunately fell in with our Camp in the night, and not answering the challenge was fired upon and mortally wounded. [The encounter]

… reduced him [Lt. Wilkinson] to the alternative of hazarding hostilities, or returning, and he accordingly descended to the Cantonment the day before Yesterday, with the Ricarra Chief and his party in safety.[11]

The tight-fisted Dearborn responded to Wilkinson's explanation of the aborted mission to the Platte on February 10: "I do not perfectly comprehend your former and present reasoning relative to the establishment of a post on the River Plat; and that of the mere conveyance of one or two Indian Chiefs to their homes; but as the thing has *ended* it requires no further notice."[12] The informant to the newspapers must have been Lt. Eli Clemson, a friend of McClallen. Clemson understood the circumstances and located McClallen to confirm that the military party escorting the two Indians and Dr. Steele had not reached the place where the trader could arrange an overland passage to New Mexico. Steele had returned to St. Louis without proving the trail to Santa Fe.

Lt. Clemson may have delivered a private letter from Wilkinson explaining that not long after McClallen left St. Louis, Wilkinson received the secretary of war's emphatic prohibition against establishing military posts without the president's express permission: "but as the thing has *ended* it requires no further notice." Reprimanded for sending his son to winter at the mouth of the Platte, the general had started a messenger by way of the Des Moines River to intercept the two men escorting the Arikara chief and warn them not to expect support from an outpost at the Platte. Already deeply committed to the next step, McClallen must have wondered why the general had not sent a galloper after him in December.

The trip with Lieutenant Wilkinson's detachment and an exciting fight with the Kansa that turned them back worked wonders for Piahito's health, and it was decided to send him to Washington. The remarkable Arikara and his conductor, Lt. Clemson, arrived in Washington on February 6, with the general's glowing introduction to President Jefferson. The general had become downright admiring.

From observation & the limited Enquiry to which I am confined by an illiterate Interpreter [Gravelines], I think you may be able to derive a fund of correct information from this Chief, relative to the region Watered by the South Western Branches of the Missouri & its Inhabitants: I understand Him to be a great traveler, a warrior & Geographer, and He is certainly a *learned* Savage...you have under cover a list of the Tribes & population of his own Nation, of the Mandanes the Gros Ventres, the Corbeau, & ten other Nations who speak different Languages. He is able to correct many parts of the Leatheren Chart which I sent you by Capt. Stoddard.[13]

That data was not mentioned on February 19 when President Jefferson sent an address to Congress reporting the progress of the Corps of Discovery.

During his stay among the Mandans, [Captain Lewis] had been able to lay down the Missouri according to its courses & distances taken on his passage up it, corrected by frequent observations of longitude & latitude; & to add to the actual survey of this portion of the river, a general map of the country between the Missisipi and the Pacific, from the 34th to the 54th degrees of Latitude....Copies of this map are now presented to both houses of Congress. With these I communicate also a statistical view, procured & forwarded by him, of the Indian nations inhabiting the territory of Louisiana & the countries adjacent to it's Northern & Western borders, of their commerce, & of other interesting circumstances respecting them.[14]

In addition to the materials sent in from Fort Mandan, the president was waiting for reports from an expedition to the Southwest that might uncover a water route to Santa Fe.[15] After hearing the president's message, Congress took a day before authorizing the printing of two hundred copies of the president's message and the documents "for the use of the Senate."[16] Given the chore of hand-setting type for what came out to be 178 printed pages, of which 123 were devoted to the Lewis and Clark Expedition, it was remarkable that the president was able to forward a printed copy to his associate John Vaughan at the American Philosophical Society on March 25. By then the cartographer Nicholas King had completed four copies of William Clark's speculative map of the West: one for the War Department, one for the State Department, another for Congress, and one for the president.[17]

Three days after the president's letter was read to Congress, the Senate approved the recess nomination of Governor Wilkinson by a margin of seventeen yeas to fourteen nays. Senator Smith had already written Wilkinson that his appointment had been authenticated. When the embattled governor replied on March 29, he tried to explain his indulgence of Dr. Steele.

> Doctr. Steele who was requested to accompany the expedition not only as a surgeon but Naturalist, proposed to me a day or two before he sailed that he would relinguish his Pay if I would suffer him to take a packet of Goods without incumbering the Boat, to which I assented & thus for saving the pay of a surgeon to the public I am charged with a base speculation.

If McClallen was aware of this development it was nothing to share with his backers. Instead, he emphasized that a mercantile adventure to Santa Fe could expect the continued support of the territorial government.[18] McClallen's capitalists had to consider that it was not the best of times for American business. Although the Barbary Wars seemed to be settling down, the overbearing British continued to harass American merchant ships at sea and intrude on the upper Missouri. There were reports from Detroit that unregenerate British loyalists were stirring up the Shawnee again.

On March 19 President Jefferson sent a message to Congress that Spanish authorities were advancing into disputed territory to occupy posts, but he was "unwilling to take measures to preclude a peaceful accommodation of differences, officers of the United States were ordered to confine themselves within the country on this side of the Sabine River" and "send a detachment from Natchitoches requiring them to withdraw."[19]

President Jefferson had not mentioned that he had confirmed five thousand dollars for a second expedition to explore the Red River, which was expected to set off from Natchez in April. From Fort Adams, Captain Richard Sparks would shepherd the scientifically minded Peter Custis of the University of Pennsylvania and the Irish surveyor, Thomas Freeman. If this Red River exploring expedition avoided a confrontation with Spanish forces, it was possible that a trading expedition might be well received on the doorstep of Santa Fe.[20] McClallen's backers calculated that trade to Santa Fe might not be all that risky and a landlocked community would welcome a store brought to their doorstep. Combining Calhoun capital with the former captain's modest profit from the first experiment meant that Baltimore had the lead in breaking into the New Mexican trade. The entrepreneurial James Calhoun Jr. beamed.

The death of his thirty-one-year-old sister, Jane, the wife of Spenser Philpot, in March may have given McClallen an excuse to make a quick visit to his family in upstate New York. The death of another daughter was a blow to Robert McClallen, whose world seemed to be collapsing. He was deeply humiliated by his default as state treasurer. As the eldest son, John McClallen explained that he had given up his military career and turned to business in order to help address those financial problems.

⊷⇥≒⊶

At some point McClallen renewed his acquaintance with the visiting Arikara chief, whose tour of the East certainly lived up to expectations.[21] But fate was unkind. Piahito came to civilization from a relatively germ-free environment, and his constitution was not prepared to deal with the noxious airs and foul water of most cities of that day. On April 7, 1806, he died in Washington and was buried among strangers.

There was more bad news. After reading reports of the president's messages in the Baltimore newspapers, John McClallen learned that Lt. Wilkinson arrived in Washington on April 28. The younger Wilkinson carried letters from the general to Senator Samuel Smith and others to the president and secretary of war. The letter to Senator Smith was meant for publication in the Baltimore papers to counter the charges being circulated by Wilkinson's enemies, specifically the obnoxious Maj. Seth Hunt, the Ste. Genevieve commandant who had seized upon the indulgence given to Dr. Steele to travel with Lieutenant Wilkinson to the mouth of the Platte. Hunt claimed this was a misuse of pubic funds to advance a private enterprise.[22]

McClallen heard the gory details of the fight with the Kansa from

Lieutenant Wilkinson as well as details of the insidious campaign that the antigovernor clique was conducting against his father. He may have also been privileged to an early forecast of how the general intended to deal with a difficult development. Because Major Hunt had raised questions about the indulgence allowed Dr. Steele, adjustments would have to be made.

On May 4 Mr. Jefferson smoothly confirmed his confidence in the governor while regretting that the appointment "blended the civil & military powers."[23] Although no changes were contemplated for the moment, two days later Secretary of War Dearborn ordered Wilkinson to "repair to the Territory of Orleans or its vicinity and take upon yourself the command of the Troops in that quarter" in answer to a Spanish intrusion on the Sabine River.[24]

Of course McClallen was not party to private or public correspondence, but Senator Smith appreciated the former captain's loyalty to Wilkinson. He may have gone out of his way by allowing the entrepreneur a glimpse of the revised Lewis and Clark map from Fort Mandan.[25] The War Department cartographer, Nicholas King, had just completed four copies of Clark's sketch showing the Missouri from St. Louis to the Platte, including the place where Lieutenant Wilkinson had his encounter with the Kansa Indians.[26]

The Pawnee Indians, whom McClallen would need to contact, lived on the Republican branch of the Kansas River. Beyond was a lot of open country until a tracing finger came to Santa Fe. McClallen noticed how the headwaters of the Rio Bravo (Rio Grande) almost connected with what Clark had drawn in as the upper reaches of the Big Horn branch of the Yellowstone River. That interlocking meant little to an overland traveler to the Spanish town, but impressions have a way of sticking. Perhaps Senator Smith also gave McClallen a copy of the printed statistical material that was published by mid-March and contained useful information relating to the Southwest.[27]

At this point the resigned officer did not have a lot of alternatives. He had to go ahead because backing out of the deal with Calhoun & Lamot would leave him out of the army with no prospects. He had already completed his purchases and there were rumors around Baltimore that Congress was considering an embargo on imports like leather, flax, hemp and silk goods, hats, clothing, millinery, woolens including hosiery, paper of all description, tin, brass, nails and spikes, even playing cards.

Plunging into the role of a civilian entrepreneur, McClallen brought his mercantile background to the selection of what to carry to the untapped potential of a New Mexican market. No one had done that before. Probably finer cloth or calico, perhaps tools or utensils that local artisans could not make would sell well. Once he had recommended flannel over linen shirts for the health of his company. Now he was back among the cloth merchants ordering cottons and silks that might appeal to a *senorita*.[28] A good part of his stock may have been taken from the nineteen bales and fifteen chests of German linens that Calhoun & Lamot received the previous year.

The entrepreneur spent the rest of the spring seeing that his outfit was properly packaged for hauling over the rutted road to Pittsburgh. Pennsylvania wagon makers had worked out a design shaped like a boat, high on both ends and sagging toward the middle so that a load jostled toward the center. Rough handling like that meant that an entrepreneur would not be taking glass or china to Santa Fe.

McClallen's associations with the well-informed Baltimore business community gave him a good idea of the political situation in the first months of 1806. He left for the West with an understanding of the pressures that the Old World was putting on the New World. Although McClallen & Company would be going into harm's way, he had no choice except to proceed.

When the wagons reached the forks, McClallen arranged for a barge that would drift down the Ohio River and could be rowed, poled, or towed up the Missouri as far as the mouth of the Platte.[29] Despite Mr. Burr's conclusion that a spring voyage was impossible due "to the want of water in the Ohio," McClallen moved the Santa Fe outfit from Baltimore to St. Louis in less time than the three months that it had taken the previous military party.

A lot depended on what Wilkinson might do to ease a passage over the dangerous plains. Because of Dr. Steele's failure to test the way to Santa Fe or the temper of the tribes along that way, McClallen would be pioneering the Santa Fe Trail. The reception he might receive in

New Mexico was uncertain. Those were heavy thoughts as the boat drifted with the spring freshet.

McClallen could not shake off how poorly prepared he was for what he was undertaking. He was a horseman acquainted with military packing but a middling hunter who had never seen a live buffalo. He had no command of French, Spanish, or the various Indian dialects that he needed to communicate. On the plains he would be totally dependent upon tribesmen he had yet to meet.

At stops along the river, McClallen began picking up rumors that Mr. Burr was up to something and that the general's name was being associated with him. He dismissed it as more of the spleen he encountered at Lexington the previous year.[30] Burr and his followers seemed to be focusing on a conquest of Mexico, maybe even the mines of Peru, but that did not seem to involve a mercantile connection to Santa Fe. Still, McClallen wondered why the general was so taken with getting a trade mission there.

The Ohio River was running high with the spring runoff and the boat made good time. At the mouth of the Ohio, he hired the experienced river guide J. Lorimore to find the best way of working up the Mississippi to St. Louis.[31] Given what he had heard since leaving there last winter, the convoluted plan to open trade with New Mexico was experiencing difficulties for which he could very well be totally responsible.

CHAPTER EIGHT

"BEHOLD THE MEXICAN TRAVELER"[1]

The ol' muddy river was not as opaque as those who drank its waters believed. Along with the silt that settled out at the bottom of the water barrel were memories of previous efforts by almost-forgotten voyageurs. River men had been spending themselves against the challenge of the Missouri for many years, bucking strong currents, undertaking impossible distances. As John McClallen made the arrangements for an adventure he had to undertake, he could not have fully understood what that meant.

Political appointees, power brokers, and opportunists were scrambling for advantage and snapping like dogs at James Wilkinson's silver-heeled boots. They called into question the legitimacy of his government, the appointments he made, his revision of a corrupt judiciary, and most viciously, his interference with the schemes of land and mining speculators. Disloyalty even festered in the army ranks when the disaffected Major Bruff tried to discredit his commanding general in a letter to the secretary of war.[2]

During the first months of 1806, Governor Wilkinson was distracted by local problems and a close vote on his congressional confirmation had done nothing to stifle the cabal conducting guerilla war against him. At the end of March, he wrote the president that he would rather step aside than cause the administration any embarrassment.[3] Instead, he was ordered to send troops down the Mississippi to deal with Spanish activities and to be prepared to take military command.

When McClallen arrived in St. Louis in early July, he found Wilkinson scrambling to finish his obligations as governor and prepare to descend the Mississippi to deal with the situation that had developed when Spanish forces advanced their territorial pretensions to the

Sabine River. Responding to Dearborn's order of March 14, Wilkinson had alerted the troops to be ready to move south by the first of May.[4] On May 6 the secretary of war ordered Wilkinson to set off for New Orleans Territory and take command of the troops there. He would inform himself of the movement of Spanish soldiers from Mexico or Havana to reinforce the troops on the frontier of New Orleans. A military and naval buildup was planned, and two hundred recruits were being sent to reinforce his army. Despite these warlike preparations, the general was cautioned to not initiate a military response.

But Wilkinson did not receive this letter until June 11, the same time he had contradictory instructions from the secretary of the treasury to put aside his military obligations in order to clear up financial details of the government that he would be leaving.[5] The delay eventually stretched to almost two months.[6] However, the general seemed confident that he would be able to resolve military matters diplomatically.

Empty barracks at Cantonment Belle Fontaine revealed that most of the garrison had been started downstream in May, even before Wilkinson received orders on June 11 to go there himself. Only McClallen's old company had been left behind. Lt. George Peter had only a short time to enjoy the sense of command before Captain James Many arrived in early January 1806. But that was only a temporary arrangement. Now Peter was simmering that he had been passed over for the captaincy in favor of Captain Walbach and didn't have many kind words about the general.

McClallen was disappointed to see dissention among the officers, but he no longer wore the uniform. He saw that General Wilkinson was pressed with the last details of his government, which included confirming the reorganization of the territorial militia. The general meant to fend off St. Louis commandant Samuel Hammond's attempt to impose a gang of his adherents as volunteers to further his campaign to gain the government. The obnoxious St. Genevieve commandant Maj. Seth Hunt was bouncing around like a yapping dog and trying to use the indulgence to Dr. Steele to malign Wilkinson's character.

McClallen might have hoped the general would pay closer attention to his trading party, which now had to proceed into the jaws of a potential war with Spain. After the return of Lt. Wilkinson's aborted expedition to the Platte, Major Hunt made an issue about allowing a civilian to accompany the military party. He howled that allowing Steele to travel with them was just an excuse to haul two thousand dollars' worth of goods at government expense.[7] Spreading to muckraking Kentucky papers, the canard made it politically imprudent for the governor to be too closely associated with another private adventure to Santa Fe.[8]

Responding to the secretary of war's second stiff admonition against planting an outpost at the Platte, Wilkinson explained that it had been meant only as a provisional depot to assist the returning Corps of Discovery and facilitate the safe return of the Arikara chief. To emphasize the gravity of what he attempted, the general included a copy of Lieutenant Wilkinson's report on the incident.

> The Savages are as ten to one—they are known to the Spaniards & unknown to us.
>
> The ultimate position of the Spaniards in New Mexico, of the United States on the Mississippi, & the intermediate hordes of Savages, may be compared to the former relations of the British posts on the lakes. [The Spaniards] will exert themselves to Erect a strong Barrier of hostile savages, to oppose us in time of War, & to harass our frontier in time of Peace.[9]

Wilkinson sourly concluded, "I am fearful this disposition of the Canzes may be excited by agents from St. Afee."[10] That concern was seconded in April when the Osage Indian agent Pierre Chouteau declared:

> If it be the intention of the government to attract to the Eastern ports of the United States or to New Orleans the trade of fine peltries, which hitherto have been taken to Canada it is necessary in order to attain this to cultivate the affection of the Sioux and of [illegible] those living on the northern limits, and to win the affection of an Indian nation, one must make presents. In fact the "Aytanes [Comanche]," a very numerous and powerful nation living in the immense prairies which are supposed to reach beyond the western limits, must become, owing to their position, the most important ally of the United States.[11]

The Kansa, at the urging of the Spanish, had spoiled the plan to deliver Dr. Steele into Santa Fe, and the second phase of that convoluted operation had already arrived from Baltimore. Unless an alternative could be devised, Captain McClallen felt that he was being left up in the air. If the general failed to find a peaceful solution, a McClallen & Company pack train in unknown country would be at great risk.

⊷≡⊶

Although involved in military obligations, closing up his official and private accounts, and fending off a growing list of political enemies, Wilkinson was still attentive of the private mercantile adventure. As early as May 3, he had already conceived and was organizing another military expedition. Three days after returning from his mission to the upper Mississippi, Lt. Zebulon Pike learned that he was "bound on another voyage," which he understood was originally intended for two other "gentlemen of the army." Pike had no idea why the arrangement had fallen through.[12]

The lieutenant was allowed just six weeks to rest, attend his neglected wife, and supervise the rendering of his field charts of the upper Mississippi. On June 24, 1806, Pike received orders to escort some recovered Osage prisoners home and arrange a peace between the Osage and Kansa Indians. He would convince the Osage to act as intermediaries in opening a connection to the Comanche and then proceed to the Pawnee villages on the Republican branch of the Kansas River to confirm their loyalty. From there his party would move south to locate the Comanche and bring them to a conference that would ensure Americans safe passage through their territory.[13]

As McClallen was the only entrepreneur planning a trip to Santa Fe, he felt vastly encouraged that the main objective of Pike's mission was a positive connection with the Comanche. They were seen as the controlling element on the southwest plains. Consistent with what Wilkinson had been discussing with Dearborn for the past year, conciliating the Comanche was an answer to Spanish efforts to erect an Indian barrier. When the expedition reached the Arkansas River, Pike's second-in-command, Lieutenant Wilkinson, would separate and explore down that stream while Pike continued as close to Santa Fe as circumstances permitted without giving offense to the Spanish. Then he would descend the Red River and meet General Wilkinson at Natchitoches, southeast of present Shreveport, Louisiana.[14]

Ominously, Wilkinson added that before going on to explore the outer bounds of Louisiana, Pike should send his reports and a rough map back to St. Louis for transmission to the general at Fort Adams, and copies to the secretary of war. The expense of an express rider to carry dispatches was insurance "against a total loss by misfortune."[15]

Directed to affect an interview and good understanding with the Pawnee and the Comanche, and to explore and make geographical and natural history observations, it is unbelievable that Lieutenant Pike was unaware of the plan to send a parallel trading expedition to open the Santa Fe market. Officers at Cantonment Belle Fontaine certainly discussed arrangements being made by one of their own. St. Louis might have been a poor factory of documents, but competitors chewed over anything having to do with the Indian trade. McClallen had too many details to attend to. There was no way that he could have disguised his intentions.

Coming dangerously close to the previous attempt, at the last moment the Cantonment Belle Fontaine surgeon volunteered to accompany Pike. John Hamilton Robinson was another of those handy medical men whom the general favored. When Wilkinson had stopped at Kaskaskia to take his neglected oath of office as governor, Robinson and two of his brothers were living there. That may have been less than a coincidence because earlier in 1805 their father, David Robinson, wrote President Jefferson, asking his opinion about publishing a journal he kept during previous travels in Louisiana.[16]

While the army was still settling into the new cantonment, Dr. Robinson moved to St. Louis, where the general engaged him in the temporary capacity of post surgeon. Steps were initiated to regularize the appointment and apparently confident of a sinecure, in December Robinson married a local girl.[17] But a permanent appointment was denied, and the temporary arrangement was due to end on June 30, 1806.

Robinson was just the sort of malleable young man that the general liked to rely upon.[18] Said to be a nephew of the slain Alexander

Hamilton, it was unlikely that Robinson could have been considered a Burrite.[19] And he was willing to leave his pregnant bride to accompany Lieutenant Pike on an extended expedition. Small parties like Pike's did not always have the attendance of a trained physician, but Robinson had no other apparent qualifications. At some point in Pike's travels, Dr. Robinson was expected to break off and attempt to enter Santa Fe on his own.[20] Infiltrating Dr. Robinson was the third instance of General Wilkinson's determination to get an agent into Santa Fe, but the association was not revealed until July 13, two days before the expedition started.[21]

Pike, Robinson, and McClallen for that matter, might have been apprehensive of what to expect from the Spanish, but Wilkinson assured that the party was in no danger because they carried documents that would make them as safe in Santa Fe as in Philadelphia.[22] McClallen felt that was putting a lot of faith in the orders that Pike carried, which directed him to avoid offending the Spanish.[23] Or to collect an outstanding civilian debt.

Soon after the departure of the Corps of Discovery, the Morrison brothers of Kaskaskia and St. Charles outfitted Jean Baptiste LaLande with a small trading outfit to go to Santa Fe. Becoming aware of the plan, the former Spanish lieutenant governor Delassus warned his superiors, who detained the adventurer. After two years, LaLande had not returned. While the Pike expedition was camped across from St. Charles, Pike and Dr. Robinson visited the Morrison store, where it was arranged that the doctor would carry a collection order that might justify an entry into Santa Fe.[24]

An unidentified correspondent found Cantonment Belle Fontaine such a delightful and promising place that he considered spending the greater part of the summer there, "as it is the garde of the country." In a letter dated July 20, 1806, the writer confided that he spent "a few days at the governor's quarters, who is preparing here for his descent of the river to Natches, or perhaps lower."[25] Although Governor Wilkinson's enemies were still exploiting the indulgence of Dr. Steele, the writer failed to mention a similar accusation of favoritism against McClallen. Nor that a private entrepreneur would be moving parallel to the Pike expedition toward the same objective.

McClallen had a lot to accomplish before he could leave. St. Louis was a small town, just two hundred houses strung along three main streets, and not much passed unnoticed in a population of around a thousand. An unusual expedition like McClallen & Company was not organized without most citizens being aware. Merchants like Auguste Chouteau, Hunt & Hankinson, or the Baltimore-based Comegys & Falconer kept their account books closed, but any townsman who dropped in could pick up clues. Christy's new tavern could be a dangerous place for secrets if a recently hired boatman allowed the Monongahela rye to get ahead of discretion.

A small purchase in the store of John Hankinson and his partner, the New Jersey native Wilson Price Hunt, could lead to a casual discussion. The Baltimore merchant John Comegys knew the Calhouns, and his store may have been the source of the peltry that his partner, Peregrine Falconer, consigned to them from New Orleans. But a well-founded adventure going to New Mexico was news. To supplement the Baltimore outfit, McClallen needed additional items pleasing to the Pawnee or the Comanche, whose help he would need. The storekeeper who sold him blue beads, horse gear, and pack saddles might promise to be discreet, but a clerk or a hanger-on picked up enough information to earn a free drink at the tavern. Speculation continued long after the boat disappeared around the first bend in the river.

Most gossip concerned the overdue Corps of Discovery or the general's ongoing disputes with Major Bruff, Major Hunt, Judge Lucas, or that conniving young weasel Carr, all members of a cabal hostile to the governor. But McClallen's activities did not pass unnoticed.[26]

Anglophobia had been simmering since early June when the thinly authenticated United States citizen and Indian trader James Aird returned to St. Louis to meet his British supplier Robert Dickson. On June 10, Aird started three boats to the Yankton trade, but a perverse wind sank one of them, and the replacement outfit would be unable to leave until the end of September.

Most parties departing for the middle river were concerned about Kansa belligerence. Moving fast on the freshet, boats loaded with valuable returns did not stop at risky places. It was parties slowly ascending the river with valuable goods that were attractive targets. McClallen intended to wait until parties going ahead tested the temper of the tribes. No river traveler could be certain of the mood of the tribes along the river, and McClallen delayed long enough to give lieutenants Pike and Wilkinson an opportunity to placate the Osages, inhibit the hostile Kansa, and impress the Pawnee.[27]

The crew McClallen hired in Pittsburgh was not acquainted with the trying Missouri River, so a new crew of trustworthy Missouri River boatmen had to be hired to replace them. McClallen would have to rely on those French-speaking swaggerers who proudly called themselves voyageurs. Like the Corps of Discovery two years before, boatmen were drawn from the Francophone St. Louis community or from the smaller village of St. Charles.

They were men who knew each other, attended the same balls or work parties, heard mass together, and went around with their friends on New Year's celebrating the *La Guignolee* tradition of house calls and treats. Most of their families were connected by tangled skeins of kinship stretching back to almost-forgotten parishes of the lower St. Lawrence, or to Indian tribes. They had lived under the Spanish flag in an encapsulated world perched on the edge of the wilderness without losing affection for the French lily banner. As inheritors of the traditions of the *coureur des bois* (runners in the woods), national affiliation rested lightly on them.

The usual estimate was that one Creole boatman was required to move every ton and a half of cargo. The fifty-five-foot-long Corps of Discovery keelboat had required twenty-two rowers, but eighteen had been enough to move the seventy-foot-long keelboat that Pike took up the Mississippi the previous year. It only took six oarsmen to drive James Aird's heavily laden thirty-foot bateau (light rowboat) against the Missouri. Based on that, the McClallen & Company boat would require fourteen rowers and a steersman.

Selecting them required an expertise and command of language that McClallen lacked. Unfortunately, sources of help no longer included the Chouteau brothers. Pierre Chouteau's visit to Washington had convinced the secretary of war that he could not disassociate himself from former interests in the Osage trade, and the general became suspicious of his motives relating to Pike's expedition. At the last minute another ambitious trader, Manuel Lisa, tried to interfere with Pike's party.

In competing with other established entrepreneurs in the St. Louis or St. Charles hiring hall, McClallen could only leave the hiring to the boat captain, or *patron*. The men he selected would obey a steersman whose experience they could trust. But engagés who knew how to pull an oar and navigate the river were not experienced in throwing a packer's hitch. Nor were boatmen usually armed. If it came to a fight with Indians, McClallen needed men willing to defend the investment. Those requirements revealed that McClallen was headed for New Mexico instead of the usual middle river trade. Those he hired, or turned away, went home and told their wives and families, and the name of John McClallen was better known over backyard clotheslines than it would be in records.

The map that Major Bruff acquired from the three traders was just a sketch, but it contained important information about the proximity of the headwaters of the Platte, Arkansas, and Red rivers. Lieutenant Pike made a copy.[28] So did McClallen because it outlined the way he must follow to go to Santa Fe. The similarity of what Pike was sent to do as an explorer, and what McClallen was undertaking as a private adventurer, depended on them operating from the same map.

Everything that lay ahead would be new to McClallen: different men, unfamiliar language, and uncertain arrangements, all without the authority of the epaulet on his shoulder. As he tried to confine his thoughts to the last-minute problems of organizing the adventure, there were moments when what lay ahead crowded in like an afternoon shadow. A mere sketch revealed nothing about the conditions he would have to endure or about the savages he would have to charm.

At the last moment, two St. Louis entrepreneurs complicated matters. Storekeeper Wilson Price Hunt exposed the plan of a rival trading adventure to the governor. A Spanish Creole in a French community, Manuel Lisa's opportunism and suspect ethics never gained the respect of the St. Louis mercantile establishment. His previous meddling with the Chouteau family lock on the Osage trade backfired when the American administration took over and new rules were put in place. Lately Lisa had attached himself to old Jacques Clamorgan, the former director of the defunct *La Compagnie de Commerce pour la Decouverte des Nations du haut du Missouri.* When Pike was ascending the Mississippi, he met a Michilimackinac supplier who was bringing a large outfit of Indian trade goods to Lisa and Clamorgan. But on the first of July, Lisa and Clamorgan contracted with the Philadelphia firm Geisse, Taylor & Snyder for twelve thousand dollars' worth of goods, an unusual source of stock for the Indian trade because the house supplied finer things, similar to what past captain McClallen recently brought from Baltimore for the New Mexican market.[29]

Lisa tried to delay Pike's expedition by obtaining a warrant for the arrest of Pike's interpreter, Barony Vasquez, for a debt. A frantic exchange of letters between the general and Pike provided security for Vasquez. Branding Lisa a "Black Spaniard," Wilkinson condemned him and Pierre Chouteau for interrupting "national movements by their despicable Intrigues."[30] Lisa later engaged Baptiste Duchouquette to go to the Osage on the excuse of collecting some debts.[31] That was suspicious because the agent was accompanied by the experienced southwest plainsman Joseph Rivet, who had connections to Santa Fe.[32]

At the beginning of August, Wilkinson enlarged on what he knew about the Lisa and Clamorgan plan to the secretary of war. Because some of the McClallen & Company accounts were with the Hunt & Hankinson store, Wilson Price Hunt was aware of what McClallen was doing. He told the general that Lisa and Clamorgan approached him about becoming a partner in an adventure they were planning to Santa Fe, but he declined.

That was exactly what John McClallen intended to do. The projected route was the same that he intended to follow, may even have been taken from yet another copy of the French trader's map. The details that the general forwarded were specific, too specific for Pike to claim ignorance of the role that his expedition would play in the scheme to open Santa Fe. Four days later, Wilkinson provided Pike with a description of what Lisa and Clamorgan planned to do. It almost exactly duplicated what McClallen was undertaking.

> It is reduced to a certainty that Manual & a Society of which he is the ostensible leader, have determined on a project to open some commercial Intercourse with St. Affee, and as this may lead to connec-

tions injurious to the United States, & will I understand be attempted without the sanction of Law, or the permission of the executive, you must do what you can consistently to defeat the Plan. No Good can be derived to the United States from such a project, because the prosecution of it will depend entirely on the Spaniards, & they will not permit it unless to serve their political as well as personal Interests.

Wilkinson had learned of this from Wilson Price Hunt, who had declined becoming a partner in a scheme another entrepreneur was developing. It was a matter of protecting the interest St. Louis storekeepers had developed by providing a fellow American goods on credit. Wilkinson continued.

> ... the ensuring Autumn & Winter will be employed in reconnoitering & opening connections with the I.ya.tans [Comanche], Pawnis &c: that this Fall or the next Winter a grand magazine is to be established at the Osage Towns, where their operations will commence. That Manual is to be the active Agent. Having formed a Connection with the I.ya.tans [Comanche], they will carry forward their Merchantdize within three or four Days travel of the Spanish Settlements, where they will deposit them under the guard of three hundred I.ya.tans [Comanche] Manual will then go forward with four or five attendants taking with Him, some Jewellry & fine Goods ... with these he will visit the Governor to whom He will make presents & implore his Pity, by a fine Tale of sufferings which have ensued the Change of Government, they are left here with goods to be sure, but not a Dollars worth of Bullion, and therefore they have adventured to see Him for the purpose of praying his leave, for the Introduction of their property into the Province. If he assents then the whole of the Goods will be carried forward, if he refuses then Manual will invite some of his Countrymen to accompany Him to his deposit & haveing there exposed to them his Merchandise, He will endeavor to open a forced or Clandestine Trade, for He observes the Spaniards will not dare to attack his Camp.[33]

When the letter caught up with Pike on August 18, he immediately developed a headache. Through that blue haze of pain he must have obliged Dr. Robinson to explain himself more fully.[34] Nothing survives to suggest that Pike expected to rendezvous with a private trading party at the Pawnee villages, but it is reasonable that he intended to placate the Pawnee and set up the cooperation of Indian packers and animals that McClallen & Company would need. Then he would go on to line up the Comanche. After Dr. Robinson made the initial contact with the New Mexicans, it would be safe for the trading outfit to follow. Although Pike never mentioned the mercantile attempt to reach Santa Fe, both he and Dr. Robinson knew about it before they left.

After failing to gain financial cooperation from Hunt & Hankinson, Lisa and Clamorgan turned to other capitalists. On August 10 Auguste Chouteau provided the security for an outfit worth $16,000, $12,649 worth of British merchandize that was purchased from the Michilimackinac supply firm of George Gilespie & Company, through the offices of the intermediary Myer Michaels. Goods from that fur trade outfitting center were intended for the Osage or Comanche trade.[35]

With Lisa and Clamorgan plunging ahead, John McClallen realized that his trading adventure would be trailed by an unwelcome competitive burden. If rivals managed to catch up, he would be in a race to that virgin market. As July slipped into August, Wilkinson was still sending in drafts, completing and transmitting accounts, even forwarding Pike's report respecting the trade of the North West Company on the upper Mississippi. On August 6 he encouraged Pike, "Should fortune favor you on your present excursion, your importance to our Country will I think make your future life comfortable."[36] But that was the general's stock promise.

In mid-August Governor Wilkinson turned the administration of Louisiana Territory over to Secretary Browne and started down the Mississippi to resume his duties as General of the Army. He excused the delay because his lady was seriously ill and until her health improved, he could not release their son to go with Pike.[37] He had stalled long enough to see Pike and Wilkinson started on an apparently legitimate small military expedition, just large enough to impress the Osage and Pawnee, maybe put the fear of retribution into the troublesome Kansa, but not large enough to upset the Spanish. If everything worked out as intended, Pike would initiate a friendly relationship with the Comanche and frustrate Spanish efforts to influence them against the United States.[38]

After Wilkinson left on August 16, Territorial Secretary Browne assumed the function of acting governor. Browne, Aaron Burr's former brother-in-law and confidant, also understood the McClallen & Company intentions because McClallen made an arrangement with him for forwarding his letters and for the reception of the returns from his winter trade with the Pawnee.

When McClallen finally got off on August 22, most of the business community already knew that he was taking a cargo of trade goods to the Mexicans. St. Louis skeptics were not that convinced that an inexperienced peddler with a pack train of calico would break down the gates of New Mexico. If Lieutenant Pike's expedition brought a hostile reaction from the Spanish or if they mistreated the entrepreneur, there was a very real possibility that the republic might find itself at war with Spain. The risks that McClallen & Company were undertaking loomed large.

Only after McClallen & Company started up the river did Secretary Browne give Lisa a license to trade. And that just authorized him to go to the Osages, a restriction that ensured the only man moving on the right path to Santa Fe was former captain John McClallen.

CHAPTER NINE

LEWIS AND CLARK AND PINCH ME

The party that departed St. Charles amounted to fourteen oarsmen under the command of the boat master. A French and Pawnee interpreter and McClallen's black waiter brought the total to seventeen. The former officer must have found his rag-tag crew colorful in *toques* and kerchiefs, but only one of those sun-darkened, short, square voyageurs left a documentary record. On August 27, 1806, just before McClallen & Company left the next day, the baker's son, Isidore Monplaisir, drew tobacco, two cotton handkerchiefs, and a half yard of blue cloth with thread from the Hunt & Hankinson store and charged it to McClallen.[1]

As the crew settled into levering the laden boat against the current, they had an advantage because the Missouri was past its spring surge. In his youth, McClallen saw cargoes discharged from Hudson River sloops rowed up the Mohawk River in batteaux not unlike his present boat. As a young lieutenant on the way to Fort Niagara, McClallen remembered going against that current.

McClallen had crammed what Lewis and Clark took three years to accomplish into the short month or so between his return from Baltimore and his departure in August. Details of properly packing the outfit in St. Louis had to be right because there would be no turning back. Passing Cantonment Belle Fontaine, the former officer could not resist a farewell salute to his company, which was under the command of a new captain. The adjoining Indian trade factory had been completed last December, but goods to stock it arrived only in the spring. The resident factor and his assistant watched the trader pass because they had an inventory of trade goods worth sixty thousand dollars to sell.

It had been ten years since the French observer and spy Victor Collet rendered a negative reaction about St. Charles. The cradle of boatmen was a mere village of one hundred and twenty ill-constructed houses for a community whose "ordinary occupations are hunting and trading with the Indians: a few hire themselves out as rowers: and it would be difficult to find a collection of individuals more ignorant, stupid, ugly, and miserable."[2]

Most of McClallen's boatmen came from St. Charles, so there was an overnight stop at the riverside town for last farewells. Next morning, the "St. Afee" merchant's crew cleared to the usual partings with sullen *femmes* or fluttering *jeune filles*. Although boats laden with grand expectations had been putting off from that shore for many years, the departure of McClallen & Company was unique. Instead of just another outfit going to the Indian trade, those packs carried stuff meant to please *senioritas*. Not a comforting thought for wives who mistrusted the fidelity of their husbands.

When the boatmen set their oars and pulled against the muddy river, McClallen, whom the men referred to in river terminology as their *bourgeois*, was finally free of the roiling politics of St. Louis.[3] A former member of the greatest club of all, the army, McClallen could not have departed without being noticed. If friends came over to the river front to see him off, they never wrote about it.

McClallen might be considered the bourgeois, but the operation of the boat was the prerogative of the patron, the boat master. The usual habit of departing boats was to steer into the first likely place, the Tavern Cave perhaps, and immediately consume their trip liquor ration. Workmen in that hard time of human power drank to become anesthetized, and McClallen's crew knew that they would be bucking the current for six hundred miles. If they were willing to be human machines, there was no begrudging them a drunk.[4] The rowers were soon wallowing in the mud as drunk as hogs.

Next day, as McClallen's hung-over boatmen stemmed the opaque water, he realized why they blocked out what lay ahead. Although the devil had gone out of the current this late in the season, the river was choked with a dangerous maze of snags, sawyers, and sinkers. Where the men were unable to row or pole, they dropped over the side with a long line jointly attached to the bow and mast, and towed. That meant stumbling beneath undercut banks that might collapse at any moment or wading in water full of unseen holes and poisonous water snakes. Around any bend boat-swallowing sands could be a rolling disaster.

After a long day of struggling around overhanging trees or climbing over drift on the narrow beaches, the men were soaked and muddy. In camp they threw themselves down on the dried scum of the previous freshet and ate on a dusty mud bank without a clean place to set down a chunk of pone. But they were voyageurs, what was misery to them?

Totally dependent upon men whom he hardly knew or could barely understand, McClallen realized these boatmen were more than mindless rowers. It required experience and sharp observation to read the river, to foresee the sawyers and sinkers lurking under the olive water, or to step around potholes while marching with the *cordelle* (towline). At the bow, the *avaunt* was the best of them, finding a course through driftwood dragon teeth, fending off torpedoes of racing logs, or probing the depths with his pole. They sang their silly French songs in defiance of the silent, greedy waters.

On a hot day McClallen wore his small clothes: shirt, vest, and deerskin breeches. Going ashore to kill game, he put on a coarse linen hunting frock. He had never considered himself a hunter, or that much of an outdoorsman actually, and living by the hunt was a new experience.

In other moments, McClallen reevaluated what he had gotten himself into. The rolling hills flattening into western plains made Louisiana a vast territory where sluggish rivers were the best-known landmarks. Three European colonial powers had mishandled that promise until, in a presumptuous deal with Napoleon Bonaparte, President Thomas Jefferson put the young nation on the continental track. What maps there were thirsted for confirmation of a continental fountain of rivers. In 1803, the definition of what a skeptical frontiersman might have called "buying a pig in a poke" fell to Mr. Jefferson's secretary, Captain of Infantry Meriwether Lewis.

McClallen knew that several trading adventures licensed by Secretary Browne were ahead. Joseph Robidoux and Robert McClellan intended to operate on the river above the Platte, and the sly British trader James Aird had sent two boats to the Yankton trade and was following with another. That was no concern of McClallen because the only traders who he had to consider were those going to the lower Platte.[5]

There was no certainty that the hostile Kansa who embarrassed Lieutenant Wilkinson last year had been pacified by Lieutenant Pike. McClallen had to bypass that potential route and go on to the shallow Platte. That would be too low this time of the year to allow his boat, so McClallen needed to obtain horses from the Indians living near the mouth and pack overland to the Pawnee village on the Republican branch of the Kansas River. Somehow he would convince their chiefs to run interference for him through the uncertain Comanche. A good deal depended on what Pike might convince them to do.[6]

Midday on September 17, 1806, the toiling McClallen & Company boat had covered over two hundred and fifty miles and passed the Grand River, which entered the Missouri at its most northern bend. Just beyond the mouth of a stream where the rowers solemnly declared that snakes were known to gobble like turkeys, they met the returning Corps of Discovery. After a long two years, Captain Lewis, his partner in command, William Clark, and twenty-eight travel-worn soldiers were headed home with a full possible bag of bear stories. The Corps of Discovery surfed from the Rocky Mountains on a current so strong that the boats made fifty-two, seventy-three, sometimes as much as eighty miles in a day. Sweeping down the Missouri, the two captains were eager to know how the republic had fared during the past two and a half years.

After meeting in midstream, both parties went ashore.[7] In the first excited exchanges, the worn-looking members of the expedition chuckled at John's declaration that they "had been long since given out by the people of the US Generaly and almost forgotten." Well, here they were, like the mythological Greeks with contrary winds tied up in a bag, returning to release a full-blown myth upon the nation.

After gargling McClallen's whiskey, the corpsmen tied into a treat of biscuit and chocolate. When the two captains asked where McClallen was headed, they were told that

he was on reather a speculative expedition to the confines of New Spain, with a view to entroduce a trade with those people, his plan is to proceede up this river to the Enterance of the river platt there to form an establishment from which to trade partially with the Panas & Ottoes, to form an acquaintance with the Panias and provail [on] Some of their principal Chiefs to accompany him to Santa Fee where he will appear in a stile calculated to atract the Spanish government in that quarter and through the influence of a handsome present he expects to be promited to exchange his merchandize for Silver & gold of which those people abound.[8]

That was particularly interesting to Lewis, who had contemplated something like it during the winter 1803/04 while he waited for Spanish permission to proceed on the Missouri. President Jefferson discouraged it.[9] Meriwether Lewis waited two years before using Clark's notes to write his impressions of the meeting with McClallen.

I also met, on my way to St. Louis, another merchant, by the same name, a Captain M'Clellan, formerly of the United States corps of artillerists. This gentleman informed me that he was connected with one of the principal houses in Baltimore, which I do not now recollect, but can readily ascertain the name and standing of the firm if it is considered of any importance; he said he had brought with him a small but well assorted adventure, calculated for the Indian trade, by way of experiment; that the majority of his goods were of the fine, high-priced kind, calculated for the trade with the Spanish province of New Mexico, which he intended to carry on within the territory of the United States, near the border of that province; that, connected with this object, the house with which he was concerned was ready to embark largely in the fur trade of the Missouri, provided it should appear to him to offer advantages to them. That since he had arrived in Louisiana, which was last autumn, he had endeavored to inform himself of the state of this trade, and that from his inquires he had been so fully impressed with the disadvantages it laboured under from the free admission of the British merchants, he had written to his house in Baltimore, advising that they should not embark in this trade unless these merchants were prohibited from entering the river.[10]

The expedition began as a "literary exploration" that required several members of the Corps of Discovery to keep daily journals. Sgt. John Ordway penciled additional details.

about 2 oClock P.M. we met a large Boat Commanded by one Capt McLanen loaded down with Marchandize about 15 hands & an Intrepter & Clark [clerk]. they are bound for the Spanish country by way of River platte to the panies Indians & purchase horses and cross the Mountains leaving their goods on this Side and git the Spaniards to come and bring their silver & gold and trade it for goods as they are full of money and no goods among them of any account. and if Mr. McLanen has Success this voiage no doubt but that trade will be advantageous to the United States hereafter... Mr. McLanen gave our party as much whiskey as they would drink and we Camped. Mr McLanen gave us a bag of Buiscuit &c.

Thursday 18th Sept 1806. a clear morning. we gave Mr. McLanen a kegg of corn took our leave of him & his party and Set out eairly and proceeded on.[11]

The impression recorded by Sergeant Gass confirmed that the party included "fifteen hands, an interpreter and a black," and that he intended to "discharge his men on this side of the mountain and get some of the Ponis, who live on the river Platte to accompany him to the Spanish country."[12]

The exchange of information may have been mutual if McClallen had a copy of the Congressional publication of the material Lewis and Clark had sent back from Fort Mandan. That showed what the nation already knew about their travels, not quite what was intended when the first journals were sent back.[13] The two explorers recovered their good humor when he told them that Governor Wilkinson had proclaimed Louisiana outside the indulgences previously allowed to British traders. Although a problem with the Spanish on the Sabine River loomed, Wilkinson was keeping the pressure on by sending Pike to arrange a permanent peace between the Osage and Kansa and to establish a good understanding with the "Ya-i-tans or Cammanchees."

After the information-starved explorers heard the most recent news, Lewis and Clark outlined what they had seen since. As they descended, they counted over a hundred traders and voyageurs headed up the river.[14] Not long after passing the mouth of the Platte, they met Alexander La Fass and three Frenchmen who meant to trade with the Pawnee.[15] A pirogue (dugout canoe) of Chouteau's was also going up the Platte to the Pawnee Nation. Another river trader, Joseph Robidoux, would probably stop at St. Michael's Prairie in order to spread his business between the Pawnee, Omaha, and Otos.[16]

With the exception of Robert McClellan, most of the traders on the river were strangers to Lewis and Clark. Given his intimacy with the governor and Secretary Browne, those adventures did not surprise McClallen, but he hoped that they would not complicate his need to gain the trust of the Pawnee on the Republican branch.

Former captain John McCLALLEN was the first of their own kind that Lewis and Clark met, a former member of a very select brotherhood and a man who Meriwether once confirmed to be a good officer despite his Federalist inclination. Second Lieutenant Clark heard about John's recent resignation with particular interest because that opened a slot on the promotion list for a new captain in the Regiment of Artillery.[17]

In the gathering dusk, as the Monongahela rye whiskey lighted fires in the faithful sergeants and tired privates, Lewis and Clark gave themselves over to reflections. Meriwether felt that he had fulfilled the key requirement of the president's instructions to find "the most direct & practicable water communication across this continent for the purposes of commerce."[18]

From the vicinity of the Great Falls of the Missouri, there was a feasible passage through the mountains, an Indian trail that Lewis followed as he returned to the east side of the mountains. But the mountain trail (the Lolo Trail) from Traveler's Rest to Lewis River was not as convenient as the president hoped and would not do as a practical link to the Columbia River. Clark calculated that the distance from the mouth of the Missouri to the place where that trail came out on the west side as a mere 2,730 miles.

Clark's return from the Three Forks of the Missouri was across a divide and down the Yellowstone River. Several other Indian trails came together near an island close to present Billings, Montana, which he learned was known as "the Lodge where all Dance." Nearby was the mouth of a river leading southwest. Clark thought that would be a good location for a trading post because beleaguered Shoshone and other western tribes could come there with minimum exposure to the rapacious "blackfoot Indians and Minnetares of fort de Prairie."[19] He believed that rivers flowing south connected to the Spanish provinces because a Shoshone they met signed that his people "could pass to the Spaniards by the way of the Yellowstone River in ten days."[20]

Passing the Mandan villages on their return, Lewis and Clark learned that North West Company proprietors had the audacity last year to send one of their clerks to shadow the corps from the Yellowstone.[21] Earlier in 1806, two proprietors penetrated deep into United States territory to meddle with the Cheyenne.[22] If gunrunners or liquor traders opened posts near the Great Falls, it was only a matter of time until they turned friendly tribes against the states.[23] Meriwether's recent brush with hostiles was a forecast. His bad experience with eight "Minnetarees of Fort des Prairies" convinced Lewis that there should be a post at Marias River to deny intruders access to the mountain portage. More than a boundary was at stake, but it was worrisome that there was no one left on the upper river to protect the interests of the republic.[24]

The two captains knew that they had accomplished something beyond recording geography and spectacular landmarks. Lewis believed that he had mostly completed Mr. Jefferson's expectation of an overland way to the Pacific but regretted not exploring the fork they named for Clark. That might be a potential alternative to the impossible Lolo Trail over the mountains that they had followed. Someone else would have to explore that possibility.

What concerned Lewis was the impression that British traders from the north were imposing upon the nation's resources and subverting tribes that were now wards of the United States. Just what that imperial ass Alexander Mackenzie proposed in his book. He was guessing, but their exploration confirmed that most of the fur trade of the greater Northwest could be drained downstream on the Missouri. If British intruders were to be opposed, the upper Missouri was where the nation needed to focus its efforts. Clark was disappointed that his report calling for a string of military posts along the river as high as the Great Falls had been ignored. If the republic intended to secure its borders, it *had* to establish a presence on the upper Missouri!

During that long night when the stars were spinning overhead, they churned over the British threat. Those traders were still among the tribes, still spreading their deadly influence. It was intolerable to have greedy imperialists inciting the wards of the nation. Lewis explored the upper tributaries of Maria's River, which was below the Great Falls and bypassed the mouth of the Milk River closer to the Mandan villages.

He was disappointed in his hope of extending the US claim as far north as 50 degrees north latitude. But there was still hope that the Milk River might "furnish a practicable and advantageous communication with the Saskatchewan River" and justify a boundary farther north.[25] In a Monongahela whiskey–induced mind, Meriwether sketched an American empire spanning the continent. In William Clark's mind, it was rivers teeming with beaver that would inspire their countrymen to answer that challenge.

But mountain portages, vague descriptions of rivers, and British intruders were no concern for a man headed to Santa Fe. He had enough to deal with in his own blind foray into the unknown. When they had exhausted themselves relating experiences and arguing solutions, McClallen rolled into his blanket wondering what the adventure to "St. Afee" would yield for him. Would Robinson have prepared a way for him?

While the officers drank and talked by their fire, McClallen's boatmen were a rapt audience for the voyageurs Cruzette, LaBiche, and LePage. Having seen the elephant, they related their adventures in the expansive style of certified *hommes du nord*, men of the greater Northwest. The Mandan chief's interpreter, Rene Jessaume, added more about the overland connection to the British trading posts on the Assiniboine River. Several of the boatmen who stayed at the Mandan villages after the corps continued west went north of the Missouri during the summer of 1805. Pierre Roi even helped a British clerk carry his returns to the British posts where he met "freemen" who had been left out in the recent merger of rival Montreal trading firms. Cast loose in the country, they had to live by hunting like Indians.

Another was a young man who accompanied General Wilkinson's private adventurers, Rivet and Grenier, who had been sent to explore the "Unicorn River" in September 1805. A British trader had given him a small outfit to take to the Arikara, but he had wasted it and feared staying to face the consequences. To escape retribution, he had joined the returning explorers.[26] Although they were not particularly concerned about insults to the republic, McClallen's boatmen picked up a good deal of background about the upper Missouri.

Next morning, because both parties had to get going, the bleary-eyed travelers guarded against renewing discussions. McClallen ignored his aching head to write a letter to send back assuring his supporters that all was going well.[27] Four days later, when the returning explorers stopped at Cantonment Belle Fontaine, Lewis left a small box of papers and books with Lieutenant Peter to be delivered to Washington.[28] It is possible those dispatches also carried McClallen's hasty letter to Calhoun in Baltimore.

What John McClallen took away from that brief meeting did not disclose much about what lay ahead for him. None of them expected that the exploration of Pike would have much impact on the nation, but opening commerce could be significant. They were soldiers doing their duty, and McClallen was a former soldier with connections that he couldn't quite escape.

The boatmen knew that the most difficult part of the river was thirty miles ahead. That was where an island squeezed the river into a two-mile-long *cheval-de-frise*, a spiky barrier of snags and sinkers. Water racing through that narrow channel undercut the southeast shore, putting men carrying the towline at risk of a toppling bank. That was the choke point where the Kansa had ambushed Lieutenant Wilkinson. At least he had soldiers to command. All McClallen had, should trouble develop, was fourteen untried boatmen who weren't even properly armed. The immensity of what he had undertaken was beginning to sink in.

CHAPTER TEN
AT THE RUBICON

By William Clark's estimate, it was 384 miles from Snake Creek, where the two parties met, to the mouth of the Platte River near present Omaha, Nebraska. Lieutenant Pike's party must have succeeded in carrying out General Wilkinson's order to "accomplish a permanent peace between the Canzas [Kansa] and Osage Nations" because McClallen & Company rowed past the mouth of the Kansas River about September 25 without encountering any river pirates. By now McClallen thought Pike must be at the Pawnee villages on the Republican branch of that stream, preparing them for his arrival.

When the party came to the mouth of the Platte in mid-October, they found the trader Alexander La Fass and one man camped on the shore. La Fass was guarding his outfit while he waited for two of his men who had been sent overland to the Pawnee Republic. They expected to meet two other Frenchmen, Andre Sulier and Henri Visonet, who spent the summer with those Indians, and to obtain packhorses.

When the two *avant coureurs* returned, they were accompanied by a stranger named Charlo who was carrying dispatches and letters from Lieutenant Pike. John McClallen was appalled to read that General Wilkinson's expectations of tribal peace, and his own future, were blown all to hell.[1]

After successfully returning fifty-one Osage prisoners to their homes and placating their chiefs, the general's arrangement for a messenger to return from the Pawnee fell through. The obstinate interpreter Noel Maugraine learned that Osage warriors had driven the troublesome Kansa to abandon their village. Now the latter were roaming and looking for revenge, and Maugraine refused to accompany the Americans any farther. Instead he hired a substitute, only identified as Charlo, at his own expense, to carry Pike's letters from the Republican Pawnee.[2]

Fearing trouble, Pike's Indian guide led the military party by a circuitous detour that took almost a month to reach the Republican branch of the Kansa River. On September 22 Pike encountered Pawnee outriders and learned that Comanche killed six of their people. Because the tribes considered themselves at war, Pike's orders to contact and placate the Comanche tribe were complicated.

When lieutenants Pike and Wilkinson arrived at the Pawnee village, tribal leaders told them that a great many Spanish soldiers had been there three or four weeks previously. Three hundred Spanish regulars, covering the prairie like a flock of blue birds, bragged that they were part of an even larger force that had been left on the upper Arkansas River because of worn-out horses.[3] The young officer in command had been adamant that American parties would not be allowed to proceed toward New Mexico, and he threatened that his superiors would return in the spring to "teach the Indians what was good for them."[4] Taking two luckless traders, Sulier and Visonet, away as prisoners, they left a Spanish flag flying over the round-domed houses.[5] Fearing that a Spanish army was hovering on the horizon, the Indians urged Pike and his men to return the way they came.

Pike and Wilkinson were weighing that disconcerting development on October 4 when the two advance agents from Alexander La Fass arrived after hiking one hundred and sixty miles from the Platte River to borrow horses that would carry a trading outfit to the village.

During the first six days of October, Lieutenant Pike wrote reports to the secretary of war and General Wilkinson, brought his accounts up to date, and penned personal letters. Recent developments made it too risky to send a courier back through the Osage towns. Instead, Charlo could ride back to the Platte with the returning traders and find his way down the Missouri. The dispatches were to be delivered to Col. Thomas Hunt, commanding at Cantonment Belle Fontaine, who would forward the military correspondence.[6]

Because the Pawnee and Comanche were at war, Pike recognized that it would be impossible "to effect any communication" with the tribesmen who controlled the plains toward Santa Fe.[7] If the Pawnee elders were so intimidated by Spanish threats that they discouraged a military party from proceeding, how would they react to an American trader who intended to bypass them with an outfit of goods? McClallen had to be warned that his mercantile adventure to Santa Fe was frustrated.[8]

In addition to a surreptitiously obtained copy of the Baron von Humboldt's map of Spanish possessions, Lieutenant Pike had probably seen a copy of William Clark's imaginative 1805 map. That showed the headwaters of the South Platte River rising only a short distance from the upper Arkansas.[9] Because the fast, shallow Platte was considered un-navigable, it is possible that Pike advised McClallen to get horses and meet him on the upper Arkansas.[10]

It took the three men about a week to ride to the mouth of the Platte. By mid-October, Pike's warning impacted McClallen like a blow. Everything depended on getting the outfit of specific goods to Santa Fe. Instead, he was a victim of unforeseen circumstances sliding into financial disaster.

When the plan of opening the Santa Fe trade was developing the previous year, it seemed like a way of initiating a mutually beneficial relationship with the landlocked New Mexican province. That theory was seriously challenged when Lieutenant Wilkinson and Dr. Steele were stopped by hostile Kansa. Now a large Spanish force had intimidated the Pawnee, and there was no way of knowing what they might convince the dangerous Comanche to do. Indians were being pressed to guard the Spanish frontier, and it was unlikely that Dr. Robinson would be able to convince Santa Fe officials to tolerate an uninvited overland trader. Those odds were much too great.

McClallen weighed the alternatives. Prospects for trading nearby were unpromising because two other outfits had already gone a few leagues up the Platte to the Oto and Pawnee villages, locking up that business for the winter. Alexander La Fass had horses to pack his outfit to the Republican branch, but McClallen would have to hire animals locally at a premium. Even if he did it, there were no assurances that he could convince the Spanish-intimidated Pawnee to risk getting him past their Comanche enemies. He could not take a small, poorly armed party to destruction.

McClallen's boat was too heavy to take up the shallow Platte so late in the season. Snaking between sandy flats, the river would inevitably strand his outfit like a dead buffalo. Switching to horses was out of the question because the price he would have to pay locally for pack animals would be ruinous.

If he took the outfit back to St. Louis, he could not expect to wholesale profitably to competitors aware of his dilemma. Most of that cargo was superfine cloth that might have sold at Santa Fe for twenty-five dollars a yard, or fine cloth for twenty dollars. Other goods, iron, steel, or confections, should have brought high prices.[11] But what was the market for German linen or fine calico among pioneer women who were struggling to build homes on a new frontier?

His best option was to find a place to wait out the winter and see what developed next spring. According to Spanish observations, there were an "infinite number of wandering tribes," all were very numerous, all very warlike.[12] What McClallen knew about them was limited to his observation of Piahito. That "Savage deliniation on a Buffalo Pelt of the Missouri & its South Western Branches including the Rivers plate & Lycorn or Pierre Jaune" was still in the back of McClallen's mind.[13]

Piahito had been sent east and paraded around foul eastern cities until the poor devil caught something that a warrior's body could not resist. The unwelcome assignment of reconciling Arikara tribesmen to the death had fallen to the interpreter, Joseph Gravelines, who was authorized to carry a gift of five hundred dollars in goods from the trade factory.[14] But after the incident with hostile Kansa, Gravelines was no longer confident that a couple of soldiers in a pirogue were a sufficient escort. When sixty-eight-year-old Pierre Dorion returned from a peacemaking mission on the Des Moines River, he offered "to land Gravelines at his destination." Loaded with condolence presents, they set off with the trader Robert McClellan for his trading post at the Omaha villages and were traveling ahead of McClallen & Company.

McClallen understood that several tribes up the river also had connections with the Spanish settlements, and he might be able to find another trail that avoided the Pawnee blockade. Instead of risking the Platte, he would continue up the Missouri and find a place to winter with Indians. He could trade the goods he brought along to bribe the

Pawnee for hospitality and even enough peltry to offset some of his debts.

⇥≡⇤

The blocked entrepreneur was wrestling with that possibility when a small pirogue landed on the Platte mouth sands. As they had promised Lewis and Clark, François Rivet and François Grenier were returning to report to their sponsor, General Wilkinson, who had outfitted them to hunt on Riviere la Corne for two years. Others of their party had broken off to go to the Cheyenne, but their examination of rivers beyond the Mandan villages had been disappointing.[15]

Grenier spent several winters among *les Mandaines* and could recite the history and prospects of business on the upper river.[16] As long as British traders from the north took enough robes and horses to supply their needs, the Arikara, Mandans, and Hidatsa were never going to be productive beaver hunters. There had not been enough beaver left along the Missouri to support the ten men Regis Loisel sent to trap between his Cedar Island house (near present Pierre, South Dakota) and the Arikara towns. Despite the fear of hostile Sioux, debt-obligated trappers had to risk going up feeder streams to make sets to trap beaver. Some worked as far west as the Black Hills but barely made wages. When Loisel's clerk, Pierre-Antoine Tabeau, went aboard the returning corps keelboat, he took with him the last of that business on *les hauts de la Missourie.*

Rivet knew about the middle river because he had traded there in the past. He made three trips to the Mandans, and even above, in the service of the Americans. While they were at the Mandan villages, Rivet and Grenier learned that the North West Company clerk, Joseph Antoine Laroque, had been off with *gens du Corbeaux* (Crow) returning to the Yellowstone River. After a disappointing hunt up the Missouri as far as the "Roshjone" (Yellowstone), Rivet and Grenier left their traps at the Mandan villages and were returning from the Arikara when they met the returning Corps of Discovery and promised to follow.[17]

McClallen was not entirely surprised to intercept the two adventurers because they had departed about the same time that the plan to send someone to Santa Fe was being discussed. He appreciated what they told him about the upper river. As they came down, Rivet and Grenier observed that the Yankton Nakota (Sioux) made their winter camp along Plum Creek, thirty-six miles north of their former location at the Riviere Jacques (the present James River). But they discouraged McClallen from going on to the untrustworthy Teton Sioux. With so many competitors trading in the region, those tribesmen might become ugly.

Meanwhile, Auguste Chouteau's trader Henri Delaurier had taken over an old house at the mouth of Riviere Jacques (Yankton, South Dakota is at its mouth) with a boat loaded with linen shirts, hats, whiskey, and a swivel gun on the bow in case the customers became troublesome.[18] The British trader James Aird stopped his two boats a bit below at the Vermillion River where he might attract some Yankton and Brule Sioux business.[19] Robert McClellan returned to the Omaha where he contended with as many as three competitors.[20]

McClellan had the Sioux interpreter Pierre Dorion and the Arikara interpreter Joseph Gravelines as passengers. The old interpreter Dorion had an invitation for a council in St. Louis to deliver to the Tetons. Gravelines was carrying condolence presents for the death of their chief Piahito to placate the Arikara. Dorion and Gravelines would probably go on to the Yankton camps to spend the winter with Dorion's family. If McClallen was looking for someone to ease him through the winter, Dorion and his mixed-blood sons enjoyed good connections that might keep other traders at bay.

In return, McClallen assured Rivet and Grenier that Governor Wilkinson had gone down the Mississippi and there was no reason for them to return to St. Louis to report to him. They might as well join his party and return upstream.

The Platte was McClallen's Rubicon because going back to St. Louis meant admitting defeat and enduring bankruptcy. The problem was that his fifteen boatmen had been hired only on one-year contracts to carry him to a place on the Platte where he could contact the Republican Pawnee. Some must have been engaged to help pack the outfit there, or even as far as Santa Fe, but the others expected to return home with the boat.

Voyageurs were not fighting men. Not all of them were armed and those who were probably carried heavy rifles that were good for hunting but slow loading for defense.[21] A few may have had the fore-sight to bring along beaver traps to set while they waited out the winter.

Lacking a drummer to stir their spirits, the former military recruiter McClallen pointed out that if they went back now, they would lose wages for the winter. Rivet and Grenier needled that the Platte was the traditional dividing line between *mangeurs du porc* (pork-eating ama-teurs) and *hommes du nord* (real men of the north), and only boatmen who passed this meridian were entitled to call themselves *hivernauts* (winterers). Besides, the passage rite required a Neptune ceremony and drinks all around.[22] The boatmen agreed to go a bit farther.

The boat crawled upstream against an onrushing season. At night the moon wore a ring and in the morning ice already scummed the oars. At this time of the year, most of the tribes along the river left their cornfields rasping in the wind to await a hardening frost while they went on the plains for the fall buffalo hunt. The occasional figure that appeared silhouetted on the high banks was just nothing more than an ill-mannered crow cawking at passing strangers.

Hiking to stretch his legs and hunt, McClallen looked out from the top of the bluffs over a dead, useless country that seemed to stretch out forever. Only an occasional tree or grove of wind-shaped thorn bushes broke that horizon. A meat hunter found deer in the breaks close to the river.

McClallen & Company had no reason to be secretive, but a histor-ical mystery was developing. It was odd that other traders or trappers along the river failed to notice their passage. James Aird left the Ver-million River to drop downstream and meet his clerks, Ramsay Crooks and James Reed, who were coming along behind McClallen & Com-pany. The British trader and the deflected merchant and company should have met somewhere on the river, but Aird never mentioned it.[23]

McClallen should have sought information from the experienced Robert McClellan. After refusing to be drawn into General Wilkinson's plan to open a Santa Fe connection, "Bob" McClellan experienced a humiliating loss of his trade to the competitive Joseph Lacroix. This year he returned to the Omaha determined to compete as ruthlessly. He was equipped with Wilkinson's authorization to arrest unlicensed com-petitors.[24] But when Robert McClellan wrote to the governor of Louisiana Territory next spring, he did not mention John McClallen.[25]

The Detroit trader Charles Courtin and his small crew also settled somewhere in the vicinity. When he wrote the next summer from the Arikara villages complaining of Indian mistreatment, Courtin did not mention the previous passage of McClallen & Company. Below the Platte, the location of McClallen & Company should have been a curiosity with intriguing political undertones; above, because of the difficulties of communication, they became a shadow.

Yankton Sioux who ranged east of the Missouri River along the James, Vermillion, and Big Sioux rivers and the headwaters of the Des Moines, a large territory encompassing the eastern half of present North and South Dakota, were accustomed to trading with the British who infiltrated from the Mississippi and St. Peters rivers. That business siphoned away beaver, martin, wolf, otter, fisher, and bear skins to Montreal while deer skins and heavier buffalo robes, of which the tribes had plenty, were floated to St. Louis.

Two years previous, the Yankton camp was composed of about forty buffalo-skin lodges painted red and white. Each lodge housed from ten to fifteen individuals. By September 1806, that mobile camp had grown to eighty lodges strung along Plum Creek, a few miles north of the mouth of the Niobrara River and thirty-six miles north of their usual winter camp near present Yankton, South Dakota.[26] During the night he spent with Lewis and Clark, McClallen heard their complaints about the untrustworthy Teton Sioux who had twice threatened the Corps of Discovery and last year abused Charles Courtin and Dorion. So Plum Creek was the high watermark for a beginner who needed the cooperation of the more considerate Yankton.

Perhaps those people distanced themselves from other trading houses to avoid too much liquor. Beyond clothing of deer, elk, buffalo, and beaver skins, handsomely decorated with porcupine quills, the Yankton cherished few material possessions. When they took the hunting trail, some of their belongings were still hauled on small travois (drags) pulled by wolfish dogs.[27] Although they still ranged on the east side of the Missouri, they were also plainsmen.

Customers who traveled widely were not what the developing trade economy of the middle river needed. During the winter of 1806/07, fifty thousand dollars in the amount of trade goods may have been carried to the trading area between the Platte and Riviere Jacques, an abundance that was more than the tribes previously experienced. But Indian hunters only killed what they needed, and their mobile life discouraged runaway materialism. The nine Yanktons Lewis and Clark encountered just below the Niobrara already had five fusees (trade guns) and enough ammunition that they could waste it shooting at a keg floating down the river.

A consumer economy approaching surfeit accentuated competition between suppliers who desperately needed pelts to answer their downstream obligations. There were a number of significant operations contesting for a limited trade. That James Aird brought four boats proved how much British traders were willing to invest to obtain beaver to satisfy the demanding Montreal market.[28]

Most of the parties that the returning Lewis and Clark met in early September treated them to a drink, which meant that they were carrying liquor despite Governor Wilkinson's attempt to control a socially damaging practice. When desperate traders started the bungs from those eight-gallon kegs of whiskey, the situation could get dangerous.[29]

Bypassing those trading places without generating comment, McClallen & Company went to the Yankton winter camps on Plum Creek, where they had the advantage of Pierre Dorion's connection to those people.[30] Over the years Dorion had done his best to mitigate the foibles of passing boat parties while raising a large, mixed-blood family whose sons married among the Iowa and the Sioux.

McClallen and his crew settled into the Plum Creek community by spending the goods intended to bribe the Pawnee. Those chiefs who had visited downstream in 1805 were clothed and honored according to custom and were still wearing the tattered remnants. To make the proper impression, McClallen put on his well-worn uniform coat and conducted his arrangements through the interpretation of Dorion and Rivet. He began learning the differences of a highly individualistic people. After trading for many years with the French and the British, the Yankton knew more about white men than McClallen could hope to absorb about them.

In the etiquette of the winter lodge, ten to fifteen of John's hosts slept packed close together, naked under their cozy buffalo robes and tattered blankets. The Yankton were past the illusion that their women could absorb the sexual power of strangers; what they got instead was venereal disease. When McClallen's host gave him a bed in the winter lodge, he was expected to share it with a girl who was a temporary gift, a winter's generosity to a stranger. Rivet's explanation that *mon capitaine* was expected to show respect to his hosts by enjoying a comforting bed warmer must have been difficult from someone brought up as a Presbyterian and trained to be an officer and a gentleman.

As McClallen became part of the established mercantile life of the middle river, he found that was more subtle than the stereotypical simplicity of a buck-skinned bargainer with a blanket full of knives and beads, and a handy whiskey keg. The Indian trade was a difficult, potentially dangerous profession that demanded skill, diplomacy, instant analysis of unusual circumstances, and snap evaluations of character. Tribesmen, who lived in a totally different social system, might be friendly one moment and outrageous the next. Shopkeepers to exotic customers needed foresight, hindsight, and a degree of restraint not found in most men. The former captain of artillery had a lot to learn.

During the short days and interminable nights in the winter lodge, the Albany merchant's son, the former servant of the republic, the general's tool, moved in another world. Once past the obscene conditions of community living, McClallen came to appreciate his hosts. In a few short months he learned to accept the stifling smoke, sweat masked by bear's oil, and brown flesh.

Black men were not unknown on the middle Missouri. McClallen's body servant was one of the few persons in the winter camp who spoke English, and they were a long, long way from genteel Baltimore. Their limited exchanges were all that McClallen had to escape the overwhelming strangeness. How the transplanted waiter felt can only be guessed.

A guest like McClallen was obliged to help hunt. McClallen's rifle was more accurate than a trade fusee, so he earned his keep. When hunting brought him to a high point, he looked out over a wintery, sere landscape that seemed to stretch away forever and felt a crushing sense of loneliness.

As the winter wore out, the hoarfrost-covered lodges of the Yanktons sheltered a great many possibilities. Too far away for guidance from General Wilkinson or Territorial Secretary Browne, McClallen faced the prospect of unloading what he could of the specific Santa Fe outfit and returning downstream next spring.[31] Or, finding another way to reach New Mexico?

McClallen was not a scholar of western geography. As long as the Mississippi was Louisiana's eastern boundary, it had not mattered where the West ended. The known geography depended on less than reliable observations or the hearsay of those who generally believed that the undetermined bounds of Louisiana stopped at the Rocky Mountains and that most western rivers descended from some common height of land. There was some truth in the speculation, as the fountain is now considered to be Three Rivers Mountain in the Wind River Range.

⚊⚊

Charged with protecting an as-yet-undefined border with the United States, concerned Spanish officers believed that the Missouri River rose somewhere in the Northwest, uncomfortably near the province of New Mexico and its valuable mines. The boundary of the Spanish Internal Provinces was somewhere "west of its confluence with the Platte."[32] French flights of imagination had soared even higher in June 1802 when a metaphorically minded former captain of the (Spanish) regiment of Louisiana, Louis Villemont, conceived of an "aerostatic chariot" (balloon) flying over the mouth of the Ohio River. He was trying to communicate to the "Citizen Minister" of Napoleonic France why the vast potential of the Mississippi and Missouri rivers should not be given up. Eight years before, Villemont had been sent to visit places in the United States, including the vicinity of St. Louis, where he probably gained access to geographical reports or gathered information from the interrogation of deserters from British posts on the upper Missouri. He wrote,

> If... you will examine the chain of mountains which goes straight to the West after having followed it for about a thousand leagues you will meet the source of the impetuous Missouri. March along its course which after 900 leagues of circulation will come to terminate at St.

Louis at 39 degrees north (latitude). You will see on the right bank New Mexico and the rich metals which are exploited there; on the left [bank] prairies from 200 to 300 leagues in extent...of 22,458 square leagues suitable for all kinds of agriculture, at the same time joined to the large villages of Indians, of *republiques*, of beavers, martins and large quantities of other fine furs of the most prescious [sort].[33]

In a second letter Villemont added, "Louisiana has for a long time found, the same as New Mexico, its conservation in its own isolation."

Initially, the United States was no better informed. In March 1804 President Jefferson wrote, "I should propose to send one party up the Panis river [North Platte] thence along the highlands to the source of the Padoucas river [South Platte] and down to its mouth."[34] After spending the winter of 1804/05 at Fort Mandan, William Clark speculated that "within an area about 20 miles square...were the sources of the South Platte, along with the headwaters of the Rio Bravo or Rio Grande and the Yellowstone; and slightly east were the headwaters of the Arkansas."[35] That was the sketchy and often inaccurate information that John McClallen inherited and which William Clark could never bring himself to correct.[36]

In the Yankton winter lodge, opinions about western geography verged on the political. Dorion explained that Riviere Jacques headed in a half-league portage to a tributary of the Red River of the North, which British traders used to reach the Sioux. Other British came over-land from the Assiniboine River to the Mandan and Hidatsa villages. Captain Lewis meant to stop them by gaining the cooperation of the Yankton and Teton Sioux.

After hunting as high as the Roche Jaune, Rivet and Grenier met the returning Corps of Discovery and learned that Captain Clark had descended the Yellowstone without incident. He believed that its main tributary, Le Grosse Horne, probably connected with Spanish waters. There was a possibility to stir the imagination of a blocked Santa Fe trader.

CHAPTER ELEVEN

"AWAY YOU ROLLING RIVER"

The story of an astonishing adventure began in the suffocating, smoky closeness of a Yankton Sioux winter lodge. During the winter McClallen studied with new interest the congressional publication of the data that Lewis and Clark compiled at Fort Mandan and sent back to President Jefferson. When McClallen obtained a copy of the publication from General Wilkinson's supporter Senator Smith, he was only interested in the information about the Kansa, the Pawnee, and the other tribes he expected to meet on the southwestern plains. During the winter with the Yankton, McClallen refocused his attention on Clark's guesses about the Yellowstone River.

The redirected Santa Fe trader read about western tribes with unpronounceable names and ominous reputations. Old Dorion and Rivet enlarged on what he might expect to encounter. Although Captain Clark branded the Teton Sioux as "the vilest miscreants of the savage race" and "the pirates of the Missouri," Rivet and Grenier passed them without incident. It was encouraging that the tribes of the Yellowstone River welcomed a British trader in 1805 and asked him to return to trade.

In February 1807, Dorion left to go to the Teton Sioux and to invite them to a conciliatory meeting in St. Louis. Given how good feelings seemed to be developing, continuing up the Missouri River was no riskier than trying to cross the plains through Spanish-allied warrior nations. With any luck McClallen could still turn a setback into an accomplishment

Absorbing the combined experience of Rivet, Grenier, and Lewis and Clark led John McClallen to consider continuing up the Missouri and following the vaguely described Yellowstone to a point where a short overland portage would bring him to waters leading to Santa Fe's backdoor. Indians reportedly made the trip in less than a couple of weeks and returned with items of New Mexican origin. Instead of depending on the untrustworthy Pawnee, McClallen should find Crow or Snake Indians willing to sell horses at a reasonable price or even lead him to the Spanish settlements.

Locked in the isolation of the winter camp, John McClallen had no way of knowing of developments downstream since he left St. Louis. That blindness cleared sometime before the ice went out when a former member of the Corps of Discovery rode into camp.

John B. Thompson had left St. Louis in March.[1] By leaving so early in the traveling season, he hoped to intercept Forest Handcock, Joseph Dickson, and John Colter, who were expected to be returning from the Yellowstone River. According to arrangements made previously when Colter left the Corps of Discovery, Thompson planned to meet Colter with a new outfit so they could continue trapping for another year.[2] That Thompson undertook a winter journey alone seems unlikely. Later evidence shows that there were two former corpsmen who met with McClallen, but identifying them requires the elimination of three possible companions: Jean Baptiste LePage,[3] Pierre Cruzatte,[4] or some suggest John Collins.[5]

Because the river was still frozen in March, the party traveled overland across the headwaters of the Grand River and on toward the Missouri. The straight-line distance from St. Louis to the Plum Creek is about five hundred miles, and winter travelers averaging twenty miles a day on foot or on horseback could have made the trip in about a month. Given this assumption, Thompson arrived at the Yankton winter camp sometime in early April, about the time that McClallen & Company was preparing to leave.

After his experience with the Lewis and Clark, Thompson knew more about the western country than anyone on the upper river. He carried the way to the western mountains in his head. Better still, he spoke English and was able to relate downstream events up to the time that he left in March. Thompson said that the St. Louis community was unaware of the Pawnee blockade or what had become of Lieutenant Pike or of former captain McClallen. In addition he related how grandly the Corps of Discovery had been received in St. Louis. During the last week of September the glory of having crossed the continent meant drinks all around. Most of the seventeen toasts presented at the dinner held at Christy's tavern concerned national politics with grandiose expressions about "unity or division, freedom without bloodshed, the baneful influence of private ambition" and not unexpected in that entrepôt of the West, "the pursuit of wealth." Thompson grinned that while the "Heads of Department" were described as "pillars supporting the world's best hope," the less idealistic members of the expedition were hoping to have "the fair daughters of Louisiana" bestow their smiles on "hardihood and virtuous valor."[6] It had been glorious.

Some enthusiasts like George Sibley, the assistant government agent at the Belle Fontaine Indian trade factory, caught the sense of the moment. "It's been hinted by Captain Lewis who it is supposed will have the management of our Indian Affairs that several trading houses will be established by Government pretty high up on this River & the Mississippi, next Spring."[7] Former members of the corps discussed going back to get in on the bonanza beaver trapping.

Before leaving for Washington, captains Lewis and Clark left an impression of the necessity of discouraging British intrusion. In the heady atmosphere of sudden celebrity, they proposed a string of military/trading posts to discourage those competitors. McClallen heard that with a wry smile; it was exactly what the secretary of war had prohibited General Wilkinson from doing.

Not long after lieutenants Pike and Wilkinson left the Osages, a fever epidemic claimed two hundred of the tribe, and the devastated survivors took out their frustrations on a couple of unlucky trappers. But there had been no news about McClallen's party when Thompson left St. Louis in March.

After the turn of the year, the big news around St. Louis was "the Burr conspiracy" to initiate a filibuster against Spanish possessions. Mr. Burr's henchman, Colonel de Pestre, was seen visiting several notables, Mr. Auguste Chouteau for one, and rode out of town accompanied by acting governor Browne's son-in-law Robert Wescott. Later, Dr. Steele, the lead miner John Smith T, Sheriff Henry Dodge, and Robert Wescott tried to deliver a cargo of lead to Mr. Burr's army of filibusters at the mouth of the Ohio River.

When Judge Otho Shrader issued an arrest warrant for the deadly Smith T in mid-January 1807, no one was found brave enough to serve a writ on this killer. Steele evaporated, young Dodge was excused as a dupe, and Wescott was left holding the bag while his father-in-law tried to reassure the townspeople that there was no danger of insurrection. Auguste Chouteau declared that the militia should be called out.[8] Later it was rumored that General Wilkinson apprehended Burr on the lower Mississippi and put an end to the plot.

McClallen must have wondered if that had anything to do with the general's determination to establish a connection to Santa Fe?[9] Surely the general would not have sent his son with Pike's patrol if he expected that they might be captured and provide an excuse to start a war. Was his mercantile adventure to Santa Fe meant as a disguised military reconnaissance?[10]

Before Thompson left St. Louis in March, he heard that Manuel Lisa had dropped his plan to go to Santa Fe and was now organizing an expedition to skim the cream of the upper Missouri beaver trade before anyone else got to it.[11] That was understandable because the letters Lieutenant Pike wrote from the Pawnee village the previous October gave McClallen no reason to doubt that a large Spanish force planned to return to the already intimidated Indians next spring "and teach them what was good for them." Although the Iatans (Comanche) were at war with the Pawnee, that was no guarantee that they would welcome an American trader headed for Santa Fe. And the price of Pawnee horses turned out to be much higher than he had expected in St. Louis.[12] But, if Lisa still entertained an idea of going to Santa Fe, then McClallen & Company had to stay ahead of him. Those clues encouraged the idea of continuing up the Missouri. Although McClallen had only a general understanding of the Yellowstone River, he believed that its southern tributaries descended from the same mythic fountain of continental waters as streams leading to the Spanish provinces.

Somehow he convinced his boatmen to go along with that preposterous idea. Rowing another 614 miles upstream to the Mandans was within reason, but how many more miles would they have to strain against a current that had its origin in the snows of the continental mountains? Part of convincing the boatmen to go on required swapping his heavy keelboat for a lighter boat. How many of the remaining boatmen bought into this new plan is uncertain since only two men associated with McClallen & Company can be identified as returning to St Louis.[13]

An arrangement was made with Chouteau's neighboring trader, Henri Delaurier, to take the keelboat back to St. Louis.[14] Over the winter McClallen traded most of the outfit meant to buy Pawnee horses for Yankton hospitality and furs. Now he sent the accumulated packs back to St. Louis. Peltry that might be worth as much as six thousand dollars would offset expenses and placate his creditors while also assuring his boatmen funds would be available in St. Louis to pay their engagements.

Before the boat left, McClallen needed to inform his downstream connections about his intention. Dipping his pen into freezing ink, he marshaled his thoughts and wrote a letter explaining his plans. He had sent a previous letter to St. Louis with the returning Corps of Discovery when the road to Santa Fe still appeared to be open. Now he had to correct that and explain his new plan.

After the arrangement with Delaurier was made, McClallen & Company's remaining precious outfit was stowed in the bateau that had been traded for the keelboat. As soon as the winter weather eased, they went on the Missouri River again.[15] His winter-stiff boatmen were stemming the flood of continental waters. In the morning, the men arose from their frost-crusted buffalo robes and danced around the fire to get their blood circulating. Pushing off, they dreaded the *embarrass* that required them to step into the frigid water with the towline. Drifting ice clunked against the oars as they rounded the infamous grand detour and rowed past Regis Loisel's vacant trading house on Cedar Island near present Pierre, South Dakota. *Le bon Dieu* only knew where the untrustworthy Teton Indians might be lurking.

An insidious letter had already preceded McClallen & Company north by way of the upper Mississippi. Few in St. Louis could have known that the previous September one of the first reports of the Lewis and Clark expedition had been copied. When the Corps of Discovery arrived in St. Louis, Captain Lewis had the Cahokia postmaster hold the postal rider for half a day while they completed their first reports.[16] Five days after dating the first batch of dispatches, he wrote another letter that had to lay in Cahokia until the next post rider appeared. The temptation was more than postmaster John Hay could resist.

After secretly copying that description of what they had discovered, and what it meant, on October 14, 1806, Hay added a terse introduction: "Dear Sir, Annexed is the sketch I mentioned to you in my last of the 7th inst.[just before] I will give it to you verbatim."[17] Hay was half French and a former fur trader on the Assiniboine River. His purloined copy of Lewis's letter went up the Mississippi to Prairie du Chien and on to former British friends at Michilimackinac. Copies undoubtedly made their way over the lakes to inform the nabobs of Montreal, or through Lake Superior to enlighten wintering traders when they returned from their distant posts to the newly established inland headquarters at Fort William on the north shore. British traders read one of the first reports of the Corps of Discovery before President Jefferson had their dispatches in hand and read Lewis's observations and suggestions for competing with British traders. It was a remarkable piece of industrial, or more properly, international, espionage. For many years the purloined letter was forgotten, but McClallen would soon feel its impact when it was in the hands of a British fur trader.

⊷⊶

The best clue to what transpired on the middle Missouri during the winter of 1806/07 is a letter the Omaha trader Robert McClellan wrote about the time that John McClallen's returning boat passed his post, apparently without stopping. In April 1807 Robert McClellan reported on recent developments to whoever was the present governor of Louisiana Territory.

> Dear Sir, The Indians that set out with Me last summer arrived safe at there villiages Excepting Washinkasaby A Mahaw who has been committeed Many Years deyed by the way. The Nations in this quarter are all pesable. I have learned from the Souix Nation that Mr. P. Dorion delivered the Speach sent by government to the Teotones chiefs who would give no answer. they have said they would ley on the banks of the Misouri this Summer for the purpose of Stopping boats Should any attempt to pass.[18]

The departure of Wilkinson left Robert McClellan uncertain if the next governor would support what he had done under Wilkinson's authorization to arrest any unlicensed traders.

> there has nothing Came under my Notice worth mentioning to government in this quarter Agreeable to my instructions I have Examined the licenses of the Trayders in this Nation. there appears to be none deficient but a certain Francis Hortus of St. Louis who Solemly declaires he has obtained Licenses and Lodged them in the hands of his father at St. Louis. this must be Enquired after.

The struggling traders of the middle Missouri River had been energized by the downstream passage of the returning Corps of Discovery and what Lewis and Clark told them about the beaver potential of the upper Missouri and its major tributary, the Yellowstone. Charles Courtin, who previously endured a difficult winter trying to deal with the Tetons, was one of the first to ignite. Robert McClellan continued,

> there is also a Certain Mr. Corta a Kenedian who obtained Licenses to Trade with the Suoix & Poncaws for the year 1806, Proceeds on a voyage this spring up the Missouri Expecting to Reach the fall before he stops.
> Dear Sir, I have arranged my business for to visit the upper parts of the Missouri as soon as I posably can after My arrival at St. Louis. Should government permit me whom I trust will indulge My request Knowing that I will Investigate Every thing that in the smallest degree may Regard these intrest. Should Government think proper to send the Mandaine Chief to his Respective home I will with Pleasure take him under my charge and there will be but little danger to fear. I shall have two boats well mannd and armed.
> Dear Sir, I have the pleasure of being your obtmt Sevt, Robt McClelan[19]

"Bob" McClellan was a better visionary than he was an Indian trader. Over the winter he convinced James Aird's ambitious young clerk, Ramsay Crooks, to join him in taking two boats and eighty men up the Missouri. Crooks carried the letter Robert McClellan had written to St. Louis and on the first of May applied to Territorial Secretary Frederick Bates for a trading license. By then other boats were also arriving from the upper river and it was no longer a locked vault of information.

Alexander La Fass may have been among the earliest to appear with a verbal report on Lieutenant Pike's negative experience with the Republican Pawnee who tried to discourage passage toward New Mexico. Correspondence that arrived at St. Louis about this time included a letter that Pike wrote last October to a friend in the Belle Fontaine garrison. It was May 17 before Territorial Secretary Bates, who was now acting governor, reported Lieutenant Pike's experience with the Pawnee Republicans. Bates had been appointed territorial secretary, replacing Browne, and was acting in that capacity until the new governor, Meriwether Lewis, arrived in St. Louis.[20]

> We last evening received accounts which render it very probable that Lt. Pike together with his whole party has been cut off. I have seen a letter from a trader at the Otto, fifteen leagues from the village of the Panis, which states that One part of the Americans who went on the Mexican expedition has been killed.... The Spanish party which preceded him out a few days, no doubt prepared the minds of the Indians for this violence.[21]

The arrival of McClallen's trading returns and Pike's dispatches were a curious coincidence. Territorial Secretary and acting Governor Bates was not a man to overlook that someone associated with the previous governor had no license to winter or trade with the Yanktons. Because information from McClallen went to his downstream agent, former territorial secretary Browne, Bates was not a party to what McClallen was planning to do.

If McClallen guessed that information about the Pawnee blockade might be valuable to the planning of the rival Lisa and Clamorgan, he may have withheld the letters Lieutenant Pike wrote from the Pawnee village in early October. Soon after boats and Indians began arriving from upriver, Clark paid Pike's messenger Charlo for his services and presumably passed on the dispatches and letters.[22] That was the first news St. Louis had of what Lieutenant Pike had encountered, and that commanded the attention of the community although it was by then eight months out of date.

Unknown to interested parties in St. Louis, as it was to John McClallen on the upper Missouri, Zebulon Pike and his small military party spent the winter shivering in a crude fort that he thought was on the headwaters of the Red River but was actually on a tributary of the Rio Grande. Dr. Robinson, who was supposed to find a way to enter Santa Fe, left the cottonwood palisade on the Rio Conejos to try to enter Santa Fe. He did not escape notice by New Mexican outriders and by the first of March Lieutenant Pike and his men were in "protective custody." On March 9 the Americans were sent on to Gen. Nemesio Salcedo at the seat of his government in Chihuahua.

During their relatively pleasant stay, Pike and Robinson heard rumors that an American officer had passed on his way to Mexico City. That could not be McClallen, who had been warned to stay away from the Pawnee. However, it turned out that the courier was one of Wilkinson's adherents, Walter Burling, who carried the general's expectation of being paid for having avoided a destructive war over the territorial confrontation on the Sabine River and squelched a possible American invasion.[23]

Although Wilkinson's action in September 1806 has been described as a betrayal of a fellow conspirator, he actually performed his duty to the nation by breaking up the filibuster plans of Aaron Burr, who intended to launch a military expedition from New Orleans against Vera Cruz. By May 20, 1807, about the time McClallen & Company was moving up the Missouri again, Wilkinson wrote Pike, filling the lieutenant in on the claims being made that Pike's expedition was a "premeditated cooperation with Burr" and warning the young officer to be "extremely cautious" in what he said when he finally reached the Mississippi again. Wilkinson was just leaving for Burr's trial in Richmond, Virginia, where he intended to confront the "arch traitor and his host of advocates."[24] Spain was not about to pay Wilkinson (or Number 13) for his services, but he would find himself heavily taxed in Virginia by false accusations and public humiliation at Burr's trial.

At Burr's Richmond trial, the anti-Wilkinson clique would have its revenge for how the general had sabotaged the ambitions of political elements in St. Louis. In continuing to seek anything to discredit the former governor, Wilkinson's enemies fixed attention on the cargo that Captain McClallen brought west in 1805 to show that the general used public funds for private interests. Wilkinson found a friend in James Calhoun Jr., who testified to the private financing of John McClallen's outfit. Calhoun swore that his firm had advanced an outfit to McClallen and paid the bills for its transportation from Pittsburgh to St. Louis.[25]

In the first months of 1807, Territorial Secretary Joseph Browne's chance of being the next governor had been slim, and it got slimmer through March as he tried to muffle activities related to the schemes of Aaron Burr. Although the new Territorial Secretary Frederick Bates arrived in St. Louis on April Fools' Day, it was a week before he received the territorial accounts from his predecessor. Because Secretary Browne handled the details of licensing traders and collecting a fee, some kind of register should have documented something about the departure of McClallen & Company in August, or about the unidentified party that left in March. But Browne withheld those records, perhaps in case he had to prove anything concerning an involvement with Burr later.[26]

After being relieved of his official duties, Joseph Browne withdrew to the mining area around present-day Potosi, Missouri, and did not return until May to attend the trial of his son-in-law Robert Westcott, on accusation related to Burrite activities. The former territorial secretary was in St. Louis when McClallen's winter trade arrived in May 1807 and, as previously arranged, he received it. Unfamiliar with the fur trade, Browne optimistically overestimated the value and gave a note for six thousand dollars in favor of Calhoun & Company.[27]

Proof of the return also came from McClallen's hireling Isidore Monplaisir, and other returning boatmen, who were in town on May 4 when Auguste Chouteau settled an account. "By John McClellan [*sic*], Due Bill, $90" with the Hunt & Hankinson store. Ten days later, Chouteau provided Monplaisir with a gross of buttons that he also charged to John McClallen & Company. The boatman also received four dozen brass rings, strouding cloth, a red-handled knife, and a damaged shirt totaling $9.75, to which was added $10 "for liberation before the expiration of his time." Monplaisir's additional bill for $6.25 brought the debt to $26, which Hunt and Hankinson settled by June 3.[28] Those dealings prove the return of the keelboat and furs.

Browne forwarded the peltry to New York for sale, but when the barrels of furs arrived, the Baltimore Calhoun family seized on the property and had their New York attorney sell it. After expenses of $30.70, the sale yielded only $1,019.30, which left $1,966.08 outstanding from Browne's note. To force payment, on May 25, 1808, the Calhouns called in Browne's bond by asking the St. Louis operation of another Baltimore firm, Falconer & Comegys, to collect.[29] Six months later, when Browne died at Potosi, he took to the grave whatever he understood of the arrangement between former captain McClallen, the departed governor Wilkinson, and himself.[30]

⇥ ⇤

By May 1807, the soft gold rush was on. The previous summer of 1806 Manuel Lisa had no chance of getting a license from Territorial Secretary Browne, but three days after receiving some of the territorial books, Secretary Bates licensed Lisa to trade and hunt on the upper Missouri. Abandoning the plan with his partner Jacques Clamorgan to enter the Santa Fe trade, Lisa now intended to take two boats and forty or so boatmen up the Missouri.

The outfit, valued at sixteen thousand dollars and acquired from a supplier with British connections, was mostly financed by the Kaskaskia merchants William Morrison and Pierre Menard, who already held some of Lisa's debts. Because George Drouillard, the former hunter for the Corps of Discovery, owed them, he was sent with Lisa to watch their interests. Drouillard brought in other former corpsmen as trappers, namely, John Potts, Peter Wiser, and Jean Baptiste LePage. The expedition left St. Louis on April 19, 1807.[31]

Bearing the title of agent for western Indians, William Clark returned to St. Louis in late April and wrote to the secretary of war on May 18 to report the departure of the military parties returning the Sioux delegates and the Mandan chief.

Two large Companies of Traders and Trappers set out from this place about the first of the month intending to ascend the Missouri to the Rocky Mountains, and remain in that Country two or three years—One other party set out from this place in march—one small party set early in the Spring from the Mahas Nation, and I am informed a party of British traders have passed over by land from the North, all aiming for the Same point the head of the Missouri.[32]

Despite Robert McClellan's pessimism, Pierre Dorion brought fifteen Yankton and Teton chiefs to St. Louis, where the recently appointed western Indian agent, William Clark, read his speech to them on May 9.

Tetons. your bad Treatment to me on my way up the missouri three summers ago, and the bad Treatment since to (Courteau) a trader who visited your County was very displeasing to your great Father and he ordered his traders not to go to your country until he sent some of his warriors to open the way and protect them.[33]

The Lisa/Drouillard adventure was already on the river, followed by a military mission organized by Clark. Lt. Joseph Kimble would see the Yankton and Teton Sioux delegation safely returned to their homes, and Ensign Nathaniel Pryor would continue on with most of the soldiers as an escort for the Mandan chief Sheheke.[34]

The soldiers traveled in conjunction with two private enterprises financed by Auguste Chouteau. William Dorion was taking twelve men and an outfit to the Yanktons where Henri Delaurier traded last winter. From there, Chouteau's son, Auguste Pierre Chouteau, would accompany Ensign Pryor to open an upriver business with the Mandan/Hidatsa.[35] The military guard included the former corpsmen George Gibson and George Shannon. Joseph Fields may have traveled with the thirty-two boatmen driving a keelboat and a pirogue for Chouteau. The combined Ensign Pryor/A. P. Chouteau expedition of fourteen soldiers and twenty-three traders left St. Louis on May 18. In all, ten former members of the Corps of Discovery returned to the upper Missouri River in 1807.

Despite being unrelenting competitors, Robert McClellan and

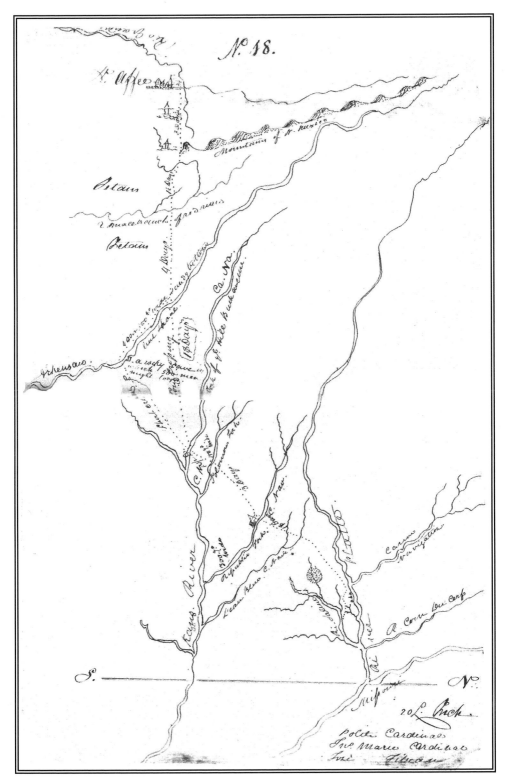

Pike's copy of the Spanish trader's route to Santa Fe.

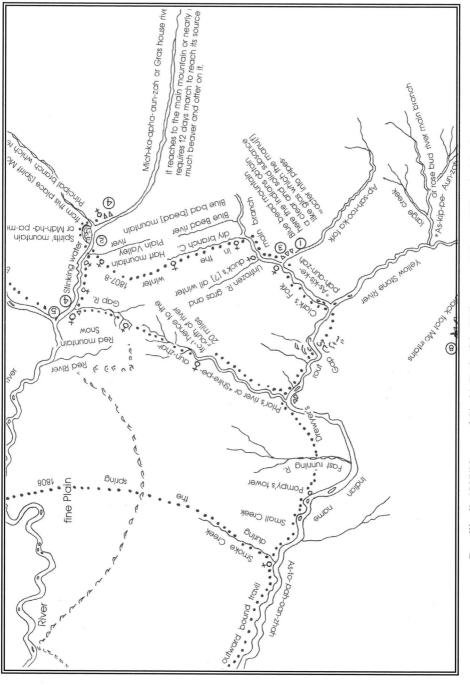

Drouillard's 1807/08 map of Clark's Fork of the Yellowstone, Missouri Historical Society.

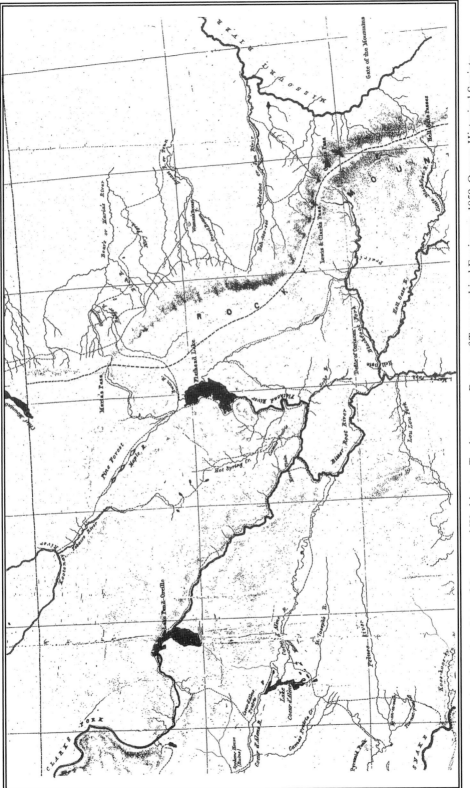

Alternations based on State of Oregon and Washington Territory map, Bureau of Topographical Engineers, 1859, Oregon Historical Society.

Left (top): Missouri River a few miles above the Yankton winter camp on Plum Creek, a few miles north of the mouth of the Niobrara River. Author's photo.

Left (center): Mouth of Clark's Fork of the Yellowstone River. Author's photo.

Left (bottom): Piskin (buffalo jump) above the Great Falls, overlooking the area where McClallen was killed. Author's photo.

Replica of Missouri River keelboat at Fort Benton, Montana. Author's photo.

Propelling a keelboat upstream. Drawing courtesy of author.

Tactique des Chasseurs.

Les pieds noirs et les Têtes plates font amicalement des échanges mutuels

Top: Father Nicholas Point, *Tactique des Chasseurs.* Salish methods of hunting buffalo on the east side of the Rocky Mountains. Courtesy of Jesuit Missouri Province Archives.

Bottom: Father Nicholas Point, meeting between Piikani and Salish. Courtesy of Jesuit Missouri Province Archives.

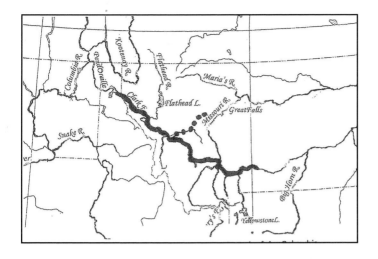

Three maps showing
McClallen's route and
deflection:

a. Platte to Clark's
Fork of Yellowstone

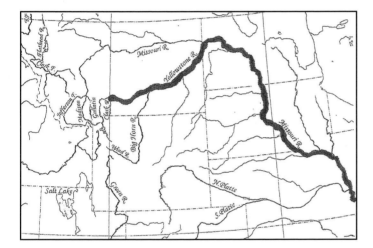

b. Yellowstone to Lake
Pend Oreille

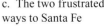

c. The two frustrated
ways to Santa Fe

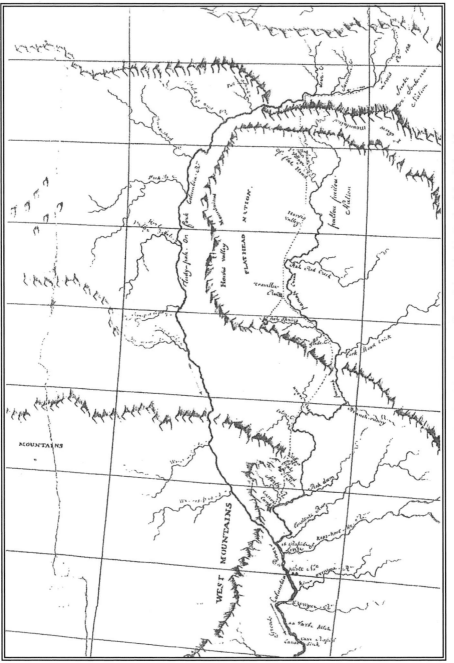

Private Fraser's map showing his understanding of the Clark's Fork of the Columbia.

James Aird may have traveled downstream together, meeting the expeditions headed up the river. They reached St. Louis in June and Aird hurried on to Mackinac by July 30. As one British trader later wrote to another from Michilimackinac,

> ... yesterday Mr. Aird arrived 30 days from St. Louis and has brought his furs with him, but not enough to pay ... he gave into the Company's Store at St. Louis the remainder of his Goods, which he says may be near to £1,200 Currency.... From what Mr. Aird says it appears there will be difficulties in the way of traders going to the West of the Mississippi, it is however believed here that they will be got over, as the Indians must have supplies which the Americans cannot at present furnish ...[36]

In a sense this distant observer was correct. The most advanced party on the upper Missouri River, actually already well up the Yellowstone River at that time, was McClallen & Company, which was not outfitted for the Indian trade or for trapping. Had there been anyone in St. Louis or Canada at that time who had enough understanding of western geography to grasp what McClallen was attempting to do, they would not have been capable of accepting his hair-brained premise.

CHAPTER TWELVE

"REATHER A SPECULATIVE EXPEDITION"

After slipping past the Teton Sioux without incident, McClallen & Company came to the three Arikara towns crowding the river, one strategically planted on an island. At least three in the boat party had been here before. But would they be able to placate villagers hungry for trade goods and as yet unaware of the death of their chief, Piahito? The less said of that the better because the chief's interpreter, Gravelines, was following with the United State's official condolences and presents. McClallen's party rowed on.

The major center of upper river exchange was several collections of mud-domed villages clustered around the mouth of the Knife River. Outsiders had been coming to trade with the Mandan/Hidatsa tribes for over a quarter of a century. Captains Lewis and Clark had spent the winter of 1804/05 recording ethnographic data without grasping the villagers' sophistication or that they were not entirely pleased with American captains telling them that they were now the children of a white father in a distant place. Still, the river people were pleased to see a boat arrive so early, confirming the promises that Lewis and Clark made the prior August.

Like the Arikara, the Mandans were anticipating the return of one of their chiefs whom the explorers took away the year before. But the new arrival disappointed their expectations by saying that he was just passing by, and was not interested in their skins or furs. He opened a pack to show that he had nothing to trade except bolts of gaudy, thin cloth. Those trade-savvy villagers preferred the good woolen blankets, powder, and ball that British traders brought overland from the Assini-boine River to the north.[1]

McClallen had been sensitized to General Wilkinson's determination to stop intruding British traders. Lewis and Clark told him that when a Hidatsa delegation traveled to a peace meeting with the Cheyenne, they were accompanied by two North West Company principals. Pretending to be horse traders, they crossed the overland connection between the Assiniboine River and the big bend of the Missouri, returning to their northern trading houses just before the Corps of Discovery arrived.[2] Indians reported they did not seem pleased with what they learned. That may have been the reason the North West Company pulled down their house at the mouth of La Souris River that had been a starting place for trading parties coming to the Missouri. The timbers were floated eighteen miles downstream to rebuild a post that looked north for its trade.

When the nearby Hudson's Bay Company Brandon House master, John McKay, tried to follow, he was threatened by Assiniboine Indians who feared that the traders were deserting them.[3] The villagers feared they would not return with the goods that they needed.[4] That winter only six Hudson's Bay Company traders visited the Mandans to trade for furs, buffalo robes, and horses. Worse, at the end of April the returning baymen were intercepted and pillaged by jealous Assiniboines.[5]

As word spread through the towns of the arrival of a new party, a number of curious Canadians came out of the dark lodges. Clothed in greasy leather and dirty, hooded blanket *capots* (hooded blanket coats), they were almost indistinguishable from the tribesmen whose hospitality they had imposed upon. Once they had been proud hommes du nord, but after the Montreal companies cast them off as excess personnel after a merger, *freeman* was not a term they wore with much pride. They had a few traps that the British advanced to them in the expectation of increasing production of beaver, but they could never repay their debts. Even stingy outfits advanced on credit were heavy obligations for men living on the edge.

John B. Thompson recognized the interpreter Toussaint Charbonneau, who had descended the Yellowstone in 1806 with Clark's party.[6] Although Lewis and Clark discounted him as a lazy fellow with careless ways, Charbonneau and his Shoshone wife returned with glowing descriptions of an upstream beaver bonanza. The men who listened to Charbonneau's yarns were a mix of free trappers left from Regis Loisel's abandoned operation or former financially indebted engagés of the British trading companies. After the 1804 merger of Montreal interests, many men took their discharges in the country because they were reluctant to abandon native wives and mixed-blood children. No longer under contract and cast loose in an unforgiving world, those "freemen" had to live by hunting and trapping. That made them more productive trappers than native hunters, who only took enough skins to satisfy their needs.

But they were still dependent on a cynical corporate policy. Debt-obligated trappers had to take their packs to the same North West Company traders who abandoned them and now refused to pay for their furs in cash. They took payment in expensively marked-up goods, which kept them caught in an apparently inescapable debt cycle. During the winter of 1806/07, the lack of provisions along the Assiniboine River brought freemen to near starvation. Some became so desperate that they traded their Indian wives or children to Hudson's Bay men and went to the buffalo country of the northern plains to survive.

Their precarious existence was difficult because the Montreal trading operations sent in contracted downstream Indian hunters, who set efficient steel traps and soon cleaned out the beaver along the Assiniboine River.[7] Local native hunters also resented the imported eastern Indians. In 1802, trapping on the south branch of the Saskatchewan became deadly when resentful Falls Indians (Atsiina) slaughtered fourteen intruding Iroquois.[8] After the North West Company clerk François-Antoine Larocque returned from the Yellowstone River tributary of the Missouri River in 1805, desperate freemen saw that as a new area to exploit.

Calculating the number of freemen trying to survive between the Assiniboine and the Missouri is difficult.[9] North West Company clerk Charles McKenzie mentioned a freeman who was equipped in 1805 to take a trading outfit to the Arikara and who failed to return by spring 1806.[10] At the Indian villages in June, McKenzie advanced supplies to freemen who intended to hunt beaver and bear on the Missouri above. But there are no reliable lists.

Traders found freemen difficult. On the lower Red River to the east, the North West Company proprietor Alexander Henry complained about obnoxious freemen who hung around without doing anything.

"This season we are troubled by an augmentation of freemen from Canada, etc. Their total numbers on this river amounted to 45; more worthless fellows could not be found in the northwest."[11] Passing the forks of the Red and Assiniboine in early September, the Hudson's Bay Company Brandon House master, John McKay, mentioned that the place was "swarming with freemen, all wanting to engage in our service. I would have nothing to do with them. I have enough of their witchcraft already. I sent them to their countrymen [Hugh] Haney, he may settle with them as he pleases."[12]

One of those freemen was old Louis Capois Hoole, who professed to have fought with a French contingent supporting Jacobite pretensions at the Battle of Culloden during "the 45" and later at the fall of New France. In 1775/76 he had been a Canadian militiaman when invading Americans took on the redcoats. Having never known a military victory, Hoole left the dull life of a "new habitant" and family man under British rule for whatever the Northwest fur trade promised.[13]

Engaged under a McTavish, Frobisher & Company contract in 1788, Hoole arrived on the lower Assiniboine River at the same time as another fixture in the Mandan trade, Hugh McCracken, and a Canadian named Chrisostome Jonquart. The latter deserted to the Missouri, where he informed Spanish authorities of British activities in their territory.[14] Mentioned eighteen times in the records of the North West Company, Hoole had made at least four overland passages to the Mandan/Hidatsa villages and accompanied the North West Company surveyor David Thompson there in 1797.

During those visits Hoole heard stories about the wealth of beaver on the upper rivers from "Old Menard," who had been as far up the Pierre Jaune (Yellowstone River) as the high falls that drop from present Yellowstone Park. From traders like Jacques d'Eglise or Jean Baptiste Truteau, he gained an inkling of how the trade was developing in St. Louis. Years before Americans came to explore, he was one of the floating community of *petite traiteurs en derouine* who acquired a collective knowledge of the promise of the Yellowstone or upper Missouri rivers. What those petty traders lacked was a leader to take them there.

Such men were beneath the notice of Lewis and Clark, whose thinly veiled opinions about discouraging British intrusion in 1804/05 were directed toward the North West Company management. Back in the fall of 1805, governor James Wilkinson had issued orders limiting the exploitation of Upper Louisiana to United States citizens. When John McClallen encountered the freemen, he realized that, lacking any other market, those trappers would continue taking their catches to the British houses on the Assiniboine. Stopping the extraction of a valuable national asset required drawing them away from British influence until there was an American post to buy their packs.

Promoting a proposal that they follow his party to the Yellowstone took more than a military recruiter's talent for beating the drum and tapping the keg. McClallen stood by while his French-speaking associates presented the argument and promised... *le bon Dieu* only knows what. McClallen may have felt like Ali Baba putting together a gang of forty thieves. The opportunity to hunt in new territory was irresistible, and going with the American officer promised safety in numbers. About thirty trappers agreed to throw in with his party.

They were feral Canadians, mixed-bloods and dispossessed Algonkian speakers from lost border wars, Iroquois still hunting far from the longhouse, and maybe even converted captives from some pointless tribal military adventure. Most were the dregs of distant, or outdistanced, societies, wilderness men leaving native wives and mixed-blood children to go off on a hunt for *Manitou* knows how long. They were fathers and brothers and sons of the fur trader's skin game, clippings of the British traders' desperation for beaver. Babbling in incomprehensible French or tribal dialects, they made John's travel-worn boatmen look like angels.

They had what McClallen's party lacked—British-made traps, British trade guns, and tattered English blankets. He didn't care if they were at best only nominal Americans.[15] McClallen's authority over his boatmen was only contractual, and he now associated with strangers whom he could not command with any certainty. The habit of command that he learned in eleven years as an officer did not come off with his worn uniform, but it still required a great deal of self-confidence. John McClallen still intended to find an overland passage to New Mexico and could not have realized that he was about to lead the first trapping brigade into the Rocky Mountains.[16]

Most of the freemen already had horses. Before McClallen reached the place where he would have to turn toward New Mexico, he would need to obtain horses necessary to pack his outfit to Santa Fe. Shrewd Mandan and Hidatsa sold horses to visiting British traders at the high price of around a gun and a hundred loads of ammunition, but cheaper mounts could be traded from the Crows. Until they reached the Crow country along the Yellowstone, the boatmen would continue rowing the bateau while the trappers rode along the shore.

At the Mandan villages or somewhere on the rivers above, the motivation that brought John B. Thompson back to the upper river to connect with a friend challenged a major western legend. The proof depends on the petty trader Charles Courtin and his small party that was trailing with the much-traveled interpreter Joseph Gravelines in tow. They were bringing confirmation of the death of Piahito to his people.[17]

McClallen & Company had moved on by the time Courtin and the interpreter Gravelines arrived at the Arikara villages on June 3. The presents that the United States sent weren't quite enough to console the tribe's loss of a leader. A combination of loss, rage, and greed led the Arikara to threaten to loot Courtin's outfit.[18] Ten days later, Joseph Dickson, one of the two trappers whom the Corps of Discovery met the year before arrived in a canoe loaded with beaver.[19] The abused Courtin wrote on June 22:

> Directly this [*la Langue de Biche* or Hind Tongue] went to the canoe and Began by plundering his meat & his Rifle then went to uncover his Peltrys & furs and taken it away. While Dickson was opposing himself to such a mischief, the Indian who had taken away the Rifle fired at him and happily missed him, but wounded another Indian in the foot.[20]

Despite this rude welcome, Dickson hung around until his sometime partner Forest Handcock drifted in on June 22 to deliver an invitation from the Mandans to come and smoke in peace with them.[21]

After enduring nineteen days of intimidation and humiliation, Courtin wrote a letter describing the situation and warning that it might take a hundred armed men to bring the Arikara to reason. Courtin trusted a copy of the letter to Dickson and left another with a friendly Arikara chief. Handcock dropped off near the mouth of the Platte, but Dickson continued downstream and delivered Courtin's letter to Territorial Secretary Frederick Bates in St. Louis sometime before August 2, 1807.[22]

Conspicuously missing from Courtin's letter is any mention of the third beaver trapper, the former corpsman John Colter who joined Dickson and Handcock in August 1806 with the intention of returning to the Yellowstone to trap. His presence, or absence, should have been worthy of notice because John B. Thompson was looking for him. Courtin's letter challenges the belief that Colter continued down the Missouri to meet the Lisa/Chouteau expedition at the mouth of the Platte.[23]

At the Mandan villages or on the river above, John B. Thompson, bringing the powder, ball, traps, and whatever else they needed to continue operating in the wilderness, connected with Colter. Thompson repeated the rumor he heard before leaving St. Louis in March that Manuel Lisa was organizing a large trapping party to ascend the Yellowstone. If the two former corpsmen wanted to skim the bonanza beaver trapping before competition arrived, they had a rapidly shortening time to do so.[24]

McClallen & Company could have intercepted Colter at the Mandan villages on the Missouri, or on the lower Yellowstone. In April 1805 it took the Corps of Discovery nineteen days to go from the Mandans to the mouth of the Yellowstone. There was no missing where the yellowish-brown water of the Yellowstone entered the deeply drab Missouri near present Williston, North Dakota. Finding this important confluence did not exactly reveal the gold of Mexico, but it was a reminder that cheered McClallen as he left the relatively familiar Missouri for unknown and uncertain waters.[25]

McClallen had no map to follow and only vaguely remembered descriptions from Lewis and Clark that he heard when he had no idea that he would end up ascending the Missouri. However, the two former corpsmen had descended from the Great Falls and remembered passing the mouth of the Yellowstone. Colter had recently hunted up that major tributary with Handcock and Dickson. Rivet knew the Missouri as far as he and Grenier had gone, and the freemen knew something of the geography that they might have experienced themselves or heard from others who had. That was how frontiersmen got around in unknown territory—using little clues and instinct.

As the bateau navigated long sandbars on either side of the entry and then a high bluff opposite of a well-timbered bottom, the initial impression was a fantasy world of melted bluffs and wind-sculpted earth pillars, a mineral world just barely frozen in time. Colors were predominantly grey banded with strips of ochre along the rim rock that gave the river its name.

The monochrome valley was already brightening as the bankside cottonwoods leafed and lush meadows greened to nourish grazing herds of buffalo, elk, and antelope. Bighorn sheep looked down from the fantastic heights. As the river widened, brushy islands began to appear and the horsemen riding along the shore could not have missed signs of beaver "havocks," where the workings of those animals were obvious. "Beaver sign" was not an adequate description of the three-foot or thicker stumps left after a colony downed a huge cottonwood tree. Lacking the charm of frolicking river otters or the sullen menace of the great white bears, the redeeming quality of those passive creatures was instinctual industry. Their workings were the beginning of a beaver bonanza beyond a trapper's wildest expectations. If the enthusiasm that Larocque expressed after returning from his trip up the Yellowstone had been a sly way of inducing Assiniboine freemen to trap where British traders were unwelcome, that had backfired. Americans were coming to claim those resources.

On their small Indian ponies, the Canadians trailed extra animals that carried their meager outfits and precious steel traps jangling in buffalo skin bags. McClallen shipped Indian corn and dried squash to feed his crew, but the freemen were expected to be self-sufficient. During the time of grazing buffalo herds, that was not a problem and plainsmen regularly took off with nothing but powder in the horn and shot in the bag, confident of killing something to eat along the way. Deer, elk, and bighorn sheep were innocent of the gun, and an experienced hunter could lure a curious antelope within range with a bit of cloth fluttering on an erect ramrod.

The catch was that fresh meat didn't last long in warm weather, and the downside of protein independence was daily uncertainty. Eating what they had, while they had it, hunters were known to consume prodigious quantities of meat, enough to last until their bellies crowded their backbones. Raised in settled upstate New York, John McClallen was not that much of a hunter, and he became an outdoorsman from necessity. Shooting supper was easy, and McClallen's boatmen gorged on broiled elk steaks and charred buffalo hump ribs.

The bourgeois knew that he was just the shepherd of a straggling gaggle of wild geese. That was just as well, as the thirty freemen were not the sort to take to rigid habits of military discipline. At the unavoidable times when the former captain of artillery had to exert command over his crew, there was no burly sergeant to enforce it. McClallen no doubt envied the enlistment papers, government pay, and promises of land that kept the Corps of Discovery members in line; he had to rely on mutual interest, group pressure, and whatever degree of persuasion survived interpretation from English into fur-trade French.

As a French-speaking intermediary, François Rivet was invaluable, but McClallen was unsure how much English he actually understood. Over the past months the captain learned enough *voyageur français* to communicate with the boatmen for practical purposes. More abstract expression was beyond him.

⟵⟶

On a sleepless night listening to the snores of the exhausted boatmen, McClallen was tortured with doubts. The geography he learned from Piahito and from his men, or gleaned in a few compacted hours with Lewis and Clark, was barely enough to sustain his confidence. Lacking a map, he was creeping out on a shaky limb of poorly understood theoretical geography. As far as he knew, Wilkinson still expected him to appear in Santa Fe, but plans made in St. Louis a year ago didn't mean a damn in this forsaken place. As his only link with the world behind, Territorial Secretary Browne was not a man to inspire much confidence if he was involved in downstream politics.

Instead of New Mexican treasure, McClallen's followers were

intent on sweeping up the soft gold pelts of beavers. As far as McClallen's laboring boatmen were concerned, the mountains were not giving up treasure easily. They pulled against snowmelt pouring down into the Yellowstone that turned riffles into rapids and quiet pools into cauldrons. In June the Roche Jaune was still brimming with the spring runoff and there were few backwaters or eddies to lessen the current. They were the first boatmen to ascend the Yellowstone by climbing a ladder of rivers. The Powder River was the first major stream to enter from the south, the second was the Tongue, which entered near the site of present Miles City, Montana. A six-mile succession of shoals near the mouth of the Tongue had a descent of three feet. William Clark had speculated on their return trip that a pirogue or large canoe could pass safely, but to get McClallen's boat over the Buffalo Shoals, his men went onshore and dragged it with the cordelle (towline). Bull-headedly bucking the continental tilt took quite a bit longer than the two weeks that Clark's party had needed for their rapid descent. When a large rock loomed near the river (Pompey's Pillar), McClallen hiked over to find among Indian etchings of animals, Clark's name, and the date July 25, 1806, not quite a year earlier.

This was the country of the Crow Indians, who believed it was the perfect place, the center of the world.[26] During Larocque's 1805 visit, he estimated there might be as many as twenty-four hundred Crow living in three hundred tents. They divided themselves into River Crows and Mountain Crows.[27] Clark, who saw no Indians, had heard from other sources about the Paunch Nation (Snakes) or the Casahanas who may have been Arapaho.

During summers, most Crow crossed trails through the Big Horn Mountains, which could be seen rising toward the southwest, to run buffalo along the Tongue River. Others continued east to the early summer trade fair at the Mandan/Hidatsa towns by following an overland route away from the Yellowstone.[28] Old people, families, and those left to guard them might stay in camps along the river. The stout-bodied, long-haired people whom McClallen & Company began meeting as they moved upstream were social, fond of company, and decent in their speaking. He was able to communicate with them because the freeman Hoole knew enough of the similar Hidatsa language to grasp similar Crow words. Ever wary, they shared their cherished homeland with a small band of Snakes and were on trading terms with tribes known as Flatheads, Nez Perce, and other western tribes willing to cross the mountains for meat. A few Flatheads recently accompanied indulgent Crow to the Mandan/Hidatsa trade fair.

McClallen was following a well-established channel of intertribal trade that passed native goods from as far west as the Pacific coast in exchange for foreign imports traded at the Hidatsa/Mandan complex. Lateral distribution reached north to the Saskatchewan or as far south as the Spanish settlements. Like the ancient caravan roads of the Old World, this path of commerce was just as political, and potentially dangerous.

During their 1805 visit to the Hidatsa, Crow traded two hundred guns and ammunition. They passed their worn old fusees (trade guns) to distant western tribesmen at outrageous prices, slyly neglecting to point out that it was access to powder and ball that kept firearms useful weapons. When self-invented gladiators on half-wild ponies warily circled each other deciding if a coupe was worth the risk, guns could turn a brief ennobling encounter into a killing. One source of trouble was Atsiina from the northern plains, the Minnetari of Fort des Prairies to Lewis and Clark, Falls Indians or *Gros Ventres* to the British traders. Atsiina had a habit of drifting into the Big Horn country to meet their Arapaho "cousins" and could always find an excuse to harry Crow Mountain Indians. The pot was kept bubbling when Hidatsa or Assiniboine raiding parties coursed along the Yellowstone to pick fights with western buffalo hunters.

The strangers ascending the Yellowstone should have had no reason to fear the local tribes. Unlike Missouri River peoples who were already spoiled from contact with white men, the Crow were intermediaries of the trade channel. Although they enjoyed a scalp dance, Larocque thought that there was more conflict in their own lodges, where the marital habit of multiple wives led to inevitable romantic entanglements and a harsh tradition of divorce. An inoffensive American party should expect a safe passage.

The McClallen & Company boat wallowed past the mouths of the Powder and the Tongue rivers, shallow, sandy streams too unpromising to be considered water roads to the south. Even the river the Mandan called Arsata, General Wilkinson's fabled Unicorn River now known as the Big Horn, turned out to be a disappointment because informants warned that it flowed through a treacherous canyon that no right-minded boatman should risk.[29] Probing for a navigable stream leading south, McClallen kept going on upstream past the site of present Billings, Montana.

Even in a vast, empty world, forty strangers moving up the river did not go unnoticed; particularly a boat that might be bringing the goods that the visiting British clerk promised two years ago.[30] During Larocque's tour, he saw seventy lodges of the far-ranging Atsiina and their Arapaho kinsmen camped on the Big Horn. They must have been part of three hundred lodges that went south in 1804 after trading with the North West Company on the south branch of the Saskatchewan River.[31] In May 1807, about a month ahead of McClallen's party, those predecessor snowbirds, wearing striped Mexican blankets and riding animals with Spanish brands, were returning and had crossed the Yellowstone River. McClallen's outriders should have found the place where they forded the river, but they had left a clue to confirm the possibility of reaching the Spanish settlements from the Yellowstone.[32]

McClallen's boat came to a large island where beaver kept the trees trimmed back about fifty feet from the shore. This was the place where the Crow usually gathered in the fall to hold their annual sun ceremony. It was known locally as "the lodge where all dance."[33] Larocque turned back from his excursion with the Crow at this point in mid-September 1805 and the following spring Clark described "a large lodge...a council lodge, it is of a Conocil form 60 feet in diameter at its base built of 20 poles each pole 2 ½ feet in Secumpheranc and 45 feet Long built in the form of a lodge & covered with bushes" and built last year.[34] All they found were shreds of a stuffed buffalo skin hanging from the center of the structure and other artifacts scattered about. Clark went on convinced that this meeting place would be a good location for a trading post.

Before turning back, Larocque made promises to those he traveled with about returning with a trading outfit. That promise had been disappointed until news spread along the river that a boat was coming.[35] When tribesmen came to see what it was about, John McClallen gained access to the geographically informed residents whom William Clark missed and a better understanding of what he planned to do by following a river south to the Spanish settlements.

About the first of July 1808, McClallen & Company reached a place where another island split the Yellowstone and a cold, lightly muddy stream led off toward the south. Clark's River was one hundred and fifty yards wide at the mouth as it caromed off an eroded cliff. At this time of the freshet it seemed navigable, but Indians who had winter camps along it warned that the river eventually turned west and entered high mountains. Navigation was possible, but John McClallen learned disconcerting information from obliging Indians who remained for the summer along the Yellowstone while most of their tribe's people went east to hunt buffalo on the Tongue.

By gestures or maps drawn in the sand, they showed him that the distance to the Mexican settlements was far greater than he expected.[36] The striped Spanish blankets, bridles, and battle-axes that they displayed did not come from direct exchanges but "on a second or third hand and they themselves have no direct trade with the Spaniards."[37] The blue beads that decorated their clothing were made at a nearby mountain.[38]

McClallen set out to open trade with the Spanish settlements, something that his Indian informants had been doing for years. Their culture was already infiltrated with imported objects and branded animals. But the diverted Santa Fe trader could not risk a longer distance than he expected until he had enough horses to do it.[39] McClallen realized that the distance to the Mexican frontier settlements, let alone to Santa Fe, might be as far as he had already traveled from the Yankton camps.[40] At that cold moment, McClallen realized that he might as well have been marooned on the moon.[41] The impossible reality was that he brought those bolts of cloth and stupid gewgaws, his fortune and his future, to a place of no return.

CHAPTER THIRTEEN

PEACE IN MOUNTAIN TIME

B y the first of July 1807, the high water of the freshet had passed and the water levels of the Yellowstone were falling. McClallen's boat scraped over shallows until the rock-shredded bottom grounded on a rocky sandbar beyond the strength of his exhausted boatmen. The Santa Fe trader had reached a place beyond General Wilkinson's powers of persuasion and had stranded his fortune and his future on a rocky shore.[1] His gamble to get to Santa Fe by going around the Pawnee/Spanish blockade failed because of his imperfect under-standing of the distances involved. Twice before he had been crushed by adverse events and rose to the challenge. Captive in a bubble of uncertainty, vulnerable to any thorn, after a 2,487 mile detour, McClallen & Company was not going to New Mexico this year.

It is difficult to imagine a lonelier place. The Yellowstone surged by, sucking in the muddy waters of Clark's River. From a bluff overlooking the mouth of that river McClallen could look west toward a distant wall of snowcapped mountains. Clark's River curved toward whatever stood between him and the Spanish provinces. Splitting a toothpick from a twig, John McClallen reconsidered his options.

The older Indians and their families spending the summer near the Sun Dance Island in the Yellowstone generously shared their geo-graphical understanding. The freemen who threw in with the party at the Hidatsa villages knew enough of that language to penetrate the similar Crow dialect. It was soon apparent that Spanish blankets and iron bits came from New Mexican outposts rather than directly from Santa Fe. The journey to the provincial capital as traveling tribes mea-sured it was many sleeps more, through mountains and across deserts that required an experienced guide. But their young men who had adventured there were away on the buffalo plains for the summer. By the time they returned it would be too late to find a guide and undertake such a daunting journey.

John McClallen was marooned at the end of his long detour. He could take his boat up Clark's Fork until it turned west into the mountains, but from there he would have to move his goods overland. Buying packhorses was a problem because the Crow did not take checks and his outfit of fine goods was of questionable value to those Indians and not much use to the trappers who accompanied him. Nevertheless, some of the calicos intended to entice senoritas would have to decorate Indian maidens, or their vain suitors.

McClallen & Company was stalled at the mouth of the Clark River near present Laurel, Montana, when a party of painted horsemen materialized on the skyline. Through his spyglass, McClallen saw rags of red uniform coats that British traders gave to flatter them.[2] Apprehensive freeman recognized undependable Atsiina warriors who were accompanied by mounted Blood Blackfeet (*Kainaa*). Those northern plainsmen had a habit of visiting the Big Horn country and were likely up to no good.

In records careless of the generalization "Blackfeet," observers failed to make the distinction between the associated tribes of the *Piikani, Kainaa,* and *Siksika.* Smallest of those linguistically related groups, Bloods were often mentioned in relation to nefarious activities. Had the newcomers known, it was odd to find Bloods associated with Atsiina so soon after the latter returned to the northern plains from an extended visit in the south. Buffalo were so easily hunted that a kind of protein intoxication left young warriors free to seek glory in war games. These visitors had heard that strangers had been visiting the Crow and were promising to bring a store. Whatever their intentions were in coming to the Yellowstone, those horsemen were unable to resist astonishing reports of a trader's boat actually ascending the Yellowstone.[3]

Innocent of that background, McClallen was not as suspicious as he should have been. When the horsemen cautiously approached, McClallen pulled out his old captain's coat. By now that worn blue uniform showed the erosion of too many camps and too many councils. The tarnished shoulder board dangled and traces of hospitable dog feasts, a dish of choice to greet a stranger, glistened on the lapels. McClallen's black valet had done what he could to keep up McClallen's image as an officer and gentleman, but camp life was hard on social illusions. With as much gravity as his sorry appearance allowed, the captain and his interpreters stepped out to meet the visitors.

The wary horsemen signed that they came to see the store. When they visited the British houses, their northern friends welcomed them with strong water. Where was the captain's hospitality?[4] Sensing more of a demand than a request, McClallen shook his head, shrugged his shoulders, and signed with a gesture his liquor was all gone...evaporated...used up. The kegs were empty, but he had some colorful cloth for their women if they were willing to sit down together and smoke.

Of course McClallen could not speak to them directly and depended on a chorus of gesturing interpreters like Rivet, Hoole, Colter, or Thompson. The Indians were astonished to find a trader's boat on the Yellowstone and concerned that Crow might be getting a trading house and what that would mean in terms of arms and munitions. Warming to the strangers, the visitors asked if the strangers came to trade. They signed that northern traders were reluctant to take robes, or wolf pelts for that matter, which was all that roving buffalo runners had to offer, and paid stingy prices for the skins they did accept. Seeing an opportunity to discredit intruders, McClallen explained that Americans were most desirous of obtaining beaver pelts but were also interested in receiving buffalo robes. The visitors nodded appreciatively.

The Bloods signed that the northern traders at the mountain house were crossing the mountains to open business with western tribes.[5] The Bloods were concerned about the arming of the Kutenais or Flatheads, whom they customarily abused. Did the Americans have guns to trade, and powder? McClallen responded that he meant to visit the Mexicans, who already had those items, but other Americans were following him who would offer good prices; say, just five beaver skins in exchange for a gun, and other goods in proportion. The prices that McClallen quoted caused the guests to cover their mouths in wonder.

That night, John's party shared meat with the visitors; they learned that their guests were far from roaming diplomats. The Bloods and Atsiina started with the intention of raiding Crow horse herds or taking

Snake scalps, trophies of about equal value. But this unexpected encounter with McClallen and his party spoiled their carefully contrived war medicine. They would have to return to their camps to report this new development and let their elders digest what they had seen.[6]

McClallen slept on the unwelcome news that British traders were expanding westward. It confirmed the rumors he heard circulating at the Mandan/Hidatsa towns. McClallen had not forgotten Captain Lewis's rant about foreigners stealing national treasure or Clark's fear that the British might claim a strategic place at the Great Falls to cut off business on the upper Missouri. If they built a trading post on the west side of the mountains, the British could dominate the Columbia drainage, moot Captain Robert Gray's 1792 discovery of the river, moot Lewis and Clark's exploration.

In the previous year, 1806, the returning Corps of Discovery had encouraged the western tribes they met to seek peace with their neighbors. When the visiting Bloods and Atsiina sat in the campfire light, they signed that their *Piikani* kinsmen were arranging a peace council with western tribes. McClallen realized this development could be an opportunity for someone to reaffirm the peaceful intentions of the United States. But there was no one in the country to do it in an official capacity.[7]

As the fires turned to ashes, former captain of artillery John McClallen had another sleepless night. As the first United States officer in the West after the return of Lewis and Clark, here was an opportunity that he could not ignore. A dutiful soldier could not turn his back on a chance to encourage peace between tribal dependents of the republic. Control of Upper Louisiana and the country beyond the mountains depended on who gained the confidence of those tribes. If former enemies were trying to arrange a peace, was it McClallen's duty to insert himself into the meeting and second those intentions?

⭤

During his military career, McClallen had been an artilleryman stationed on lonely posts guarding the sea approaches to the nation's important cities: Government Island protecting New York. Fort Moultrie, Charleston. Fort McHenry, Baltimore. St. Louis had been his first posting buried in the interior to guard against enemies who could come only over seas of grass. That had been his role as a defender, always ready even without being called to action.

The first step was to exploit the opportunity to challenge British intruders. On the morning of what he calculated was the tenth of July 1807, former captain John McClallen got out his field desk and sat down under a cottonwood that had escaped the voracious beaver. Lacking presents to impress the Indians, or alcohol to undermine them, the best he had to answer the challenge of British expansion was paper and pen. He headed the letter with an address that suggested a grasp of the bounds of Upper Louisiana: Fort Lewis... Yellow River... Columbia.

Tying the Yellowstone River to the distant Columbia seconded and broadened United States pretensions to the Pacific slope. The British trader who read it could not deny that Yankee Captain John Grey had discovered and named the Columbia River or that Lewis and Clark had explored its drainage. They had built a fort at the mouth of the Columbia River and lived there through the winter of 1805/06. By emphatically claiming the important point of usage, on July 10, 1807, John McClallen raised what would become known as the Oregon Question.[8]

He wrote a long, detailed set of regulations governing the conduct of foreign traders in United States territory.[9] Headed for Santa Fe when he left St. Louis, it is unlikely that McClallen carried a document from General Wilkinson pertaining to British traders he was not expected to meet. But he used what he understood of the general's intentions as an outline. He wrote,

> We the undersigned by the Power delegated to us by General Braith-
> waite Commander of the new ceded Territo(r)ies northward of the
> Illinois do hereby make known and declare the Instructions we have
> received relating to Foreigners who may at present be carrying on a
> Traffic with the Indians within our Territories for Peltries &c, or who
> may in future carry on a Traffic with the said Indians—

This introduction was followed by ten specific regulations governing how foreign traders were expected to conduct their business in northern Louisiana and across the mountains in the drainage of the

Columbia River. In the ninth paragraph he declared, "We have therefore given a Copy of the above instructions, Rules, and Regulations to be observed in the Indian traffic to the principal chief of each of the indian Tribes the most likely to see these foreign Traders." He meant the Atsiina and Bloods who brought the news of British intentions and who would go to their houses to trade. It was the last paragraph that was the shocker.

> 10th. The new ceded Territories to the American States northward and westward of the Illinois, comprehend the Mississourie Red River and all the Lands westward to the Coast of California and the Columbia River with all its branches; of which we have now taken Possession and on which we are now settled down to the Pacific Ocean; extending northward to about 50 Degrees north Latitude, according to the Boundaries settled at the Treaty of Peace between the united States and the Court of Great Britain, although it is by no means allowed here nor does any of our Expressions bear the Sense that Great Britain has any special right to any of the Lands on the Pacific Ocean or to the Commerce of any of the Rivers that flow into the said Ocean, all of which we shall comprehend as within our said Territories until some further Explanation takes place on this head between the united States of America and the Court of St. James.

> Signed
> Fort Lewis,   James Roseman Lieutenant
> Yellow River   Zachary Perch Captain &
> Columbia   Commanding Officer
> 10th July, 1807.[10]

McClallen expanded the idea of a continental nation farther west and north than Meriwether Lewis had dared, farther than Thomas Jefferson might have put on paper at a time when relations with overbearing Britain teetered on the edge of war.[11] When McClallen wrote he had no way of knowing that the Jefferson administration was tinkering with bans on international trade. His understanding came from Wilkinson's actions to bring intrusive British traders on the upper Mississippi and middle Missouri to heel, combined with what he had picked up about Lewis's resentment of British traders.

McClallen risked an unauthorized appropriation of authority in attaching official significance to his letter. Lewis and Clark had the certainty of their mission and the president's blessing to stiffen their resolve; Pike and Robinson had the general's sanction. But John McClallen was a private individual meddling without authority in international relations. To imply authority, McClallen inserted General Braithwaite, a fictitious invention, because he had no way of knowing who replaced Wilkinson and avoided associating his mentor with something extralegal.

There was a long chance that Lieutenant Pike or Dr. Robinson might still be out there, stretching their orders in light of the Spanish-induced Pawnee blockade by waiting for McClallen in the Spanish mountains.[12] Unwilling to put that association on paper, he reinvented himself as Captain Zackary Perch, a fishy play on the name of Zebulon Pike, and he named his fictitious second-in-command, Lieutenant James Roseman, to resemble Pike's associate, Dr. John Robinson. If the Bloods and Atsiina continued south, a copy might come into Pike's hands and let him know what had become of McClallen & Company. Those cocky alliterations suggest that McClallen still hoped to connect with Lieutenant Pike's southwest expedition.[13]

It took McClallen several hours to formulate and copy what was meant as a circulating letter aimed at more than one target.[14] About the time that John McClallen composed regulations for the Northwest Indian trade, Meriwether Lewis began a long document of his observations and reflections on the past, present, and future state of Upper Louisiana. Upon his 1807 return, Jefferson had elected Lewis governor of the Louisiana Territory. In recapitulating his meeting with McClallen, Lewis had no idea where the Santa Fe merchant was or what he was attempting when he wrote,

> The British traders have gone even farther in the northwest, and even offered bribes to induce the Indians to destroy each other; nor have I any reason to doubt but what the same thing will happen on the Missouri, unless some disinterested person, armed with authority by government, be placed in such a situation as will enable him to prevent such controversies.... If the American merchant does not adventure, the field is at once abandoned to the Northwest company....[15]

In August 1807, when Lewis was still working out an expert and studied view of the immense territory, John McClallen was the only man in the West capable of defending the interests of the United States.

Inventing trading regulations was a stretch because McClallen & Company was not prepared for that business, and his handful of boatmen were not equipped with traps or arms needed to undertake the hunt. McClallen realized that he had made a tactical error in drawing the freemen away from the Mandan connection. Allowing them to accompany him up the Yellowstone brought them to a place where they might contribute to the British western expansion. In distant Virginia, Lewis also saw that problem:

> Thus, those distant Indians will soon be supplied with merchandise: and while they are taught the art of taking the furs of their country, they will learn the value, and until they have learnt its value, we shall run no risk of displeasing them by taking it. When the period shall arrive that the distant nations shall have learned the art of taking their furs, and know how to appreciate its value, then the hunter becomes no longer absolutely necessary to the merchant, and may be withdrawn: but in the onset he seems to form a very necessary link in that chain which is to unite those nations and ourselves in a state of commercial intercourse.

McClallen meant to scare off British traders trying to establish a presence at the Great Falls by warning that the United States had taken possession of the outermost bounds of Louisiana and by clearly stating that the nation meant to immediately assert its rightful presence all the way to the Pacific.[16] McClallen may have given the visiting Indians a copy to carry when they went to the British houses, but there is no evidence that a letter sent along the east side of the mountains ever reached traders on the Saskatchewan.[17] Six months later, a Hudson's Bay Company trader at Edmonton House spoke with the Bloods and Atsiina who bumped into the Americans on the banks of the Missouri the previous fall.[18] They told James Bird that the Americans proposed a general meeting in the spring "with All the tribes they have hitherto warred with, in order to settle a Peace with them, and for the Purposes of Trade." Bird was pessimistic because "they delight too much in War to deprive themselves of Enemies by making the Peace proposed."[19]

It was a coincidence that James Bird's proposal to build a house more convenient to those he knew as the Muddy River and the Southern Indians (the *Piikani* and the Cree) filtered through the northern plains grapevine to the Mandan/Hidatsa villages. Bird meant a trading post closer to the upper Missouri River, where those productive beaver hunters liked to range. Although the Hudson's Bay Company lacked the resources and manpower to fulfill that promise, those rumors contributed to McClallen's obligation to frighten away or intimidate British traders.

Taken literally, McClallen's letter suggests that he still intended to reach the Spanish possessions and he was only making a gesture in the national interest. The copy he gave to the visiting Bloods and Atsiina was meant to forestall a British establishment near the Great Falls, the one that Meriwether Lewis feared.[20] That copy disappeared.

What the Bloods reported about British expansion beyond the mountains raised a larger problem for McClallen. Nothing in his past record indicates that McClallen was an idealist. But he had been a soldier and had learned a strong sense of duty. Only two letters, both copies made by the hands of others, survive to suggest how John McClallen was thinking as the currents of destiny took hold, but there is an echo of the drum calling a soldier to his duty. Left unchallenged, British traders might gain the same deadly influence over tribes west of the mountains that they bloodily exploited during the Indian wars in the Ohio country. He had already been deflected by a Spanish-inspired blockade and he could not stand by as the British created a hostile barrier to the Columbia River.

◄═ ═►

McClallen still intended to slip into Santa Fe by the backdoor, and mid-July was early in the traveling season. Given the good relations with the Crows, he stood a chance of convincing someone to guide him to the Spanish settlements. But they understood his predicament and set a high price on their horses. Better deals could be made with western buffalo hunters like those the former corpsmen knew previously. Meeting them could be an opportunity to encourage a peace initiative, discount British influence, and deal for cheaper packhorses.

McClallen had already asked too much of the boatmen lolling in the shade of the willows. They agreed to follow him because they were in too deep to go back. Like the trapper hunkered beside their grazing ponies, they lived day by day in an immediate world of direct need and uncertain gratification. Staying alive in a dangerous world required narrow focus, and they felt little commitment to abstractions of national interest or international policy. But the visit of the deadly Bloods and Atsiina chilled their intention to split off and hunt on the upper Yellowstone.[21] Wintering with hospitable Indians beyond the reach of those devils was a better option.

The Santa Fe cargo was cached in a hole in the ground. McClallen watched experts dig several "bottle shaped" holes in places that looked safe from high water, carefully keeping the fresh dirt on hides to leave no clues. The precious cargo was wrapped against leakage, put into the hole, covered, and camouflaged so evidence of activity was not obvious. Instead of a deposit slip, McClallen noted intersecting landmarks. As well as possible, the battered boat was hidden in the willows. Then, McClallen & Company went on up the Yellowstone River trailed by thirty or so freemen.

An obliging Crow or far-ranging Flathead guided the straggling brigade from the mouth of the Clark River until the river bent south toward a dark cleft between two mountain ranges.[22] He signed that the river fell out of the sky into a deep gorge (Yellowstone Falls) and beyond there were boiling pools and burning rocks. Taking that as a breath of hell, the boatmen shuddered and crossed themselves.

July is still spring in the high country. Wild roses were blooming and goose hatchlings were clustered around their mother in the river. Passing a small bottom, McClallen's party saw a log fort with walls covered by standing bark. That defensive work was built as the last resort of beleaguered warriors flying before enemies.[23] There was no way of knowing who those contestants might have been, but it was the first evidence of warlike activities ahead.

A well-used Indian trail was rutted by dragged *travois*, an Indian carrying device of two crossed poles over the back of a pony attached to an A-frame that dragged their belongings and butts behind. McClallen's straggling line of hikers and horsemen crossed a low divide to the most eastern branch of the upper Missouri, which the politically sensitive Clark named after Secretary of the Treasury Albert Gallatin. The trip to the Three Forks was just forty-three miles, but the meandering Gallatin River was cut by a maze of channels where William Clark had felt "swamped in this beaver bottom." Splashing through that soggy grassland, McClallen's brigade came to the place where the Gallatin joined the Madison and the Jefferson rivers to form the landmark Three Forks of the Missouri. That place was halfway between present Bozeman and Butte, Montana.

This was where the Old North Trail squeezed close to the river, a natural ignition point for conflicts between western tribes coming to hunt buffalo and northern plainsmen jealous of their territorial prerogatives. Unable to resist the opportunity, McClallen's practical-minded trappers melted into the shady, hospitable oasis, casting about for signs of beaver along the river banks. They would learn in time that the thick brush threaded by deer and elk trails probably concealed terrible yellow grizzly bears...or Indians.

According to the former corpsmen, the Shoshones (Snakes) had found this part of the world too dangerous after Hidatsa raiders captured two of their women. Two springs earlier, the band of around four hundred Shoshones lost twenty men, killed or captured. Nowadays, they risked coming down the Jefferson Fork only as far as the Beaverhead Rock.

That did not discourage other western tribes from crossing the mountains. The Salish who the former corpsmen knew as Ootlashshoots had been on their way to the fall buffalo hunt when they met the Corps of Discovery west of the mountains in the Bitterroot Valley. Eighty of the four hundred hunters traveling in thirty-three lodges were warriors ready to defend their camp or the herd of five hundred horses that they drove along, an irresistible temptation to rustlers. Usually they were accompanied by other like-speaking peoples from along the lower Clark's Fork.[24]

Western tribes came to the buffalo plains to hunt, make winter meat, and trade with Crow middlemen who used the sniffy term *Flatheads* to disparage their customers who preferred their own name, Salish (*Selis*).[25] Their sinew-backed bows were superior tools for running buffalo, but not as intimidating in war as a gun. Northern plains-men, jealous of their arms advantage, denied access to the trading houses on the upper Saskatchewan in order to keep them poorly armed and munitioned.

In the buffalo country the western tribes customarily set up forti-fied hunting camps near the herds, killing as many buffalo as possible in surrounds, pounds (corrals), or by driving stampeding animals over a *piskan* (buffalo jump). After falling, the crippled animals were easy to slaughter.[26] Butchers worked fast, always checking over their shoulders for the approach of enemies. Back in the camp, women and children split and dried the meat that would be packed in bags and carried back across the mountains.[27]

Smoke from those drying fires rose like beacons. Turning north in the wide valley of the Missouri River, McClallen & Company located a Salish hunting camp and approached carefully, displaying signs of peaceful intentions. Flatheads spoke a language no one in the party understood, but the former corpsmen had picked up a few *Sahaptan* words during the time they spent with the Nez Perce (*Nimi'ipuu*). That helped bridge the communication barrier when a Nez Perce traveling with the hunting community recognized the two former corpsmen. He came from the "Pellate Paller" band that spent the most time with the corps. He might have been one of the five young men who guided the corps and its train of sixty-odd horses across the Lolo Trail leading east to the Bitterroot Valley in the spring of 1806.[28]

Putting aside the worn-out butcher knives obtained from their more advantaged Crow neighbors, the men and women of the Salish hunting camp stepped forward to greet the strangers. In speaking to them McClallen depended on the few Nez Perce words that Thompson or Colter picked up a long year ago, augmented by a good deal of hand talking and pantomime. The western tribes were delighted to see Americans again; it showed that the other captains had spoken true, but where were the goods for the trading house? Where were the guns?[29]

To placate them, McClallen reemphasized the benevolence of the distant great father and restated the need for tribal harmony. Although he had to communicate through the imperfect medium of signs, the rapt congregation seemed impressed because they planned to go to the peace meeting. The American captain was welcome to accompany them because he would validate the proceedings and had already proposed another council next spring to the Bloods and Atsiina.[30]

Safe conduct to virgin beaver trapping certainly appealed to the eager freemen, who were not sure where they stood in that potentially deadly world. As soon as the beaver started growing winter coats, trappers could scatter and make sets in western streams that had never seen a trap.

◆═ ═◆

Tribal warfare was a combination of territorial defense and an excuse to test the mettle of young warriors, a kind of deadly gamesmanship. Rumors in 1806 of attacks on the Salish had been exaggerated. It was conflicts between rival northern plainsmen that had the Blackfoot heartland roiling. In April 1807, a Blackfoot (*Siksika*) chief confided to the Edmonton trader James Bird that "his countrymen all wish for Peace" because they feared the traders would deny them brandy and tobacco. War inhibited hunting, and the *Piikani* tried to avoid being drawn into the disputes that impacted their tribal friends the Cree, whom the British traders called "Southern Indians." *Piikani* were threatening to arrange a truce with the western tribes so they could concentrate attention on their overbearing Blackfoot, Blood, and Atsiina neighbors.[31] *Piikani* discounted the unfortunate encounter with Lewis's small party in the spring of 1806 as just another horse-capture exploit gone bad. Those foolish young men got what they deserved when the strangers resisted a move on their horses.[32]

McClallen had no way of knowing that the small party of Charles Courtin, the trader who experienced difficulties with the Arikara, was now proceeding up the Missouri toward the Great Falls, but he expected the Lisa/Drouillard expedition to bypass the Arikara and enter the Yellowstone River. The freemen with McClallen could hunt beaver west of the mountains and return to the new trading house on the Yellowstone.

McClallen's party traveled with Salish buffalo hunters who knew mountain travel as a way of life. Because bull hides were preferred for lodge covers, they made early hunts in the spring and returned later in the summer to dry winter provisions. The hundreds of horses they drove across the mountains included favored buffalo-running ponies and remounts. Families accompanying the hunt required horses for themselves and at least two to carry the lodge, poles, and camp gear. A poor man might have only a half dozen animals, while a rich family may have had as many as thirty. Homeward bound, the caravan was laden with *parfleches* (large leather envelopes) that bundled around fifty pounds of dried buffalo meat. Ponies staggered under loads of two hundred pounds or more. Years later, a literary-minded trapper described the parade:

> Listen to the rattle of numerous lodge poles trailed by packhorses, to the various noises of children screaming, women scolding, and dogs howling. Observe occasional frightened horses running away and scattering their loads over the prairie ... and in every direction crowds of hungry dogs chasing and worrying ... small animals.[33]

After meeting the Ootlashshoots in 1806, William Clark wrote:

> The Indians inform us that there is an excellent road from the 3 forks of the Missouri through a low gap in the mountains to the East fork of Clarks river which passes down the fork to its junction and up the West Side of the main fork to Travellers Rest Creek which they travel with their families in 6 days the distance being about 150 miles.[34]

That was the way the returning hunters, trailed by the McClallen party, used to cross the mountains. Toward the end of July returning hunting parties could climb the height west of present Helena, Montana, that later became known as McDonald Pass. They dropped down into the long valley of the Clark's Fork and exited through the dangerous Hellgate. They emerged from the shadowed walls of a tight canyon into the broad meadows of the lower Bitterroot Valley.

CHAPTER FOURTEEN

TOP OF THE WORLD

N ew worlds to conquer. Pink crags towered over the two men who arrived at a broad alpine meadow cut by the twisting channel through the snow of a little stream that flowed west.[1]

Clattering up the rocky bed of a diminishing stream, they were pleased to find that it originated in a soggy mountain meadow covered with patches of melting snow. From here the waters took a new direction ... west.

Although others had passed this way before, the winded geographer David Thompson appreciated the significance of straddling the continental divide. On June 22, 1807, he optimistically considered that he was "along a rill, which here rises & whose Current descends to the Pacific Ocean. May God in his mercy give us to see where its waters flow into the Ocean & return in Safety."[2] Ironically, the pass across the northern Rocky Mountains above and north of Golden, British Columbia, that Thompson used took the name of a competitor.

A poor Welsh kid educated in mathematics at a London charity school, David Thompson had been apprenticed to the Hudson's Bay Company. During the winter of 1787/88 he accompanied other traders *en dourine* (going about to drum up trade) who were sent to live with the beaver-hunting *Piikani*. Appalled by their potential for savagery, the young clerk was told that those far-ranging people made journeys to the Spanish lands. After Thompson shifted to the rival North West Company, he was employed as a surveyor to determine a dividing line between the British Northwest and Spanish Louisiana.[3]

This crossing of the northern Rocky Mountains was nothing new. Two half-engaged men, Charles La Gassé and Pierre Le Blanc, wintered in 1800/01 with the Kutenai Indians. The following summer

Duncan McGillivray sent Thompson and James Hughes to find a trail across the mountains above Rocky Mountain House on the upper Saskatchewan River, but they failed. In the summer of 1806, Pierre Bercier, Thompson's guide, crossed with the mixed-blood clerks Jacques Rafael Finlay (Jaco) and Nicholas Montour to slash out an Indian trail wide enough to pass loaded horses. Was it with a sense of history that Thompson's brother-in-law, John McDonald, sent the country sons of two North West Company founders to open the road to the western sea?[4]

The 1804 merger of two rival Canadian companies left the North West Company facing the debts of their expensive competition and the need to find new sources of lucrative beaver, the only fur that paid the cost of distant transport. Just when the partnership could devote its resources to a westward extension of trade, a new problem developed.[5] The United States purchased the Louisiana Territory from the French and sent a small military party up the Missouri, where they spent the winter of 1804/05 at the Mandan villages.

Captains Lewis and Clark failed to conceal their distaste for British traders. Captain Lewis let slip to British clerks that if the headwater streams of the Missouri justified it, they hoped to locate the boundary between the United States and British possessions as far as 50 or even 51 degrees north latitude. Although the minutes of the Nor'westers annual summer rendezvous on the north shore of Lake Superior fail to record it, the passage of the Corps of Discovery must have been a topic of serious discussion among the wintering partners. That summer two North West Company proprietors traveled to the Missouri and concluded that an inferior level of trade leading to a potential international incident was not worth the risk.[6]

As agents of downstream partners, Duncan McGillivray and his brother William saw advantage in the creation of a British presence west of the Rocky Mountains. Strengthening claims of discovery, exploration, and usage might reflect favorably in London when they hoped to extract a right of transit from the Hudson's Bay Company. For some time plans had been considered for breaking into the China market from a West Coast port.

Although Thompson's previous performance as a trail finder at

Rocky Mountain House was disappointing, the astronomer and recent partner was recommended to lead the expansion. When North West Company partners assembled for their 1807 annual meeting, the move across the mountains was under way. By then most partners who came to the rendezvous had read and passed around postmaster John Hay's remarkable piece of business espionage, a purloined copy of Captain Lewis's letter describing a connection to the Columbia River and the Missouri as a potential trade route.[7] The American officer confirmed that a transcontinental link running from the upper Missouri River to the Pacific offered a convenient and economical outlet for peltry. He also saw the Missouri River diverting the British trade of the northern plains south to St. Louis. That ominous possibility added incentive to Duncan McGillivray's intention of expanding the British presence across the mountains.

In response to the Lewis letter, McGillivray returned to Montreal and composed the pamphlet titled "Some Account of the trade carried on by the North West Company," which was meant for the edification of a not entirely interested British government.

> Not satisfied with the immense region on the eastern side of the Rocky Mountains throughout which their trade is established, they [the North West Company] have commenced a project for extending their researches and trade as far as the South Sea; and have already introduced British manufactured goods, among the nations on the Western side of the Rocky mountains; intending to form a general establishment for the trade of that country on the Columbia river, which as has already been observed, receives and conducts to the ocean all the waters that rise West of the mountains. The trade as it is carried on at present beyond the mountains, instead of yielding any profit, is a very considerable loss to the Company, as the furs will not pay for the transport to Montreal where they are shipped; nor can any establishment be formed immediately on the side of the Western Ocean; as the natives in consequence of some very ill-treatment by some American adventurers trading on the coast about 10 years ago, are extremely hostile to the whites.... Should the Company succeed in this project a new field will be opened for the consumption of British manufactured goods; and a vast country and population made dependent on the British Empire. It is conceived however that all this

cannot be accomplished without the aid of the British Government; which will scarce be withheld from an effort of such commercial and political consequence.[8]

McGillivray's optimism was shadowed by the American threat when he wrote

> The integrity of British North America, is in the hands of the traders; and will continue so, while the present system of traffic, organized and regulated as it is, is not materially changed, not withstanding the labours of the ascendent party in America, to weaken and divide it. Embassies, bribes, promises and experiments, have all been rendered abortive by the vigilance of the British traders whose interest is inseparable from that of the government in relation to the Indians.[9]

McGillivray's point man for the extension of imperial pretensions may not have been all that enthusiastic for what promised to be an onerous undertaking. Thompson spent the winter of 1806/07 at Rocky Mountain House trying to reconcile the tribes that traded there to an expansion that would surely arm enemies they were accustomed to dominating. As the inheritor of a plan already under way, Thompson had to proceed no matter his feelings about those fearsome warriors.

When Thompson left Rocky Mountain House on May 10, 1807, deep snow on the east side of the mountains stopped his advance party for over a month. Gasping men and blown horses were still picking across patches of frozen snow as late as June 26. The pack train descended a dark, dripping mountainside covered with a deceptive carpet of moss. Lightly set stones might shift under hoof or open a crevice to a fragile leg. Slipping and floundering down the beds of swollen brooks, the horses skinned their legs and gouged their sides. Leaping over tangles of fallen trees risked impalement on a broken branch. The constant bucking and plunging of the struggling animals loosened the pack cords and the men wallowed in icy water and slippery mud to readjust the loads.[10]

The pack train came down what Thompson called the Blaeberry River near present Golden, British Columbia, to a river flowing northward. Working upstream to a lake near the head of the river, the

Nor'westers began building a house until local Kutenai (*Ktunaxa* or *Ksunka* "water people," Thompson's Kootenae) advised on a better location. Thompson could not escape his apprehension of a *Piikani* reaction. On August 9, 1807, Thompson and his small party were busy building the house when "4 tents of Kootenae... who have passed the greater part of the Summer in the Mountains among the Buffalo," returned. They had been hunting east of the mountains with their Flathead friends. Four days later other returning tribesmen brought Thompson disturbing details.

> At noon 2 Kootenais men from the great Band arrived, the news they brought caused such crying & shrieks among the whole that we thought an attack at hand — Came to [undecipherable word] but they informed us it was on acct of a Battle between the Flat Heads & Piagans in which 13 of the latter & 4 of the former were killed — that the Americans in number abt 40 are making a military & trading Post in the south Branch of the Columbia, whither the Flat Heads, after the Battle had retired — but that still 5 of them were with the old Chief & a large band of Flat Bows who are all expected here in 10 nights hence.[11]

It was bad news that the Indians Thompson hoped to attract had already been in council with the dreaded *Piikani* and that they were under the influence of a large party of Americans. Then an obliging Indian handed the flabbergasted trader an astonishing document.[12]

> We the undersigned by the Power delegated to us by General Braithwaite Commander of all the new ceded Territo[r]ies northward of the Illinois do hereby make known and declare the instructions we have received relating to Foreigners who may at present be carrying on a Traffic with the Indians within our Territories for Peltries &c, or who may in future carry on a Traffic with the said Indians—1st. By a standing law of Congress, and now more especially to be enforce, no Traders under whatever Denomination, whether Americans or Foreigners are permitted to sell or give Spirituous Liquors of any Kind to the Natives under any pretence whatever, under the Penalty of forfeiting all the property in their Possession, the half of which belongs to him that is the Informer, the other Half to him that is authorized

& shall receive the said Property: and for the second Offence, forfeiture of Goods and imprisonment of Body.

2nd. No Trader has a right to hoist a Flag of any kind whatever at his place of residence, whether Camp or House; Any Offence of this kind will be considered as an Insult on the American Nation and punished accordingly. If it is found necessary for the sake of Peace &c to display a Flag, permission must be requested of the Commanding Officer of the nearest military Post, who, if he finds the request reasonable will permit the American Flag to be hoisted, but that of no other Nation.

3rd. No Indian Trader under any pretense has a right to give Flags, Medals or any other honorary Marks of Distinction to any Indian whether Chief or not. Whatever marks of Merit or Honor an Indian shall merit will be bestowed by the Commanding Officer, and by him alone. All other Persons are hereby prohibited from so doing, under pain of being fined for said offence or Offences against the Jurisdiction of America.

4th. As much Inconvenience and Confusion is found to arise from the Competition of Traders, who often lavish their Goods to the great hurt of their Creditors, it is hereby made known to all Indian Traders, native as well as foreign, that no one shall presume to sell beyond the price fixed by the Commanding Officer. For the first Offence, the offending Trader shall be severely reprimanded, and for the Second, his Magazine of Goods shall be shut up and he, himself, with his Servants prohibited from any further Commerce with the Natives: his Property shall be under the Seal of the Commanding Officer till the Season permits his Embarkation for the place from whence he came.

David Thompson had been present at the 1806 Fort William rendezvous when the assembled wintering partners read similar regulations presented the previous winter to their Leech Lake trader by a Lieutenant Pike. That was an almost immediate reflection of what captains Lewis and Clark implied during their 1804/05 stay at the Mandan/Hidatsa villages. Continuing to read the circular letter from another American officer, Thompson had no reason to doubt its authenticity.

5th. No trader or any of his Servants shall revenge an Injury, Affront, Misdemeanor &c that shall be done unto them by the native Indians, otherwise than may concern his direct personal safety or property; but shall make his Complaint to the Commanding Officer, who will punish the Offender according to Justice.

6th. As all Indian Traders in the American Territory enjoy the Protection of America and its Salutary Laws, Justice requires that they in return shall contribute towards the support of the Armed Force that protects them; all Indian Traders who are native Americans and come direct from the United States with their merchandize &c, having paid the ordinary Duties at the Custom House, are free from any farther Duty on producing the Custom House Voucher; all Foreigners shall pay 10 P Cent on the Imports and 8 P Cent on the Exports, or 20 P Cent on the Goods imported; but inasmuch as the Subjects of Great Britain trading direct from Canada, on Account of the reciprocal Commerce and good Neighborhood between the Inhabitants of the said Province and the Citizens of America, have an Indulgence above others, the Commander in Chief, by the Powers vested in him, has thought proper to abate the Duty on all foreign Goods &c to 12 p Ct., on the Imports direct from Canada; the Exports to be free. Merchandize coming from Canada that have paid the American duties, either at Detroit or Michillimacana on producing the Custom House Voucher are to pay no farther Duty. Every Indian Trader must deliver to the Commanding Officer an exact Account of his Exports and Imports.

7th. And whereas the great Distance between some parts of the new ceded Territories and Civilized Towns may prevent the foreign Traders from having it in their Power to pay all Times their Duty on their Merchandize, Peltries &c in Money, the Commander in Chief has thought proper to permit the Duty to be paid in Kind, the Duty on Imports in Goods, provided they be such as many be of Use to the Military Posts; the Exports to be paid in Furrs being every ninth Skin, according to the Book of Custom House rates.[13]

8th. Indian traders whether native or foreign are requested to furnish themselves with the Laws of Congress, relating to Commerce in general and the bye Laws of the upper Provinces, relating to the Indian Trade, in particular as, thereby the[y] will probably save themselves and the Commanding Officer much Trouble.

British traders were already accustomed, albeit grudgingly, to paying duties when their goods passed through Michilimackinac and on to Prairie du Chien. Presumably customs houses would be set up on the head of the Mississippi, or even at the Mandan villages. But this presumptuous officer carried that further by intending to collect duties in goods from the stock that Thompson brought across the mountains. If he had the manpower to enforce that, it would ruin chances of making the expansion profitable.

> 9th. By Information received at the Monden Village on the Missis-sourie we were given to understand that, some of the Subjects of Great Britain are about to carry on a Trade and traffic with the western Indians we have therefore given a Copy of the above Instruc-tions, Rules and Regulations to be observed in the Indian Traffic to the principal Chief of each of the Indian Tribes the most likely to see these foreign Traders that, the said Traders may not pretend Igno-rance that they are within the Jurisdiction of Congress and conse-quently obliged to obey all its Laws & Regulations &c. It is expected of the indian Traders or Traders who may see these our Instructions &c that, they will take a copy, leaving the Original in the Hands of the Indian Chief.[14]

But the last paragraph was most concerning because it expanded the territorial ambitions of the United States far beyond anything pre-viously declared, far beyond what Thompson's partners or the British Empire could swallow.

> 10th. The new ceded Territories to the American States northward and westward of the Illinois, comprehend the Mississourie Red River and all the Lands westward to the Coast of California and the Columbia River with all its branches; of which we have now taken Possession and on which we are now settled down to the Pacific Ocean; extending northward to about 50 Degrees north Latitude, according to the Boundaries settled at the Treaty of Peace between the united States and the Court of Great Britain, although it is by no means allowed here nor does any of our Expressions bear the Sense that Great Britain has any special right to any of the Lands on the Pacific Ocean or to the Commerce of any of the Rivers that flow into

the said Ocean, all of which we shall comprehend as within our said Territories until some further Explanation takes place on this head between the united States of America and the Court of St. James.[15]

Signed
Fort Lewis,   James Roseman Lieutenant
Yellow River   Zachary Perch Captain &
Columbia   Commanding Officer
10th July, 1807.[16]

As a surveyor who had already tried to establish a boundary between the Assiniboine and Missouri rivers, Thompson realized that the last paragraph challenged British claims to the Columbia River and its drainage, perhaps to the Pacific Northwest. When the downstream agents forwarded it to London, it would certainly stir a reaction in the halls of government. Unwilling to risk a reaction, even to himself, Thompson carefully skirted around the unwelcome development in his continuation of the Rocky Mountain House journal.[17]

For a long month, the damned letter hung over Thompson like a cloud. An opportunity came to send it back across the mountains when he started a party back across the mountain portage to Rocky Mountain House with dispatches and the trade to date.[18]

Using his rough journal for reference, Thompson rewrote a twenty-six-page report that he headed "Narrative of the expedition to the Kootenai & Flat Bow Indian Countries, on the sources of the Columbia River, Pacific Ocean by D. Thompson on behalf of the N. W. Company 1807." This was addressed to Mr. Duncan McGillivray, "Director of the N. W. Coy & the gentlemen of Upper Fort des Prairies" and covered his experiences from May 10 until September 23, 1807. In elaborating on the terse entry for August 13 in his daily journal, Thompson filled in additional information.

... about 3 weeks ago the Americans to the number of 42, arrived to settle a military & trading Post at the confluence of the two more southern & considerable Branches of the Columbia & that they were preparing to make a small advance Post lower down the River. 2 of those who were with Capt. Lewis were also with them, of whom the poor Kootenaes related several dreadful stories. This establishment of the Americans will give a new Turn to our so long delayed settling of this Country, in which we have entered it seems too late; but, in my opinion the most valuable part of the Country still remains to us.[19]

This and the field journal entry are the only records of what was a shocking development for Thompson, although he may have expressed his feelings more fully in letters that accompanied the narrative. There had to be something to explain the list of regulations that accompanied his packet of dispatches. Thompson's clerk, Finnan McDonald, and five men carried those documents when they left on September 23. Two days after they departed more details were delivered by "two chiefs of the Lake and Kootenae Indians." After smoking they filled in about the council with a large party of *Piikani*, Bloods, and Blackfeet who came in late July.

> The Peagans said they & their Allies were come by order & request to Make Peace with the Saleesh & Shawpatin Indians—that they all remained about 6 or 7 Days peacefully smoking, each Party having agreed upon a mutual Oblivion of all past Injuries & ever for the future to act as Friends & Allies, without any reserve whatever.[20]

During the council someone passed on a rumor of trouble on the east side "that the Blackfeet had plundered Fort Augustus on the Saskatchewan River to equip themselves more ably for War" and had gone to war on the Crow Mountain Indians."[21] Thompson feared that his vital supply line from the Saskatchewan was cut off but did not attempt to recall the dispatches.[22]

About the end of October 1807, McDonald and his men reached Rocky Mountain House, where they gave the dispatches to three engagés who were going downstream, picked up a packet of letters and additional supplies, and headed back to Kootenae House.[23] Along the way down the Saskatchewan, the three expressmen allowed the Hudson's Bay Company trader John Peter Pruden to read what seemed to be intended as a circular to all British traders. Pruden made a copy and sent that down to the Edmonton House factor James Bird. On November 10 Bird copied the letter into his journal. It would be the only version of the inconvenient document to survive.[24]

The document traveled to the North West Company headquarters with the winter express that was scheduled to pass Fort Vermillion on the middle Saskatchewan at the end of January 1808. But before it reached Fort William on the north shore of Lake Superior in early April, Duncan McGillivray was dead and it was his brother William who read about the disconcerting appearance of another American party.

The United States and the British Empire had come head to head in the persons of a surveyor/reluctant fur trader and an entrepreneurial former army officer. The two men came from different backgrounds and experience, but they shared a discomfort in being where they were and that they had fallen into what could very well become a conflict of great international significance. Thompson couldn't wait to get out of the fur trade. McClallen still hadn't realized he had stumbled into it.

CHAPTER FIFTEEN

FOLLOWING WESTERN WATERS

I n the past year John McClallen had learned a lot. He had learned to trust Indians. If his experience started badly because of the Pawnee blockade, that was really a political abstraction without a direct threat. McClallen had agreed to undertake the mercantile opening of a trail to Santa Fe that had to pass through tribes of the southern plains, people who were most often described with fear and hatred. He had heard the horror stories of the revolution, the Indian rebellion, and the conquest of the old Northwest as the bloody folklore of Indian dispossession. His first personal experience was being absorbed into the life of the Yankton Nakota winter camp, and he left it next spring with his innocence intact. He threaded the Arikara, Mandan, Hidatsa, and Crow lust for trade goods and weapons because he demanded little of them except basic hospitality. Meeting two of the most dangerous tribes of the northern plains, he parted from them in peace with the impression that their *Piikani* neighbors were seeking peace with the Flatheads. He threw in with returning Salish buffalo hunters, confident that it was his duty to extend a Pax American. It is unlikely McClallen ever read Voltaire or felt part of the enlightenment that motivated President Jefferson, but he was in his way a frontier Candide.

When the Salish buffalo hunters returned to favorite wintering places along the lower Bitterroot River in the vicinity of present Missoula, Montana, the eager freemen trappers spread out and began working those virgin beaver streams. Those Nez Perce (*Nimi'ipuu*) who chose not to attend the planned peace council followed the Lolo trail back to their homes on the Clearwater River. But the Salishs, Kalispels, and Kutenais turned north across a low divide.[1] Trailing down a gentle canyon, the laden caravan picked up a stream flowing west.[2] The journey for most of those buffalo hunters stopped when they came to a large river said to flow from a large lake to the north.[3] A well-known trail went on north past that lake to the Kutenai (*Ktunaxa*) country. Because the horse pastures on the rolling hills were usually free of snow during the winter, herders favored camps in the vicinity.[4] This was the lower end of the Flathead Valley.

The Salish called the impressive mountains rising to the east Coulhicat. The Mission Mountains as they are known today still appear to be an impossible barrier, but McClallen's hosts signed that a trail followed a river through those mountains.[5] Equally impressive mountain ranges beyond were threaded by horse trails, no more than a hoof print wide that crossed steep slopes of greasy shale, which might release in an instant. A rider, looking down to the stream twisting between huge rocks far below, put his trust in his pony. Dangerous in the summer, those icy trails were used in the winter by raiders coming to steal horses.

The return of the buffalo hunters was usually a time for welcoming and relaxation. But in the early fall of 1807, an important council had been called. *Piikani* enemies were seeking an end to the destructive round of horse raids, retaliations, and tortured confrontations in the buffalo country.[6] Their motive was not entirely altruistic. In the early summer of 1806, about the time that Captain Meriwether Lewis had his brush with eight young *Piikani* horse drovers, about one hundred and sixty lodges of Cree, Assiniboines, Blackfeet, and Bloods set out to attack the Atsiina, who were returning to the south branch of the Saskatchewan after being away for some time visiting their Arapaho relatives. The combined army intended to discourage their return, but the unlikely coalition did not get far before a falling-out over a horse led to a melee in which twenty-five Blackfeet or Bloods and three Assiniboines were killed, and the Cree fled.[7]

Although *Piikani* evaded involvement in the hostilities, they were upset when four tents of their Cree friends coming to trade at the British houses were intercepted and massacred by two or three hundred revenge-seeking Blackfeet. The largest of the three associated tribes, the *Piikani*, were fed up with their Blood and Blackfoot neighbors' habit of passing through their territory to raid for Flathead horses. The trouble those raids caused usually fell upon innocent *Piikani* bystanders.

Despite the unfortunate incident with Lewis's party the previous year, the *Piikani* had been impressed by promises to open trade in their country. A handy store would give them a reliable source of ammunition that their troublesome neighbors could not control. Captain Lewis's promise seemed to be confirmed by the appearance of another American officer on the Yellowstone, making similar statements to the Bloods and Atsiina.

During the trip from the upper Missouri River, John McClallen became acquainted with the Salish and Nez Perce buffalo hunters. As the peace council assembled, he had a few days to meet and evaluate the *Piikani*, who were the most southern and mountain-oriented of the generalized Blackfeet.[8]

Their appearance would not have been much different from the images that the artist Karl Bodmer would capture a quarter of a century later. The elders who conducted the negotiation were wrapped in painted buffalo robes; their young attendants carefully groomed and painted to impress their Salish counterparts, and girls. If there was dancing in the evening or gambling, elders were careful to keep the excitement under control because this was an opportunity to stop disruptions that were destructive to all parties.

McClallen learned about the arrangements for a council when he met the Bloods and the Atsiina in early July. But when the *Piikani* came they were accompanied by Blackfoot and Blood observers who had a stake in horse raiding. Winters on the northern plains were hard on their herds, and they often made up losses by rustling Salish horses. Not all that interested in trans-mountain harmony, they attended to protect their disruptive habits.

McClallen was the first American most of the participants had known. A British trader's contemporary vocabulary included the Blackfoot term *Homuksestooan* for Americans but did not give the Kutenai term, *Suyapi*.[9] In fact most of the participants had only a vague grasp of international difference. However, a uniformed officer and a guard of soldiers gave the gathering added significance. Appreciating the sense of ceremony, McClallen had his flag tied to a cut sapling and held by one of the former corpsmen, just as young warriors supported the feathered coup staffs of their chiefs. His presence confirmed a benevolent policy and both factions welcomed the implication that strangers were interested in their welfare. Instead of a tribal world perpetually at its own throat, McClallen saw former enemies come together in a sincere attempt to negotiate a mutually beneficial understanding.

For a week stiffly formal elders, backed up by gravely watchful men of standing in the community, conducted the gathering. Vibrating just behind them were young men who exuded pretentious pugnacity. Salish women and children stood on the periphery, outside the decision making as spectators. Formal posturing and ritual smoking set the stage for a dramatization of their positions. The elders moved slowly because this was a serious undertaking. During the nights while elders compared impressions and discussed possibilities, the drums thumped and the young people gambled or danced. Hampered by the barrier of language, McClallen sat with the old men absorbing what he could as they strained to come to terms with the new world that he represented.

Learning the art of Indian diplomacy, McClallen may have modified the speech that General Wilkinson gave him to deliver to the Pawnee or Comanche. The former corpsmen's grasp of a few *Sahaptan* words or their experience in sign language helped, but subtleties could not survive the tortured translation. Most of McClallen's presentation depended upon the impression he exuded: concern, wealth, generosity, and mutual respect.

When it was his turn to speak, McClallen just stood before the assembly, and, as earnestly as possible, made a plea for peace and a spiel for commerce. As his interpreters mimed, the elders nodded gravely and pretended to understand baffling concepts that were worlds beyond their experience, far beyond their limited intention.

Nor did the tribesmen, who spoke different languages, completely understand each other. The universal gesture language was good enough for long-distance exchanges on the buffalo plains, but it lacked the subtlety necessary for diplomacy. A product of a transplanted authoritarian tradition, McClallen failed to grasp how little influence those leading men actually had over their independent-minded constituents. Innocent of the complexity of tribal politics, the self-appointed envoy saw the council as a kind of performance rather than a negotiation, a mutual exercise in unintelligibility. At best the meeting was just a nonbinding demonstration of intention, a theater of diplomacy that hoped to communicate the dream of friendship.

Despite those limitations, the treaty almost succeeded. David Thompson heard the story secondhand and recorded what happened next.

> each Party having agreed upon a mutual Oblivion of all past Injuries, & ever for the future to act as Friends & Allies, without any reserve whatever. When the Peagans & their Allies were raising camp the Blackfoots began to put on a hostile plundering appearance, & as the women had got at some distance they began by seizing upon a very swift Mare, tossing the Owner off her Back—a young Saleesh Indian. But the latter losing no Time, sent an Arrow thro' the Heart of the Aggressor, which directly brought on a Battle.

Later he added details in another version of the incident.

> ...that a very large Band of Peagans, Blood & Blackfoot Indians had crossed to this Side of the Mountain & made Peace with the Flat Heads; but as they were preparing to depart, the Meadow Indians began to pillage, which raised a Tumult, & ended by the Flat Heads taking Arms & killing 13 of the Aggressors & obliging the others to fly with precipitation. Four of the Flat Heads were killed & several wounded.[10]

In a horrific moment McClallen and his men saw eighteen Indians laid low. The man holding his flag was run down and nearly brained. This was the first time that the former army officer witnessed bloodshed in anger. Later he complained that "the Pilchenees wounded one of our brave Soldiers."[11] The visiting delegation fled.

The killings were only the beginning of an appalling demonstration of savagery as Salish women grotesquely vented their terror by hacking at the bloody bodies or the caked parts of bodies, hell on earth. Through a long night, their keening and drumming kept McClallen and his shaken followers on edge.

Violence showed that their friends were more than background spear carriers in a second-act exploration opera. A vital people, the

Salish were trying to live peacefully in a cozy but vulnerable mountain enclave. The same mountain passes that allowed them to go to the buffalo also left them open to raiding enemies. Atrocities would continue to keep their homeland in turmoil unless McClallen could find a way to renew the peace initiative.

McClallen made another copy of the trading regulations and trusted it to an obliging Nez Perce who planned to accompany Kutenai returning to their homes. Following a route past Black Horse Lake (present Flathead Lake) led overland to another river that paralleled Clark's Fork. Following what is now known as the Kootenay River would bring them over a short portage to the place where the British trader was building a house near present Windermere, British Columbia.[12] That was the long trail that brought David Thompson a bombshell.

⫶⫶

As the morning shadow of Coulhicat retreated across the deer meadows and spring creeks, the valley of the Flatheads lightened to a new day. In his circular letter John McClallen had already laid out the scope of United States authority by claiming "all the Lands westward to the Coast of California and the Columbia River with all its branches; of which we have now taken Possession and on which we are now settled down to the Pacific Ocean; extending northward to about 50 Degrees north Latitude." All the patriotic author had to do was make it stick.

Mapless in a suddenly shattered paradise, McClallen had a workable understanding of the streams Lewis and Clark followed from the two former corpsmen. In his instructions to Captain Lewis, President Jefferson charged the Corps of Discovery with the primary goal of finding a practical passage between the Missouri and the Columbia rivers. Who could say how many times the two former corpsmen had heard that when their spirits were flagging. After twice enduring the pass leading west from the lower Bitterroot Valley, they were not enthusiastic for a sixty-mile-long mountain trail that snow closed for much of the year. After two trying crossings of what later became known as the Lolo Trail, they felt that it failed to answer President Jefferson's desire for a practical connection between continental drainages.[13] If the

United States wanted a hold on the Pacific shore, that had to be by way of the Missouri River to the Columbia River.

When the Corps of Discovery returned to the lower Bitterroot Valley in the spring of 1806, they were headed home and it was too late to explore Clark Fork. They rationalized that some obstacle downstream prevented salmon from ascending.[14] While Captain Clark turned south through the Bitterroot Valley, Captain Lewis headed east on the trail Salish used to go to the buffalo hunt on the east side of the mountains. Lewis confirmed Cokalarishkit to be an easy one-hundred-and-eighty-mile direct overland route to the Great Falls. When he reported to the president that they had found "the most practicable rout" for Mr. Jefferson's mountain portage, he must have regretted failing to explore Clark's Fork.[15] With Santa Fe on his mind when he met the explorers, McClallen had not paid much attention to their regrets about missed geographical opportunities. From what McClallen could gather, the river of the Salish flowed west to a large lake that might float a boat to the Columbia. But he couldn't trust the judgment of horse Indians when it came to navigation.

After doing what he could to discourage British meddling with the wards of the nation, McClallen was in position to explore a better connection to the Columbia River. The road to the buffalo did not end at the Salish Horse Plains' winter camps.[16] During the buildup to the treaty meeting, McClallen observed other returning buffalo hunters who wore beads and ornaments that came from ships calling in at the mouth of the Columbia. Indian maps drawn in the sand showed that after being joined by the Flathead River, Nemissoolatakoo (Clark Fork River) flowed west. McClallen decided to follow the river and determine if it was capable of floating a boat.

Locked away from other developments, neither Thompson nor McClallen had any way of knowing that the North West Company explorer Simon Fraser was finally writing off the Fraser River as a practicable passage to the Pacific. British hopes of reaching an ocean outlet now depended on what David Thompson could discover. Unnamed rivers and mountains were the unresolved mysteries of an undefined world.

The Salish liked to winter their herds on relatively snow-free pastures in an area they knew as Comkanee after a large yellowish boulder that resembled the upper part of a human torso.[17] Nowadays that is near a little Montana town named Paradise. A typical winter camp might have included about fifty lodges of Salishs, Kalispels, and a few Kutenais.[18] Other hunters headed west, driving horse herds and laden pack strings along the Flathead River until it joined the Clark Fork River. In the grip of his destiny, McClallen saddled and followed.

The trappers had scattered to work promising streams. John B. Thompson and John Colter had come a long way to make their fortunes, and they may have gone trapping with freemen like Rivet, who had developed an interest in a Salish widow. That left McClallen with his body servant and some of the boatmen. As the small party headed out, the Salish women sang *sakaha*, the trails, for them. They were not traveling alone because other hunters were returning from the fall hunt to their western homes. Those nameless bands would afterward be known by the labels that French trappers gave them. McClallen was accompanied by several boatmen who lacked traps. The body servant was the second black man to descend the Pacific slope.[19]

The first imposing barrier was a place on the north side of the river east of present Thompson Falls, where an infamous Bad Rock crowded close to the water. The shale and rocky slope rising hundreds of feet above the water had to be crossed by a narrow trail that required travois to be disassembled and dragged. A later traveler wrote

> I had seen landscapes of awful grandeur, but this one ... surpassed all others in horror. My courage failed at the first sight, it was impossible to remain on horseback. My mule was sufficiently kind to allow me to grasp her tail, to which I held on firmly until the good beast conducted me safely to the very top of the mountain. There I breathed freely for a while and contemplated the magnificent prospect that presented itself to my sight.[20]

A long flat plain fringed with groves of pines opened beyond. On the west side of that meadow, the river broke over an impressive rapid.[21] Below, the river widened, and with depth darkened and took on the emerald color of snowmelt waters. After a night of distant thunder and lightening flashes, a suggestion of moisture seemed to intensify the summer colors.

McClallen and his followers accompanied western tribes who traveled with the Salish for safety in numbers, the as-yet-unnamed Kalispels, Spokanes, Coeur d'Alenes, or some Sanpoils from the Columbia River willing to travel a great distance for a change in their salmon diet.[22]

The Clark Fork River flowed through a low, swampy floodplain named Nacemci that in late summer and early fall was a fine place to graze trail-worn ponies. During the berry harvest it was a favorite place for gatherings and ceremonies. The stored berries or baked roots that their women gathered there had a smoky, figgy taste. Stay-at-homes welcomed the returning buffalo hunters and admired their loads of dried meat. For the past two years they had been hearing about strangers. McClallen took every opportunity to question informants about the country ahead.

On a brisk September morning they came to a lake that stretched away west like a mountain-girt fiord. In times beyond recall that great trench had been gouged by ancient glaciers and scoured by ice-dammed floods. Low-hanging clouds cast the surface in a monochromatic iron grey, and all around, mountains crowded, cold blue shadow behind cold blue shadow. The season was closing in and the green slopes were already punctuated by yellow tamarack and aspen.

Two years later, the buffalo road that McClallen and his party followed along the north shore was described by Thompson.

> The Ground near the Lake is low & often muddy & wet, with high Hills a short distance within plenty of water Fowl, but no shelter for the Sportsman. For these 5 days past the Leaves have been withering much on the Hills, half of them are already fallen off & those of the Willows &c. are in the same state...the Poplar, Aspin, Birch, Alder &c are getting yellow & a few falling off.[23]

The trail kept close to the lakeshore, sometimes picking through marshes and bulrush meadows that were probably drowned during high water when travelers were forced to use another way higher on the steep hillside. Near the west end of the lake, attractive meadows marked the meandering course of a river coming in from the north and the Indian trail that followed it.[24]

Local buffalo hunters usually returned in late summer or early fall in time to resume fishing or deer hunting. The river leading out of the lake cascaded through three channels in a solid rock ledge, now the base of the Albeni Falls Dam. Just above those falls, McClallen's guides pointed out the wide Sineacateen ford, where some of the returning hunters broke off toward the south to cross the Spokane River and thread through raw basalt channels gouged by ancient floods.[25]

It was the trail leading west that interested John McClallen. A local Kalispel obliged by drawing a map in the coarse palomino sand that seemed to dash the hope of connecting to the Columbia. Not far downstream the river turned far north and eventually plunged over an impassible waterfall. That was why salmon never came up Nemissoolatakoo.[26]

However, the Kalispels did obtain dried salmon from a great fishing place farther west. That trail started from the large Kalispel camp below the falls and crossed a range of low mountains to a long valley tending northwest. It ended at the Fishing Basket Falls (Kettle Falls on the Columbia River) where Sanpoil (*Skoyelpy*) took salmon by the thousands, gutted them on reeking middens and hung the split bodies on racks to dry. An overland trip of only a couple of days brought a traveler to the place where it was possible to paddle to the bitter water.

McClallen realized that less than a hundred miles lay between him and the Columbia River.[27] His only survey instrument was his old military compass, but McClallen was sure that route was well within the parameters of 49 or 50 degrees north latitude. He had found a practical connection between the Missouri River and the Pacific Ocean and completed Mr. Jefferson's desire for a mountain portage.

Toward the end of September, the obliging Nez Perce, who carried McClallen's circular letter to the British trader, returned by way of a trail along the Pack River that entered the west end of the large lake. This young man reported the British trader's lack of response. As other tribesmen were considering a trip north to see the house that was being built, McClallen saw an opportunity to send another letter to the unresponsive British trader. He needed to determine if the *Piikani* peace initiative was still in play.

The name Poltito Palton Lake entered the geographical puzzle when McClallen used it in his second letter.[28] Realizing that the connection to the Columbia was as significant to United States interests as the Great Falls or the Three Forks of the Missouri, McClallen had to keep the bluff going without a face-to-face confrontation that would reveal his bluff. He wrote another stiff warning.

Poltito Palton Lake   Sept 29th 1807
To the British Mercht. Trafficking with the Cabanaws.
Sir,

I have been informed by a chief of the Poltito palton that the regulations intrusted to him for the instruction of such British Merchants as may traffic with the Indian under the Jurisdiction of Congress have been delivered to you, and of course an answer was expected whether you chose to abide by such Regulations as are or may be promulgated for the good order of Society and Civilization of the Indians. Your silence Sir I am to construe into a tacit disrespect, and thereby am apt to think you do not acknowledge the authority of Congress over these Countries, which are certainly the property of the United States both by discovery and Cession. If such is your ideas you must learn Sir that we have more powerful means of persuasion in our hands than we have hitherto used, we shall with regret apply Force, but where necessary it will be done with vigor, so as fully to enforce the Decrees of Congress, and support the Honour and Rights of the United States— and if my private opinion be of any weight, you nor any British Merchant will be suffered to traffic with our Indian Allies. As soon as our Military Posts are fortified, strong Patrols will be sent out to survey the Country and where necessary and eligible American Merchants will be placed who will second the philanthropic views of Congress in the Civilization of the Natives. You will see Sir the necessity of submitting and with a good grace,—you may evade our useful Regulations for a year but the time is certainly at hand when the authority of Congress will be as fully established over these Countries as over New York or Washington.

The Pilchenees with their blood-thirsty allies made an inroad into the Territories of the Poltito palton our friends and wounded one of our brave Soldiers. We expect Sir you will no longer supply those Marauders with Arms and Ammunition and also signify this our desire to the other british Merchants at the same time we hope whenever we may find it necessary to chastise these scoundrels you will assist us with men and as far as your abilities will permit.

Signed Jeremy Pinch Lieut.[29]

After his disappointment with the Salish-*Piikani* peace meeting, McClallen's party had dispersed to trap and he was free to continue doing what he could to reinforce an American presence. His exploration of the Clark Fork River from the Flathead Valley to the end of what we know as Lake Pend Oreille covered new territory and proved a practicable route from the Missouri River to the Columbia, a major accomplishment in transcontinental geography. But it remained to be seen whether those efforts were sufficient to discourage British expansion.

CHAPTER SIXTEEN

"I COULD NOT ALTOGETHER INDIANIFY MY HEART"[1]

McClallen's letter to Thompson does not indicate how he intended to return to the lower Bitterroot Valley. Having satisfied himself with a satisfactory portage route from the Missouri to the Columbia, he was ready to settle down and expand his relationship with the Salish and Nez Perce. But the explorer found the tribes dying. They were racking and hacking with swollen throats until, weakened by the convulsions, they suffocated. Terror of an unknown death was in their eyes. McClallen had seen it before. Not long after the first Osage delegation returned to St. Louis from visiting the president, "young and old, were seized with a species of influenza."[2] The survivors took it to the Osage towns where more died. McClallen must have recognized the Ootlashshoots had whooping cough (pertussis). He could not help wondering if he, or his men, had inadvertently brought death to their hosts.

This appears to have been the first pandemic disease to strike western Indians since the small pox disaster to the tribes in 1781. The monster appeared at the Mandan/Hidatsa villages before he arrived. Two years previous, in 1805, a North West Company clerk noted a similar scourge torturing those nearby people and described

> a violent Cough, or Chincough among the Missurie Indians which carried away, by their own calculations 130 souls old & young in less than a month's time. The old men & women whose constitution was worn out, fell an easy prey unregrated [unregreted?] to this disease & the Children had not strength enough to resist its violence. Indeed many a person of middle age were carried away in the carnage—It was not a strange thing to see two or three dead in the same lodge at once.[3]

By the winter of 1806/07 the affliction had worked its way across the northern plains to the Rocky Mountain House, where David Thompson noticed symptoms affecting the bands that came to trade. He was as appalled as McClallen when his man Bercier returned from the great band of the Kootenae in September reporting that those tribesmen "informed me that a violent Distemper had taken the Flat Heads which had communicated itself to the Kootenais & Flat Bows & had brought the major part of them so low, as to prevent them from decamping & that many of the Children had already died of it." Three families that straggled to Kootenae House confirmed that all were ill and many reduced to mere skeletons.[4] Thompson had seen the disease among the Indians who traded at Rocky Mountain House and like McClallen may have wondered if he or his men were responsible for its appearance in the West.

Attributing the outbreak to his favorite scapegoats, the *Piikani*, Thompson dredged up an old myth that had its origin during the French and Indian Wars.[5] After the fight at the peace meeting, "The Spoils of the Peagans & their Allies being gathered up and worn by the Saleesh & brought on the distemper before noticed, which had been previously among the Peagans & their Allies, & lodging in the hair Robes, & had spread the infection."[6]

The two strangers west of the mountains may not have connected their appearance with the introduction of a disease to which the Indians lacked acquired resistance, but that was the old story of the precursor of tribal dispossession, population reduction—the last thing either of them wanted.

⊷⊷

David Thompson was not having that great a winter. This was his first major responsibility since becoming a partner in the North West Company and he had to attend to business before anything else. Part of being a corporate man was enduring an uncomfortable winter in the middle of nowhere. Thompson was uncertain how the expansion of trade west of the mountains would be accepted by the tribes that traded at Rocky Mountain House. He still carried the imprint of the first winter he spent with the "Peeagans" and the memory of warriors returning from raids and the ghastly celebrations of their war games-manship. It had been twelve years since Duncan McGillivray took him back to those same camps to obtain permission to introduce contract Iroquois beaver trappers. They convinced themselves that a placative "Pekenow leader named Sac o tow tow" gave them permission. But when Iroquois trappers were sent up the south branch of the Saskatche-wan River, the Atsiina (Falls Indians) killed fourteen of them. Thompson spent his first winter west of the mountains fearing a similar *Piikani* reaction to the intrusive establishment of Kootenae House.

On August 9 and 13 Kutenai tribesmen returning from the summer buffalo hunt reported a battle with the Peagans. Despite the blown-up peace council, parties of *Piikani* continued circulating in the Kutenai country. On August 27, a dozen men and two women brought a little food to the house builders, which convinced Thompson that they were sent by their war chief Kootenae Appee to see what he was doing. He took their reassurances as dissimulation.

In the evening after those visitors departed, a Kutenai warned that another thirty Peagans were coming with nothing to trade. Thompson began putting up palisades around his buildings. The twenty-three men and some women who arrived on September 5 hung around until the lack of food drove them away on the thirteenth. Thompson was convinced that they were jealous of a post to benefit of the Kutenai.

Meanwhile, the disease-ridden Kutenai had been crawling toward the new house, accompanied by ten Salish who turned back in fear of the Peagans. When they finally arrived on September 25, two chiefs gave Thompson a fuller version of the peace council fiasco.[7] That was frustrating because Thompson had sent off the clerk Finnan McDonald and two men two days before carrying the letter from the American officer and a narrative of developments up to that point. The packet had to reach Rocky Mountain House in time to be sent down to Fort Ver-million to catch the winter express to headquarters.[8]

On September 29, the date when McClallen wrote his second letter from the west end of Lake Pend Oreille (near present Sandpoint, Idaho), Thompson was questioning visiting Flat Bow Indians about the mysteries of the western geography. Their leader, Ugly Head, provided

Thompson with "a Sketch of their County & to near the Sea, which they say I may go to from hence & be back in a month hence [*sic*] were it Summer time."[9] But the informant warned that it was too late in the season and that the people along the way were harsh and brutish.[10]

As a practicing astronomer, accustomed to sighting on the stars, David Thompson liked to know precisely where he was. His journals, complex with compass sights and mathematical notations, show how diligently he worked to bring scientific order to an undefined world. But compared to the formal record keeping of the Hudson's Bay Company employee, the journals kept by Nor'westers were erratic. Although most proprietors of isolated posts wrote for their own amusement, if at all, Thompson continued the habit he had learned as a young bayman. Unfortunately, he did not bother to make file copies of his correspondence and he also knew how to leave embarrassments out.[11]

On October 2, 1807, Thompson started south with Ugly Head, hoping to test the navigability of a river flowing south. But after two days they came to the place where the Flat Bow trail cut overland and the explorer saw no reason to follow it. He was back at Kootenae House by the sixth and that was the extent of his exploring. He would not attempt it again for six and a half months.[12]

On October 24, Thompson entered in his journal the barren comment that the engagé Charles Loyer had arrived from across the mountains, proof that he was not entirely out of communication with his supporters, although the uncertainty of exchanges must have been maddening. About the same time, Thompson's not entirely reticent Kutenai informant reported that the Blackfoot and Blood Indians were determined to make war upon his people for furnishing arms to the Salish. That was likely to include traders, so Thompson began setting night watches while feeling "at the Mercy of the Supreme Being as the arbiter of Life & Death."[13] On the October 29 he wrote another letter to "Messrs. McGillivray, McDonald and Hughes" and sent this off with two "half-Kootenais" who were crossing the mountains with some returning *Piikani.*

The first problem Thompson faced was feeding himself, his green clerk Finnan McDonald, seven or eight engagés, two women, and six children. Unlike the northern woods, this was a country without rabbits for the women to snare, and where salmon came up the river according to their own schedule. In late August he obtained some provisions from visiting *Piikani*, and later Kutenai hunters delivered four deer.

When Finnan McDonald and the party sent to Rocky Mountain House returned in early November 1807, they brought back trade goods, clothing, and a keg of French brandy. Thompson's personal order had included a pair of brass candlesticks, a pound each of cinnamon and cloves, a bottle of "Eau de Luce" toilet water, twenty pounds of marled soap, twenty-four bottles each of peppermint for digestion, and Turlington's balm for every other ailment.[14]

The prospects for trading in this previously "undeveloped" region were discouraging, and McDonald had only carried "80 MB [made beaver, an accounting term] in bear and swanskins as the first returns sent to Rocky Mountain House."[15] Thompson noted, "the natives seem eager to open commerce with us," but they were not productive beaver hunters and needed to be taught how to take and properly prepare pelts. After seeing that the Lake Indians turned in only 128 beaver skins, Thompson knew that the western tribes would have to be educated in how to hunt and how to prepare beaver pelts. He sent two men, Boisvert and Boulard, to live with the Indians and teach them, and to do a little trading. In March 1808, Thompson wrote letters to supporters across the mountains calling for the introduction of contracted or debt-obligated steel trappers, Iroquois preferably. When those trappers were turned loose to take beaver, Thompson figured the prospects should improve.

Thompson was surprised when Finnan McDonald returned with an unexpected gift from the Cahokia postmaster John Hay. It was a copy of one of the first reports describing the American explorations that Hay intercepted and sent to his British friends. In the flickering firelight of winter-bound Kootenae House, Thompson read a copy of "Capn. Lewis's account of his journey to the Pacific Ocean." It was the description of the country that Thompson meant to discover. The first of two disconcerting paragraphs took the edge off Thompson's hopes for geographical fame.

> In returning thro' the Rocky Mountains, we divided ourselves into several parties digressing from the Route by which we went out with a view more effectually to explore the Country, and discover the most

practicable Route which existed across the continent by way of the Missesouris & Columbia Rivers: in this we have been completely successful, Therefore have no hesitation to say & declare that such as Nature has permitted we have discovered the most practicable Route which does exist across the Continent of North America in that direction; such is that by way of the Missesourii to the foot of the Rapids below the great Falls of that River a distance of 2575 miles, thence by land passing the Rocky Mountains to a navigable part of the Kooskooskee [Clearwater River in Idaho] 320 M. & the Kooskooskee 73 M. Lewis River [Snake River] 152 M. & the Columbia 413 M. to the Pacific Ocean 3555 miles.[16]

Another paragraph threatened to stifle the expectation of developing more business, or even hanging on to what the Nor'westers presently exploited.

I consider this Track across the Continent as presenting immense advantages to the Fur Trade—as all the Furs collected in 9/10 of the valuable Fur Country of America may be conveyed to the Mouth of the Columbia & shipped from thence for the East Indies by the 1st of August in each year, & will of course reach Canton [China] earlier than the Furs which are annually exported from Montreal reach Great Britain.

On December 11 Thompson manfully set himself to copying the damn letter into his discovery book.[17] Ironically, the last time he used that worn journal was in late June 1801 to record his failure to find a passage across the mountains.[18] The handwriting of the new entry was precise and careful, with no suggestion that Thompson's hand trembled as he copied those words that meant very little to discover was left for him.[19] After he finished, Thompson had time for what he termed "thought upon thought." His answer to the real (or imagined) *Piikani* threat was to build posts "out of their Power" in the promising Flathead country but an aggressive American officer and forty-two Americans were already there. After having received the aggressive list of trading regulations, an actual confrontation chanced creating an international incident.

During the long dark evenings while his unconcerned men snored, David Thompson sat staring into the fireplace. He was only "the voyage of a Summer Moon" away from the sea and a great accomplishment in exploration, but others had already beaten him to that mark. He was back to his old nightmare of playing draughts (checkers) with the devil, as he had as an apprehensive young man. He wanted more out of the skin game than a partner's share: fame perhaps, recognition at least. He had made too many sightings on the stars and had worked too hard to create the mathematics that reduced the wilderness to a known fact to be denied his heart's desire.

Thompson wrote his Christmas letters and sent them on to Fort Augustus on December 7, 1807, with two of his men. As a Christmas present, Thompson received another threatening letter from the American officer dated "Poltito Palton Lake, Sept 29th 1807." It was delivered by a delegation that included a Flathead chief, a Poltito Palton leader, and three Kutenai. There may have been some prearrangement in their arrival on December 21, just three days after five *Piikani* appeared from across the mountains reporting that the northern plains tribes were fighting among themselves. When the old Kutenai leader and four lodges of his sickly followers arrived, there were more discussions "about Peace & War." According to Thompson, the Flatheads boldly stated that they "would either bravely meet them in the Field when and where they chose, or if they wished for peace they were welcome to come and settle the terms &c."[20] Obviously, the *Piikani* made that difficult winter journey because they were still interested in peace.

Christmas was not that big a holiday for the Welsh surveyor, who passed a quiet day with his mixed-blood wife and small children. Next morning when the Peagans put on snowshoes to return to their winter camps, Thompson sent tobacco and a pipe to their leaders asking them to remain quiet during the winter because he did not intend to remain in this country. What Thompson meant was that he hoped to put himself beyond their reach. Then he sat down and wrote a response to the American letter that the visiting Poltito Palton finally delivered.[21]

Dec. 26, 1807
To Lieut. Jeremy Pinch
Sir,

Two days ago I received your polite Favour of the 29th Sept and must confess myself neither authorized nor competent to give a direct answer to the Question proposed, nor am I politician enough to settle the Boundaries of our respective Countries. If prior discovery forms any right to a Country, Lieut. Broughton of the British Navy many years ago explored the Columbia for 120 miles from the sea and was the first that made known its Geography. The high Duties you require will be submitted to the consideration of all the Partners of the N. W. Compy.—and if complied with, they will pay custom for the Merchandise that may be sent here, at Michilimacance, as is usual for all other Merchandise intended for the Indians in the American Territories, and the Custom House Certificates will be produced when required. I am etc. David Thompson[22]

Despite Thompson's carefully calculated and measured response, the presence of a United States officer upset him enough that he took the unusual action for him of copying the second letter and his exasperated response into his journal, along with a bitter personal expression. "It seems this officer was on a party of Discovery when he wrote the above. His Poltito paltons are the Green Wood Indians, ... his Pilcheness the Fall Indians, I suppose, as it was they who wounded the soldier ... not one of these petty officers but what has as much arrogance as Buonaparte at the head of his Invincibles."[23]

On December 29, 1807, while the visiting Flatheads were still around Kootenae House, Thompson arranged that they would work beaver during the winter and locked them into the deal by advancing trade goods on credit. He promised to come in the spring to receive the returns. The returning delegates also carried Thompson's curt reply to the threatening American.

Thompson could have deduced that this second appearance of American officers on the Pacific slope had to be temporary. During the Salish visit, Thompson questioned those who had been in contact with the Americans since summer and learned that the small army was not quite what its commander made it to be. Most of them were Canadian freemen who were unlikely to participate in territorial disputes. His hunters would have to carry their packs as far as St. Louis to realize a gain.

Thompson was more concerned about the *Piikani* and their persistent search for peace with the western tribes. There had to be something ominous in the five *Piikani* delegates who braved the mountain snows in late December to meet western Indians. It was not reassuring that they were met by the same delegation of Salish, Nez Perce, and Kutenai who delivered another threatening letter from the American officer. What did that aggressive officer mean when he threatened "we have more powerful means of persuasion in our hands... you nor any British Merchant will be suffered to traffic with our Indian Allies."

Looking for directions from headquarters in early February, Thompson sent two men to the west end of the mountain trail to receive letters. They returned disappointed, but a month later a party of six *Piikani* appeared bringing letters from Fort Augustus on the Saskatchewan River, dated around the end of the year 1807. Those included the latest tribal war news. Although the Cree, simmering from an unendurable insult, were assembling to strike all the northern plainsmen, for the present they entertained no hostile intentions against the western tribes. Presumably that included the Kootenae House trader, but a disturbance at Thompson's supply base could cut off necessary supplies.

Isolated from the society of other traders and committed to an expensive experiment that could prove costly to all the other partners, David Thompson felt the "uncertainty of reward" and the unsettling "fluctuating Politics of Kam" (Kaministiquia, the North West Company headquarters on Lake Superior) might cut off the support he needed. Cut off from the "letters or resolves &c from Cumberland House" at the bottom of the Saskatchewan, he looked to his supporter, Donald McTavish, for hints about those proceedings at the annual meetings. But it had taken three months for the Christmas letters from the Saskatchewan to reach Thompson, and that was only through the courtesy of more *Piikani* winter travelers.[24]

Having made a difficult winter crossing of the mountains to deliver some kind of response to the Salish, the *Piikani* were eager to return home. Thompson wrote a hurried public letter to Hughes, McDonald, and McTavish describing the difficulties of establishing trade in the country, and of educating the Indians to take beaver.[25] It was disappointing that the locals were not all that productive and increasing returns required the introduction of ten or twelve Iroquois steel trappers.[26] By the end of the season he hoped to have thirty packs, but based on how things were going, he would need two years to properly develop the business in the new country.

Thompson did not expect to draw trade from the Indians of the Columbia River because they were supplied by sailing ships that called in at the mouth. However, he estimated that there were a total of around seven hundred Flathead, Green Wood, and Grand River Indians, of whom only sixty of seventy were Flatheads. The Kalispel had the most promising country for beaver production but were said to be quarrelsome. Thompson wrote, "All these Indians have been so harassed with war from the other side [of the] mountains and have always had a very unequal combat... they look on our arrival as a blessing from Heaven."[27] By that he meant his trade in guns and ammunition.

Settling accounts to show a profit was going to be a problem. The goods brought over from the Saskatchewan posts to get the expansion started were worth £1,020 at Fort des Prairies prices. The wages of the men added another £434, which with interest made a total expense of £1,500. Thompson initially expected to get sixty packs, and privately admitted as few as thirty.

The following spring he planned to follow the Kootenay River collecting furs, even the beaver clothing worn by the Indians. As he traveled, he would pay close attention for a better location for a trading post that would be central to productive tribes. In a second, private letter to his supporter, Donald McTavish, Thompson railed against the shortsighted partners and felt that he was being kept in the dark about the "fluctuating politics" within the organization. There had been serious difficulties with the expansion of the trade, obtaining food, and teaching the Indians a new economy dependent on their learning to hunt commercially. "With regards to Discovery, I have done little, for Commerce I have done much." Thompson ended with a reaffirmation of his determination to persist, "You know... that I know fairly what I am about."[28]

Three days after the Indians started east with Thompson's March letters, the clerk James McMillan ran in on snowshoes with a dog team bringing additional supplies. He was soon headed back across the mountains with Thompson's response to whatever information came in that packet. His food supply must have improved after the turn of the year 1808 because he put one of his men to work digging a hole in the hillside to make a "glacier," layering quarters of meat and ice that would remain frozen. Looking ahead, Thompson bought two large dogs as a traveling food supply when he recrossed the mountains in the spring. Although Thompson skirted mentioning the importation of arms, it cost him a new gun and tobacco to obtain a horse.

Lacking peltry to offset the costs of the expansion, Thompson needed to call in the debts that he had allowed to visiting Salish at Christmas. The Flatheads or the two engagés sent to them had not appeared. Although he had been west of the mountains for almost nine months, Thompson was still a theoretical geographer dependent upon Indians for his understanding of the region. Given what he learned from visiting Indians, coupled with a diagram furnished by the Lake Indians, he gathered that the American captain had been on another river that ran parallel to the Kootenay River.

> As to my passage across the mountains, [the trail he used to get to Kootenae House] it certainly ought to be worse than that of Captain Lewis... the Defile [passage] he passed is by the Flatheads allowed to be a very good one and in a plentiful Country comparatively speaking whereas that by which we pass is agreed by all to be the worse, and only used as being out of the way of the Meadow Indians: between where I am and where Captain Lewis passed, there are 3 good Passages, the best at L'Hanam a Bout close to which I have already been, but all unfit for us on account of the Meadow Indians.[29]

Thompson had deduced from Hay's purloined Lewis letter that there was an easier way across the mountains than the trying trail he followed. The only reason for using it or another that he explored previously was because of the threat he perceived from the *Piikani* who resented what he was doing.

In paraphrasing information extracted from the Lewis letter, Thompson failed to address the question of the American officer blocking expansion. During that lonely winter, David Thompson and the officer he knew as Captain Perch confronted each other by implication without meeting in person. But the presence of an American officer clearly impinged on the plan for engrossing the Columbia drainage, and of developing an outlet to the Pacific. Thompson must have felt grim, but he refused to admit that his first move of the new western skin game was already in check.

Perhaps Thompson felt that he had covered that subject adequately in the copy of his journal that he sent in the previous fall and augmented with letters sent since. The March letters should have included details on how he planned to resolve the problem Captain Perch posed, but he failed to outline his plans, which left his supporters hanging. Although Thompson was not one to let much of himself leak into his journal, it is ironic that almost all that is known about Captain Zachary Perch comes from the trail-worn documents of his only opponent.[30] And that was not very much.

⊸⊨ ⊨⊶

During those months John McClallen lay in a Salish lodge somewhere on the other side of an exasperating lack of communication. Recognizing that Indians were under no obligation to be postmen, he waited for three or four months without knowing the reaction to his second warning to the British trader. Pend d'Oreille and Nez Perce leaders returning from the Christmas meeting at Kootenae House may not have bothered to carry Thompson's response to Captain Perch. But their report that the *Piikani* peace initiative was still on surely spread up the Clark Fork.[31]

Because trapping was better in the surrounding creeks of the lower Bitterroot Valley, most of McClallen's freemen stayed with those Salish rather than going to the camps on the Horse Plains that most Flatheads preferred. Until ice closed those streams, the Canadian trappers skinned and ate the beaver they found in their sets. When checking sets in cold water became pure torture, they moved into the Bitterroot Salish lodges. Before the winter was over, those illness-decimated families probably regretted their hospitality.

Bitterroot Salish tucked their winter lodges in the willows along the lower river, facing south to catch the sun when it finally cleared the jagged skyline. There were (or had been) about four hundred living in thirty or more lodges. A traveling band has the chance of coming across game along the way but a permanent location soon exhausts the local food supply. Stores carefully calculated to last out the winter were being used up to feed their guests.

The freemen helped by hunting, but the loud echoes of their guns drove alarmed animals away from bowmen. At best a winter-thin deer was just a couple of meals, and a larger elk lasted only a few days. Beyond the burden upon their carefully calculated larders, the leering trappers were a threat to the chastity of their daughters. When the matron of the lodge looked away, foolish girls snuggled in beds of imported buffalo robes and smiled at the trappers.[32]

Gambling was a universal language. Hand and stick games, played to the accompaniment of drumming and singing, could be intense. A lonely leader with too much on his mind was tortured by thoughts. Having long since exhausted the conversational potential of his valet, John McClallen joined the French to kill a few hours playing cards. Most of his conversations with Francophones were as limp as the worn cards they dealt.

The Salish elders in the winter lodge repeated a litany of abuses by enemies from across the mountains. Not all of them were *Piikani* because most of the associated Blackfeet liked the excitement of stealing Flathead ponies. Horse raids kept Salish families in constant tension. Rustlers came through the mountains to slip into their herds, snare a likely mount, drive off as many ponies as they could, and race for home. If Salish pursued the thieves too vigorously, they risked running fights or ambushes.

Neither Meriwether Lewis and William Clark, nor David Thompson, nor McClallen had what could be called complete communication with those beleaguered Salish tribesmen. Conversations depended on sign language and a few recognizable words. The only brief exchange that Lewis and Clark had with the Salish they met in the upper Bitterroot Valley passed through four or five translators. Sometime around September 25 and 29, 1807, Thompson had mentioned several conversations with the Kutenai and Lake Indians, but he later admitted that "me & my Guide converse together partly by signs & partly by words." Commenting on the difficulty of communication, he wrote, "what I say in French is to be spoken in Blackfoot then in Kootenae, then in Flat Head,

&c, &c, so that the sense is fairly translated away before it arrives at the person being spoken to."[33] Thompson began coaching two interpreters, one who had already spent the previous winter west of the mountains.

What McClallen might have learned from the Salish or Nez Perce about the British trader needs to be taken with caution. For over a year he had been living among people whose languages baffled him, trying to converse in simple words backed up by strained gestures and pantomime. He relied on the two former corpsmen who had picked up some Sahaptan words from the *Poltito Palton* band but had no previous opportunity to learn the lilting Salishan tongue. Reliance on the "universal" sign language risked misunderstanding local or regional variations.[34] Despite an over-inflated myth of its utility, talking with gestures was a compromised way to communicate.

As a consequence, McClallen spent the winter of 1807/08 in a fog of partial understanding that was frustrating for a former officer accustomed to giving direct orders. For the answer to a critical question, he had to wait out a frustrating daisy chain of translations with no confidence that what he had asked, or heard, was correct. Beyond former corpsmen or his body servant, he had no one to hear his concerns as he worked out a plan for the following spring.

McClallen built on the previous experience of John B. Thompson and John Colter. When the expedition split up at Traveler's Rest in 1806, Thompson went with Captain Lewis along the road to the buffalo as far as the Great Falls. Colter accompanied Clark's party back to the Jefferson Fork and then paddled the recovered pirogues down to the Great Falls. Between them, they knew the upper Missouri pretty well.

What McClallen lacked was an understanding of the extent of British traders' influence over the western tribes. Could there have been meddling that resulted in the breakup of the peace council? If the Salish or Nez Perce gave him information about British activities, then his activities surely filtered north and revealed the composition of his party. McClallen realized that a scattered gang of thirty trappers could not be depended upon to uphold the interests of a nation to which they owed nothing. Given the opportunity, they would trade their packs of beaver at the most convenient store. Having brought them west of the mountains, the best McClallen could do was steer those freemen back to the Yellowstone, where Manuel Lisa must have built a post. When they were beyond British subversion, McClallen & Company could take the overland trail to Santa Fe. That was what he initially intended to do, open an overland trading route to the New Mexican province. In the long, dark hours that McClallen spent among the hospitable Salish, he reevaluated his situation. The side trip down the Clark Fork filled in his understanding of the country and its connection to the Columbia River. The navigability of the Clark Fork River completed the link from the Missouri to the Columbia, which was Mr. Jefferson's much-desired mountain portage. McClallen had found it. Being accepted as the discoverer of that much-coveted connection between the two great rivers depended on the reception and appreciation of his geographic explorations. But public recognition alone would never generate the money he needed to relieve his father's debt. The expectation of wealth in New Mexican specie for the goods he left cached on the Yellowstone was still his best alternative.

Tribal advisors, seconded by the former corpsmen, assured McClallen that Cokalarishkit, the road to the buffalo, was the shortest route to the Great Falls. Unraveling the puzzle of the western waters was not the reason that McClallen crossed the mountains. He had temporarily postponed the trip to Santa Fe in order to encourage the *Piikani* peace initiative. But he found that tribal politics were more complex than well-meant gestures. The gory failure of tribal diplomacy had been a shock. No matter how well intended the tribal leaders were, they could not control passionate young warriors. In the flash of a knife, a few malcontents overturned the treaty. Horse raiders continued to keep the Salish and Kutenai country under siege, and only the lack of arms and ammunition kept those intertribal games from becoming even deadlier.

Although Lewis and Clark, and now McClallen, promised a trading house where guns and powder would be available at a cheap price, it was the British who threatened to open an armory. McClallen remembered the Bloods and Atsiina interest in the price of weapons when he met some of them on the Yellowstone. Did they break up the peace council because it threatened their arms advantage? If a western arms race was developing, Americans had to control it. Bringing the Salish and the *Piikani* together again was the best hope for renewing a trans-mountain peace, thereby checking the disruptive Bloods and Blackfeet and blocking British interference.

John McClallen was ready to get on with his own concerns. He had completed the exploration Lewis and Clark failed to do, established good relations with all the western Indians he met, and from all appearances checked the advance of British traders. The task of placating the northern plainsmen east of the mountains and renewing the *Piikani* peace initiative was the only duty to the nation remaining.

CHAPTER SEVENTEEN

COKALARISHKIT, THE PROTEIN ROAD

The names that Lewis and Clark laid on the land were a conceit. Entering another's house, they had presumed to rename the furniture. The tribal names of landmarks grew out of familiarity, usage, and mystical rationalizations that were in keeping with the lives they lived. Innocent of the quadrant or the chronometer, the Indian map of the Pacific Northwest was created from stick diagrams or lines drawn in the sand. That understanding came from an entirely different frame of reference, from a people who went about their lives oblivious of continental mysteries and free of distant political abstractions.

An older history is written in horizontal lines that girdle the mountains bracketing the water gap where Clark Fork flows into the lower Bitterroot Valley. On the mountainside behind the present city of Missoula, Montana, can be seen the beaches of great lakes backed up behind ice dams that blocked the river during past ice ages. When impounded waters breached those barriers, the floods (and there were many) gouged out the depths of Lake Pend Oreille in northern Idaho and scoured down to bedrock basalt the channeled scablands of the Columbia Plateau, an area covering the states of Washington, Oregon, and Idaho from the Cascade Mountains in the west to the Rocky Mountains in the east. Now another dam was opening, and soon strangers would flood in to almost scour the native peoples from the face of the land.

By following well-worn Indian trails, John McClallen had confirmed the essential geography of the convoluted river systems that would soon be the arteries, veins, and capillaries of the beaver trapper's heart's desire; and with any luck it would be a bloodline of world commerce.

In a still puzzling burst of personal initiative, the soldier inside the fictitious skin of Capt. Zackary Perch accepted being the point man of the republic. Those insights came from the politics and ambitions molding Louisiana, from both the intrigues of General Wilkinson and the sense of national destiny of Captain Lewis. For John McClallen, living for eight months among western tribesmen knotted a lot of loose ends together. He understood how necessary it was to protect the tribes from each other and from the inroads of strangers.

Victims of inherited purpose, John McClallen and David Thompson were trying to make the best of their circumstances. Over the winter they sparred with words at long distance without knowing each other or realizing their similarities. McClallen's past made him a military commander without an army; Thompson was an astronomer losing sight of his star.

The Salish or the Nez Perce who returned from the winter visit to the British trader at his trading post reported that he appeared to be doing little to encourage a peace. Kutenai were still being harassed by horse raiders. They might be the malcontents who broke up last year's peace meeting, and they could not be allowed to kill the peace initiative.[1]

Peace overtures resurfaced when the Bloods and the Atsiina who intercepted McClallen on the Yellowstone reported their meeting to the Hudson's Bay Company trader at Edmonton House. In January 1808, the Hudson's Bay Company factor on the Saskatchewan, James Bird, noted that an American officer had proposed a general meeting in the spring "with All tribes they have hitherto warred with, in order to settle a Peace with them and for the Purposes of trade."[2] Obviously, he was the same officer who wrote the trade regulations that Bird had previously copied into the house journal.

Bird knew that beaver were numerous between the south branch of the Saskatchewan and the Missouri, but that he or a party could not go there with so few men. The North West Company also viewed that opportunity "with wistfull eyes," but "to make one great effort" would require at least forty men.[3] While disputes between the Cree Indians and other northern plainsmen kept them distracted, Bird waited to see how Mr. Thompson prevailed west of the mountains.

Instead of forty men, the North West Company had only one observer in the *Piikani* winter camps. Those were the Indians Thompson most feared would take exception to the North West Company opening trade with western tribes. That was Jacques Raphael Finlay (or Jaco), the country son of a founder of the company, whose performance at a clerk's salary to break trail for the western expansion had displeased David Thompson. The indignant trader recommended that he forfeit his pay and position. Either on orders from the Fort Augustus proprietor, James Hughes, or on his own initiative, Jaco took his family south along the east side of the mountains to the Bow River, where they wintered with *Piikani* who were scattered in the friendly parks along the Spitchee (Highwood) River west of present Calgary.

Piikani returning from west of the mountains must have told Finlay about the frustrated peace council, and how the Bloods and the Blackfeet broke it up. During the winter, he saw other parties of *Piikani* departing to cross the mountains and returning to report that the western tribes were still in favor of a peace. If Jaco forwarded information about Thompson's progress at Kootenae House, there is no record of it when he returned to the Saskatchewan houses in the spring.

In his March letter to Fort Augustus, Thompson continued to disparage Finlay's efforts at road building and canoe construction. Passing Rocky Mountain House on June 25, 1808, Thompson took perverse satisfaction in buying just one pack of beaver pelts from Finlay, all he had to show for a winter's work.[4] But by then, Thompson was still calling for Iroquois trappers to increase the poor show of the first winter west of the mountains. As far as he knew, the American officer had as many as forty or so trappers.

◂═ ═▸

After McClallen's Canadian freemen spread like a sheen of oil over the waters of the lower Bitterroot Valley, a new breed of mountain trappers was born, and a new mythology was created. Setting the first traps in western waters, those nominal Americans worked out the techniques and limitations of the whole new beaver hunt. Greasy, weathered outcasts from corporate ruthlessness, they remade themselves as the first mountain men.

By spring they had accumulated packs of valuable fur, potential fortunes that were not realized until the stiff bundles of stretched pelts could be delivered to a market. Captain McClallen could not provide the essentials they needed to continue hunting. They may have been reluctant to go to the British trader at the Kutenai country because they had learned from past experience that North West Company buyers gave good prices for beaver but charged high for the supplies a free trapper needed. Because the North West Company refused to pay in cash, a debt-obligated trapper could never save enough real money to get out of the country.[5]

To find a market, these mountain men would trap across the Three Forks and down the Yellowstone in search of the trading adventure that John B. Thompson told them left St. Louis the previous March. If Manuel Lisa followed McClallen & Company to the Yellowstone, there was the possibility of a closer store.

The strain that forty or more strangers put on the Salish meat supply made an early hunt across the mountains imperative but not unusual. Later observers saw the hunters depart as early as February. At that time of the year the bulls were still wandering apart from the cows and the calves, and their thick hides were preferred for lodge covers or leather. David Thompson had yet to stir from Kootenae House when the Americans in the lower Bitterroot Valley prepared to accompany the early hunters.

Salish survivors of the coughing sickness left the Horse Plains to the singing of the plaintive "*sakaha*, the trails." Following what would be known later as Jaco River east, they took the right fork (Finlay Creek) toward a low divide. Crossing to a prearranged meeting in the lower Bitterroot Valley, they were joined by Nez Perce and sang *Kaes, chasinim*, which meant "to attach themselves to the party."[6] A later fellow traveler described the moving community.

> Since these hunts were long affairs, the hunters took with them everything they possessed. Each wigwam counted usually seven or eight persons, and these, together with their possessions required the use of about twenty horses. [Those] wound between two chains of mountains which sometimes drew together to offer at close range a view of what was most majestic about the wilderness, sometimes separated to reveal a series of infinitely varied and distant perspectives. This is what was called the great hunting trail.[7]

Buffalo hunting parties had followed those trails for so long that the way was mapped in their souls. Wide places where families tried to avoid the dust might be as many as fifteen parallel trails wide, drawn by the dragging tepee poles.[8] After a cold crossing of Nemissoolatakoo (the Clark Fork River), the travelers moved through the gap in the mountain wall along the east side of the Bitterroot Valley. The long valley beyond led toward the most direct way to the Three Forks. Most of the thirty freemen and probably the two former corpsmen, with precious packs to protect them, would travel with the buffalo hunters as far as the Three Forks.

It was here that McClallen joined the march. One can only guess that François Rivet, the black body servant, and eight unidentifiable men stayed with McClallen, who intended to complete an important diplomatic mission before returning to his caches and continuing to Santa Fe. He was driving the horses he needed to pack overland. The rest of the party he brought last fall would go with the buffalo hunters. On the morning when the parties separated, McClallen & Company turned east.[9]

That journey began in an ominous canyon where steep, dark slopes crowded the trail close to the Blackfoot River. Two years before, in 1805, Captain Lewis was discomforted when his Nez Perce guides made excuses to avoid risking that dangerous passage.

> These people now informed me that the road which they shewed me at no great distance from our Camp would lead us up the East branch of Clark's river and a river they called Cokahlarishkit or the *river of the road to buffaloe* and thence to medicine river and the falls of the Missouri where we wished to go. they alledged that as the road was a well beaten track we could not now miss our way and as they were affraid of meeting with their enimies the Minnetares.[10]

After eight tense miles, McClallen's small party was glad to clear that pinched passage.[11] Beyond, the river valley gradually opened into broad, undulating meadows spotted with groves of aspen, poplar, and cottonwoods. The river looped gently through a serene, gentle landscape where unconcerned antelope grazed, and in the distance wild horses raised their heads and snorted. A small tributary stream coming in from the right wound through a wide pleasant valley where edible camas bulbs grew in the marshes. Another rocky creek coming from the left descended from high mountains. That was one of the trails that enemies used in their nefarious adventures. When Lewis's party passed in the spring of 1806, the hunter George Drouillard determined that a war party, taking care to conceal their fires, had been camped there.[12]

As the mountain-bordered flats gradually stepped higher, there was a risk of encountering snow. Hunting parties had to find grass to strengthen their ponies before challenging the passes. The first flurries of snow usually fell in December, but the accumulation was never too deep and went off again as early as March. But it can freeze in the high places as late as June or July. McClallen & Company had to chance snowdrifts in unavoidable places that might appear to be solid enough to bear an animal but could be undermined by snowmelt. A horse breaking through the crust could flounder hysterically, cutting itself or breaking a fragile leg.[13] If McClallen wanted to reach Santa Fe, he had to protect his packhorses.

Near the top of the climb, forested mountain slopes squeezed the trail along a dwindling creek with many difficult switchbacks. Finally, the party came to a high point, and from his saddle McClallen looked out over a rolling country. Shadows defined the billowing hills where a prominent square butte dominated the panorama. Beyond, in the distance, the thin, silver meanders of the Missouri River could be seen. When Lewis came this way, he marveled at the largest herd of grazing buffalo that he had ever seen. Now the carpet of new buffalo grass supported calving herds.

The small party was entering the land that the wolf made, where the first buffalo came out of the earth and were punished for despoiling the first man by having to wear humps. Its secrets were as dark as an uncaring warrior's heart because those who contested on that common ground jealously guarded their prerogatives. Northern plainsmen were accustomed to crossing the Big (Missouri) River and Ponokai Sisokchta (Elk River or Yellowstone River) as they trailed south to the Crow tribe's world looking for long-haired scalps. Others followed the Old North Trail along the mountains to kill Shoshones around the Three Forks.[14] Some went as far as the Spanish frontier settlements.

There was a little valley that western hunters favored on the upper

Dearborn River that drained down to the Missouri. Steep, rocky cliffs made a secure corral for a small bottom of about five acres with enough grass to sustain the horses of around fifteen lodges, enough to put up a fortified camp to resist an attack.[15] But northern rustlers usually came in the night. There might only be a nervous nickering from the grazing ponies, perhaps an animal cry in the dark, and the sudden sound of receding hoof beats. In horse-capture gamesmanship, the plains of the upper Missouri were an annually replenished stockyard.[16] And here was McClallen & Company with an enticing herd that he intended to use to pack his cached outfit to New Mexico.

The small party angled toward the distant tree line of Medicine (Sun) River, stopping halfway to water the ponies at a small creek. McClallen understood that *Piikani* usually hunted north of the Great Falls along the Bear (Marias) River, but because the bulls were scattered in small groups in the spring, hunters or roving scouts might be encountered anywhere.

McClallen needed to find *Piikani* in order to renew the alliance that had been so close to realization before the Bloods and the Blackfeet had spoiled it. He hoped to convince them that Father Jefferson's heart was good and that he had sent his son to encourage peace between his new children. The death of a young *Piikani* caused by Captain Lewis previously should not discourage the possibility of a convenient trading house.[17] When a truce ensured their safety, the Americans would bring a reliable powder supply, and other desirable things, at better prices than the greedy British king's men.

Those were good intentions, but McClallen lacked an overview of the Blackfeet world to understand what he was proposing. Although the usual ranges of Blackfeet stretched from the Saskatchewan River to the Missouri River, most kept their winter camps along the south branch of the Saskatchewan. Blackfeet and Bloods preferred the sheltered draws around the mouth of the Red Deer River, but the *Piikani*, half of the total tribal population, favored cozy places closer to the mountains along the Highwood River.

To spread out the pressure on available resources, winter camps were small, just family groups or bands. The immediacy, personality, and responsibility of communal life was like the smoke from the tepee fires that hung over those camps, something a stranger could not discern. Because they lost so many to the earlier smallpox pandemic, those camps were full of young people. Although responsible men looked to the common good, there were always ambitious warriors jockeying for power. Personal passions could ignite in a moment, and those who were alienated sometimes voted with their feet, creating a social churning that kept a world without a constitution in perpetual turmoil. Wisdom went up the smoke hole when young men boasted of last summer's hunts or horse-capturing adventures. Because personal leadership counted for more than political abstractions, there was no central authority within the camps for McClallen to approach. The *Piikani* world was already conditioned to commerce because of their long association with Cree middlemen, who had taught them to hunt beaver. Going to the traders added to their wealth.

In the sheltering river valleys of the south branch, Blackfeet, Bloods, and Atsiina spurned stepping down from a pony to dig oversized rodents from their houses. Wolf and fox skins were a by-product of their buffalo hunting, but lately the traders had stopped taking them. Killing fourteen imported Iroquois trappers six years before had less to do with the preservation of a natural resource than with the rejection of obnoxious outsiders, but it checked the North West Company's expansion southward.

In 1807 northern plainsmen were aware of several parties of American trappers. Because of the previous summer's contact with the boat party ascending the Yellowstone, Bloods and Atsiina knew that McClallen & Company crossed the mountains with the Flatheads. Blackfeet also encountered a small party coming up the Missouri to trap. By winter, rumors circulated that others built a trading house on the Yellowstone at the mouth of Amukikini Isisakta (the Big Horn).[18] Before the winter was over, Blackfeet, Bloods, and Atsiina were learning how easy it was to intimidate and rob terrified trappers.[19]

Riding down from the continental crest, John McClallen had the satisfaction of knowing that he had located and proved a practical overland route that could make the Great Falls the head of Missouri River navigation. Making that a practical avenue of commerce required meeting and reconciling the tribes to each other. Unfortunately, his small herd of horses could be an irresistible temptation to any ranging raiders. However, he had passed through the tribes of the Missouri, Yellowstone, and Clark's Fork without incident. The brawl between tribes that broke up last fall's conference did not have to be the final curtain on peace if he could locate and speak with responsible elders. McClallen felt that he could still convince the parties to arrange an accommodation.

Somewhere along the Missouri River between the Great Falls and the Three Forks, a party of Bloods intercepted his small party of ten. After a mounted scout spun his pony to signal from a rise, the rest of the painted band cautiously approached. The two groups of horsemen sat staring at each other from long distance while making tentative gestures. The warriors were counting the guns and the horses. They were signaled to come closer so preliminary conversations could be made through signs at a safe distance. Perhaps the Indian leaders dismounted and cautiously approached. To demonstrate that his party meant no harm, McClallen had his men lay down their weapons while he went forward holding out gifts. The parties merged.

CHAPTER EIGHTEEN

A STEP INTO THE ABYSS

In March 1808, John McClallen's British rival was still wearing out the winter at Kootanae House. Almost as soon as he arrived west of the mountains as the point man for North West Company expansion, David Thompson had found himself posted as an intruder. Captain Perch appeared out of nowhere with an army of forty-two men while, at one point, Thompson was left with just four engagés. When he read the cocksure Captain Lewis's prediction of a boundary drawn across the northern plains at 50 degrees north latitude, Thompson was unprepared to dispute that presumption and risk creating an international incident. The exploration he did in the fall of 1807 was just a gesture.

In March he was already calling for ten or twelve Iroquois hunters to trap between the mountain portage and Kootanae House, twice as many between there and the Pend d'Oreille country. Thirty or so trappers should put him on a competitive footing with the Americans. But the Fort Augustus master, James Hughes, sent only five, and they soon tied in with Jaco Finlay, who returned to the country he pioneered as a freeman trapper.[1]

As providers of peltry, the Kutenai were disappointing, and Thompson had to do more to inspire them to take beaver. At the end of March, he sent two of his men to collect the debts he allowed to visiting Flatheads (Kalispels also known as Pend d'Oreille). When they did not return, it was time to do some exploring. On April 20, 1808, Thompson left Kootenae House with a small canoe party to test the navigability of McGillivray's River and ensure that the Indians did not throw away the beaver clothing they wore during the winter. Those greasy coats were just as valuable as a raw skin. And he needed to determine what the Americans were doing.

The two men he sent to bring in the Flatheads had disappeared. When Thompson reached the ten lodges of Old Kutenai Chief, he learned that as they were coming to his camp the two had been overtaken by forty-seven *Piikani* who followed them. A fight developed in which one of the high-handed *Piikani* troublemakers was killed and another had his arm broken. The Old Chief and the horse he was riding were wounded while failing to prevent the stampede of thirty-five Kutenai horses. Thompson took the incident as proof that the eastern Indians were trying to sabotage the expansion.

On May 12 Thompson engaged the obliging Flat Bow chief Ugly Head to go south and bring in the Kalispels. Meanwhile he and his crew spent the next five days exploring the lake of the Flat Bows. When they returned to the camp, Ugly Head reported that the road to the lake of the Kalispels (McClallen's Poltito Palton Lake) was flooded and it was impossible to bring anything over that soggy trail.[2] The disappointed trader ruefully wrote in his journal "thus all my fine Hopes are ruined."[3] Nothing crept into those pages to suggest that he knew what had become of his American opponent.

With just three small traveling packs of mixed furs to show for his trip, Thompson set out to follow the overland route that he refused to try the previous October. The small party was soon lost, hungry, and bogged down. Lame from struggling over fallen trees and wading in cold water, Thompson sent his two men back to the Kutenai camp to find someone who knew the way through the awful country. While Thompson stayed put, waiting for help, he "passed the time in sad reflections."[4]

The plan for opening a western trade was not developing as he had hoped. The difficulties of provisioning a distant outpost and getting supplies across the Rocky Mountains seemed too difficult. Trapped on that sodden trace under dripping forests and towering mountains, it must have occurred to the British trader that he could die there in pursuit of the skin of an overgrown rodent. The astronomer's exploratory accomplishment came down to the glimpse of a few stars that he could see between the tops of overhanging trees. Thompson allowed only hints of those dark thoughts in his field journal, but there is no doubt that they burdened his mind. Two days later, the indispensable Ugly

Head caught up and led the party out of the wilderness for the price of a capot (blanket coat), a yard and a half of red strouds (woolen cloth), a large knife, a small axe, ten balls, and powder. Adding to that cost was the loss in a rushing river of one of the packs, half of beaver and two bear skins.

When the party returned to Kootenae House on June 5, Thompson found that Finnan McDonald had already started the women, children, and the packs made during the first year of trading down the river in a large canoe. They were across the mountains by June 22, but Thompson still had to run down the Saskatchewan River, cross Lake Winnipeg, and push upstream to the Rainy Lake inland depot. That was a long trip just to accept the next outfit that might have been more efficiently sent up the Saskatchewan with other upper Fort des Prairies goods. But operating policy required a trader to personally receive the next outfit.

The appearance of another American officer close on the heels of the Corps of Discovery was an unwelcome forecast of trouble. The Nor'westers did not need another little black fly biting them, and Thompson needed to get advice from headquarters.[5] In July 1807, about the time that Captain Perch wrote the circular letter setting out trade regulations, the expedition journal of Patrick Gass was coming off the press. As the product of a hack Pittsburgh editor, the first publication about the Corps of Discovery was not completely trustworthy.[6] It was laden with references to Alexander Mackenzie's *Voyages from Montreal*, the only reference book the editor had available. By the spring of 1808, the wintering partners of the North West Company were already reading it and passing around the purloined copy of Captain Lewis's first letter. Most were appalled by the recommendations that he made to President Jefferson for the northern expansion of territory and the transport of furs, even British, by way of the Missouri River. That was a direct threat to their operations, not only across the mountains but also to the Saskatchewan trade or beyond. After a long winter to consider how that would impact their expensive western experiment, several of those tough Scots were having second thoughts about an investment they had made reluctantly.

The winter express had passed Pembina on the Red River of the North on March 31, 1808, and went on via Leech Lake in central Minnesota to Fort William. That delivered Thompson's September packet from Kootanae House, including the trade regulations laid down by Captain Perch and Thompson's narrative of events. Thompson's comment to Duncan McGillivray that the American establishment "will give a new Turn to our so long delayed settling of this Country, on which we have entered it seems too late" was no comfort for those who entertained doubts about the profitability of a Columbia enterprise.[7] They were shocked that the Americans put Lewis's recommendations into effect much sooner than anyone thought possible.

Thompson's supporters, James Hughes, John McDonald, and Donald McTavish, attended the rendezvous and argued that it took more than one season to prove the prospects of a new territory. An American check on their expansion across the mountains might reflect unfavorably on other concessions that this trading partnership hoped to obtain from the British government.[8]

David Thompson had no opportunity to answer criticism of his first trial of the west. By the time his canoe reached Rainy Lake, the meeting at Fort William would be over. The decisions made there about how the North West Company would proceed would have been based on the information he sent down with the winter express. The last words James Hughes or John McDonald had from Thompson were the letters that he wrote in March when he still expected to make thirty packs from his winter trade.

Riding down the Saskatchewan River, Thompson began a pencil draft on the empty pages at the back of his field journal of what he needed to communicate to Duncan McGillivray. It was a recital of what he had done since ending the "Narrative of the expedition to the Kootenai & Flat Bow Indian Countries" on September 22, 1807. Thompson ruefully pointed out that he would be late returning to Kootenae House and unable to extend operations to the promising Flathead country until the next year. "The Flat Heads &c were only 12 days March from us... & the Lake Indians (Lower Kutenai) only 6 days & yet both as completely shut up by Mountains as if they were on the other side... & the waters rising in Summer have nearly the same effect." Nearly obscured in the faint, smudged lines of the draft was Thompson's admission that the appearance of Captain Perch had disrupted his plans. "I shall now leave to your Judgement if we can with any propriety come to the River of Lakes."[9]

As his canoe ascended the voyageur mainline, Thompson met canoes headed to winter posts. By the time he passed Portage de L'Isle on July 29, 1808, he knew that his supporter, Duncan McGillivray, had died in Montreal the previous April. Duncan McGillivray pushed the expansion that his uncle Simon McTavish sent him to initiate in 1800, and his last contribution to that vision was a document titled "Some Account of the trade carried on by the North West Company."[10] Before he died, McGillivray wrote that "the trade that is carried on at present beyond the mountains, instead of getting any profit, is a very considerable loss to the Company; as the Furs did not pay for the transport to Montreal, where they were shipped." Duncan, or his brother, William McGillivray, added, "Should the Company succeed in the project a new field will be opened for the consumption of British manufactured goods; and a vast country and population made dependent on the British Empire."[11] If Thompson bothered to make a fair copy of the penciled draft in the back of his notebook, it was passed to Duncan's brother, William.

Donald McTavish and James Hughes, returning from the meeting, met Thompson on the water road and warned him on August 2 about the unenthusiastic agreement to continue. However, Thompson's ailing brother-in-law John McDonald was returning to Montreal on medical furlough and should be able to encourage the downstream agents to continue supporting the extension of trade. That should help claim objections to an unprofitable first year.

McDonald's departure left James Hughes as the proprietor for Upper Fort des Prairies department on the Saskatchewan River. Someone was needed at Fort Vermillion and Alexander Henry, aka "the younger" to distinguish him from his famous uncle of the same name, was an old hand in the Northwest trade.

As the trader on the Red River, Henry had been out of the direct line of the previous exchanges between Lewis and Clark and North West Company partners on the Assiniboine River.[12] While the Americans were still across the Rocky Mountains, Henry and another partner had sent the clerk François Antoine LaRocque to accompany the Crows to the upper Yellowstone. Just before the return of the Corps of Discovery, Henry and Charles Chaboillez visited the Mandan villages on the Missouri, where they found United States flags flying. They had extracted useful information from the Indians about western geography and their attitude toward the Americans. After returning to their posts, the two North West Company proprietors recommended abandoning the unprofitable Mandan trade. Henry forwarded his recommendations to headquarters with the 1806/07 winter express and also expressed them at the 1807 summer rendezvous. When he returned to his post, he may have learned that some bothersome freemen may have gone up the Yellowstone with another American party.

When the 1807/08 winter express passed his post in March, Henry read Thompson's "narrative" written for Duncan McGillivray and the trading regulations set down by Captain Zackary Perch. There were other letters from James Hughes or John McDonald leading Henry to deduce that this Captain Perch was the same as the officer who passed through the Mandan villages in the spring of 1807, scooping up freemen and taking them up the Yellowstone River.

Although views on how to answer United States pressure were important, Henry did not bother to go to the 1808 annual meeting and sent his letters with the Lower Red River brigade. Later he insinuated insultingly that the "grand Divan" at the bottom of the Winnipeg River held up his dispatches to Fort William until they were not worth the paper he had written them on.[13]

On August 3, 1808, three Indians came from Rainy Lake in ten days with the news of the death of Duncan McGillivray and the departure from the Saskatchewan, due to illness, of John McDonald. Before Thompson reached the inland depot, Henry had already been reassigned to take over the Lower Fort des Prairies district.[14] Thompson was sent back to finish what he had started, and Henry was told to put some muscle into the middle Saskatchewan trade.

Within five days Alexander Henry was ready to move from the posting he held for eight years. Passing down the Red River into the south end of Lake Winnipeg, his light canoe drove north close on the track of Thompson and the Columbia River brigade. Henry overtook them in ten days at Wicked Point on Lake Winnipeg. They traveled together or at least in proximity, but the new Fort des Prairies master did not mention "the Philosopher" Thompson again until they arrived together at Fort Vermillion.

That is curious because Henry should have had a lot of questions about the Saskatchewan operations. When he arrived at Fort Vermillion, he found the Painted Feather band of Blackfeet, Bloods, and Strong Wood Assiniboine clamoring for first chance at the new outfit. Henry neglected to mention in his journal that some of those northern plainsmen met American trappers on the Missouri and robbed them of the furs that he did not hesitate to accept. That certainly included more information about American activities, but he did not mention it until the next year when he was disappointed that those northern plainsmen failed to steal more.[15]

The shadow of Captain Perch still loomed and no one could be certain how his trading regulations would impact business. On that very interesting question, James Hughes is mute, Thompson is frustratingly reticent, and Henry avoided revealing clues in his personal journal. He broke off daily entries for the winter of 1808/09 with the dismissive "Here I passed the winter during which nothing extraordinary occurred further than the common routine of the Trade at this place."[16]

What Henry neglected to mention was that loot taken from Americans came to the Saskatchewan trading houses in the fall of 1808. The Painted Feather and Cold bands of Blackfeet usually brought in less-desirable wolf or fox skins, but this year during a war excursion to the south, they took a considerable booty in beaver.[17] Their trade was too profitable to refuse, and Henry displayed no qualms about receiving it.[18]

Henry, Hughes, and Thompson were at Fort Vermillion from September 14 to 17, 1808, while the furs taken from Americans on the upper Missouri were being accepted. Given what Henry knew about those who traveled up the Missouri in 1807, and what all three of the British traders—Henry, Hughes, and Thompson himself—grasped, they must have deduced that Captain Perch was the unlucky American.

Loot also showed up farther on the river at the combined North West Company's Fort Augustus/Hudson's Bay Company Edmonton House, but if James Hughes kept a journal at Fort Augustus, it has not survived. However, Indians who came to the Hudson's Bay Company house on

October 2, 1808, told the Edmonton House master James Bird that Bloods, Atsiina, and Sarcee Indians had robbed and killed Americans.

> [S]everal Blood Indians arrive'd with provisions &. These People it appears from a variety of Accounts, & from the spoils now in their Possession, discovered in their Summer War excursions, on a southern branch of the Missoury, two small settlements which they plundered of goods to a considerable amount, besides about 300 Beaver Skins. One of the men belonging to these settlements was killed & the rest (ten in number) after being stripped were permitted to escape—From some papers brought in by the Indians, the immediate Traders seem to have been Canadians; but from the situation of the Houses, & from the American Colors, which were taken from them, it is concluded that they must have been Subject to the United States.... Several Sussus arrived, most of the beaver they brought seems to have been taken from the settlements above mentioned. Several of them are mark'd with the Initials of the names of their former owners (who we suppose to have been Freemen).[19]

On October 20 and 29, 1808, Muddy River Indians (Bird's term for *Piikani*) arrived at Edmonton House with only a few beaver skins. *Piikani* usually delivered around four hundred beaver pelts, and Bird believed that they were still distracted by the disputes with neighboring tribes. Later, Atsiina admitted plundering a small American settlement on the Missouri and killing two men for seventy beaver of inferior quality.[20] Bird's journals do not indicate that the beaver-hunting *Piikani* were involved in those abuses.[21]

What Bird heard pointed toward the American officer who wrote the trade regulations copied into the house journal last November. The Nor'westers were reasonably assured that the inconvenient Captain Zackary Perch no longer blocked their expansion plans. But Thompson returned to Kootenae House too late to do anything except send his clerk to collect returns from the Flat Bow Indians that he had missed the previous spring. As far as the British traders were concerned, Captain Zackary Perch had been a will-o'-the-wisp and his influence was cut short by his death. That news became known to the Saskatchewan River traders during the summer. Not until the winter of 1810/11 did

Thompson allow himself to speculate "as the Peagans killed an officer and 8 soldiers out a tribe of 12 do [same], if this accident has not drove them back, they will probably get the start of me." But he was referring to the later killing of Missouri Fur Company trappers at the Three Forks of the Missouri.[22]

━═ ═━

Was Captain Perch killed in a random act of violence? Or did the Bloods he met along the upper Missouri River recognize him as an instigator of the Salish-*Piikani* peace initiative? Only a few bare facts are not enough to explain that last glimpse of an enigmatic man.

Peripheral evidence shows that for a brief moment John McClallen made himself the point man of a continental nation, at a time when other interests were trying to fragment that vision. Had the ambitions of a desperate North West Company been allowed to claim the Pacific slope without challenge, this book might have been written in a far larger British Columbia, rather than in the state of Washington.

After being deflected from the Spanish frontier, McClallen took on the British Empire. Representatives of those two national interests arrived on the Columbia drainage at almost the same moment. The coincidence was the accident of circumstances that reflected very different motivations. David Thompson crossed the pass into the Kutenai country as the representative of corporate interests with just a tip of the beaver hat to imperial pretension to the Pacific slope.

McClallen followed Salish buffalo hunters into western Montana out of a sense of duty to his country, a decision that can be specifically dated to July 10, 1807. As the first American officer in the West after Lewis and Clark, he led the initial surge of United States expansion beyond Louisiana. He did it because there was no one else to uphold national authority. Surely his exploration and confirmation of a practical route to the Columbia would have been worth a footnote in the literature of discovery. Was that all there was for John McClallen, a long climb up the gallows stairs and a step into the abyss? His reward was anonymity in the buffalo grass.

An improbable death date survived in the memory of the McClallen family. "John McClellan [sic], born 29 Jun 1772 in Albany, New York, died 22 Mar 1808 in Batavia, East Indies, at the age of 35."[23] That false assumption meant that his family never knew what he tried to do.

Traders in the depths of the wilderness were better informed. Through the courtesy of Mr. Bird, "Commander in Chief of the Honble H. B. Co Forces in F[ort] D[es] P[rairie]," Alexander Henry received newspapers that had been sent from England. In March 1808 Sir Alexander Mackenzie recommended to the secretary of state for war and the colonies that the "NWCo. should have exclusive right of Trade on the Columbia and its tributary waters...it being evident from the exertions of the American Government, this it is their intention to claim under the right of the Discoveries of Captains Lewis and Clark ...exclusive Privileges to the intermediate Country."[24] Newspapers as late as May 23, 1808, reported that there appeared to be an amiable understanding between Great Britain and America.[25]

Soon after David Thompson returned to Kootenae House on November 3, 1808, he sent Finnan McDonald and seven men to collect the missing Salish returns and whatever furs the Lake Indians collected since his spring visit. But the boat party was caught in the ice and had to spend the winter in two leather tents above the falls of McGillivray's River. McDonald's suffering paid off as he acquired thirty-two field packs. Part of those returns was the uncollected advances that Thompson made to the Flatheads in December 1807. The two freemen who Thompson sent previously to induce the Lake Kutenai to take beaver returned with some packs.[26] Other peltry came over from Clark's Fork with freemen who stayed after the departure of Captain Perch, or who returned after his death. Rather than following most of the freemen back to the Yellowstone River, François Rivet went back to his Salish widow and they soon conceived a son.[27]

From the Three Forks of the Missouri down the upper Yellowstone to Manuel Lisa's house at the mouth of the Big Horn was about one hundred and forty miles. It must have been a busy place in the spring of 1808. Former members of the Corps of Discovery, George Drouillard, John Potts, Peter Weiser, Jean Baptiste LaPage, and Colter's former associate Forest Handcock must have prowled along it with other anonymous Lisa engagés, making sets as they came there to do and

taking beaver in their prime. They may not have been entirely surprised to meet French-speaking freemen who had been across the
mountains with the American captain and returned carrying packs of
pelts taken from the Bitterroot or Clark's Fork. Some, maybe John B.
Thompson or Colter, had been as far west as the great lake of the
Poltito Paltons, or heard about it from others who had and readily told
that place was within striking distance of the river of the west. That
made them a new breed of voyageur who never read Alexander
Mackenzie's published brag or, being illiterate, anything else, but who
knew what they had seen was an accomplishment. Unable to write, their
pride was lost on the winds.

As many as forty witnesses could testify to the events of 1807/08.
Those included the Mandan freemen and St. Louis engagés who went to
the trading post that Manuel Lisa established on November 27, 1807, at
the mouth of the Big Horn River. During the winter, a curious artifact
resurfaced at Fort Remon. Short of guns to trade, Lisa was obliged to buy
one from Jean Baptiste Bouche in a deal that required Lisa to throw in a
silver watch worth forty-five dollars. Sometime before August 1806, Lisa
had bought it from Capt. John McClallen. But the opportunity to mention what became of McClallen passed without comment.[28]

The former hunter for Lewis and Clark, George Drouillard, made
two trips in the Big Horn basin, drumming up trade from the wintering
tribes.[29] Drouillard was in contact with the same people who advised
Captain McClallen about the geography six moons before. In the spring
of 1808, the trappers scattered along the upper Yellowstone began
meeting the Canadian freemen returning from west of the mountains.
After trading the beaver taken in the Salish country for supplies, those
wandering Ishmaels were absorbed into the Lisa operation. According
to Lisa's later recollection, John Colter ranged five hundred miles
during the winter of 1807/08 in search of the winter camps of the
Mountain Crow band. To bring in Shoshones, as he later claimed,
would have required him to hike over mountains buried in deep snow
to their customary winter camps along the Snake River. But there is no
documentary record of Colter until he joined a trapping party that
returned to the Three Forks after the keelboat departed in July. Later
accounts of his association with Lisa are based on hearsay.[30]

Most of the trappers spread along the upper Yellowstone returned to Fort Remon to reoutfit before Lisa and Drouillard left for St. Louis in July 1808.[31] Thirteen discouraged travelers returned to St. Louis with the keelboat. Many of the trappers remaining on the Yellowstone after July 1808 were freemen who accompanied McClallen. They were remembered at the Mandan/Hidatsa villages as previous visitors who had not been seen for eighteen months.[32]

⊷⊶

In a remarkably fast trip, Manuel Lisa and George Drouillard arrived at St. Louis by August 5.[33] Drouillard wasted no time in communicating the latest developments in the upper country to his former commanders as well as a map of the geography. Captain Lewis was now governor of Louisiana Territory and Clark was the agent for western Indians. Before coming to St. Louis, Lewis had compiled his thoughts on how to address that responsibility in a study he headed "Observations and reflections on the present and future state of Upper Louisiana," in which he recalled his meeting with "Captain M'Clellan."[34]

The newspaper Governor Lewis helped establish published its first edition on July 22, 1808. Two weeks later, the *Missouri Gazette* printed the first half of the governor's analysis of the western trade under the unmistakable nom de plume "Clatsop." The article recalled Captain McClallen's intention of going to Santa Fe. By August 5 Drouillard surely informed the governor and General Clark that McClallen had not gone to New Mexico as expected. Instead he had been in the Rocky Mountains for the past year, trying to uphold the interests of the nation on his own initiative. A daring lone man confronting British traders should have been big news. But no evidence has emerged to indicate that Lewis or Clark ever mentioned what they learned about that loose cannoneer in the West.

It is possible that John Colter had not returned to Fort Remon before Drouillard and Lisa departed in July. But his associate, John B. Thompson, rode back to St. Louis as a passenger on the keelboat. Thompson needed cash and immediately went to Governor Lewis or General Clark to obtain his land warrant for service on the expedition.

On August 12, 1808, six days after the keelboat reached St. Louis, John B. Thompson assigned this land warrant to his former associate George Gibson.[35] Surely in the face-to-face meeting with Lewis or Clark, Thompson revealed what McClallen had done in the West. But those activities diminished the impact of the book about the expedition that had yet to be written and published. A year later, Lewis was dead and the secret, if there were a secret, died with him.

CHAPTER NINETEEN

POSTSCRIPT TO LOST LETTERS

In what developed into a "no-story" story, this is a last chance to address two lingering questions: the frustrated attempt to open the Santa Fe Trail and the beau geste to block British expansion on the Pacific slope. Spanish reaction to having the Louisiana Territory as a neighbor caused McClallen's Santa Fe adventure to fail. But was there a hidden Wilkinson connection between John McClallen's adventure to Santa Fe and the military expedition of Lieutenant Pike? Pike's travels to the Southwest are usually seen as an exploration with international complications. Unfortunately, his geographical observations were flawed and led him to mistake the South Platte for the North Platte and to believe that from a height near the head of the Arkansas River he could see the Yellowstone. That imperfect understanding was not a factor in McClallen's detour because he never knew about it, but it created a lasting embarrassment to the cartographical contribution of William Clark, who relied on Pike's published maps.

Pike and McClallen depended on copies of a trader's map showing the overland route to Santa Fe. Both saw, with General Wilkinson's indulgence, the purloined copy of Baron von Humboldt's map of the Spanish possessions and William Clark's speculative map of 1805. Because they were both headed to the same place, it is possible to speculate that Pike's expedition was a covering operation shielding the private adventure designed by General Wilkinson and conducted by McClallen. That plan was too much like what the general previously arranged for his son Lieutenant Wilkinson and Dr. Steele to bear much public scrutiny. However, it is unlikely that Lieutenant Pike and Dr. Robinson were unaware of McClallen's intentions.[1]

Expecting McClallen to find a way around the Pawnee blockade,

Pike and his men spent the cold winter of 1806/07 in the mountains waiting for him. After a break in the weather, Dr. Robinson left Lieutenant Pike's stockade house to walk to Santa Fe. During his interrogation by Governor Joaquin del Real Alencaster, the doctor was appallingly direct in stating that the United States was intent on claiming all the country whose waters drained into the Mississippi River. Although he had no idea of what had become of Lewis and Clark, Robinson maintained that the "Misury" River had been successfully explored to its sources and was to be populated with the purpose of embracing all its trade and the commerce of the Indian nations, even those far distant.[2]

That was quite an expansive statement from a mere bill collector. Guessing that Robinson may have been sent by "Wilkinson himself," Governor Alencaster sent his guests in confinement, including Pike, who had been brought in by New Mexican soldiers, on to Chihuahua, where Robinson tried to convince Governor Nemesio Salcedo that he desired to become a Spanish subject. To prove it, Robinson was willing to lead an expedition to the northern part of the province in search of unwelcome intruders.[3] That would have been McClallen & Company.

Santa Fe was a traditional magnet for liars, and the apprehensive Governor Salcedo ordered outposts established along the east side of the Sangre de Cristo Mountains, manned with soldiers ready to warn of an overland invasion. Considering the building tension, had McClallen & Company approached with a pack train, there might have been serious consequences. But then, and probably from the beginning, an invasion of New Mexico was the last thing on General Wilkinson's agenda, and he never revealed why he wanted to get an agent inside Santa Fe.[4]

After a brief captivity and grilling in Chihuahua, Governor Salcedo forwarded Pike and Robinson to United States forces at Natchitoches, where they arrived on July 1, 1807. Pike was still at Natchitoches on August 18, 1807, when Indian agent John Sibley met a delegation of Comanche. After giving them assurances of the friendship of the United States and distributing presents, Sibley draped himself and the principal chief in a United States flag. The Comanche replied that "they were very desirous of having our Flag and it was the Same to them Whether Spain was pleased or displeased... and they would all die in defense of it."[5]

Pike had in hand a letter that General Wilkinson wrote on May 20, 1807, filling in "Captain Pike" on the latest developments.

> You will hear of the scenes in which I have been engaged, and may be informed that the traitors whose infamous designs against the constitution and government of our country I have detected, exposed, and destroyed, are vainly attempting to explain their own conduct by inculpating me; and, among other devices, they have asserted that your's and lieutenant Wilkinson's enterprise was a premeditated co-operation with Burr. Being on the wing to Richmond in Virginia, to confront the arch traitor and his host of advocates, I have not leisure to commune with you as amply as I could desire; let it then suffice to you for me to say, that of the information you have acquired, and the observations you have made, you must be cautious, extremely cautious how you breathe a word.[6]

James Wilkinson was the original Teflon man. At Aaron Burr's trial, he survived grilling by a battery of lawyers, and it was years before the truth about agent Number 13 and the "Reflections on Louisiana" reemerged from Spanish records. Oddly, what damned James Wilkinson in the American mind wasn't his traitorous activities, but that he had betrayed the traitor Burr. Although his enemies railed against him, as historians looking for an easy target still do, the commanding General of the Army helped preserve the republic by avoiding a potential war. In a convoluted way, secret Number 13 may have made himself the instrument of a carefully contrived peace.

During his brief tenure as governor of Louisiana Territory, Wilkinson had ordered the exploration and identification of the boundaries of that as-yet-uncertain expanse. After mooting the Spanish military threat through diplomacy, he may have expected an appreciative US administration to shift his government from lackluster St. Louis to Orleans Territory, where he could exercise a lucrative secret option to export grain to Cuba.[7] If his record is taken without prejudice, in the performance of his duties, James Wilkinson was a dutiful officer of the republic. Ironically he died in Mexico City in 1825 while trying to put through a scheme to colonize lands in Texas.[8] Any answers regarding the actual intent of McClallen's mission to Santa Fe were buried with him.

General Wilkinson sacrificed his follower Philip Nolan to his fixation with the Southwest by sending him repeatedly into forbidden territory. He was prepared to chance Dr. Steele, Lieutenant Pike, Dr. Robinson, and Captain McClallen to his inexplicable need to penetrate to Santa Fe. Ironically, it was the old entrepreneur Jacques Clamorgan who completed the trip to "St. Afee."

After committing in 1806 to a debt of twelve thousand dollars' worth of goods in partnership with James Clamorgan, Manuel Lisa grasped that McClallen & Company would beat them to Santa Fe. As an alternative, he began organizing an expedition to the Yellowstone. Twelve days after taking out a license to trade with the Indians of the Pawnee Republic, Clamorgan learned that Lisa had verbally broken their agreement.[9] Overcoming his exasperation, the old man went on, accompanied by three Frenchmen and a Negro slave, to do it himself. Despite Spanish-intimidated Indians, the trading expedition passed from the Pawnee Republic to Santa Fe, where they arrived on December 12, 1807, with four loaded mules. Clamorgan continued to Chihuahua and sold his merchandise there for a modest profit.[10] The old entrepreneur returned to St. Louis by way of Texas on July 26, 1809.[11]

Santa Fe was a name that still excited another Wilkinson. In 1810, the general's nephew Benjamin Wilkinson left St. Louis to go to New Orleans, where he planned to take a ship to Baltimore. Before leaving he shared something with the St. Louis public house keeper and justice of the court of quarter sessions, William Christy. When Christy called on him at his house in Belle Fontaine, he was told that a local man named Ira Nash had been sent to make mercantile arrangements in the Spanish provinces. After receiving a favorable letter from Nash, Benjamin Wilkinson invited Christy to join in a business where "fortunes might soon be made" in Santa Fe.[12]

During this time territorial expansionist thinking was convoluted and often nefarious. In the first two decades of the nineteenth century, Dr. John Robinson continued to be one of those Americans capable of audacious actions and a sometimes perverse patriotism. In 1810, Mexico rebelled against Spanish rule. On June 19, 1812, Major Pike recommended Robinson to Secretary of State James Monroe for an attempt to get Mexican governor Salcedo to confirm the boundary between the United States and the New Mexican provinces. That diplomacy may have included encouraging Salcedo to join a revolt against the vice regency in Mexico City. When the results were disappointing, Robinson published a broadside fomenting a filibuster and military action.[13] Although ordered by James Monroe to desist, Robinson continued to make forays with the revolutionaries. Robinson returned to New Orleans in March 1817 and died two years later. His obituary was published in the *Missouri Gazette* of November 24, 1819: "His pursuits have been constantly directed to the grand object [liberation of Mexico] and would have succeeded had he met with men equal to himself in wisdom to plan, and courage to execute."[14]

Blocking British territorial expansion in the north turned out to be a smoldering time bomb. When he finally understood the lateral distance between the Yellowstone River and the Rio Grande, John McClallen set aside his idea of entering New Mexico by the backdoor. He made that assessment on the ground, looking up the muddy Clark's Fork of the Yellowstone, then performed a remarkable military "change front" by wheeling west to address British ambitions in the Pacific Northwest.

John McClallen was in Baltimore and Washington in early 1806 putting together the outfit that he planned to take to Santa Fe at a time when the northern boundary of the United States was "supposed" to be the same as the nebulous bounds of the previous Spanish Louisiana. Before the Corps of Discovery left St. Louis, the former surveyor-general Antoine Soulard made a copy of his *Topographie des Huits du Missisipi et du Missouri*, which was dated 1804 and was labeled "*Possession Espagnole* north of L. Winepig and R. Oupas [the south branch of the Saskatchewan River]."[15] It is uncertain if Captain Lewis was aware of President Jefferson's concern about a northern boundary or that the United States ambassador to London would soon be ransacking bookshops looking for proof that accepted understanding put the northern boundary at 49 degrees north latitude. While the expedition was returning in the summer of 1806 James Monroe and his associate, special envoy William Pinckney of Baltimore, were negotiating a number of concerns far more demanding than a northern boundary.[16] What they came up with about the northern boundary was rejected by Secretary of State James Madison, who was far more concerned about the British traders who were coming from the north and gaining inroads among tribes in American territory.[17]

When Meriwether Lewis returned to Washington in early 1807, he was even more concerned about British intrusions of the as-yet-undetermined northern boundary of the vast territory he was soon to govern. He and Clark depended on personal observations rather than cartographic theory or unverified maps. His negative attitude toward intrusive British traders was observed by them during the winter of 1804/05 and was reinforced in his mind during the expedition's return in 1806. His first reports to the president were emphatic and it was a subject that Lewis returned to in his *Observations and Reflections on the Subject of Governing and Maintaining a State of Friendly Intercourse with the Indians of the Territory of Louisiana.*[18]

What information former captain McClallen might have gathered during his time in the east in early 1806 concerned the Southwest border, not the north, and would have been political gossip. The attitude he took up the Yellowstone reflected whatever Lewis communicated to him during their short meeting on the lower Missouri. Because he had no direct interest in the fur trade, it is difficult to find the reason this private citizen decided to confront British expansion by gaining the confidence of western tribes. All he had as a justification for his actions was the Wilkinson edict that all traders be licensed. If British traders were not licensed, then they were poaching upon United States territory. What he did that was unique was to extend that territorial claim west of the Rocky Mountains.

As early as mid-September of 1808, the North West Company's David Thompson knew that Captain Zackary Perch no longer stood in the way of his move to the Salish country. The following summer he went south to Lake Pend Oreille, where he built Kullyspell House on the north shore, followed by Saleesh House just above the falls of Clark's Fork. Conveniently close to the Salish winter camps on the Horse Plains, the location also attracted the survivors of McClallen's party, feral men like François Rivet or Louis Capois Hoole, who confirmed McClallen's death at the hands of Indians opposed to peace. By then, those freemen had been reinforced by another American party.[19]

After hunting on the upper Missouri and moving south around the Three Forks for two years, the Detroit trader/trapper Charles Courtin and four or five men left as many as fifty packs *en cache* to be retrieved later and crossed the mountains in 1809 to winter with the Salish.[20] Although there were exchanges between engagés and freemen, Courtin did not approach David Thompson at nearby Saleesh House, nor did the British trader approach the American in the Indian camp.[21]

In February 1810, Courtin needed to take his packs of beaver to St. Louis to settle his debts.[22] Traveling with the early buffalo hunt, Courtin set out to return to the caches that he left at the Three Forks. Sometime before February 25, 1810, the party was ambushed and Courtin was killed.[23] After recovering most of the scattered packs, the Indians turned them over to survivors of Courtin's party, who asked Thompson to adjudicate a distribution of the salvage.[24] Thompson was no more hesitant than Alexander Henry to trade the peltry of slain Americans, and he generously dispersed the pelts that he knew he would receive. That resulted in so many packs that Thompson had to move out and use Saleesh House for storage. The take represented the first significant returns of the British expansion into US territory.[25]

Thompson left Saleesh House on April 17, 1810, determined to take an overdue furlough. Instead, North West Company management sent him back to deal with the threat of Hudson's Bay Company competition, and to descend the Columbia River to confirm an agreement with John Jacob Astor's Pacific Fur Company.

During the summer of 1810, Thompson's clerk, Finnan McDonald, and one of Courtin's surviving trappers, Michael Bourdon, tried to go to the Three Forks to recover those lost caches. When the buffalo-hunting Salish encountered territory-sensitive *Piikani*, a fight developed in which Thompson's men participated and the *Piikani* lost several warriors. After suffering losses to the newly armed Salish, the *Piikani* blocked Thompson's access to his western posts and delayed his descent of the Columbia River for a year. Despite his fear of the *Piikani*, their firm reaction was bloodless.

To get around the blockade, Thompson tried a more northerly

route that bogged him down in the snows of the more northerly Athabasca Pass. Marooned and embarrassed, Thompson resorted to another disaster to explain his failure.

> The Americans it seems, were as usual determined to be before hand with us in the Columbia by ship navigation. As the Peeagans killed an officer and 8 soldiers out of a tribe of 12 do [same], if this accident has not drove them back, they will probably get the start of me.[26]

But it was not the advantage of the Americans sending ships to the mouth of the Columbia that embarrassed Thompson. It was his own loose mismanagement of Indian relations. Because he had known about the death of Captain Perch for two years, Thompson referred to attacks on the Missouri Fur Company party at the Three Forks and the death of George Drouillard. Done with skin games and ominous Indians, Thompson left the West for good in the spring of 1812.

Thirty-four years later, when the Oregon Boundary Question was being negotiated, the aging astronomer bent the truth by claiming that he had crossed the mountains before Lewis and Clark. He also invented a statement that all the American freemen who intruded into the Flat-head country were eventually killed.[27]

The potential witnesses to John McClallen's detour to destiny took their memory of him to the grave. Meriwether Lewis died on the Natchez Trace in 1809, and Maj. Zebulon Pike was killed in the War of 1812. The two former corpsmen who accompanied McClallen dropped from the record when John Colter died of natural causes in 1812, and then when John B. Thompson was killed three years later. The observant journalist Alexander Henry drowned in the Columbia in 1814. William Clark outlasted them all. Up until the 1814 publication of the narrative of the expedition, he continued adding data to his manuscript map of 1810, but he never wrote anything about John McClallen.

The author of the Zackary Perch letters could only have been John McClallen. He was the one individual present in the West in July 1807 who could have expressed that understanding of United States policy. In a remarkable example of personal initiative, John McClallen asserted national sovereignty in Upper Louisiana and boldly extended the United States rights of discovery, exploration, and usage to the

Pacific shore. Curiously, those ten regulations governing foreign traders came from a man with no direct interest in the fur trade. For a brief few months, McClallen inhibited North West Company expansion, slowing it in a way that allowed Astor's Pacific Fur Company to gain a toehold on the Columbia River.

Because former captain McClallen failed to return, the important confirmation of a practical mountain portage to the Pacific was lost. No overland road of any consequence followed Cokalarishkit to the Kettle Falls until British traders used that connection later to drain away the Salish and Kutenai trade. The upper Missouri became a historical backwater and tribal sanctuary, ignored as a water road until the buffalo robe trade demanded economically feasible transportation.

For thirteen years the North West Company enjoyed a monopoly on the fur trade of the Pacific Northwest but could not make the ambitious Columbia enterprise pay. In 1821 they merged with the Hudson's Bay Company, and three years later the new governor of the combined company made a visit west of the mountains and foresaw that the 1818 compromise of British and American joint occupancy and its extension in 1827 was not enough to hold the disputed Oregon Country for Great Britain. American overland immigration would eventually claim the country south of the Columbia River.

In January 1842, the United States Congress directed President Polk to notify London of the termination of the convention of joint occupancy. By the end of the year the British were ready to open a negotiation in Washington, and Hudson's Bay Company Governor George Simpson was obliged to do something to offset his decision to shift western headquarters away from the Columbia. He addressed an inquiry about prescience to the former fur trader Joseph Howse, who had carried the only Hudson's Bay Company outfit to the Salish during the winter of 1810/11.

Howse replied on February 19, 1843, that he could not give certain information but could only speculate on North West Company activities prior to the march of the Corps of Discovery. He did not believe that David Thompson crossed the mountains in 1800. "Mr. Bird can of course satisfy your enquires on this head."[28] Instead, Simpson turned to Thompson for a useful claim of prior discovery by stating,

I some years ago at your request communicated with the Govr & Com of the HB Co. on the subject of your maps, but having no occasion for them, they did not authorise me to make any proposition to you respecting them. It would be unavailing to bring the subject again under their consideration, but I should hope Her Majesty's Government will take them off your hands & reward you liberally for your unrewarded Labors in the course of discovery and science.[29]

As it turned out Thompson was paid one hundred and fifty pounds for a touched-up version of his maps of the Northwest, "but the advice he tendered on the Oregon Boundary Question was largely ignored."[30] By November, Archibald Barkley, the Hudson's Bay Company secretary, entered the discussion with a pessimistic view of how matters were developing.

The American rascals are running riot on the Oregon Question and I have been trying to get something on the subject...cannot get date of the first crossing of the RM by the British. Stuart says D. Thomson and McGillivray crossed in 1801 & 2...but Stuart talks at random and has no documents.

A month later, Simpson responded.

On the ground of first discovery, Jonathan, I think, has the best of it, as there is no question that Grey first "entered" the River and Lewis & Clarke I fear will be found to have first crossed the mountains (in 1805). Thompson first *wintered* in the Columbia in 1806–07 [actually 1807/08], & I left with you a letter from an officer belonging to Lewis & Clarke's expedition, dated in 1807, addressed to Thompson, warning him off, on the ground of the country being American territory.[31]

The letter Simpson referred to was the copy of the circular letter from Captain Zackary Perch that Edmonton House factor James Bird dutifully copied into the house journal. It had finally resurfaced.

Thompson continued to promote his view that he was the first to cross the Rocky Mountains. In a letter addressed to the British minister in Washington, Richard Pakenham, Simpson doubted a letter published in the *Montreal Herald* of April 16, 1844, that Thompson crossed the mountains in October 1800.

Two years ago he informed me he did not cross until 1806 and was then warned off by an officer of Lewis & Clarke's Expedition, on the ground that it was United States Territory, by a letter which he gave me & which I forwarded to the H. B. House where it is now deposited. [This must have been McClallen's second letter and reply which came from DT's journal.] Mr. Thompson then told me he did not possess either Journals or papers which could establish any material facts with respect to the discovery of the country from the East side of the mountains.[32]

On May 9, 1845, the aged David Thompson entered the dispute in a letter to Sir James Alexander of the British Royal Engineers.

In 1801 the North West Company determined to extend their Fur Trade to the west side of the Rocky Mountains, and if possible to the Pacific Ocean; this expedition was intrusted to me, and I crossed the Mountains to the headwaters of McGillivray's River; but an overwhelming force of the eastern Indians obliged me to retreat a most desperate retreat of six days for the dreaded western Indians being furnished with Arms and Ammunition. The Report of my attempt and defeat, soon reached Washington and in 1804 the Executive of the U. States organized a plan of discovery, to be conducted by Captain Lewis and Clarke.[33]

The aging Thompson's attempt to invent a prior British claim to the Columbia drainage led him to manipulate facts, just as he did in versions of his narrative.[34] He had been sensitized to the mythic line of 49 degrees north latitude during his first service to the North West Company in 1797/98 and was helping the survey of the international border in the province of Ontario from 1817 to 1827 when the joint occupancy of the country west of the Rocky Mountains was agreed on in 1818 and under consideration for renewal in 1827/28.

The old man confused the facts in the final months of the long-delayed boundary question, but he was not the only one. When it became evident that the British government would concede the 49th parallel as a boundary, Hudson's Bay Company Governor Simpson also stretched the truth. He had been promoting a British military force to protect the company's interests on the Columbia. In asking for protection for company property, he expected British citizens in the Pacific

Northwest to rise in defense of the empire. Many were the old freemen or their descendants who provided Thompson with a resident trapping force in the Salish country. They had been freemen too long to buy into imperial pretensions.

Nor could the diplomats rely on David Thompson's belated claim of discovery prior to the expedition of captains Lewis and Clark. As the boundary decision plodded toward the inevitable, Hudson's Bay Company Secretary Barkley privately responded to what Simpson hoped to get from Thompson.

> Your old papers I had carefully laid by. The letter you allude to was from a Lieut. Pinch to Mr. D. Thompson dated Sep 1807. On the same sheet was Thompson's reply, dated Decr. 1807 but the letters were not original. They were copies in T's handwriting. Copies with some other information relative to the early trading on the West side by the NWCo. were sent to Lord Abn. [Aberdeen] In consequence of an application from the F. Office. It is a most extraordinary thing that Thomson cannot tell when he first crossed the Mountains or commenced trading there. I fear he is not well inclined to the Co.[35]

Dated at Hudson's Bay House on February 23, 1846, Barkley's packet included copies of the letter from Lt. Jeremy Pinch, which seemed to show that a second American officer had preceded Thompson to the Columbia River. Three days later the Hudson's Bay Company secretary sent Thompson's reply to Pinch, with a note from the copyist suggesting that it had been taken from an original journal of Thompson's. The name Pinch appears to have been a misreading by Thompson, or some copyist at some point, of the name Perch.

On June 15, 1846, after several years of diplomatic negotiation, the United States Senate approved a boundary treaty that was soon proclaimed in England.[36] The 49th parallel of latitude, which had divided North America since 1818, was extended to the Pacific. Dismissed as an unsolvable historical enigma, the neglected adventure of former captain of artillery John McClallen was overshadowed by the iconic journals of the Corps of Discovery. The former officer's activities were an inconvenient anomaly to accepted versions of western exploration. It was, inescapably, a no-story story.

That is not to say that the list of trading regulations that John McClallen wrote from the Yellowstone River in July 1807 or the warning letter that followed from Lake Pend Oreille in September were the only documents blocking British ambitions for a favorable Oregon boundary settlement thirty-nine years later. As baffled negotiators anticipated in 1818 and renewed in 1827, the ultimate factor in a decision would be population movements. Although the disputed Oregon Country lay under the uncomfortable compromise of joint occupancy during those years, except for the brief flares of Captain Perch, Charles Courtin, the St. Louis Missouri Fur Company, and the Pacific Fur Company, the Columbia drainage was mainly exploited by British mercantile interests.

Despite the pronouncement in the House of Lords by Thomas Douglas, Earl of Selkirk, that the old rules regarding territorial claims of the Age of Discovery no longer applied and that literal occupation of territory was now the operational principle, the British fur trade proved ephemeral when faced with American overland immigration. The boundary commissioners had to argue other important considerations: access to the Pacific from good ports, a boundary cutting across major rivers, other oblique problems introduced as bargaining chips, national and imperial pride. But it was people who finally crowded out one of the world's great corporations.

I like to think that the spark that glowed briefly in the Salish country during the winter of 1807/08 smoldered between the pages of the Hudson's Bay Company records until it warmed the last debate. The enigmatic Captain Zackary Perch was the invention of a brave man who for a moment accepted an unexpected duty to the nation that cost him his life. John McClallen's only monuments are those two neglected letters. The real enigma is not who he was but what deep sense of patriotic duty caused him to make that personal sacrifice.

Despite his untimely death at the hands of tribesmen unwilling to give up war gamesmanship, John McClallen made a lasting contribution to the nation by briefly derailing Thompson's expansion and leaving a document to prove it. McClallen's plan to redeem the family honor was cut off by tribal politics. Surviving his son by ten years, Robert McClallen ended up living in a boarding house at the end of Dock

Street in Albany, New York. After the death of the oldest son, the family still lived around Albany. His surviving brothers and sisters should have generated some kind of memory of John McClallen, but they were young when he left to join the army. As far as they knew, their brother had gone off into the West and was killed by Indians. All that the Albany McClallen family seems to have retained was a coldly specific date, March 22, 1808. Even that account of his death became hopelessly garbled over the years because it became confused with another person of the same name.

The tragedy was that the bubble of Captain Zackary Perch floated among prickly pears, easily burst, and was immediately forgotten. His forgotten bones were lost in the breathing buffalo grass. John McClallen's lasting legacy was the rawhide knot of trappers who followed him into the mountains. One of the last was the freeman who followed McClallen from the Mandan villages. Old Louis Capois Hoole's string finally ran out and "His body was found by the Flatheads, close to a beaver dam; a ball had penetrated his temples, and the few white hairs that remained on his aged head did not prevent his inhuman butchers from stripping it of the scalp."[37] Although the Salish were careful with their wives and daughters, the first babies of McClallen's men and their Indian lovers might have been born about the time that McClallen died. François Rivet returned to his Salish widow.[38] Never more than nominally American, those latter-day coureurs de bois stayed to found a mixed-blood subpopulation. For the next four generations western freemen practiced a self-reliance and independence of spirit that still characterizes their descendants in the region. Facing the future together, the lives of western freemen and the Salish gave a human dimension to the history of the Pacific Northwest.

Oblivious of diplomatic maneuvering, the Salish and Nez Perce continued to use the road to the buffalo. Jesuit missionaries, who accompanied the hunt after 1842, left vivid descriptions of the intertribal exchanges still roiling on the northern plains. Removed from the road of the overland pioneers, the northern plainsmen had another eighty years of protein wars, horse capture games, and never-ending conflicts. As the great herds gradually diminished, those tribes, broken by hunger, were starved onto reservations.

POSTSCRIPT TO LOST LETTERS

There is not much left in the Salish country to mark those forgotten passages. A highway runs up the Blackfoot River, where mining interests connive to despoil the serenity. Racing along that road, it is surprising how fast you cross the divide and suddenly see the rolling hills, the square butte, and the distant thread of the Missouri spread before you. It is almost as it was when John McClallen and his faithful boatmen saw them.

ACKNOWLEDGMENTS

My recognition of the Zackery Perch enigma and reconstruction of a neglected American martyr has taken more years than I would like to admit and has consumed many cheap composition books and roller-ball pens. That curiosity was pushed along by my good friend Alvin M. Josephy Jr., who had already taken a shot at the question in his great study, *The Nez Perce Indians and the Opening of the Northwest*. Another good friend, Lloyd Keith, heard more about John McClallen than a man should endure on those long drives that we took together to conferences and symposiums. Both of them have gone down the long trail now, and I miss their gentle chipping at my uncertainties. Distance saves my fellow author Thomas Danisi from daily reminders of McClallen, but he has always been ready to step up to a question that can be answered only in St. Louis. Shirlee Anne Smith, Judith Beaty, and Ann Morton were generous in opening the resources of the Winnipeg archives of the Hudson's Bay Company that have provided a northern reflection on activities south of the line. Stephen Jackson-Clark went into the National Archives on my behalf. John Logan Allen helped me understand how William Clark's "error of the Southwest" redirected McClallen & Company from Santa Fe to the Salish Country. Stefen Bielinski of the Colonial Albany Social History Project has helped unravel the Henry and McClallen families of that old Dutch fur-trade town. Dr. William Foley graciously contributed the foreword. Publishing is a cooperative endeavor, and editor in chief Steven L. Mitchell has been a good friend guiding the manuscript to publication. It was good working again with Joe Gramlich, who did the final scrubbing. I thank Michael Haynes for the artwork. Less specifically, but no less vital, are those whose names are included in the bibliography, contributors, as good historians are to the ever-growing fund of the past, and the archivists and librarians who generously open those pages for a researcher.

This book is for my grandchildren, Esther Bea and Ray Jackson Doss.

JOHN McCLALLEN TIMELINE

1742 and 1749. The Henry and McClallen families came from Maghera, Londonderry, in Northern Ireland.

January 29, 1772. John, son of Robert and Jane McClallen, is born in Albany, New York.

February 1792. Robert McClallen helps incorporate the Bank of Albany.

June 2, 1794. John McClallen is commissioned a lieutenant in the Corps of Artillerists and Engineers.

October 1796. Lieutenant McClallen is stationed at Fort Niagara but refuses invitation of former quartermaster general James O'Hara to join potentially lucrative private business.

July 24, 1798. McClallen is commissioned a captain and posted at Fort Jay on Governor's Island, New York.

April 1799. McClallen is brigade major under Gen. William McPhearson during tax protests.

March 1798. John's father, Robert McClallen, is appointed New York state treasurer.

October 7, 1800. Captain McClallen is "arranged" to the 2nd Battalion to assume the command of the "late" Captain Frye's company in South Carolina.

June 1802. McClallen is assigned command of Fort McHenry, Baltimore, Maryland, and forms relationship with prominent merchant family.

Early 1803. McClallen learns of his father's thirty-three-thousand-dollar default as New York state treasurer.

Summer 1804. McClallen meets commanding General of the Army James Wilkinson at Fredericktown, Maryland.

Early 1805. McClallen arranges with James Calhoun Jr. to take experimental out-of-trade goods to St. Louis.

May 23, 1805. McClallen and his company leave Pittsburgh, Pennsylvania, for St. Louis in the Louisiana Territory.

July 1805. They are on station at Cantonment Belle Fontaine, north of St. Louis.

In early September 1805 McClallen becomes part of Wilkinson's convoluted plan to send a mercantile adventure to Santa Fe.

October 20, 1805. General Wilkinson sends a small detachment to winter at the mouth of the Platte. By December 1, 1805, Captain McClallen starts east to resign his commission and obtain outfit of trade goods he will take to Santa Fe.

December 30, 1805. General Wilkinson reports the Platte River detachment was turned back by hostile Kansa Indians.

June 24, 1806. Lt. Zebulon Pike is ordered to arrange peace between Osage and Kansa Indians and to proceed to placate the Comanche who control the way to Santa Fe.

August 28, 1806. McClallen & Company leave St. Louis in a keelboat. Company consists of fifteen boatmen, an interpreter, and a black clerk or body servant.

September 17, 1806. McClallen & Company meet the returning Lewis and Clark expedition and gain perspective on their observations of the West.

Mid-October 1806. At the mouth of the Platte McClallen intercepts dispatches from Lieutenant Pike and learns that Spanish-intimidated Republican River Pawnee will prevent him from traveling to Santa Fe. While deciding how to proceed McClallen meets two men Wilkinson previously sent to explore the Yellowstone River and Big Horn River. They convince him to continue up the Missouri River and winter with Indians until he decides what to do.

Winter 1806/07. McClallen & Company stay in the Yankton Sioux winter camp along Plum Creek, where McClallen has his first experience of Indian life.

Spring 1807. McClallen sends the furs he has traded during the winter to St. Louis, where the boat arrives on May 4. He has decided to continue up the Missouri and Yellowstone and enter Santa Fe by an overland route.

At the Mandan villages McClallen & Company is joined by around thirty Canadian freemen recently discharged from British trading companies. All proceed to the Yellowstone and ascend it to the mouth of the Clark Fork River. After being visited by Blood and Atsiina Indians and learning that British traders are expanding operations west of the Rocky Mountains, McClallen feels it is his duty as a former officer to attempt to block this.

July 10, 1807. McClallen writes a ten-paragraph circular letter governing the conduct of foreign traders in United States territory and expanding that claim to the Pacific Ocean.

McClallen follows returning Salish buffalo hunters west of the mountains with a party of forty-two men, including the former corpsmen John B. Thompson and John Colter.

Late July 1807. McClallen participates in a peace council between the western and eastern tribes, which is disrupted and ended by Blackfeet and Bloods hostile to a *Piikani* peace initiative.

August 9, 1807. The British trader David Thompson learns of a battle between the Salish and *Piikani* Blackfeet and that a large party of Americans is now in the Flathead country.

He receives the trading regulations McClallen wrote the previous July.

Early September. After the breakup of the peace council McClallen and a small party explore the Clark Fork of the Columbia as far as Lake Pend Oreille, where he writes a second, stern letter to the British trader dated **September 29, 1807.** McClallen returns to the Salish winter camp in the Bitterroot Valley where he finds tribespeople suffering from fatal pertussis (whooping cough).

Winter 1807/08. Wintering among the friendly Salish, McClallen is determined to renew the peace initiative by locating and encouraging the *Piikani.*

Spring 1808. Most of the party return to the upper Missouri with their catch of beaver pelts, but McClallen and ten men turn east to follow the Salish road to the buffalo to the vicinity of the Great Falls of the Missouri, hoping to find the *Piikani.* Somewhere above the Great Falls McClallen's party is intercepted by Blood and Atsiina Indians who kill him, strip his followers of their possessions, and drive off the herd of horses that would have taken McClallen's cached trading outfit overland to Santa Fe.

INDIAN TRIBES AND THEIR VARIANT NAMES

There is power in naming oneself, but many native peoples were content to know themselves as just "we the people" or "the real people" and concentrated on identifying their neighbors. That led to several names, sometimes derogatory, for a group, to which were added those strangers heard or invented. A writer hopes to clarify his narrative by bringing a long string of misunderstood and often erroneous names or usages to some manageable common point. For clarity, I am obliged to use the commonly recognized name but try to include a currently acceptable *italicized* native name. That is a gesture fraught with potential argument, but the intention is to move toward respect for how a group saw itself. As sources, a tip of the hat is due to Frederick E. Hoxie, ed., *Encyclopedia of North American Indians* (Boston: Houghton Mifflin, 1996) and to the Web site http://www.native-languages.org/original.htm.

Arapaho (*Hinonoeino*, "our people"), ranged in Colorado and Wyoming, probed north for contact with Atsiina kinsmen.

Arikara (*Sahnish*, "original people"), sedentary village dwellers living along the Missouri River in South Dakota.

Atsiina (*A'ani*, "white clay people"), aka Gros Ventre, Falls Indians, ranged on the south branch of the Saskatchewan or probed south into Crow country.

Blackfeet (*Siksika*), one group of the body of like-speaking peoples (*Nititapi*) generalized as Blackfeet, who ranged from the Saskatchewan to the Missouri or beyond.

Bloods (*Kainaa*), generally south of the Blackfeet proper and often associated with Atsiina.

Cheyenne (*Tsitsistas* or *Tsetschestahase*, "the people"), ranged from the Missouri River as far west as the Black Hills.

Comanche (*Numinu*, "the people"), large body of associated tribes and bands on the Southern Great Plains.

Cree (*Iyiniwok/Ininiwok*, "the people"), aka Northern Plains Cree or Southern Indians.

Crow (*Apsdallike*), ranged along Tongue, Powder, and Big Horn rivers south of the Yellowstone.

Hidatsa (*Nuxbaaga*, "original people"), more or less sedentary village people, just south of the big bend of the Missouri River but known to range widely north and west.

Kalispell ("camas people") aka Pend d'Oreille, ranged along Clark Fork from Flathead Valley to northern Idaho.

Kutenai (*Ktunaxa* or *Ksunka* "water people"), along headwaters of the Columbia, Kootenay River, and Kootenay Lake.

Mandan, sedentary village people south of the big bend of the Missouri River.

Nez Perce (*Nimi'ipuu*), homeland along the Clearwater and Snake rivers of Idaho.

Missouri, Kansas, Omaha, Oto, and **Ponca** tribes of middle Missouri River. Siouan-speaking tribes of present Nebraska.

Osage (*Tzi-sho*, or "sky people," and *Hunkah*, or "earth people")

Pawnee, three distinct bands along the Platte River and one south on the Republican branch of the Kansas River.

Piikani (Muddy River Indians), largest group of the generalized Blackfeet ranging south from winter camps near present Calgary, Alberta, to the Snake River Valley and beyond.

Salish (*Selis* or Flatheads), homes in the Bitterroot and Flathead valleys, ranged east of the Rocky Mountains in seasonal buffalo hunts.

Sarcee (*Saahsi* in Blackfoot), a small group that migrated from the north to northern plains.

Shoshone (Snakes), ranged in the length of the Snake River Valley.

Teton Sioux (*Lakota*), nomadic tribe ranging west of the middle Missouri River as far as the Black Hills.

Yankton Sioux (*Nakota* or *Ihanktonwanna*, "little campers at the end"), east of the middle Missouri.

NOTES

PREFACE

1. Recognition of the enigma appeared in Robert C. Clark, *History of the Willamette Valley* (Chicago, 1927), pp. 122, 839–41. Clark researched records in London bearing on the Oregon Boundary decision. This was followed by an article by J. Neilson Barry, "Lieutenant Jeremy Pinch," *Oregon Historical Quarterly* [*OHQ*] 38 (September 1937): 323–27; J. B. Tyrrell, "Letter of Roseman and Perch," *OHQ* 38 (December 1937): 391–97; Jesse S. Douglas, "Jeremy Pinch and the War Department," *OHQ* 39 (December 1939): 425–31; T. C. Elliott, "The Strange Case of David Thompson and Jeremy Pinch," *OHQ* 40 (June 1939): 188–99; W. J. Ghent, "Jeremy Pinch Again," *OHQ* 40 (December 1939): 307–14; Alvin M. Josephy Jr., "The Naming of the Nez Perces," *Montana* 5 (October 1855): 1–18; Alvin M. Josephy Jr., "A Man to Match the Mountains," *American Heritage* 11 (October 1960): 60–63, 81–85; Alvin M. Josephy Jr., *The Nez Perce Indians and the Opening of the Northwest* (New Haven, CT: Yale University Press, 1965), pp. 40–45, 656–63; David Lavender, *The American Heritage History of the Great West* (New York: American Heritage Publishing, 1965). All of the articles above were described in Harry M. Majors, "John McClellan in the Montana Rockies 1807," *Northwest Discovery* 2 (November/December 1981): 9.

CHAPTER ONE: A GUNNER OF THE REPUBLIC

1. William E. Birkhimer, *Historical Sketch of the Organization, Administration, Matériel and Tactics of the Artillery, United States Army* (1884; reprint, New York: Greenwood Press, 1968), p. 27.

2. Lois McClellan Patrie and Gene McClellan, comps., *The Descendents of Michael and Jane (Henry) McClellan of Colrain, Mass.* (Bakersfield, CA: G. McClellan, 1997), p. 8.

3. Alexander Henry, *Travels and Adventures in Canada and the Indian Territories, between the Years 1760 and 1776* (New York: L. Riley, 1809; University of Michigan at Ann Arbor Microfilms, 1966), pp. 1–2, 10–11, 192–93.

4. David Armour, ed., *Treason? At Michilimackinac: The Proceedings of a General Court Martial Held at Montreal in October 1768 for the Trial of Major Robert Rogers* (Mackinac Island; Mackinac Island State Park Commission, 1972), pp. 84–86.

5. James Sullivan et al., eds., *Papers of Sir William Johnson* (Albany: University of the State of New York, 1921–1957), 5:126, 135–36, 340, 411, 553.

6. James Sullivan et al., eds., *Minutes of the Albany Committee of Correspondence, 1775–1778* (Albany: University of the State of New York, 1923), pp. 383–87. For an overview, see Robert McConnell Hatch, *Thrust for Canada: The American Attempt on Quebec in 1775–1776* (Boston: Houghton Mifflin, 1979).

7. An artifact of that time survives in the Museum of the Fur Trade, at Chadron, Nebraska. "It appearing to this Committee by proof that Robert Henry and Company, having purchased a Considerable Quantity of Merchandise last Winter at Montreal and that they have received the aid of General Wooster in transporting the said Goods from thence in expectation that such part of the Merchandise as could be of use to the Continental Army should be disposed of by them for that purpose." On February 14, 1777, Robert Henry, Robert McClallen, James Bloodgood, and Hugh Mitchel of Schenectady told the Albany board that the General Court of Massachusetts Bay had prohibited the removal of certain merchandise from there to any other state. Sullivan et al., *Minutes of the Albany Committee of Correspondence*, pp. 350, 351, 383, 387, 683, 997. The fur-trade museum has authenticated that the blanket issued to a Massachusetts soldier was preserved and it is now the earliest example of a fur-trade blanket in that extensive collection.

8. "An Albany Merchant's Stock in 1790" in Joel Munsell, comp., *Annuals of Albany*, 10 vols. (Albany: J. Munsell, 1850–59), p. 226.

9. Arthur James Weise, *The History of the City of Albany from the Discovery of the Great River in 1524 by Verrazzano to the Present* (1838; Ithaca: Cornell University Digital Library), p. 399.

10. When anti-Federalist sentiments were detected in upstate New York, a Federalist committee was established at Albany on March 12, 1788, with the merchant Robert McClallen as chairman. McClallen to Duane, May 12, 1788, in Jackson Turner Main, *The Anti-Federalist: Critics of the Constitution 1781–1788* (Chapel Hill: University of North Carolina Press, 1961), p. 236.

11. The Albany Glassworks warehouse of McClallen, McGregor and Company was started with a loan from the New York Legislature of £3,000,

interest free for three years at 5 percent interest. Munsell, *Annuals of Albany*, 3:156; *Report of the New York State Historian*, p. 403.

12. The appointment might have required a gesture of political equity as Joseph Yates, the son of their neighbor Robert Yates, was also recommended by the Republican Mr. Aaron Burr.

13. Distractions kept "father" George Washington from confirming the appointment until December 27. Dorothy Twohig, ed., *The Journal of the Proceedings of the President 1793–1797* (Charlottesville: University of Virginia Press, 1981), p. 324.

14. Captain Frederick Frye, Massachusetts, Captain of Artillery June 2, 1794 (the same date as Lieutenant McClallen's), honorary discharged, June 1, 1802, died June 30, 1828. Heitman, *Historical Register*, 1:439.

15. William Simmons, War Department accountant, certification of payment, April 23, 1795, for service from January to through March 1795, Simmons to Pickering, August 3, 1795, certifies McClallen's account for recruiting, contingent expenses, and subsistence from June 12, 1794, to April 24, 1795. John McClallen file, http://wardepartmentpapers.org/.

16. Munsell, *Annuals of Albany*, vol. 3; War Department Accountants Howell and Simmons to McClallen, December 22, 1794, and April 23, 1795, Department of War Accountant's Office (Revolutionary War Papers, RG94), http://wardepartmentpapers.org/. Some of McClallen's recruits were assigned to the company of Capt. Alexander Thompson.

17. "Invoice of public stores shipped on board the schooner Weymouth . . . to be forwarded to Lt. Q. M. McClellan, West Point, May 30, 1796," and a "Return of clothing, hand tools and hardware." Papers of Ordinance Officer Samuel Hodgdon, United States Military Academy collection, West Point.

18. Because the only available shipping on the lake was dedicated to the British military or to Montreal merchants, the Schenectady and Albany functionary Henry Glenn was obliged to charter a British boat. Captain Bruff still commanded at Niagara in mid-September 1797.

19. John McClallen to Colin MacGregor, Fort Niagara, August 21, 1796, New York Historical Society, Misc. Manuscript. Previously in May 1793 the firm McGregor, McClallen & Company had been granted a loan of £3,000 by the New York legislature to build a glass manufactory. Putting a glass furnace in an old house was not a great idea, and the plant burned down on November 27. Curiously, James O'Hara is better known as the founder of the glass industry in Pittsburgh.

20. Minutes of the Northwest Company, Canada Archives, Q, 286:123–24 in Harold Innis, *The Fur Trade in Canada* (1930; reprint, New Haven: Yale University Press, 1964), pp. 186–87.

21. Father Washington was brought out of retirement to head it, but Inspector General Alexander Hamilton held the real power. Theodore J. Crackel, *Mr. Jefferson's Army: Politics and Social Reform in the Military Establishment, 1801–1809* (New York: New York University Press, 1987).

22. William H. Powell, *List of Officers of the Army of the United States from 1779 to 1900* (1900; reprint, Detroit: Gale Research, 1967), p. 38.

23. Congressional Act of April 27, 1798, Harold C. Syrett, ed., *The Papers of Alexander Hamilton*, 26 vols. (New York: Columbia University Press, 1961–1975).

CHAPTER TWO: CAPT. JOHN McCLALLEN

1. The slot John stepped into had belonged to a Massachusetts gunner in the war for independence. Thomas H. S. Hamersly, *Complete Regular Army Register of the United States for One Hundred Years 1779–1879* (Washington: T. H. S. Hamersly, 1880), p. 47; Francis B. Heitman, *Historical Register and Dictionary of the United States Army from Its Organization, September 29, 1789, to March 2, 1903* (1903; reprint, Urbana: University of Illinois Press, 1965), p. 655.

2. On January 2, 1798, the New York legislature appointed Robert McClallen state treasurer in place of Gerard Banker, who had filled the office for many years. Joel Munsel, comp., *The Annals of Albany*, 10 vols. (Albany: Joel Munsell, 1871), 4:291, 310.

3. Edmund Banks Smith, *Governor's Island: Its Military History under Three Flags, 1637–1913* (New York: self-published, 1913; Google Books Digitization, 2006). Even in garrison, officers and their families made sacrifices to the defense of the nation. Captain Frye buried a child there on September 27, 1798, and Maj. Constant Freeman on August 5, 1799.

4. In 1797 Maj. Adam Hoops was a surveyor for Robert Morris in the ceded Indian land grab that became infamous as Holland Land Company.

5. Enclosure, McClallen to McHenry, March 11, 1799, in McHenry to Hamilton, March 16, 1799, letter book p. 142, Hamilton Papers, Library of Congress.

6. Harold C. Syrett, ed., *The Papers of Alexander Hamilton*, 26 vols. (New York: Columbia University Press, 1961–1975), 23:75.

7. Service there had been Meriwether Lewis's first military experience.

8. Captain Frye had fallen afoul of Major Hoops over an unauthorized assumption of authority at Fort Jay. The court-martial had been postponed until evidence could be obtained from another witness. McClallen's per diem of $32 was paid from March 17 to April 1.

9. Certification of payment to Washington Morton and Samuel B. Malcolm for services as judge advocates for court-martial in New York; trial of Capt. Frederick Frye, Dr. Osborn, and Captain Cockran, March 21, 1800. Frye file, http://wardepartmentpapers.org/. Frye survived and was still in command at Fort Mifflin in October 1800. He was honorably discharged on June 1, 1802, and died June 30, 1828. Heitman, *Historical Register,* 1:439.

10. McClallen to Hamilton, Philadelphia, April 4, 1799, Syrett, *Hamilton Papers,* 22:117.

11. One of several officers reported to have beaten a dissident newspaperman in Reading was Lt. Zebulon Montgomery Pike, who was twenty in 1799 when he was commissioned a first lieutenant in the First Infantry Regiment, stationed in western Pennsylvania.

12. Enclosure, McClallen to McHenry, March 11, 1799, in McHenry to Hamilton, March 16, 1799; statement of subsistence for Capt. McClallen's company from July 1, 1799, to March 31, 1800, inclusive. Syrett, *Hamilton Papers,* 22:610.

13. *Greenleaf's New York Journal,* March 7, 1798.

14. *Albany's Historic [State] Street* (Albany: National Savings Bank, 1918), p. 21.

15. Spending a year on recruiting duty may seem extensive, but McClallen's parallel as an officer, Meriwether Lewis, spent most of the first six years of his army career recruiting around his hometown.

16. Theodore J. Crackel, *Mr. Jefferson's Army; Politics and Social Reform in the Military Establishment, 1801–1809* (New York: New York University Press, 1987), pp. 29–30. Three marine officers were so offended by Randolph's comments that they cornered him in the theater and gave him a roughing up.

17. Ibid., pp. 18–33.

18. Syrett, *Hamilton Papers,* 24:334, 379.

19. General James Wilkinson's Order Book, December 31, 1796–March 8, 1808, NARA RG 94, Records of the Adjutant General's Office, M0654 [hereafter WOB], roll 3, p. 254; Crackel, *Mr. Jefferson's Army,* pp. 31–33. The wording should be taken to mean recent, as Captain Frye was not honorably discharged until June 1, 1802, and lived until the end of January 1828. It appears that the men McClallen recruited in Albany were reassigned to Captain Reid and sent to Pittsburgh.

20. According to WOB, the commission of Capt. Meriwether Lewis was dated February 16, 1801, but William H. Powell gives it as December 5, 1800. See *List of Officers of the Army of the United States from 1779 to 1900* (1900; reprint, Detroit: Gale Research, 1967).

21. Jefferson to James Wilkinson, Washington, February 25, 1801, Donald Jackson, ed., *Letters of the Lewis and Clark Expedition, with Related Documents: 1783–1854*, 2nd ed., 2 vols. (Urbana: University of Illinois Press, 1978), 1:1.

22. The evaluation of the president's intention comes from Crackel, *Mr. Jefferson's Army*, or from Donald Jackson, *Thomas Jefferson and the Stoney Mountains: Exploring the West from Monticello* (Urbana: University of Illinois Press, 1981), pp. 119–21.

23. Donald Jackson, "Jefferson, Meriwether Lewis, and the Reduction of the United States Army," *Proceedings of the American Philosophical Society* 125, no. 2 (April 1980): 91–96.

24. WOB, Fort Adams, November 29, 1801. Having narrowly escaped elimination himself during consideration of the new establishment, General Wilkinson wrote Aaron Burr from Fort Wilkinson near the mouth of the Ohio River on May 6, 1802, that he had half a mind to throw in his commission. Mary Jo Kline, ed., *Political Correspondence and Public Papers of Aaron Burr*, 2 vols. (Princeton, NJ: Princeton University Press, 1983), 2:720–21.

25. "Officer's Roster, July 14, 1801," Library of Congress Manuscript Division, Jefferson Papers, items 19697–99, 19705; Web site version, "Discovering Lewis and Clark, Evaluations of the Army's Officers," www.lewis-clark.org.

26. Fowle had been accepted on February 20, 1799, but the Senate postponed that "for inquiry" until February 23.

27. WOB, roll 3, pp. 340–41.

28. William E. Birkhimer, *Historical Sketch of the Organization, Administration, Matériel and Tactics of the Artillery, United States Army* (1884; reprint, New York: Greenwood Press, 1968), pp. 355–56.

29. After being transferred to the redesignated Regiment of Artillery on April 1, 1802, Lieutenant Fowle resigned his commission on November 27, 1802. Heitman, *Historical Register*, 1:432.

30. After spending a number of years in South Carolina, William Calhoun, the eldest son of Mayor James Calhoun, returned to Baltimore in 1803. He died five years later at Summerhill, the home of James Buchanan. *Baltimore Federal Gazette*, June 29, 1808, in Robert Barnes, *Marriages and Deaths from Baltimore Newspapers, 1796–1816* (Baltimore: Genealogical Publishing, 1978), p. 49.

31. Wilbur F. Coyle, *The Mayors of Baltimore* (Baltimore: reprinted from *Baltimore Municipal Journal*, 1919), pp. 9–13. Ann Calhoun died in March 1799 and her husband in 1816. The funeral procession for the former mayor started from his home on Baltimore Street. *Baltimore Federal Gazette*, August 14, 1816.

32. Another figure who John might have met socially was Joseph Alston, who had married Aaron Burr's daughter Theodosia on February 2, 1801.

33. It would not have meant much to McClallen at that time that Montreal fur-trade interests had been trying to break into the China trade for several years and were already considering a scheme to send ships to the mouth of the Columbia.

34. Captain McClallen received $40 a month with no allowance for forage, and three rations a day. His total annual compensation was $633.30. "Military Establishment, 1st Regt Arts & Engs, 1802," US Congress, *American State Papers: Miscellaneous* (Washington: Gales & Seaton, 1834), 37:380.

CHAPTER THREE: GEN. JAMES WILKINSON

1. During the years 1799 to 1802 the assessment rolls of Albany First Ward show the decline of McClallen's real estate holdings from $5,621 to $2,000, and his personal property from $732 to $600.

2. A four-page supplement in the *Albany Centinal*, November 27, 1803, recounted Robert McCallen's statement of his public and private concerns, supported by eleven certificates and vouchers.

3. Joel Munsell, comp., *Annuals of Albany*, 10 vols. (Albany, NY: J. Munsell, 1850–59), 4:291, 310. The state treasurer held the funds that were dispersed by the comptroller. Comptroller Samuel Jones had taken office a year before McClallen's appointment and ran up a debt of seventy-three thousand dollars borrowed from the Bank of New York and from the Bank of Albany (of which Robert McClallen was a director). Those were years when the state had to finance the defense of New York Harbor, other public works projects, and the payment of Indian annuities, which all required larger sums of money than McClallen was accustomed to handling.

4. "Robert McClallen," Colonial Albany Social History Project, http://nysm.nysed.gov/.

5. Munsell, *Annuals of Albany*, 5:234–35. This may explain the difficulty in recovering information.

6. John McCallen remained closely connected to the Albany family through recruiting visits in 1794/95 and 1799/1800 and through furloughs for family business in 1798 and 1805/06. Some final connection fixed the date May 22, 1808, firmly in family memory.

7. Theodore J. Crackel, *Mr. Jefferson's Army: Politics and Social Reform in the Military Establishment, 1801–1809* (New York: New York University Press, 1987), pp. 90, 206n53. At Fort Jay in early August Capt. George Inglesol also wrestled with the substitution of beer for spirits. At Fort Johnson, Constant

Freeman tried to head off the men's reaction by pointing out the price of Philadelphia beer in Charleston.

8. Jefferson to Congress, January 18, 1803. The instructions to Lewis read "…have conferences with the natives on the subject of commercial intercourse, get admission among them for our traders as others are admitted, agree on convenient deposits for an interchange of articles, and return with the information acquired in the course of two summers." Control of that alternative might even bleed off some of the British interior trade.

9. Both articles were reprinted in the Fredericktown *Hornet* of July 19, 1803.

10. Clarence E. Carter, ed., *Territorial Papers of the United States*, vols. 13–14, *The Territory of Louisiana-Missouri 1806–1814* (Washington, DC: Government Printing Office, 1949) [hereafter *TP*], 13:9–10.

11. Fort Adams on the Mississippi River below present Natchez was the US port of entry before the purchase.

12. General Order, April 1801.

13. General James Wilkinson's Order Book, December 31, 1796–March 8, 1808, NARA RG 94, Records of the Adjutant General's Office, M0654 [hereafter WOB], roll 3, Headquarters, Fort Adams, May 25, 1803, p. 399.

14. The general had been retained when other officers were eliminated, perhaps because his wife was a Philadelphia Biddle whose family had connections to Vice President Aaron Burr.

15. WOB, roll 3, pp. 399, 448.

16. Selected letters sent 1800–1806, Records of the War Department, Office of the Secretary of War.

17. Cushing to McClallen, March 2, 1804, NARA RG94, M185, roll 2.

18. The detachment made good time as Lt. Clarence Mulford witnessed the agency and power of attorney of Captain Lewis to Captain Stoddard on May 16, 1804. Donald Jackson, ed., *Letters of the Lewis and Clark Expedition, with Related Documents: 1783–1854*, 2nd ed., 2 vols. (Urbana: University of Illinois, 1978) [hereafter *Letters of L&C*], 2:191.

19. The administration feared that might be combined with a naval attack upon New Orleans. That was what Vice President Aaron Burr would propose to the British minister before August 6, 1804.

20. WOB, p. 489. On July 11 Vice President Aaron Burr killed Alexander Hamilton over political excesses related to the campaign. Burr fled to Philadelphia, where newspapers had the story by July 14 and the nearby Reading paper on July 17. But the Fredericktown *Hornet* had not picked up the news on July 17.

21. Dearborn to Hook, War Department, July 18, 1804, *Letters of L&C*, 1:203.

22. Thanks to Jon Kukla for a description of the celebrations in *A Wilderness So Immense* (New York: Knopf, 2003), pp. 333–35.

23. Perhaps White Sulphur Springs in modern West Virginia, noted since 1795 for elegance and decorum.

24. Wilkinson to Dearborn, October 25, 1804, Carter, *Territorial Papers*, 13:243–44.

25. Bruff to Wilkinson, St. Louis, September 29, 1804, *TP*, 13:60.

26. Once infected by the parasite, the host would carry it forever. The subject of malaria is explored more fully in Thomas C. Danisi and John C. Jackson, *Meriwether Lewis* (Amherst, NY: Prometheus Books, 2009), pp. 307–25.

27. James O'Fallon to Bryan Bruin, from Gen. Clark, December 21, 1790, in Lawrence Kinnaird, ed., *Spain in the Mississippi Valley, 1765–1794*, pt. 2, *Post War Decade, 1782–1791* (Washington, DC: Government Printing Office, 1946), pp. 397–98. Actually, whatever Wilkinson did was worth $9,640 to Spain six years later.

28. When the quasi war with postrevolutionary France required a build-up of the army, Inspector General Alexander Hamilton recommended that President Adams advance Wilkinson to the rank of major general, and General Washington had agreed, as "it would feed his ambition, soothe his vanity, and by avoiding discontent, produce the good effect you contemplate."

29. For a general background see John Edward Weems, *Men without Countries: Three Adventurers of the Early Southwest* (Boston: Houghton Mifflin, 1969).

30. Taken generally from Crackel, *Mr. Jefferson's Army*, pp. 101–104. This may have been the beginning of Wilkinson's impression of the possibility of military action against the Spanish Interior Provinces.

31. The amount was $12,000 in bribes and $8,640 to reimburse Wilkinson for what he had previously done to "retard, disjoint and defeat the mediated irruption of General George Rogers Clark in Louisiana." Kukla, *Wilderness So Immense*, p. 180.

32. "Reflections on Louisiana by Vincente Folch," in James Alexander Robertson, *Louisiana under the Rule of Spain, France and the United States, 1785–1807* (Cleveland: Arthur H. Clark, 1911), pp. 325–47.

33. It has been suggested that Wilkinson immediately approached Spanish officers about the twenty thousand dollars in arrears, but it was not until March 12, 1804, that he wrote Casa Calvo that he would submit his "Observations" in exchange for a cash payment of twelve thousand pesos in lieu of the neglected pension. However, at the beginning of the year the pension had been raised to four thousand pesos and Casa Calvo forwarded the

proposal to Pedro Cevallos, Spanish first secretary of state, on March 30. Wilkinson to Casa Calvo, March 12, 1804; Casa Calvo to Cevallos, March 30, 1804, in Thomas Perkins Abernethy, *The Burr Conspiracy* (New York: Oxford University Press, 1954), pp. 11–13.

34. Ibid. Wilkinson had the Mexican Association of three hundred men in New Orleans in mind, who were dedicated to the overthrow of the vice regency in Mexico.

35. Dan L. Flores, *Jefferson & Southwestern Exploration: The Freeman & Custis Accounts of the Red River Expedition of 1806* (Norman: University of Oklahoma Press, 1984), pp. 81–83 and note for sources. Although the full "Observations and Reflections" concerns broader international implications, historical focus has concentrated on this suggestion. Ironically, on March 31, 1804, Dearborn wrote Wilkinson announcing plans for the Dunbar exploration of the Red River and the need to provide a military escort. *TP*, 13:27.

36. Shortly after returning from the upper Missouri, the Indian trader Regis Loisel warned the Spanish administrator still in St. Louis of the danger. Former lieutenant governor Delassus forwarded a letter to Casa Calvo at New Orleans. By the time these warnings were received, the expedition was beyond interception. Loisel to Delassus, St. Louis, May 28, 1804; Delassus to Casa Calvo, St. Louis, September 1, 1804, in Abraham P. Nasatir, ed., *Before Lewis and Clark: Documents Illustrating the History of the Missouri 1785–1804*, 2 vols. (1952; reprint, Lincoln: University of Nebraska Press, 1990), 2:735–40, 736n1.

37. "Reflections on Louisiana" was incorrectly attributed to Folch in Robertson, *Louisiana under the Rule of Spain*, p. 343.

38. Wilkinson to Casa Calvo, March 12, 1804, in Abernethy, *Burr Conspiracy*, p. 11. Gilbert Leonard was a confidant in New Orleans who in 1796 helped pass a payment of $9,640 on to Wilkinson.

39. *Hamilton Papers*, 26:217. The letter traveled by Walter Burling, a county judge of Mississippi Territory, who was another of Wilkinson's circle of adherents. Two years later Burling carried another of Wilkinson's letters to Mexico City.

40. Wilkinson used part of the twelve-thousand-peso payment he received to buy 107 hogsheads of sugar, which he shipped to New York on April 25, 1804.

41. This appears to be the arrears for his previous service to the Spanish.

42. Abernethy, *Burr Conspiracy*, p. 15.

43. Pedro Cevallos, commandant of the Interior Provinces, reported from New Orleans on September 24, 1804, that he had just received a letter from "the subject known as number 13," forwarding a Washington news item of June

18 that reported that Mr. Monroe and Mr. Pinckney were in Madrid negotiating details of the boundary question. Nasatir, *Before Lewis and Clark*, 2:753.

44. Donald Jackson, ed., *The Journals of Zebulon Montgomery Pike with Letters and Related Documents*, 2 vols. (Norman: University of Oklahoma Press, 1966) [hereafter *Pike Journals*], 1:233, 452–53, 455; 2:368nn1, 4.

45. This is drawn from Milton Lomask, *Aaron Burr: The Conspiracy and Years in Exile 1805–1836* (New York: Farrar, Straus & Giroux, 1982), pp. 26–27, 34, 42.

46. *TP*, 13:40.

47. Anonymous letter dated St. Louis, November 4, 1804, *TP*, 13:70–71.

48. Flores, *Jefferson & Southwestern Exploration*, pp. 77–81.

49. *TP*, 13:59.

50. Morrison and his brothers enjoyed the financial support of their uncle Guy Bryan, a Philadelphia merchant. In late 1803, Lewis and Clark met Bryan on his way to Kaskaskia with an outfit for Morrison's store.

51. A & R Steele to Beckenridge, December 10, 1804, Beckenridge Papers, Library of Congress in Isaac Joslin Cox, "Opening the Santa Fe Trail," *Missouri Historical Review* 2, no.1 (October 1930): 34.

52. James Morton Smith, ed., *The Republic of Letters: The Correspondence of Thomas Jefferson and James Madison 1776–1826*, 3 vols. (New York: Norton, 1995), 3:1365. Browne was the former brother-in-law of Aaron Burr. Those were recess appointments that would need to be confirmed by the Senate.

CHAPTER FOUR: FLOATING INTO THE WEST

1. Dearborn to Gates, February 22, 1805, in Theodore J. Crackel, *Mr. Jefferson's Army: Politics and Social Reform in the Military Establishment, 1801–1809* (New York: New York University Press, 1987), p. 93n66.

2. Extract from Captain George Peter's deposition, in James Wilkinson, *Memoirs of My Own Times*, 3 vols. (Philadelphia: Abraham Small, 1816; reprint, New York: AMS Press, 1973), 2:cxvi. General Wilkinson had been close with Burr since returning from New Orleans by ship. For details see Dan L. Flores, *Jefferson & Southwestern Exploration: The Freeman & Custis Accounts of the Red River Expedition of 1806* (Norman: University of Oklahoma Press, 1984), pp. 77–78n121.

3. "Deposition of James Calhoun, Jr.," in Wilkinson, *Memoirs*, 2: cxvi. Calhoun was called during the 1810 trial of General Wilkinson and showed that McClallen's property and expenses were kept separate from the shipment of General Wilkinson's personal property.

4. Calhoun & Lamot received this cargo on June 6, 1805. By December

they expanded the business to include five tons of pig lead from the Missouri mines. On February 26, 1806, they received twenty hogsheads of sugar. "Abstracts of merchandise entered at the Baltimore Custom House," reported in the *Baltimore Price-Current.*

5. At least one other Baltimore interest was operating in St. Louis. P. [Peregrine] Falconer and John G. Comegys was a branch of the Baltimore house C. and John G. Comegys.

6. "Deposition of James Calhoun Jr." The explanation was given several years after the fact.

7. Calhoun deposition, ca. 1810–11, also in Ezekiel Bacon (chairman), *Report of the Committee Appointed to Inquire into the Conduct of General Wilkinson* (Washington, DC: United States Congress, House of Representatives, 1811), pp. 531–33.

8. Data on the Missouri River Indian trade from Lewis and Clark was not available until Wilkinson and McClallen reached Fort Massac.

9. Six years later, James Calhoun Jr. provided testimony to those investigating the conduct of General Wilkinson and tried to take pressure off that officer. The presumption that the general was a shadow investor is unproven, although it is tempting to speculate that some of the funds paid to Number 13 might have been used to finance the opening of trade to Santa Fe.

10. "Return of Troops destined to St. Louis on the Mississippi, or the Vicinity of that Command, Head Quarters Washington, March 1805," James Wilkinson Letters, 1757–1825, Chicago Historical Society.

11. Aaron Burr had hoped for the appointment of governor of Orleans Territory. With General Wilkinson in the role as military commandant and civil governor of the northern half of Louisiana, they would present a unified frontier abutting Spanish territory. When Burr's appointment failed to come through, he wrote Wilkinson in April to confirm their previously planned meeting at Pittsburgh. Burr suggested that his former brother-in-law Mr. Browne and the surveyor Charles Lauss would comply with any orders from Wilkinson. Burr saw no reason to correspond in cipher.

12. Some men may have been taken from Lieutenant Hooke, who was being promoted to captain and would stay at Pittsburgh to recruit the rest of his company.

13. United States Congress, *American State Papers, Miscellaneous* (Washington, DC: Gales & Seaton, 1834), 38:114. The military agent Moses Hooke paid $199.65 for Wilkinson's boat, and a total of $262.96 for cartage from Washington City, Philadelphia, and Baltimore. He was soon promoted to captain and ordered to recruit a company.

14. May 7, 1805, at Pittsburgh, General James Wilkinson's Order Book, December 31, 1796–March 8, 1808, NARA RG 94, Records of the Adjutant General's Office, M0654 [hereafter WOB], roll 1, pp. 539, 541. On May 11 Lt. James Biddle Wilkinson, the general's son, was appointed his adjutant, but apparently only for the trip, as Lt. Daniel Hughes assumed that duty at St. Louis.

15. "Calhoun's Testimony," Wilkinson, *Memoirs.*

16. When Captain Daniel Bissell at Fort Massac was reassigned to Fort Adams, he threatened to resign rather than serve in a southern post. Unwilling to lose "an officer of experience, resource and hardihood," the general would send a less-favored officer, Captain John Campbell, to that fate. Wilkinson to Dearborn, St. Louis, July 27, 1805, in Clarence E. Carter, ed., *Territorial Papers of the United States*, vols. 13–14, *The Territory of Louisiana-Missouri 1806–1814* (Washington, DC: Government Printing Office, 1949) [hereafter *TP*], 14:167.

17. WOB, roll 3, pp. 399, 401, 448, 539.

18. *TP*, 13:109, 127.

19. Wilkinson informed Dearborn that the boats were fully loaded, "that on which my private property and Family are embarked having on Board six field pieces and other Public Property to the amount of ten tonnes." Ibid., 13:134.

20. First Lt. James Wilkinson, Second Infantry Regiment, had been appointed aide-de-camp to the general in chief (his father) on December 1, 1804.

21. Lt. Benjamin Wilkinson had been with the general as paymaster at the Choctaw Treaty in late 1801, as was the aide-de-camp Lt. J. B. Walbach. The lieutenant had resigned his commission. *Senate Journal*, March 24, 1804.

22. *TP*, 13:135. The uniforms were being held for the recruiting service.

23. Benjamin Hovey moved from his Massachusetts birthplace to Tioga County in 1790. He served with Burr in the twenty-first session of the New York Assembly and was commissioned brigadier general of the militia in 1802. Hovey and his son-in-law James Glover appear to have been land speculators in Ohio or Indiana. Burr recommended Glover for appointment in the Republican spoils following the 1801 election based on his intention of moving into the Ohio Country. Mary-Jo Kline, ed., *Political Correspondence and Public Papers of Aaron Burr*, 2 vols. (Princeton, NJ: Princeton University Press, 1983), 1:542, 545, 567; 2:934–35. On January 17, 1805, General Hovey and several associates petitioned Congress for a grant of twenty-five thousand acres of land to finance the construction of a canal around the falls of the Ohio River. Thomas Perkins Abernethy, *The Burr Conspiracy* (New York: Oxford University Press, 1954), p. 22.

24. Extract from Captain George Peter's deposition, Wilkinson, *Memoirs* 2:lxvii. There might have been a bit more than that to the meeting. In coming down the Ohio ahead of the government party, Aaron Burr had stopped in Cincinnati to confer with Senator John Smith and Jonathan Dayton, who were interested in the canal project. It was arranged that the canal company would put up a subscription for funds and Burr immediately borrowed twenty-five thousand dollars against that as-yet-uncollected capital. McClallen's warning about Hovey suggests that he was unaware of those developments. For background see Buckner F. Melton Jr., *Aaron Burr: Conspiracy to Treason* (New York: John Wiley, 2002), pp. 74, 76–77.

25. US Congress, *American State Papers: Miscellaneous*, 37:116–19. Peter also stated that the goods were shipped from Fort Massac to St. Louis in public boats, which required an additional boat for the public property. But in a later hearing James Calhoun presented the bill by which McClallen paid for the services of the river guide, J. Lorimer.

26. Abernethy, *Burr Conspiracy*, p. 28. Burr carried letters of introduction to Wilkinson's old New Orleans connection, Daniel Clark, to the lingering Spanish functionary, the Marquis de Casa Calvo, and to Gilbert Leonard, one of the few men who knew the identity of Number 13.

27. As it turned out Colonel Butler died in September and Colonel Thomas H. Cushing took command of the Second Infantry Regiment. Major A. Y. Nicoli became the new adjutant general, but Wilkinson kept him close to headquarters in St. Louis.

28. Promoted to major of artillery in 1803, Bruff was sent west in the spring of 1804 to be military commandant of the Department of Upper Louisiana while his predecessor, Captain Stoddard, retained the duties of civil commandant.

29. US Congress, *American State Papers: Miscellaneous*, 37:577. Wilkinson wrote that he was tired of army service and was looking for a "snug fixture, and to hang up his sword."

30. Warfington's expedition pay ended on June 1, and he was under command to return to Captain Campbell's company. He reached Fort Massac by June 19 when Lt. John Brahan issued him some articles of uniform clothing.

31. *Aurora General Advertiser*, Philadephia, July 9, 1805; *National Aegis*, Worcester, Massachusetts, July 17, 1805; *The Bee*, Hudson, New York, July 23; *Republican Spy*, July 23; *Connecticut Courant*, July 31.

32. *American Citizen*, New York, July 17, 1805. Ironically, the Spanish officer Casa Calvo had a copy of the Lexington story at New Orleans by July 19. That must have come to him on the boat that General Wilkinson provided to carry Burr and a delegation of officers to New Orleans.

33. One may have been Private John Boley, who would soon be assigned to accompany Lt. Zebulon Montgomery Pike.

34. That raises an interesting question, as only barges had been mentioned leaving Pittsburgh. Although the Corps of Discovery keelboat had been sent to assist another military detachment in ascending the Mississippi to St. Louis, it is possible that the general changed orders and reassigned it to McClallen.

35. According to a later statement, McClallen hired the experienced pilot J. Lorimore to take his boat and cargo from Cape Girardeau to St. Louis. "Deposition of James Calhoun, Jr.," in Wilkinson, *Memoirs*, 2:cxvi. But Calhoun's statement is suspect, as McClallen was traveling on a government boat and had no reason to provide a private pilot. The twenty-five-dollar charge may have applied to the second voyage.

36. "The Arrival of General Wilkinson at St. Louis," *Republican Watch-Tower*, New York, September 7, 1805. The three-month-old news item probably enlarged upon the facts.

37. Designated for Fort Adams, Second Lt. William P. Clyma of Campbell's company, Second Infantry, survived that service and was promoted to first lieutenant on July 20, 1806. Captain Richmond and another subaltern also shared a tent.

38. The companies of Captain Richmond and Captain Lewis had been transferred from the Detroit area. Wilkinson to Colonel Thomas Hunt, Pittsburgh, May 6, 1805, General Daniel Bissell Papers, Special Collection M-9, University of Missouri at St. Louis/Mercantile Library collections. Captain Campbell's Company came from South West Point in Tennessee.

39. WOB, roll 3, pp. 548, 552. Oddly, the date of the celebration is given as July 6.

40. McClallen and Campbell remained in St. Louis until July 25 or 26. Although on detached duty in the West, Capt. Meriwether Lewis was still considered an infantry company commander.

41. Versions of the construction of the Indian Trade Factory give the supervision of the project to Lt. Colonel Jacob Kingsbury of the First Infantry Regiment.

42. The Ohioan Benjamin Lockwood was a veteran of the old Legion and Indian wars who transferred to the First Infantry Regiment in September 1802 and was dead by July 29, 1807. The infantry company he commanded was actually designated as that of Meriwether Lewis, whom the president requested to continue on the army list while serving as his secretary. In the same form, Second Lt. William Clark was carried on duty at Michilimackinac

when he was in the West. Like McClallen, James Richmond was a New Yorker, a veteran of the Legion who made captain in 1801 and was transferred to the First Infantry during the 1802 reorganization. On August 11, 1806, he was killed in a duel near Fort Adams. John Campbell may have been a Virginian whose career began in 1797 and who made captain in 1803. He lived to serve in the War of 1812 and was a lieutenant colonel at his discharge in 1815. Francis B. Heitman, *Historical Register and Dictionary of the United States Army from Its Organization, September 29, 1789, to March 2, 1903*, 2 vols. (Washington, DC: Government Printing Office, 1903; reprint, Urbana: University of Illinois Press, 1965), pp. 278, 638, 829. It was Campbell's company that Corporal Warfington was trying to rejoin, so his experiences in ascending and descending the Missouri from the Mandan villages were available to General Wilkinson and his officers after leaving Fort Massac.

CHAPTER FIVE: THE OFFICERS AND GENTLEMEN OF ST. LOUIS

1. Wilkinson to Dearborn, Fort Massac, June 13, 1805, Donald Jackson, ed., *Letters of the Lewis and Clark Expedition, with Related Documents 1783–1854*, 2nd ed., 2 vols. (Urbana: University of Illinois Press, 1978) [hereafter *Letters of L&C*], 2:690.

2. Wilkinson to Secretary of War Dearborn, Fort Massac, June 13, 1805, Clarence E. Carter, ed., *Territorial Papers of the United States*, vols. 13–14, *The Territory of Louisiana-Missouri 1806–1814* (Washington, DC: Government Printing Office, 1949) [hereafter *TP*], 13:688–90.

3. Lt. Zebulon Pike was not a raw beginner in western interests. From his post at Kaskaskia he had forwarded geographical data to Dr. Samuel Latham Mitchell, representative from New York, which the House Committee on Commerce and Manufactures reported in February 1804.

4. General James Wilkinson's Order Book, December 31, 1796–March 8, 1808, NARA RG 94, Records of the Adjutant General's Office, M0654 [hereafter WOB].

5. Instructions of Governor Wilkinson to Pierre Chouteau, *TP*, 13:184.

6. Alexander Mackenzie, *Voyages from Montreal on the River St. Laurence through the Continent of North American to the Frozen and Pacific Oceans in the Years 1789 and 1793* (London: R. Noble, 1801; reprint, Readex Microprint Corporation, 1966), pp. 397–412.

7. Maj. James Bruff bought a copy of Mackenzie's *Voyages* on September

15, 1804. Campbell Account Book, Missouri Historical Society. It was an odd item to have in stock in St. Louis.

8. From the 1798 survey by David Thompson, Mackenzie understood that the old line of the 49th degree fell short of Missouri.

9. Enclosure, Bruff to Wilkinson, St. Louis, September 29, 1804, in Wilkinson to Secretary of War, Washington, November 2, 1804, *TP*, 13:59.

10. Bruff to Wilkinson, St. Louis, May 28, 1805 in Wilkinson to Dearborn, Massac, June 15, 1805, *TP*, 13:135.

11. "The Number of Officers & Men for to protect the Indian trade and Keep the Savages at peace with the U. S. and each other, if Soldiers act as Boatmen & Soldiers would require at the Cheyenne River 640 miles from Council Bluffs, a Captain, a Lieutenant, an Ensign, one Sergeant Major, three Interpreters, four Sergeants, four Corporals, four Music and seventy-five privates. At the Rochejone River five hundred miles above there should be an agent, a Captain, an Ensign, a Sergeant Major, four interpreters, three Sergeants, three Corporals, three Music and forty-five privates. Completing the interdiction of the Missouri at the great falls another seven hundred miles above would require a Lieutenant, a Sergeant Major, two interpreters, two Sergeants, one Corporal, one Music and thirty men. The Number of Officers & Men for to protect the Indian trade and Keep the Savages at peace with the U. S. and each other," in Gary E. Moulton, ed., *The Journals of the Lewis and Clark Expedition*, 13 vols. (Lincoln: University of Nebraska Press, 1983–2001) [hereafter *Journals of L&C*], 3:377.

12. Wilkinson to Dearborn, Massac, June 15, 1805, *TP*, 13:135.

13. Ibid.

14. Wilkinson to Secretary of War, St. Louis, July 27, 1805, *TP*, 13:160, 163.

15. Wilkinson to Secretary of State, St. Louis, August 24, 1805, WOB, M221, roll 2, frame 0603–0607 1/2.

16. Wilkinson to Secretary of State Madison, St. Louis, August 24, 1805.

17. Wilkinson to Officers of the Territory, August 22, 1805, Proclamation, August 26, 1805, *TP*, 13:188–91.

18. Wilkinson to Madison, August 24, 1805, *TP*, 13:189–91.

19. Donald Jackson, ed., *The Journals of Zebulon Montgomery Pike with Letters and Related Documents*, 2 vols. (Norman: University of Oklahoma Press, 1966) [hereafter *Pike Journals*], 2:15, 17–18.

20. This is mostly gleaned from David Lavender, *Fist in the Wilderness* (New York: Doubleday, 1964), chaps. 4 and 5.

21. Meriwether Lewis recalled in 1807 that John McClallen told him, "… the house with which he was concerned was ready to embark largely in the

fur trade of the Missouri, provided it should appear to him to offer advantages to them. That since he had arrived in Louisiana, which was last autumn, he had endeavoured to inform himself of the state of this trade, and that from his inquiries he had been so fully impressed with the disadvantages it laboured under from the free admission of the British merchants, he had written to his house in Baltimore, advising that they should not embark in this trade unless those merchants were prohibited from entering the river." Meriwether Lewis, "Observations and Reflections," in *Letters of L&C*, 2:709–10.

22. Ten years before when James Mackay outfitted John Evans to ascend the Missouri, he told him to watch for an animal that "had only one horn on its forehead." Somehow, antelope and the French name Grosse Horn had become entwined. Wilkinson was talking about the Big Horn.

23. Wilkinson to Dearborn, St. Louis, September 8, 1805, *TP*, 13:199.

24. Delassus to Casa Calvo, St. Louis, August 10, 1804, in Abraham P. Nasatir, ed., *Before Lewis and Clark: Documents Illustrating the History of the Missouri 1785–1804* (St. Louis: St. Louis Historical Documents Foundation, 1952; reprint, Lincoln: University of Nebraska Press, 1990), pp. 742–45. Delassus was concerned that Major Bruff was asking questions about the shortest routes to New Mexico and Santa Fe, where some American merchants were already sending small outfits.

25. The scene that follows is speculative and used as a means of deepening the background.

26. For background see William E. Foley and C. David Rice, *The First Chouteaus: River Barons of Early St. Louis* (Urbana and Chicago: University of Illinois Press, 1983).

27. He shipped beaver worth £2273/15/4 1/12 in Halifax currency to Montreal for sale in 1803.

28. Auguste Chouteau was also sending peltry to New Orleans. Chouteau Papers, Missouri Historical Society.

29. By June 6, McClallen's backers, Calhoun & Lamot, had received their first consignment of three bales of peltry from New Orleans. That does not mean the peltry came from Chouteau but was likely shipped by the newly established western operations of the Baltimore-based Comegys & Falconer.

30. Chouteau provided that information and advice to Lt. John Armstrong in 1790. John Armstrong Memorandum, folder 6, box 2, Collection M0006, Indiana Historical Society.

31. The very interesting career of James Mackay is treated in W. Raymond Wood, *Prologue to Lewis & Clark: The Mackay and Evans Expedition* (Norman: University of Oklahoma Press, 2003).

32. For one thing, double agents do not accept checks. In the past Wilkinson hauled specie from Spanish payments back to Kentucky on mules. In 1794, when Baron Carondelet tried to send six thousand dollars to Wilkinson in 1794, the shipment was concealed in kegs barged up the Mississippi. Wilkinson's agent was killed, but Wilkinson and his associates managed to cover up the incriminating circumstances. An overland merchant might bring back his profit in gold or silver. Dale van Every, *Ark of Empire: The American Frontier 1784–1803* (1963; reprint, New York: Arno Press, 1977), p. 317n1.

CHAPTER SIX: WESTERN HORIZONS

1. Wilkinson to Jefferson, St. Louis, October 22, 1805, November 6, 1805, Clarence E. Carter, ed., *Territorial Papers of the United States*, vols. 13–14, *The Territory of Louisiana-Missouri 1806–1814* (Washington, DC: Government Printing Office, 1949) [hereafter *TP*], 13:243, 265.

2. Dearborn to Wilkinson, War Department, February 26, 1805, in Donald Jackson, ed., *The Journals of Zebulon Montgomery Pike with Letters and Related Documents*, 2 vols. (Norman: University of Oklahoma Press, 1966) [hereafter *Pike Journals*], 2:99. The tactic had been previously suggested in 1790 when Lt. John Armstrong was ordered to explore the Missouri and its connection to a river draining into the Gulf of Mexico.

3. Ibid., 1:458–59. There is also a statement describing the passage in Pike's hand, 2:113.

4. Ibid., 1:458–59, pl. 60, 2:113.

5. Joseph Gervais may have been the man the Spanish knew as Jose Calbert and who applied for permission to settle in New Mexico.

6. M. Farfong may have been a mixed-blood descendent of Jean Lafond dit (called) Mongraine. See Tanis C. Thorne, *The Many Hands of My Relations: French and Indians on the Lower Missouri* (Columbia: University of Missouri Press, 1996), pp. 94–95.

7. The plans of Laurent Durocher and the former upper river trader Jacques d'Eglise were explained in the cover letter that the Marquis de Casa Calvo attached to a memorial from Regis Loisel. He noted that d'Eglise was supposed to go up the "Misury" but had failed to appear there. See Annie Heloise Abel, ed., *Tabeau's Narrative of Loisel's Expedition to the Upper Missouri* (Norman: University of Oklahoma Press, 1939), pp. 235–44. LaLande was detained in Santa Fe and Durocher was sent on to Chihuahua to explain himself to Governor Salcedo. Those planning another Santa Fe adventure were

unaware that in October, LaLande, Durocher, and Gervais accompanied the experienced plainsman Pedro Vial, who was sent to create a Comanche, Pawnee, or Osage barrier to American expansion.

8. Wilkinson to Dearborn, St. Louis, August 10, 1805, *TP*, 13:183. The traders were licensed by Captain Stoddard three days after he reported the departure of the Corps of Discovery. Former Spanish lieutenant governor Delassus warned that Gervais had been lined up to guide Jean Baptiste LaLande and Jeanot Meteyer, who were carrying a two-thousand-dollar outfit provided by Morrison.

9. Wilkinson to Dearborn, St. Louis, August 25, 1805, *Pike Journals*, 2:232–33.

10. Wilkinson to Dearborn, St. Louis, July 27, 1805, *TP*, 13:169. Compare to his advice to the Spanish in the "Reflections on Louisiana."

11. He was the chief of ten lodges that the Corps of Discovery encountered between the Arikara and Mandan villages. Clark called him "Ar ke tar na shar," *akitaaneesaanu*, or Chief of the Town (band chief), which appears to have been a title rather than a proper name. This was the chief who accompanied the expedition to the Mandans and Hidatsas to make peace and seek an alliance against the Sioux. In writing condolences to the tribe on the man's death, Jefferson was uncertain which of the above names was correct, finally settling on "Arketarnawhar chief of the town" after writing and crossing out "Piaketa" and "Toone" or their English versions. The Arkirara interpreter Joseph Gravelines suggested that the correct pronunciation was "Ank.e.douch.a.ro." Gary E. Moulton, ed., *The Journals of the Lewis and Clark Expedition*, 13 vols. (Lincoln: University of Nebraska Press, 1983–2001), 3:156n5.

12. As a means of communicating between tribes speaking different languages, hand signing depended on a background of shared cultural understanding and abstract limitations.

13. Wilkinson to Eustis, September 3, 1809, in Donald Jackson, *Thomas Jefferson and the Stoney Mountains: Exploring the West from Monticello* (Urbana: University of Illinois Press, 1981), pp. 99, 114. Wilkinson to Jefferson, November 5, 1805, forwarding list of articles "transmitted you by Capt. Stoddard," Thomas Jefferson Papers, General Correspondence 165–1827, Library of Congress, American Memory Web site.

14. Wilkinson to Secretary of War Dearborn, St. Louis, August 10, 1805, *TP*, 13:182–83. Wilkinson seems to have reversed the figure; the trader's map made it thirty-one days' travel to Santa Fe.

15. Before Wilkinson left Washington, Dearborn specified "As no perma-

nent Military Posts, can with propriety, be immediately established, it will be improper to incur any considerable expense, for works or buildings at present." Dearborn to Wilkinson, April 19, 1805, *TP*, 13:117.

16. Lieutenant Peter reported from the Osage villages that those tribes had no objection to a United States post in their country. Peter to Wilkinson, Osage Towns, September 8, 1805, *TP*, 13:231. But Wilkinson did not receive that letter until September 22 when Chouteau returned before Peter. Concern about a Spanish attack on New Orleans would be mooted on October 25 when the British fleet destroyed the Spanish navy at Trafalgar.

17. Wilkinson to Dearborn, St. Louis, September 8, 1805, in *Pike Journals*, 2:100. Dearborn responded on October 16, 1805, "I am fully convinced by your communication, of the practicability, if necessary, of a military movement either by the Platt, the Osage or the Arkansas, to the Eastern part of Mexico; and I am not sure that a project of that kind may not become necessary." Note p. 103.

18. Wilkinson to Dearborn (Private), St. Louis, September 8, 1805, in *Pike Journals*, 2:100–101.

19. Ibid.

20. Ibid.

21. Ibid. That was almost exactly what Number 13 predicted in March 1804. Since then the outgoing lieutenant governor of Spanish Illinois had seconded that possibility in a letter to the Marquis de Casa Calvo. He wrote that St. Louis was already awash in fine dry goods attractive to that market. Unless precautions were taken, "within a short time, one will see descending the Missouri, instead of furs, silver from the Mexican mines." Abraham P. Nasatir, ed., *Before Lewis and Clark: Documents Illustrating the History of the Missouri 1785–1804* (Norman: University of Oklahoma Press, 2002), 2:745.

22. After Burr left, it was claimed that Wilkinson considered war with Spain inevitable and ordered Bruff south to Fort Adams to prepare munitions against a possible attack on Baton Rouge. Thomas Perkins Abernethy, *The Burr Conspiracy* (Oxford: Oxford University Press, 1954; reprint, Gloucester, MA: Peter Smith, 1968), pp. 28–29, 30–31. However, the contributors to that after-the-fact assumption were men unfriendly to the Wilkinson administration. Major Bruff and Militia Major Timothy Kibby later implied that they were approached about some kind of expedition against the Spanish Interior Provinces. Judge Rufus Easton testified that Burr asked him if Maj. James Bruff might be a proper person to lead a expedition to Santa Fe. The Bruff and Kibby declarations were given at Burr's trial in an attempt to discredit Wilkinson's testimony, but by then it had been revealed that the interviews Burr had in New Orleans concerned a filibuster focused on Vera Cruz.

23. It was October or November before General Wilkinson communicated with the former vice president, although during the same period Mr. Burr sent a number of letters to him.

24. Clark to Wilkinson, August 24, 1805, in Theodore J. Crackel, *Mr. Jefferson's Army: Politics and Social Reform in the Military Establishment, 1801–1809* (New York: New York University Press, 1987), p. 114. Clark's advice to "amuse Mr. Burr" became the first step in the general's disassociation from the scheme that he and his maps had set in motion almost two years before. According to his recollection, Wilkinson gave the letter to Secretary Browne to forward to Burr. Crackel believes that Wilkinson would have been foolhardy to continue with Burr in the face of this warning, and in his study of the Freeman expedition, Dan L. Flores agrees.

25. Dearborn to Wilkinson, August 24, 1805, Wilkinson Papers, Chicago Historical Society. See Crackel, *Mr. Jefferson's Army*, pp. 114–16 or Dan L. Flores, *Southern Counterpart to Lewis & Clark: The Freeman & Custis Expedition of 1806* (Norman: University of Oklahoma Press, 1984), pp. 77–80.

26. See Crackel, *Mr. Jefferson's Army*, p. 211n211 for a fuller analysis of this denial.

27. Wilkinson to Samuel Smith, March 20, 1806, *TP*, 13: 466–67; see also pp. 333, 385, 518.

28. Isaac Joslin Cox, "Opening the Santa Fe Trail," *Missouri Historical Review* 25 (October 1930): 34. Founded in 1792, Shelbyville was about halfway between Louisville and Frankfort, Kentucky. In 1800 the population was only 262 and its business mostly supplied local farms.

29. General Wilkinson had an affinity for frontier doctors. By August 10, 1805, the same day that he was thinking about establishing a post at the Platte, the general accepted the services of Dr. John H. Robinson as post surgeon at the cantonment. Wilkinson to Dearborn, August 5, 1805, *TP*, 13:182. When Robinson arrived to tend to the sick at the camp, Captain McClallen may have learned that the surgeon's family was also very interested in western development.

30. Wilkinson to Dearborn, October 8, 1805, Donald Jackson, ed., *Letters of the Lewis and Clark Expedition, with Related Documents 1783–1854*, 2nd ed., 2 vols. (Urbana: University of Illinois Press, 1978) [hereafter *Letters of L&C*], 1:262.

31. Ibid. The time lag came into play. Initially announced on August 10, the plan was not received in Washington until September 19. Wilkinson suggested it again on September 8, but the secretary of war did not receive that until November 9. On October 16 and again on November 2 and 21, Dearborn ordered that no posts were to be established.

32. In distant Chihuahua, Mexican governor Nemisio Salcedo was trying

to respond to the scenario outlined by Number 13 and reinforced by the Missouri River trader Regis Loisel. But Spanish forces never had a realistic chance of intercepting the Corps of Discovery and the best that Salcedo could do was to try to get the lieutenant governor of Santa Fe to snare the expedition when it returned. Joaquin del Real Alencaster was instructed to utilize the services of two experienced plains travelers, Jose Calbert (Gervais) and Pierre Vial, to infiltrate the Pawnee near the mouth of the Platte and convince them to intercept and take into custody the expedition of "Captain Merri [Meriwether Lewis]," or that failing, seize the "Coffers and papers the expedition may be carrying, [for] our acquiring the papers would be a considerable advantage, without our having to use troops to intercept the expedition." Salcedo to Alencaster, Chihuahua, September 9, 1805, *Pike Journals*, 2:1805.

33. Wilkinson wrote to the secretary of war on August 25, 1805, for permission to send "a Subaltern & Party to winter with the Houteaux or Ottos, at their towns fifteen leagues up the river plate and about two leagues above an Eastern Branch called Salt River." *Pike Journals*, 2:232–33. Wilkinson's mention of the Salt River is another indication he had seen Clark's maps.

34. On November 26 General Wilkinson wrote to the secretary of war extolling the qualifications of the former hussar, Lt. John DeBarth Walbach, for promotion as "the ablest horse officer in America, not only in the choice of animals, but in equipping, training, forming, and heading them in action." Coues, *Pike Journals*, 1:xxix. It must have been about the same time that General Wilkinson requested the temporary transfer of Captain James B. Many. Many was to come from New Orleans to take command of Captain McClallen's company and arrived by January 6, 1806.

35. Wilkinson to Dearborn (Private), St. Louis, September 8, 1805, *Pike Journals*, 2:100; Dearborn to Wilkinson, October 16, 1805, *TP*, 13:240.

36. Wilkinson to Jefferson, St. Louis, October 22, 1805, *Letters of L&C*, 2:691. Was Piahito trying to get across an early impression of the Yellowstone geyser basin or just the hot spot at the mouth of the Shoshone River?

37. WOB, M221, roll 2, p. 519.

38. Wilkinson to Dearborn, November 26, 1805, RG, Letters Received by the Secretary of War, registered series 1801–1860, M566, roll 3, p. 73.

39. Ibid., p. 69.

40. Secretary of War, Registers of Letters Received January 3, 1803–January 7, 1806, NARA RG22, roll 2.

41. Timing gets critical. Dispatches from General Wilkinson left St. Louis December 31 and arrived February 6. Endorsement to Wilkinson to Dearborn, December 30, 1805, *TP*, 13:359. Lieutenant Clemson and the Arikara chief left

St. Louis on December 24 and arrived in Washington February 13. McClallen appears to have traveled ahead of both.

42. Carr later wrote, "Whilst I suffer with indignation in the base means employed by this blustering sycophant, to find out something which will heighten him in the intimation of his master, I cannot but despise him with all the majesty of contempt." William C. Carr, St. Louis, December 23, 1805, to Charles Carr, Lexington, Kentucky, Carr Family Papers, Missouri Historical Society.

CHAPTER SEVEN: VICTIMS OF CIRCUMSTANCE

1. United States Congress. Eighth Cong., 2nd Sess., Senate, December 3, 1805.

2. Wilkinson to Dearborn, December 3, 1805, NARA RG, M566, roll 1, frames 0105–0110.

3. Dearborn to Wilkinson, November 20, 1805, in Theodore J. Crackel, *Mr. Jefferson's Army: Politics and Social Reform in the Military Establishment, 1801–1809* (New York: New York University Press, 1987), p. 124n3.

4. Smith was president pro tempore of the Senate. The other John McClallen was a Maryland man who would soon be appointed United States consul at Batavia, Dutch East Indies.

5. Smith to Jefferson, Baltimore, January 20, 1806, Thomas Jefferson Papers, Series 1, General Correspondence. 1651–1827, image 315, Library of Congress American Memory.

6. "Deposition of James Calhoun, Jr.," in James Wilkinson, *Memoirs of My Own Times*, 3 vols. (Philadelphia: Abraham Small, 1816; reprint, New York: AMS Press, 1973), 2:cxvi.

7. McClallen's resignation left Major Bruff as the last of the thirty-six officers who received commissions in the Regiment of Artillerists and Engineers in 1794.

8. General James Wilkinson's Order Book, December 31, 1796–March 8, 1808, NARA RG 94, Records of the Adjutant General's Office, M0654 [hereafter WOB], p. 583. McClallen probably met the former *Hussar de Rohon* in April 1798 when the experienced veteran of the continental wars served as aide-de-camp to General William Macphearson, Inspector General Alexander Hamilton, and General Charles C. Pinckney. He was commissioned first lieutenant in the artillery regiment in February 1801 and was a lieutenant serving at Fort Jay on January 1, 1805.

9. General Wilkinson would later try to placate Peter by giving him charge of an experimental unit of light artillery, but he had made an enemy.

10. Frankfort *Palladium*, January 16, 1806, reprinted in the *Republican Star* on February 18.

11. Wilkinson to Dearborn, December 30, 1805, Clarence E. Carter, ed., *Territorial Papers of the United States*, vols. 13–14, *The Territory of Louisiana-Missouri 1806–1814* (Washington, DC: Government Printing Office, 1949) [hereafter *TP*], 13:359. Ironically, General Wilkinson's scheme fell apart due to the advice that Number 13 gave Casa Calvo and Fouche in March 1804 about protecting the Spanish Interior Provinces from American opportunists. In 1805, the experienced Spanish pathfinder Pierre Vial left Santa Fe accompanied by Morrison's missing traders LaLande, Durocher, and Gervais with orders to construct an Osage, Pawnee, or Kansa barrier to American expansion. David J. Weber, *The Taos Trappers: The Fur Trade in the Far Southwest, 1540–1846* (1968; Norman: University of Oklahoma Press, 1982), pp. 35–37.

12. Dearborn to Wilkinson, November 2 and 21, 1805; Wilkinson to Dearborn, December 10, 1805; Wilkinson to Dearborn, December 30, 1805, in *TP*, 13:251–52, 29–91, 297–99, 355; Donald Jackson, ed., *Letters of the Lewis and Clark Expedition, with Related Documents 1783–1854*, 2nd ed., 2 vols. (Urbana: University of Illinois Press, 1978) [hereafter *Letters of L&C*], 1:278–80 reprints the December 30 letter and gives a recapitulation.

13. Wilkinson to Jefferson, St. Louis, December 23, 1805, *TP*, 13:316–18.

14. Jefferson to the Senate and House of Representatives, February 19, 1806, *Letters of L&C*, 1:299.

15. It is generally overlooked that a United States expedition looking for a water route to the New Mexican silver mines was jointly headed by a mineralogist.

16. Ibid. A version of the A. & G. Way edition, the 1806 Natchez edition has been published in facsimile under the title *Jefferson's Western Exploration: Discoveries Made in Exploring the Missouri, Red River and Washita by Captains Lewis and Clark, Doctor Sibley and William Dunbar, and compiled by Thomas Jefferson*, edited and introduced by Doug Erickson, Jeremy Skinner, and Paul Merchant (Spokane: Arthur H. Clark, 2004).

17. National Archives, Records of the Accounting Officers of the Department of the Treasury, RG 217, Entry 515, Audit Reports on Military Accounts and Claims, Report Book E, vol. 5, p. 25. King was paid $159. Samuel Mitchill described this map, "...soon there will be sent to Congress a better Map of Louisiana than ever appeared, compiled under the eye of Mr. Jefferson and Mr. Dearborn from the communication of Capts. Lewis and Clark and other

manuscript maps & documents of travellers." Samuel L. Mitchell to CM, February 10, 1806, folder 41.321.435, Museum of the City of New York.

18. It is unlikely the approval was influenced by the names of the thousand citizens who signed a memorial supporting the governor or those who offered alternatives. Those documents could not have reached Washington in time.

19. Jefferson to Congress, March 14, 1806, Senate Journal.

20. See Dan L. Flores, *Jefferson & Southwestern Exploration: The Freeman & Custis Accounts of the Red River Expedition of 1806* (Norman: University of Oklahoma Press, 1984), for background on this attempt to define a southwest boundary and potential access to Santa Fe.

21. William Dunlap, *Diary*, 2 vols. (New York: Collections of the New York Historical Society, 1930), 2:389, 392.

22. Wilkinson to Samuel Smith, St. Louis, March 29, 1806, *TP*, 13.

23. Jefferson to Smith, Washington, May 4, 1806, *TP*, 13:504–505.

24. Dearborn to Wilkinson, War Department, May 4, 1806, *TP*, 13:505.

25. Samuel Smith, who had been a Baltimore merchant before being elected to Congress in 1793, was Senate president pro tempore from 1805 to 1808.

26. Crackel points out that this appears to have been the only soldier lost in combat during the Jefferson administrations.

27. This supposition is based on the relationship between the three men and later developments.

28. The initial outfit that McClallen took west in 1805 was documented by the testimony that Calhoun gave in 1810 in defense of General Wilkinson, but data concerning the 1806 outfit or its value has escaped a diligent search.

29. The distance is approximately 1,350 miles overland and by river.

30. In early January and continuing through February and March, the United States district attorney for Kentucky, Joseph Hamilton Daveiss, warned the president about a developing conspiracy that involved Wilkinson and Mr. Burr. Although Daveiss seemed rabid in his reports, and Jefferson may have dismissed him as another of those trying to discredit Wilkinson, the president had an interview with his former vice president on April 15 and kept lengthy notes on what passed between them. Jefferson Papers, Library of Congress.

31. The pilot was from the Cape Girardeau family of Louis Lorimore, an Indian trader and functionary for the new regime. "Deposition of James Calhoun, Jr." in Wilkinson, *Memoirs*, appendix cxvi.

CHAPTER EIGHT:
"BEHOLD THE MEXICAN TRAVELER"

1. James Wilkinson's introduction of Phillip Nolan to Thomas Jefferson, May 22, 1800, in John Edward Weems, *Men without Countries: Three Adventurers of the Early Southwest* (Boston: Houghton Mifflin Company, 1969), p. 101. Nolan was killed on the last adventure.

2. In September 1805 when Bruff told his commanding officer that he would not be governor for six months, Wilkinson called that sedition and ordered a court-martial. On January 8, 1806, Bruff wrote the secretary of war "I have no confidence in the patriotism of General Wilkinson: and as a man I think of him with horror." Testimony of Maj. James Bruff at the Aaron Burr trial, October 6, 1807, *American State Papers*, 10 Congress, 1 Session, Miscellaneous, vol. 1, pp. 571–77.

3. By the same post he wrote his supporter Samuel Smith that the government of the territory meant nothing to him "compared to the Interests & Fame of Him who placed me here—excessive Jealousies & extreme illiberalities will spread the poison of disaffection every where, and the indulgence of a vain and affected Patriotism will destroy prematurely, the glorious fabric which we fought to Erect." Wilkinson to Smith, St. Louis, March 29, 1806, Clarence E. Carter, ed., *Territorial Papers of the United States*, vols. 13–14, *The Territory of Louisiana-Missouri 1806–1814* (Washington, DC: Government Printing Office, 1949) [hereafter *TP*], 13:466.

4. Dearborn to Wilkinson, May 6, 1806; General James Wilkinson's Order Book, December 31, 1796–March 8, 1808, NARA RG 94, Records of the Adjutant General's Office, M0654 [hereafter WOB].

5. Jealous of the prerogatives of his office and unsupportive of Wilkinson's attempt to bring a disputatious land board to heel, Secretary of the Treasury Albert Gallatin was receiving his information from William C. Carr, an avowed enemy of the governor.

6. Wilkinson to Smith, St. Louis, June 17, 1806, *TP*, 13:521. Smith had this by August 8, 1806, when he wrote a five-page letter to Jefferson blistering the cabal and advising against the appointment of Hammond in Wilkinson's place. General Correspondence, Jefferson Papers, Library of Congress.

7. *TP*, 13:213–17. If the figure is correct, that is very close to the value of the first outfit that McClallen brought from Baltimore.

8. Wilkinson initially recommended Dr. Steele to the surveyor general at Cincinnati and when that failed to gain an appointment, on July 8, 1806, made him clerk of the General Sessions of the Peace and Protonotary. *TP*, 13:388,

518. Dr. Steele later joined acting governor Browne's son-in-law Maj. Robert Wescott, the notorious rabble-rouser John Smith T, and Henry Dodge in trying to connect with Burr. See William Fahey, *A History of Missouri*, 3 vols. (Columbia: University of Missouri Press, 1977), 1:114, 120–21. Steele notarized statements that were used to explain away Wilkinson's involvement with Burr and in 1810 went to Baton Rouge, where he became registrar of land claims in West Florida.

9. Wilkinson to Dearborn, St. Louis, December 30, 1805, *TP*, 13:357.

10. That should have been no surprise since closing the door to all Americans was what Number 13 had advised the Spanish to do, but there is no proof that activities in St. Louis were connected to a Burrite invasion plan.

11. Chouteau to Wilkinson, St. Louis, April 12, 1806, in Abraham P. Nasatir, ed., *Before Lewis and Clark: Documents Illustrating the History of the Missouri 1785–1804*, 2 vols. (1952; reprint, Lincoln: University of Nebraska Press, 1990), 2:770.

12. Might that have been Lieutenant Peter, who had already traveled to the Osage, or former captain McClallen?

13. Wilkinson to Pike, St. Louis, June 24, 1806, Donald Jackson, ed., *The Journals of Zebulon Montgomery Pike with Letters and Related Documents*, 2 vols. (Norman: University of Oklahoma Press, 1966) [hereafter *Pike Journals*], 1:285–88.

14. Ibid. The order did not mention meeting another military detachment under the command of Capt. Richard Sparks that was ascending the Red River with a party of Jefferson-inspired scientists.

15. Wilkinson to Pike, Cantonment Missouri, July 18, 1806, in *Pike Journals*, 2:118–21. As it turned out the expressman, Noel Mongrain, was too closely associated with Chouteau interests.

16. *TP*, 13:182; Donald Jackson, ed., *Letters of the Lewis and Clark Expedition, with Related Documents 1783–1854*, 2nd ed., 2 vols. (Urbana: University of Illinois Press, 1978), 1:258.

17. *Pike Journals*, 1:290n5.

18. Ibid., p. 201n2. Donald Jackson suggests that Wilkinson "foresaw the feasibility in the spring of 1806 when the expedition was planned of contriving Pikes capture and using it as justification for an invasion of New Mexico."

19. Frederic Louis Billon, *Annuals of St. Louis in Its Territorial Days, 1804–1821* (St. Louis, 1888).

20. A few days before the expedition departed, General Wilkinson was said to have intimated to the St. Charles militia officer Timothy Kibby that Pike was not fully aware of the real reason for his expedition.

21. Wilkinson to Pike, Cantonment Missouri, July 12, 1806, in *Pike Journals*, 1:289.

22. This evidence surfaced only later when Wilkinson's enemies were trying to discredit him in the aftermath of the Burr trial.

23. Donald Jackson suggests Wilkinson's orders were the cover. A very readable version of Pike and Robinson's adventure from a New Mexican point of view is Paul Horgan, *Great River: The Rio Grande in North American History* (New York: Rinehart, 1954), pp. 390–422.

24. Instructions to Robinson are mentioned in Wilkinson to Dearborn, Cantonment Missouri, August 2, 1806, *Pike Journals*, 2:128–29, 132n1. At the store Pike was introduced to a Mr. George Henry of New Jersey. The twenty-eight-year-old stranger soon made it clear that he had command of both French and Spanish and wished to join the expedition as a volunteer. Donald Jackson identifies Henry as from Erwenna or Pittstown, New Jersey, where he later joined Pike's regiment during the War of 1812. He may have had some connection to the Morrisons' uncle, Guy Bryan, of Philadelphia.

25. Baltimore *City Gazette and Daily Advertiser*, August 18, 1806, p. 2, from Newsbank and/or the American Antiquarian Society Web site. Although McClallen recently came from Baltimore, there is no apparent connection.

26. Major Bruff apparently resisted being sent down the Mississippi with the troops.

27. Number 13's Natchez connection had already warned Captain-General of the Interior Provinces of Mexico Nemesio Salcedo about American expeditions. By mid-June 1806, a large Spanish force from Santa Fe was in the field. A hundred regulars from Nueva Vizcaya and five hundred militia from New Mexico were commanded by Lt. Don Facundo Malgares, who was ordered to strengthen the Indian barrier, and if it worked out, intercept the returning Corps of Discovery. Isaac Joslin Cox, "Opening the Santa Fe Trail," *Missouri Historical Review* 25, no. 1 (October 1930): 49–51. On July 29 another Spanish field force from Chihuahua intercepted the Freeman and Custis expedition at the "Spanish Bluffs 615 miles up the Red River" and summarily turned back Mr. Jefferson's exploration. Dan L. Flores, *Jefferson & Southwestern Exploration: The Freeman & Custis Accounts of the Red River Expedition of 1806* (Norman: University of Oklahoma Press, 1984), p. 206.

28. *Pike Journals*, pl. 60.

29. Richard Edward Oglesby, *Manuel Lisa and the Opening of the Missouri Fur Trade* (Norman: University of Oklahoma Press, 1984), pp. 35–39.

30. Wilkinson to Pike, July 18, 1806, *Pike Journals*, 2:118–19.

31. Lisa started Baptiste Duchouquette dit (called) Lamie, the experi-

enced plainsman Joseph Rivet, and Calex Montardie to the Osages, but Pike intercepted them and turned them back for lack of a license.

32. The "Monsieur McClellan" who Duchouquette met as he came to the Osages was the Maha trader Robert McClellan. *Missouri Historical Collections*, 3:3, p. 264.

33. Wilkinson to Pike, Cantonment Missouri, August 6, 1806, *Pike Journals*, 2:133–37. After sorting out Lisa's transparent attempt to stall Pike's interpreter, on August 6 General Wilkinson authorized the lieutenant to do whatever was necessary to break up their plans. By then Pike also suspected that Lisa and Cadet Chouteau were somehow linked.

34. *Pike Journals*, 1:306.

35. Oglesby, *Manuel Lisa*, p. 40. Later the Kaskaskia merchant William Morrison came into possession of the Geise & Company note.

36. Wilkinson to Pike, Cantonment Missouri, August 6, 1806, *Pike Journals*, 2:135.

37. See Wilkinson to Dearborn, August 2, 1806, in ibid., 2:128–31 and note.

38. The last letter of instructions from General Wilkinson concerning the rival operations of Lisa and Clamorgan was dated at St. Louis on August 6. Before he left, Wilkinson gave his avowed enemy Carr comeuppance by filing a lawsuit against him.

CHAPTER NINE: LEWIS AND CLARK AND PINCH ME

1. Receipt for a bill contracted August 27, 1806, and settled June 3, 1807, Hunt & Hankinson accounts, Auguste Chouteau Papers, Missouri Historical Society. Montplasir was a "dit" name for the old fur-trade family Dizy but was uncommon around St. Louis. There is a reference to "Monplaiser *Boulanger*" (baker) in the 1798 debts of the Spanish Missouri Company. Someone of that name was still operating on the lower Mississippi as late as 1849. Ludlow Field Maury Collection, Missouri Historical Society.

2. Annie Heloise Abel, ed., *Tabeau's Narrative of Loisel's Expedition to the Upper Missouri* (Norman: University of Oklahoma Press, 1939), p. 15n28. Lieutenant Wilkinson counted only eighty houses in 1806, which were principally occupied by Indian traders and their engagés.

3. About a month before, a Spanish force on the Red River turned back the Freeman/Custis expedition that was sponsored by President Jefferson and

known to General Wilkinson. See Dan L. Flores, *Jefferson & Southwestern Exploration: The Freeman & Custis Accounts of the Red River Expedition of 1806* (Norman: University of Oklahoma Press, 1984).

4. This description of McClallen's ascent of the Missouri is based on the author's familiarity with previous accounts.

5. Had a list survived we might know if a license was written to go to Santa Fe. Territorial Secretary Browne should have turned a list of the licenses he issued over to his replacement, Frederick Bates, but those records are missing.

6. Gary E. Moulton, ed., *The Journals of the Lewis & Clark Expedition*, 13 vols. (Lincoln: University of Nebraska Press, 1983–2001) [hereafter *Journals of L&C*], 8:363. This study uses the electronic version of the series and some references will be made by year and date.

7. This was at present river mile 257. McClallen & Company covered that distance in twenty-one days, eight less than the corps had taken in 1804. The river channel has changed considerably since 1806, but the current is still impressive.

8. William Clark's entry for September 17, 1806, *Journals of L&C*.

9. Jefferson to Lewis, Washington, November 16, 1803, Donald Jackson, ed., *Letters of the Lewis and Clark Expedition, with Related Documents 1783–1854*, 2nd ed., 2 vols. (Urbana: University of Illinois Press, 1978) [hereafter *Letters of L&C*], 1:137.

10. "Observations and Reflections," *Letters of L&C*, 2:709–10. Jackson dated these observations from August 1807. On August 2, 1808, the *Missouri Gazette* published the first part under the author's unmistakable pseudonym, Clatsop. When he wrote, Lewis had Clark's record with him and probably referred to it.

11. Milo Milton Quaife, ed., *The Journals of Captain Meriwether Lewis and Sergeant John Ordway* (Madison: Publications of the State Historical Society of Wisconsin, 1916), pp. 400–401.

12. The most recent version differs somewhat. See Carol Lynn MacGregor, ed., *The Journal of Patrick Gass: Member of the Lewis and Clark Expedition* (Missoula: Mountain Press Publishing, 1997).

13. The inventory of Meriwether's property after his death in 1809 included "one book of An Estimate of the Western Indians" that may have been a manuscript of recent experience or might have been a copy of the material sent back from Fort Mandan in 1805, which was printed by Congress.

14. Donald Jackson, *Among the Sleeping Giants: Occasional Pieces on Lewis and Clark* (Urbana: University of Illinois Press, 1987), pp. 31–32. They named

Robert McClellan with Joseph Gravelines and Pierre Dorion on board. M. LaCroix, Etienne Brant, and the Detroit-area trader Charles Courtin were going about their business as usual.

15. As the corps ascended the Missouri on June 10, 1804, they met a *cajeux* (two dugout canoes lashed together to make raft) with three French half-breeds and a mulatto returning from two or three years with the Pawnee.

16. Permit to Joseph Robidoux to trade with the Pani, Maha, and Oto Indians on the Missouri, signed by Joseph Browne, August 27, 1806, Auguste Chouteau Papers, Missouri Historical Society.

17. It had. On February 21, 1806, the Senate considered the advancement of Second Lieutenant William Clark (his actual rank during the expedition) to first lieutenant, vice (succeeding) Lt. John B. Walbach, who had been promoted captain after John McClallen resigned January 31, 1806.

18. Jefferson to Lewis, June 20, 1803, in John Logan Allen, *Passage through the Garden: Lewis and Clark and the Image of the American Northwest* (Urbana: University of Illinois Press, 1975), p. xix.

19. *Journals of L&C*, 8:221, 278.

20. Ibid. Lewis's entry for August 14, 1805, recorded a description of the Snake and rivers to the south that he guessed ran into the "gulph of California." Moulton corrected that in note 13 and added in note 14 that Shoshones could pass from the Yellowstone to the Spaniards in ten days but could not obtain firearms from them.

21. François-Antoine Larocque's "Yellowstone Journal," in W. Raymond Wood and Thomas D. Thiessen, eds., *Early Fur Trade on the Northern Plains: Canadian Traders among the Mandan and Hidatsa Indians, 1738–1818* (Norman: University of Oklahoma Press, 1985).

22. "The Mandan Tour," in Elliott Coues, ed., *New Light on the Early History of the Greater Northwest: The Manuscript Journals of Alexander Henry and of David Thompson, 1799–1814*, 2 vols. (1897; reprint, Minneapolis: Ross & Haines, 1965).

23. "Observations and Reflections of Lewis," *Letters of L&C*, 2:696–719.

24. Later Lewis wrote, "The furs of all this immense tract of country including such as may be collected on the upper portion of the River St. Peters, Red river and the Assinnibion with the immence country watered by the Columbia, may be conveyed to the mouth of the Columbia by the 1st of August in each year and from thence be shipped to, and arrive in Canton earlier than the furs at present shiped from Montreal annually arrive in London. The British N. West Company of Canada were they permitted by the United States might also convey their furs collected in the Athabaske, on the

Saskashawan, and South and West of Lake Winnipic by that rout within the period before mentioned. Thus the productions [of] nine tenths of the most valuable fur country of America could be conveyed by the rout proposed to the East Indies." Lewis to Jefferson, St. Louis, September 23, 1806, *Letters of L&C*, 1:321.

25. *Journals of L&C*, 4:124.

26. Ibid., August 21, 1806, and n. 2.

27. *Journals of L&C*, 8:65n5. It is tantalizing that Clark left the rest of page 69 blank, perhaps for the insertion of additional information that was never filled in.

28. The entry for September 22, 1806, and "Postexpeditionary Miscellany," *Journals of L&C*.

CHAPTER TEN: AT THE RUBICON

1. Previous travelers between the Platte and Republican branch made the trip in eighteen days.

2. Charlo was a young man who spoke the Panis language, "and in many other respects is preferable to" Maugraine. Donald Jackson, ed., *The Journals of Zebulon Montgomery Pike with Letters and Related Documents*, 2 vols. (Norman: University of Oklahoma Press, 1966) [hereafter *Pike Journals*], 1:331n92.

3. Lieutenant Kimball to William Clark, Camp Bellfontaine, November 1, 1807, *Pike Journals*, 2:277.

4. Pike to Dearborn, Pawnee towns, October 1, 1806, *Pike Journals*, 2:226–27. The officer was Lieutenant Don Fecundo Melgares.

5. For an interesting consideration of the circumstances see Anne M. Platoff, "The Pike-Pawnee Flag Incident: Re-examining a Vexillogical Legend," *Raven: A Journal of Vexillology*, 6 (1999): 1–8. The United States flag in use at that time had thirteen stars and thirteen bars.

6. Charlo started on October 6. There is the suggestion that McClallen received Pike's dispatches and lacking the means of forwarding them, held the packet until he sent his boat back the following spring. After assuming charge of western Indian affairs at St. Louis in May 1807, about the time boats were arriving from upriver, William Clark paid twenty dollars to "Charlo, an express" sent by Pike from the Pawnee village, per Pike's certificate dated October 6, 1806. *Pike Journals*, 2:143n2.

7. Pike's (reconstructed) Journal; Pike to Dearborn, Pawnee Republic, October 1, 1806; Pike to Wilkinson, October 2, 1806, *Pike Journals*, 2:321–31,

2:147–53. Wilkinson had Pike's letter of August 30 at Natchitoches by October 17, but did not hear more from him until he received an early report from his son on February 27, 1807, at New Orleans.

8. About mid-May, a St. Louis acquaintance of Pike received a letter reporting the Spanish visit and forwarding Pike's bills for expenses incurred on the expedition as far as the Pawnee villages. The new territorial secretary Frederick Bates informed Dearborn on May 15 and 17 that it was "very probable that Lt. Pike together with his whole party has been cut off." However, by May 2 Secretary Dearborn had already received the report that Pike wrote from the Pawnee Republic and send down the Arkansas River with Lieutenant Wilkinson.

9. When Lieutenant Pike climbed a high point, he believed that he could see the Yellowstone in the distance. *Pike Journals*, 1:365–66n161.

10. That could explain why Pike dawdled in the mountains through the winter of 1806/07. My study of this "error of the southwest" is pending publication.

11. "Pike's Observations on New Spain," *Pike Journals*, 2:50–51.

12. Those included a bewildering list of Ricaras, Mandanas, Ventrudos or Gros Ventres, Souliers [Zapatos] as peoples fixed on the Missouri. The wandering nations were Chayennes, Cayouva, Caninanbiches, Catakas, Otomies, Chaoines, Sioux, Bois Brule, Saones, Oncpapas, Ochendanne, Siriton, Ynctan, Ynctoannan, Waepiton, Minikaojoup. Farther removed were Cuerbos, Serpientes, Ventrudos, Volantes, Les Gens des Feuille, Salcy, Pieds Ganes, and Pieds Negros. Abraham P. Nasatir, ed., *Before Lewis and Clark: Documents Illustrating the History of the Missouri 1785–1804*, 2 vols. (St. Louis: St. Louis Historical Documents Foundation, 1952; reprint, Lincoln: University of Nebraska Press, 1990), 2:739.

13. Donald Jackson, ed., *Letters of the Lewis and Clark Expedition, with Related Documents 1783–1854*, 2nd ed., 2 vols. (Urbana: University of Illinois Press, 1978) [hereafter *Letters of L&C*], 2:691.

14. Secretary of War to Wilkinson, April 9, 1806.

15. In the spring of 1806 Cheyenne Indians told visiting North West Company traders that "last fall two Spaniards came up the river which runs to the S. in a wooden canoe or a boat loaded with goods, who passed the winter among them, disposed of all of their property, and sold very cheap, giving a double handful of gunpowder and 50 balls for one beaver." In the spring the two men had collected such a quantity of skins that they were obliged to make another canoe. Even two could scarcely contain the packs, with just enough room for a man to sit behind to steer. Although they rode ahead of the Corps of Discovery, their return to St. Louis apparently failed to generate comment.

Elliott Coues, ed., *New Light on the Early History of the Greater Northwest: The Manuscript Journals of Alexander Henry and of David Thompson, 1799–1814*, 2 vols. (1897; reprint, Minneapolis: Ross & Haines, 1965), 1:384.

16. Clarence E. Carter, ed., *Territorial Papers of the United States*, vols. 13–14, *The Territory of Louisiana-Missouri 1806–1814* (Washington, DC: Government Printing Office, 1949) [hereafter *TP*], 13:199. The most convincing identification of Grenier is Annie Heloise Abel, ed., *Tabeau's Narrative of Loisel's Expedition to the Upper Missouri* (1939; reprint, Norman: University of Oklahoma Press, 1968), p. 168n22. Citing Collot's Index of the St. Louis Church Register, she believes him to be François Fleury dit (called) Grenier, a hunter previously with Tabeau. When Rivet's namesake son, François Rivet Jr., was drowned at the Dalles of the Columbia River in 1830, another of those who lost their lives was Pierre Joseph Grenier dit Massa. Glyndwr Williams, ed., *Peter Skene Ogden's Snake Country Journals 1827–1829* (London: Hudson's Bay Record Society, 1971), p. 181.

17. Speculation extracted from Raymond W. Wood and Thomas D. Thiessen, eds., *Early Fur Trade on the Northern Plains: Canadian Traders among the Mandans and Hidatsa Indians 1738–1818* (Norman: University of Oklahoma Press, 1985), pp. 265, 269, 273.

18. The last entry of Henri Delaurier's account with Hunt & Hankinson was July 1, 1806. Entries resumed on May 29, 1807. Auguste Chouteau Papers, Missouri Historical Society. On May 11, 1808, Frederick Bates issued a license to trade with the Sioux to Auguste Chouteau "by agent Henry Deroulier." Thomas Maitland Marshall, ed., *The Life and Papers of Frederick Bates*, 2 vols. (St. Louis: Missouri Historical Society, 1926), 2:31.

19. After caching his outfit Aird returned downstream to meet his clerks Ramsay Crooks and James Reed. Crooks was left to trade against Robert McClellan and young Hortiz at the Omahas. During the winter of 1806/07 Crooks and McClellan worked out a new partnership. David Lavender, *The Fist in the Wilderness* (Garden City, NY: Doubleday, 1964; reprint, Albuquerque: University of New Mexico Press, 1979), p. 82.

20. Joseph Hubert dit (called) LaCroix came from LaChine and married Helen Bissonette at St. Louis in 1792. Both David Lavender and Gary E. Moulton thought that LaCroix might be an Englishman, but that must have reflected the association with Aird. Another of his boats was following in company with those of Etienne Brant and Charles Courtin. Gary E. Moulton, ed., *The Journals of the Lewis and Clark Expedition*, 13 vols. (Lincoln: University of Nebraska Press, 1983–2001) [hereafter *Journals of L&C*], September 10, 1806, and n. 3, September 14. Sometime prior to June 1806 Joseph LaCroix & Com-

pany was paid $153.76 for ransoming an Osage prisoner. NARA RG 217, p. 7476 in *Pike's Journals*, 1:287n1.

21. Contrary to the popular image, not all who entered the Indian country were armed like pirates. At Rocky Mountain House in 1811 Alexander Henry wrote that of the twenty-five men called to defend the fort, a third of them "had never taken a gun in their hands before and were perfectly ignorant of how to load them." As late as 1822/23, the leader of the Hudson's Bay Company Bow River expedition into the dangerous ranges of the Gens du Large was appalled to find that one of his men had no gun and refused to be charged for one. It was unlikely that McClallen would have risked taking trade guns into Spanish territory.

22. Pork eaters became northmen by being sprinkled (or dunked) in northern waters.

23. This depends on speculation by Lavender in his *Fist in the Wilderness*, pp. 72, 75, 77, 82.

24. John McClallen knew that General Wilkinson had authorized Robert McClellan to arrest any traders without a license on the upper river. As McClallen's license was for the Pawnee business, technically he was operating illegally.

25. This letter is treated below but at the time it was written in April 1807, Robert McClellan did not know the identity of the governor.

26. *Journals of L&C*, September 1, 1806. The two captains received this information from a brother of young Dorion's wife.

27. Five years later a traveler described the Yankton village as three hundred lodges planted on the north side of the river but those were conical huts made of split wood and sticks, covered with earth like those of the Maha and other river people. On the trail they used leather lodges. "[Dr. Thomas] Journal," appendix A, in Thomas James, *Three Years among the Indians and Mexicans* (Lincoln: University of Nebraska Press, 1984), pp. 171–72.

28. After Aird lost a boat, his clerks Ramsay Crooks and James (or John) Reed brought between twelve thousand and fifteen thousand dollars in goods to add to Aird's stock. Other traders were Auguste Chouteau's wintering agent Henri Delaurier, Joseph La Croix, Robert McClellan, François Hortiz, and Charles Courtin.

29. According to Harry Majors' analysis of parties on the river that year, there were at least fifty-six traders and men in the vicinity of the Omahas and Yanktons, perhaps as many as a hundred. Harry M. Majors, ed., "John McClellen in the Montana Rockies 1807," *Northwest Discovery* 2, no. 9 (November–December 1981): 570–71.

30. Ibid. Majors postulates that the party wintered at Loisel's abandoned Cedar Island post but negative experiences by the Corps of Discovery and Charles Courtin would have discouraged that. In February when old Dorion came up the river to convince Teton leaders to come to St. Louis and mend the bad reputation they had of harassing travelers, there was no mention of McClallen & Company.

31. It is possible that instructions were sent to McClallen with the party that Indian Superintendent William Clark noted departed for the upper river in March 1807.

32. *Letters of L&C*, 1:211.

33. Nasatir, *Before Lewis & Clark*, 1:318, 2:680–87, 690–703.

34. Jefferson to Dunbar, March 13, 1804, in Jackson, *Jefferson and the Stoney Mountains*, pp. 223, 236n1. *Padouca* was a French term initially applied to prairie 'pache but by now is used to describe Comanche or the related Arapaho. See George E. Hyde, *The Pawnee Indians* (Norman: University of Oklahoma Press, 1974), pp. 145–51.

35. John Logan Allen, *Passage through the Garden: Lewis and Clark and the Image of the American Northwest* (Urbana: University of Illinois Press, 1975), p. 238. The Spanish administration of the Spanish Internal Provinces also believed that the Rio Chato (Platte), Rio Que Corre (Niobrara), Rio Chayennes, and Rio Rocas Pagizas (Yellowstone) all rose in the mountains of northern New Mexico. Clark hadn't changed his mind after descending the Yellowstone.

36. William Clark's "error of the southwest" has been discussed by such eminent historians as Bernard DeVoto, John Logan Allen, or J. Neilson Barry. A recent reconsideration is John C. Jackson, "Updating William Clark's 'Error of the Southwest.'"

CHAPTER ELEVEN:
"AWAY YOU ROLLING RIVER"

1. This surmise flies in the face of a letter that could not have been written before the first of April when Frederick Bates arrived to take over the duties of territorial secretary. Donald Jackson contended that Bates obliged several former corpsmen by writing their petition to receive land grants in Illinois or Louisiana Territory. Thompson's name headed the list of petitioners on the back of the sheet, but there is no proof that those were actual autographs. Gary E. Moulton, ed., *The Journals of the Lewis and Clark Expedition*, 13 vols. (Lincoln: University of Nebraska Press, 1983–2001), 2:516, 522.

2. Laborer John Thompson was living in North Hamption, New Hampshire, when he enlisted in Capt. Amos Stoddard's company on February 20, 1799. Although the usual term of enlistment was five years, he was reenlisted at Boston, February 6, 1801, by Lt. G. W. Duncan, and yet again on February 19, 1804, at Kaskaskia while waiting for the transfer of St. Louis, which took place on March 10, 1804. When the Corps of Discovery departed from St. Charles on May 21, Private Thompson was "on command" to Captain Lewis, who dated his service from January 1, 1804, until October 10, 1806, with pay of $166.66 2/3. Capt. Amos Stoddard Company Book, Missouri Historical Society, p. 33.

3. The identity of a second former corpsman with Thompson is problematic. A contender could have been Jean Baptiste LePage, who signed a note to August Chouteau on April 25, 1807, and planned to pay it off by hunting deer. LePage was the only man Clark failed to pay according to the payment vouchers returned to Lewis on August 20, 1807. LePage was later associated with the Lisa and Drouillard expedition at Fort Remon in late 1809 and apparently died there. Larry E. Morris, *The Fate of the Corps: What Became of the Lewis and Clark Explorers after the Expedition* (New Haven, CT: Yale University Press, 2004), pp. 77–78.

4. Ibid., pp. 151, 247n6. Cruzatte owed an old debt to the supplier Gregoire Sarpy, who tried to collect it soon after the Corps of Discovery returned and Cruzatte had been paid for his service. When the matter was pressed again in March 1807, Cruzatte was around. On April 10, 1807, a contract drawn with Lisa's clerks promised to furnish Cales (Calix) Montargy and Pierre Cruzat to hunt for the clerks. *Antoine Dubriel v. Lisa*, Court of Common Pleas, District of Saint Louis, July 1809 in L. R. Coulter-Frick, *Courageous Colter and Companions* (Washington, MO: self-published, 1997), p. 392. Cruzatte is mentioned in notes for beaver furs at Fort Remon from June 14 to 27, 1808, which suggests he made a spring hunt in association with a trapper named Machecon. See p. 395.

5. Larry Morris bases his suggestion on Collins' skills as a hunter and scout and that he disappeared from the public record after the return of the Lewis and Clark expedition. Morris, *Fate of the Corps*, pp. 150–51, 190.

6. An interesting but unanswered question is who sold and who bought the beaver pelts that had been taken by corpsmen during the trip?

7. George Sibley, Belle Fontaine, October 25, 1806, Sibley Papers, Missouri Historical Society, pp. 2–3.

8. The St. Louis grand jury found that Wescott "begun and set on foot an expedition, to be carried on from the territory against the Dominion of Spain, a prince or state with whom the united states are at peace" and a trial was set

for the May term. Although he was under subpoena to testify, the former corpsman Robert Fraser picked up something about the conspiracy and followed Lewis and Clark to Washington.

9. The general had cut off communications with Burr and even had Lt. Daniel Hughes write a letter to Secretary of the Navy Robert Smith, Senator Smith's brother, warning of Burr's suspicious activities. Crackel, *Mr. Jefferson's Army*, pp. 114–16n64.

10. In May 1807, General Wilkinson was already on his way to Richmond as the star witness in the treason trial of Aaron Burr. Burr's battery of lawyers tried to involve Wilkinson for encouraging and abetting their client. Legal tactics saved Burr at the cost of embarrassing the general and creating the myth that he had betrayed a traitor. But in the final reckoning James Wilkinson's intrigues were just intrigues. Few Americans ever achieved as high a standing in infamy as Number 13, and done so little actual damage to deserve it.

11. Richard Edward Oglesby, *Manuel Lisa and the Opening of the Missouri River Fur Trade* (Norman: University of Oklahoma Press, 1963; reprint, 1984), pp. 37–46. As early as April 11, 1807, Paul Primeau, one of the boatmen who returned from the Mandans in the spring of 1805, planned to join Lisa/Drouillard and signed a $292.05 promissory note for his outfit.

12. Elliott Coues, *Zebulon M. Pike: Expeditions in the Years 1805–1806–1807* (New York: Dover, 1987), 2:585–89.

13. Entries in the Pierre Chouteau account books show that E[ttiene] St. Pierre was paid "*pour sa service*" as a hivernaut (wintering engagé) on May 29, 1807, which was charged against "M. M'clelan." Two days before there is an entry for Pierre Dorion Pere suggesting that he had also returned from the Yankons. Missouri Historical Society, Pierre Chouteau Account Books, vol. 3, pp. 72, 163. Montplaisir returned according to a bill contracted August 27, 1806, and settled June 3, 1807, Hunt & Hankinson accounts, Colonel Auguste Chouteau Papers, Missouri Historical Society.

14. The last entry of Henri Delaurier's account with Hunt & Hankinson was dated July 1, 1806. The account resumed on May 29, 1807, when he bought a handkerchief and a pair of men's shoes costing $11.75. By June 4 Delaurier paid his bill in full. Auguste Chouteau Papers, Missouri Historical Society. Records for 1807 show furs belonging to Auguste Chouteau being shipped from Mt. Joliet and Chicago. Milo M. Quaife, *Chicago and the Old Northwest* (Chicago: University of Chicago Press, 1913).

15. Two years before, the ice in the river broke at the Mandan villages by the end of March, allowing the Corps of Discovery to proceed on April 9. In 1853, the Stevens railway survey found that ice usually closed the upper Mis-

souri between Fort Clark and Fort Union from November 20 until around April 10.

16. George Drouillard delivered the first dispatches addressed to the president, Governor Harrison, and Clark's friends in Kentucky to Postmaster Hay on September 24.

17. Donald Jackson, ed., *Letters of the Lewis and Clark Expedition, with Related Documents 1783–1854*, 2nd ed., 2 vols. (Urbana: University of Illinois Press, 1978), 2:336–43. The only copy of this letter, in David Thompson's hand, is in the Vancouver, British Columbia, Public Library.

18. The indispensable Pierre Dorion left his family at the Yankton camp in February 1806 and traveled up the river to the Teton Sioux, where he convinced some of their chiefs to come to St. Louis and hear the words of the great father.

19. Robert McClellan to the governor of Upper Louisiana, Mahaws Cantonment, April 5, 1807, E. G. Voorhis Memorial Collection, Missouri Historical Society. When the letter arrived in St. Louis in early May, the new territorial secretary Frederick Bates readdressed it to Governor Meriwether Lewis and forwarded it to Philadelphia. By then William Clark had returned to St. Louis as Indian agent, but would be unable to save Robert McClellan from the consequences of his action in arresting an unlicensed trader.

20. Bates to Dearborn, St. Louis, May 15, 1807; May 17, 1807, Donald Jackson, ed., *The Journals of Zebulon Montgomery Pike with Letters and Related Documents*, 2 vols. (Norman: University of Oklahoma Press, 1966) [hereafter *Pike Journals*], 2:226–27.

21. Frederick Bates to Secretary of War Dearborn, St. Louis, May 17, 1807, ALS, RC (DNA-4, B-246 as cited in *Pike Journals*, 2:227).

22. *Pike Journals*, 2:143n2, 226–27, 330–31n92.

23. Wilkinson's price was one hundred twenty-one thousand pesos, but that may have included upsetting Burr's plans for a filibuster against Vera Cruz. Remuneration was the expectation of the times, as Pike twice reminded the general that he expected a captaincy for his efforts.

24. Salcedo to Wilkinson, April 8, 1807; Pike to Wilkinson, April 20, 1807; Wilkinson to Pike, May 20, 1807. Coues, *Zebulon M. Pike*, 2:815–17, 822–24, 825–28.

25. Ezekiel Bacon (chairman), *Report of the Committee Appointed to Inquire into the Conduct of General Wilkinson* (Washington, DC: United States Congress, House of Representatives, 1811), p. 531. It is possible that Calhoun may have bent the truth to spare the general and the recipes that he presented were for the shipment of the 1806 outfit.

26. "The Bonds given by persons engaged in Indian trade have not been delivered to me. Will you have the goodness to inform me whether they remain in your hands; and whether they ought not to have been deposited in my office?" Bates to Brown, June 3, 1807, Thomas Maitland Marshall, ed., *The Life and Papers of Frederick Bates*, 2 vols. (St. Louis: Missouri Historical Society, 1926), vol. 1.

27. St. Genevieve Probate Court Records. Browne also wrote a draft to Calhoun & Company for $2,984.08, which bounced.

28. In 1753 the name Monplaisir had appeared in a voyageur contract to go west for the Le Corne family. The only St. Louis reference is to a baker, not a boatman.

29. John G. Comegys was no cream puff. He and Lisa broke the peace with a fist fight over a dispute about outfitting debts, and on September 19, 1808, both men were required by the St. Louis court to post bonds.

30. For the next several years his widow struggled to close the debts of the estate, almost half of which was $2,517.22 still owed. Calhoun & Company continued trying to squeeze a bit more out of the widow. Their suit set the amount at $2,985.35 plus damages of $890.82, for a total of $3,877.17.

31. Hiram Martin Chittenden, *The American Fur Trade of the Far West: A History of the Pioneer Trading Posts and Early Fur Companies of the Missouri Valley and the Rocky Mountains and of the Overland Commerce with Santa Fe*, 2 vols. (New York: Press of the Pioneers, 1902; reprint, Lincoln: University of Nebraska Press, 1986), p. 125.

32. Clark to Dearborn, St. Louis, May 18, 1807, Clarence E. Carter, ed., *Territorial Papers of the United States*, vols. 13–14, *The Territory of Louisiana-Missouri 1806–1814* (Washington, DC: Government Printing Office, 1949) [hereafter *TP*], 14:122. When Clark wrote, he had the information from R. McClellan's letter of April 5 and what Ramsay Crooks related.

33. "William Clark Brigd General of Ml. [militia] and Indian agent for Louisiana In Council with the Chiefs and warriors of the Yanktons and Several Bands of the Tetons on their arrival at St. Louis May 9th 1807," William Clark to Secretary of War Dearborn, RG107, C-Misc., M222, 02, frames 0771–72.

34. Kimble was commissioned a lieutenant in the Regiment of Artillery on September 10, 1806, and must have joined McClallen's former company still stationed at Belle Fontaine.

35. A. P. Chouteau was a recent but resigned West Point graduate.

36. Thomas Blackwood to J & A McGill, Mackinac, July 30, 1807. Aird returned to St. Louis, where he took out a license to trade with the Oto and Maha on September 1 but was held up until the September 9 in order to testify at the trial of Robert McClellan for the arrest of an unlicensed trader.

CHAPTER TWELVE:
"REATHER A SPECULATIVE EXPEDITION"

1. See John C. Jackson, "Brandon House and the Mandan Connection," *North Dakota History* 49, no. 1 (Winter 1982): 11–19.

2. The North West Company partners were Alexander Henry and Charles Chaboillez. Elliott Coues, ed., *New Light on the Early History of the Greater Northwest: The Manuscript Journals of Alexander Henry and of David Thompson, 1799–1814*, 2 vols. (1897; reprint, Minneapolis: Ross & Haines, 1965), 1:285, 304.

3. Brandon House Journal, HBCA B22/a/15, fols. 3, 5; B22/a/17, fol. 15.

4. The Nor'westers pulled down the house at the mouth of La Souris River, where trading parties started to come to the Missouri and floated the timber eighteen miles downstream to rebuild a post that looked north for its trade. Brandon House master John McKay was threatened when the Assiniboine feared that the traders were leaving them.

5. After Assiniboines killed his former agent, Old Menard, in 1804, McKay had difficulties convincing timid Orkneymen to risk the dangerous overland passage to the Missouri. His trader George Budge returned to Brandon House on April 27, 1807, reporting that the Americans meant to settle the Missouri as high as the Mandans and it wasn't worth going there again. The Hudson's Bay Company continued to conduct business through independent intermediaries in October when McKay sent Jean Baptiste LaFrance and Hugh McCracken to the Mandans. LaFrance died of consumption and McCracken was afraid to risk returning until October 1808.

6. Charbonneau was paid $409.16 1/3 for his service from April 7, 1805, to August 17, 1806, with an extra $91.16 1/3 for the use of a horse and other equipment during the expedition. He was sixteen hundred miles up the Missouri when the 9th Congress on March 3, 1807, passed the bill authorizing extra pay and bounty lands to the members of the Corps of Discovery. Clark received funds from Lewis to make those payments and traveled to St. Louis. The funds for Charbonneau were not among Lewis's debts after his death, but it is uncertain how or when he received them.

7. Comments on this corporate-created erosion of the animal population appear in the journals of many traders on the Saskatchewan, Red, and Assiniboine rivers.

8. *A'ani*, "white clay people," according to John Horse Capture in Frederick Hoxie, ed., *Encyclopedia of North American Indians* (Boston: Houghton Mifflin, 1996), p. 225. Blackfoot speakers knew them as *Atsiina*; white traders as

Gros Ventre, Falls, or Rapids Indians; Lewis and Clark as Minnetaries of Fort des Prairies. To avoid confusion I will use the term *Atsiina*.

9. A list of New North West Company (XYC) engagés in all trading areas in 1804 had 318 names, but in the next year that dropped to forty. "Statement of Wages 1804 and 1805," B. C. Payette, comp., *The Oregon Country under the Union Jack* (Montreal: Payette Radio Limited, 1962), pp. 590–95.

10. W. Raymond Wood and Thomas D. Thiessen, eds., *Early Fur Trade on the Northern Plains: Canadian Traders among the Mandan and Hidatsa Indians, 1738–1818* (Norman: University of Oklahoma Press, 1985).

11. Henry does not mean that more freemen were coming from Canada but rather that that was their original place of origin. The coalition of the North West Company and New North West Company aka Sir Alexander Mackenzie was known at Pembina by the first of January 1805, and by late October Pelletier, Desjardins, and Bostonae Pangmen were mentioned as XYC freemen. Coues, ed., *New Light on the Early History of the Greater Northwest*, 1:424.

12. Hugh Heney is an overlooked player on the Mandan connection. Despite rumors in November 1800 that he had been killed by British traders, Heney returned to St. Louis and the formed a two-year association with Regis Loisel, on advances from Auguste Chouteau. Unable to repay his one-third interest in the arrangement, Heney showed up at Brandon House in mid-September 1804 in company with the Mandan "residenter" Old Menard who had lived with them for years. After McKay refused to engage him, he returned to the Mandans in December working for the North West Company. Heney so impressed Captains Lewis and Clark that they later tried to engage him as US Indian agent on the upper river but found he was otherwise engaged. Later he worked for the Hudson's Bay Company at Pembina on the Red River.

13. Louis Capois dit (called) Hoole and Genevieve Laforge may have married as early as 1751 and were described as a couple in 1777. Through the courtesy of Susan Boilvan Summervile; Ross Cox, *The Columbia River, or Scenes and Adventures during a Residence of Six Years on the Western Side of the Rocky Mountains among Various Tribes of Indians Hitherto Unknown; Together with "A Journey across the American Continent,"* ed. Edger I. Stewart and Jane R. Stewart (Norman: University of Oklahoma Press, 1957), pp. 192–93.

14. *Repertoire des engagement pour l'ouest conserves dans les archives judiciares de Montreal, Rapport de L'archiviste de la Provence de Quebec* (1942–43). For his interrogation by Spanish in St. Louis, see Nasatir, *Before Lewis and Clark*, 2:330–33.

15. Two of them may have been former trappers for Regis Loisel. Jean Baptiste Tibeau, who took an outfit at Fort Remon on June 4, 1808, and his associate Baptiste Marie were not listed in the initial Lisa/Drouillard party.

16. This source hangs on a letter from Pierre Chouteau to Secretary of War William Eustis, dated at the Mandan villages on December 14, 1809. Chouteau noted that "about thirty American hunters, who had used to visit the Mandan Village, not being seen nor heard of for about eighteen months." Pierre Chouteau Letterbook, pp. 146–47, Missouri Historical Society. Chouteau wasn't the only source of gossip about the upper Missouri in late 1809. At Fort Osage Capt. Eli Clemson picked up a rumor from a boat returning from the Mandans. It was generally believed that the British had established a trading post at the Three Forks of the Missouri River and were encouraging the Blackfeet to harry trappers. Capt. Eli Clemson to Wm. Linnard, Fort Osage, November 18, 1809.

17. After a difficult winter in 1805/06 with the Teton Sioux, Courtin returned to St. Louis, turned in his packs to be forwarded to Canadian debt holders, and obtained a new outfit from a local financier. Lewis and Clark met him as he headed up the Missouri on September 14, 1806, three days ahead of McClallen & Company.

18. At that time Courtin owed Hugh and Richard Pattinson of Sandwich, Upper Canada, the sum of £3043/5/1 that had accrued since 1802, although returns from his 1805/06 winter with the Teton Sioux would earn £283/1/6 when sold in London on July 31, 1807. Tesson Collection, Missouri Historical Society.

19. In February 1804 the Femme Osage landowner Forest Hancock signed a note to Manuel Lisa for an outfit worth twelve hundred dollars, a bit more than what would have been necessary to equip a trapper. He and Joseph Dickson had agreed to make a two-year trapping excursion up the Missouri.

20. Bates to Dearborn, St. Louis, August 2, 1807, "Enclosing a communication from a Mr. Courtin relative to the bad disposition of the Ricaras, &c &c," NARA RG107, B-280/3.

21. See also Frank H. Dickson, "Hard on the Heels of Lewis and Clark," *Montana* 26, no. 1 (January 1976): 14–25. Courtin knew both of these men from the miserable winter they spent together at the Brule Tetons in 1805/06.

22. Lewis and Clark took thirty-three days to descend from the Arikara towns to St. Louis, so Dickson probably arrived by July 24, and it required time to translate Courtin's letter before Bates forwarded it on August 2. It was about a nineteen- or twenty-day trip to the mouth of the Platte, which would have put Dickson and Handcock there about July 10. By then Lisa/Drouillard had already passed the Platte.

23. L. R. Colter-Frick, *Courageous Colter and Companions* (Washington, MO: self-published, 1997), pp. 41–43. Hiram Martin Chittenden in his *The American*

Fur Trade of the Far West, 2 vols. (New York: Press of the Pioneers, 1835; reprint, Lincoln: University of Nebraska Press, 1986), 1:114–16, 2:704–705, drew from Lisa's 1811 statement to a visiting writer the recollection that Colter joined him at the Platte. Lisa had not known Colter previously, but George Drouillard was associated with Colter during the Lewis and Clark expedition and failed to mention Colter, or his exploratory accomplishments, in the report that he gave to their former captains on August 5, 1808. This contemporary evidence suggests that Colter and Thompson were the two former corpsmen who Indians later recognized traveling with McClallen. Rivet and Grenier were also along, but western Indians would not have known them. For a recent reconsideration see John C. Jackson, "Revisiting the Colter Legend," *Rocky Mountain Fur Trade Journal* 3 (2009): 1–19.

24. When the Corps of Discovery returned to the Mandan villages in 1806, both Clark and Sergeant Ordway indicate that "our officers settled with him" (Colter) on August 17. That seems to have been for $179.33 1/3, the amount of Colter's pay from October 15, 1803, to October 10, 1806, a generosity since Colter left the expedition on October 17, the same day that Charbonneau was paid $409.16 2/3 for his service. That does not appear to have been the ammunition or other small supplies contributed to Colter by the two captains or his fellow corpsmen as gifts. Whether Colter was paid in cash or with a draft is uncertain. A draft would not have been useful to a man returning to the Yellowstone, but Colter could have signed it over to someone he trusted, John B. Thompson likely, who could take it downstream and use it to buy an outfit that would sustain them for another year of hunting on the Yellowstone. Before Lewis died, he listed a debt of $320 owed to Colter for his gratuity allowed by the government. When Colter returned to St. Louis in November 1810 he made suit against Edward Hempstead, administrator of the Lewis estate for the sum of $559. The March 1811 court judgment was for $377.60 plus court fees of $15.51. St. Louis Circuit Court Historical Records Project, http://stlouiscourtrecords.wusl.edu.

25. There is no record of McClallen's ascent of the Yellowstone, but details had not changed much since Clark's party descended the previous year, and his journal provides a framework for this reconstruction.

26. *Apsaruke* more commonly *Absoroka,* lately *Apsáalooke.* The standard study is Robert H. Lowie, *The Crow Indians* (New York: Holt, Rinehart and Winston, 1935; reissue, 1956; reprint, Lincoln: University of Nebraska Press, 2004).

27. "Larocque's Yellowstone Journal," p. 206n108.

28. William Clark sketched it as a dotted line on one of the maps he drew at Fort Mandan.

29. Running through a broad-timbered valley bounded on one side by river-carved bluffs and on the west side by sculpted rocks, the Big Horn would have appeared promising to a uniformed boat party. The Lisa/Drouillard party that followed found plenty of cottonwoods for building and located their fort under a rocky bluff that offered views of the Yellowstone and Big Horn valleys.

30. In 1805 Larocque made arrangements for contacting the Crow when he returned with an outfit. Smoke signals on the hills were the agreed signal, and the next year as Clark descended the Yellowstone on July 18 he noticed signals in the plain to the south, southeast.

31. Larocque recognized their description of a man with a crippled arm as a fellow North West Company trader. In a deserted camp of thirty lodges he also found chief's coats and stroud cloth that came from Hudson's Bay Company houses on the upper Saskatchewan.

32. Edmonton House Journal, May 8, 1807, HBCA B60/a/6, fos. 6, 8; Wood and Thiessen, *Early Fur Trade*, p. 192n77. There are many examples among northern tribes of the New Mexican exchange but those contacts were likely with frontier settlements that extended into Colorado and not as far south as the Santa Fe area.

33. Near the mouth of the Clark Fork of the Yellowstone. Wood and Thiessen, *Early Fur Trade*, p. 192, place it close to present Laurel, Montana. For Clark's description see Gary E. Moulton, ed., *The Journals of the Lewis and Clark Expedition*, 13 vols. (Lincoln: University of Nebraska Press, 1983–2001) [hereafter *Journals of L&C*], 8:209n2, 220n3.

34. Clark's party passed about July 24, 1806, *Journals of L&C*, 8:191–92.

35. "Larocque's Journal," in Wood and Thiessen, *Early Fur Trade*, p. 220. That journal was still unwritten and would not be published for many years, but McClallen would have received similar information when he questioned his informants about the way to Santa Fe.

36. Although the sign language has become almost mythic, it was open to misunderstanding. As an example, the idea Larocque formed that it took the Flatheads only two days to cross the Rocky Mountains was wrong; what he misread was the time that it took to cross what is now known as the Bozeman Pass between Billings and Bozeman, Montana.

37. LaRocque's "Yellowstone Journal," pp. 189, 192, 220.

38. Meriwether Lewis's notes to George Drouillard's map of the Big Horn basin.

39. When the anthropologist Robert Lowie studied the Crow in 1907 it had been a hundred years since John McClallen led his companions up the Yellowstone and learned to his dismay that the actual geography was very dif-

ferent from what he imagined. He had no more reason to question their statements than did the former corpsman George Drouillard, who would survey the headwaters of the Clark River later that fall.

40. In a time before reliable maps, McClallen faced a trip through unknown country that could be from eight hundred fifty to one thousand miles. He had no way of knowing that he would have to follow up the Clark River or the Big Horn, find a way through or around the Wind River Range, pick up the headwaters of the Green, and follow it past the Duchesne/White River area to the old Spanish Trail crossing of the Colorado, pass the upper Dolorous, cross the San Juan, and come down the Chama to Santa Cruz and Santa Fe. Indian raids on Spanish herds may have only come as far as the present Colorado/New Mexico border.

41. Clark's Estimate of Distances. There is a pictograph on a rock near the Musselshell River, just north of present Billings, Montana, depicting white men standing and poling a boat. That is not a drawing of Clark's party because they descended the Yellowstone paddling dugouts. Later that fall, the Lisa/Drouillard expedition only came as far as the mouth of the Big Horn. "The Explorer's Petroglyph," 24ML402, courtesy of Stuart Conner, Billings, Montana, November 11, 1996.

CHAPTER THIRTEEN:
PEACE IN MOUNTAIN TIME

1. McClallen had no way of knowing that seven months prior Lieutenant Pike and Dr. Robinson had been apprehended for trespassing on a tributary of the North River (Rio Grande), briefly imprisoned, and recently returned to the lower Mississippi.

2. In 1805 Larocque noted the presence of Atsiina and an unlucky Assiniboine horse raiding party. W. Raymond Wood and Thomas D. Thiessen, eds., *Early Fur Trade on the Northern Plains: Canadian Traders among the Mandan and Hidatsa Indians, 1738–1818* (Norman: University of Oklahoma Press, 1985), p. 191.

3. Larocque saw between two hundred seventy-five to three hundred lodges of Atsiina camped on the Big Horn in 1805. The following year Clark's party descending the Yellowstone River only saw Indians watching from high places and assumed it was Crows who ran off their horses.

4. McClallen was probably short of alcohol because he started with only what was necessary to oil his crew. There was no need to carry whiskey to the New Mexican well of Taos lightning (frontier whiskey).

5. This was a rumor that the North West Company trader David Thompson intended to go from Rocky Mountain House to trade directly with the Kutenai Indians on the west side.

6. "Fall and Blood Indians who were on a war expedition last autumn [1807] and discovered an American Settlement on the Banks of the Missoury. The Americans they say received them in a very friendly manner, made them presents and invited them to a general meeting next spring [1808] with all the tribes they have hitherto warred with, in order to settle a peace with them, and for the purposes of trade. They tell us that the Americans promise to sell them a gun for five beavers & other Articles in proportion, that they value Buffalo robes &, but add that the Americans have no spirits." Statement to James Bird, January 22, 1808, Edmonton House Journal, HBCA B60/a/7, fol. 22.

7. Actually, the *Piikani* had another motive. Peace with the western tribes would allow them to pay full attention to troublesome northern plainsmen.

8. Not as far-fetched as it might seem. The letter resurfaced in 1846 when negotiations were in process to decide the extension of the international boundary from the Rocky Mountains to the shore of the Pacific. Secretary A[lexander] Barclay to Foreign Office, Hudson's Bay House, London, February 23, 1846, in Robert Carlton Clark, *History of the Willamette Valley, Oregon* (Chicago: S. J. Clarke, 1927), 1:838.

9. J. B. Tyrrell, "Letter of Roseman and Perch, July 10th, 1807," *Oregon Historical Quarterly* 38, no. 4 (December 1937): 391–94.

10. The only copy of the letter is in the Edmonton House Journal, January 22, 1808, HBCA B60/a/7, fol. 12. Hudson's Bay Company policy required trading posts to keep daily records of occurrences, which were sent to London for the information of the board of governors. Tons of these handwritten and unpublished journal books and correspondence books have been preserved and provide an irreplaceable source of historical data. They are presently located in Winnipeg, Manitoba, Canada.

11. Of course it was a beau geste that the North West Company would smother so completely that the only evidence of its existence was preserved in a competitor's house journal.

12. They had been apprehended and deported by New Mexican authorities.

13. McClallen might have speculated that Lieutenant Pike realized the Pawnee blockade would deflect him and left a detachment in case the trader showed up. When the circular letter was being written, Pike and Robinson had been captured, interrogated, and were in Natchitoches on their way back to United States authority.

14. The only known recipient minimized its reception. David Thompson's admirers still try to keep that inconvenient document from overshadowing his accomplishments.

15. "Observations and Reflections on the Present and Future State of Upper Louisiana, in Relation to the Government of the Indian Nations Inhabiting That Country, and the Trade and Intercourse with the Same, by Captain Lewis," in Donald Jackson, ed., *Letters of Lewis and Clark Expedition with Related Documents, 1783–1854*, 2nd ed., 2 vols. (Urbana: University of University of Illinois Press, 1978) [hereafter *Letters of L&C*], 2:711, 715.

16. Clark had also been inspired to write letters at this place last year. In addition to recopying the letter composed at Traveler's Rest inviting the British trader Hugh Heney to enter United States service, he also addressed the Crows. Smarting from the recent loss of half of his horse herd, Clark forgave them their trespasses with the caution that the white father had more soldiers than there were leaves on the trees. See Gary E. Moulton, ed., *The Journals of the Lewis and Clark Expedition*, 13 vols. (Lincoln: University of Nebraska Press, 1983–2001) [hereafter *Journals of L&C*], 8: 211–15.

17. Edmonton House Journal, November 10, 1807, HBCA B60/a/7, fols. 6–8d. The plains Cree and *Piikani* who traded at Edmonton House in October and November 1807 failed to mention an encounter.

18. Falls and Blood Indians statements to James Bird, Edmonton House Journal, January 22, 1808, HBCA B60/a/7, fol. 22.

19. Although he was unaware that his informant's tribesmen had already sabotaged the meeting, Bird correctly foresaw why that would fail.

20. "Lewis to President Jefferson," *Letters of L&C*, 2:336–43; "Post expedition Miscellany," *Journals of L&C*, vol. 3.

21. Atsiina (*A'ani'*) were known to the apprehensive Captain Lewis as "Minnetaries of fort du Prairie," to Hudson's Bay men as Falls Indians, and to history as Gros Ventres. Disreputable for killing fourteen contracted beaver trappers in 1801, they were suspected of the 1805 attack on a North West Company brigade departing the south branch.

22. The Absaroka and Beartooth ranges, which form the grand canyon of the Yellowstone River.

23. Clark's "Yellowstone Journal," July 17, 1806. See Web edition of the journals.

24. Nez Perce (*Nimi'ipuu*) properly knew the Ootlashshoots as *Sha-lees* (Salish). Moulton believes *Tushapaws* may have been a Shoshoni term for "people with shaved heads," presumably as close as their language allowed to the sign for *Flathead*.

25. The Ootlashshoots appear to have been the Salish Red Willow band who usually wintered in the lower end of the Bitterroot Valley. The Tushapaw, who usually wintered in the Flathead Valley, may have been eastern *Kalispel*. The term *Flathead* has a long history in relationships between opponents dating back to Iroquois disdain for southern Algonquins. The usual explanation links it to the sign language gesture for *Salish*, a flattened hand held over the brow.

26. The bone middens (refuse dumps) of those ancient hunting sites are many yards deep.

27. For a description of the tradition of the hunt, see William E. Farr, "Going to Buffalo, Indian Hunting Migrations across the Rocky Mountains," *Montana: The Magazine of Western History* 53, no. 4 (Winter 2003): 2–21; 54, no. 1(Spring 2004): 26–43.

28. The journals suggest that one may have been a brother of the Nez Perce chief Cut Nose and two were from the lodge of Broken Arm, young men of good character respected by their people. Two others were searching to make sure their Salish friends had not been destroyed by northern raiders. *Journals of L&C,* June 8, 1806, nn. 1, 3.

29. Sergeant Ordway ended his journal on September 23, 1806, with this estimate of trade goods:

> *pelate pallow* and [*illegible*] nations west Side of the [Rocky?] Mountains have horses with [*illegible*] for Sale the goods [which?] they want for them is follows. Small light [*illegible*] mounted guns powder & balls, brass or copper kittles Small or middling Size knives Beeds blue & white blue is Set the [first?] by all Indians in this [region?] red cloath calicoes &c Squaw axes tommahawks medl. awls Buttens tin cups & pans [*illegible*] of copper or brass trinkets or Combs Silk linen lace or [twill?] white [*illegible*] of different kinds Red paint needles Swords or big knives [*illegible*] of Iron & files of which they make arrow points to Suit themselves &c war axes is in great demand as they purchase a fiew from the Indians on the Missourie. [*illegible*] wide quality or binding but ribbens & tape is of no account among them but they will trade for anything that they know is of Service to them. I think twezers would be a fine thing as they pluck ther beards and ey brows all out [*several words illegible*].

From *Journals of L&C.*

30. HBCA B60/a/6, fols. 6d, 9. In November 1806, David Thompson, the North West Company officer at Rocky Mountain House, sent his man, Prince

Valarde, to the Bloods and in mid-January 1807 with a similar message to the *Piikani*. Thompson was trying to deflect potential enemies from congregating at the post and interfering with his intention of extending trade across the mountains. David Thompson, Journal of the Rocky Mountain House Occurences, October 11, 1806, to July 26, 1807, Ontario Archives, bk. 18.

31. Edmonton House Journal, 1806/1807, HBCA B60/a/6, fols. 8d, 9.

32. Bird's entry in the house journal reflects no sense of simmering resentment. HBCA B60/a/6, fol. 6. For further discussion that the Muddy River Indians held no grudge for the unfortunate incident, see John C. Jackson, "The Fight on Two Medicine River: Who Were Those Indians, and How Many Died," *We Proceeded On: Lewis and Clark Trail Heritage Foundation* 23, no. 1 (February 2006): 14–23.

33. Warren Angus Ferris, *Life in the Rocky Mountains 1830–1835*, ed. Leroy R. Hafen (Denver: Old West Publishing, 1983), p. 182.

34. *Journals of L&C*, 8:394.

CHAPTER FOURTEEN: TOP OF THE WORLD

1. Barbara Belyea, ed., *Columbia Journals: David Thompson* (Montreal: Magill-Queens University Press, 1994; reprint, Seattle: University of Washington Press, 1998), pp. 44–48.

2. Journal of the Rocky Mountain House Occurrences, 1806/07, October 11, 1806–July 26, 1807 by David Thompson, bk. 18, which is continued as bk. 19, Archives of Ontario. Belyea, in her editing of selections, relies on bk. 20. Belyea, ed., *Columbia Journals*, pp. 45, 214.

3. For general background on Thompson's previous career, see Richard Glover, ed., *David Thompson's Narrative, 1784–1813* (Toronto: Champlain Society, 1962) or the recent republication in three promised volumes by William E. Morreau, *The Writings of David Thompson* (Toronto: Champlain Society, 2009). Also useful is Jack Nisbet, *Sources of the River: Tracking David Thompson across Western North America* (Seattle: Sasquatch Books, 1994).

4. Thompson did not immediately criticize Finlay for failing to perform as expected in his field journal AO18 but made a stronger condemnation in a later version, AO20, at a time when the expansion wasn't going all that well.

5. Thompson neglected to enlarge on this prior understanding in his retrospective *Narrative*, probably to heighten the impression of a later discovery. That book reveals no indication that he profited from the geographical information collected by the Hudson's Bay Company trader Peter Fidler from sev-

eral Indian informants at Chesterfield House on the south branch of the Saskatchewan during the years 1800 to 1802.

6. Elliott Coues, ed., *New Light on the Early History of the Greater Northwest: The Manuscript Journals of Alexander Henry and of David Thompson, 1799–1814*, 2 vols. (1897; reprint, Minneapolis: Ross & Haines, 1965).

7. Donald Jackson, ed., *Letters of the Lewis and Clark Expedition, with Related Documents 1783–1854*, 2nd ed., 2 vols. (Urbana: University of Illinois Press, 1978), 2: 336–43.

8. Duncan McGillivray, "Some Account of the Trade carried on by the North West Company, 1808," *Report of the Public Archives of Canada, 1928* (Ottawa: King's Printer, 1929), pp. 70–71 as cited in James P. Ronda, *Astoria and Empire* (Lincoln and London: University of Nebraska Press, 1990), pp. 18–24.

9. The "Account" is in the hand of Duncan McGillivray with annotations in the hand of his brother William McGillivray. A. S. Morton, ed., *The Journal of Duncan McGillivray of the North West Company* (1929; reprint, Fairfield: Ye Galleon Press, 1989). Appendix 22-23 describes this document.

10. This was Thompson's first experience in the demanding art of mountain packing, and he designed awkwardly rigid, twenty-eight-inch-square by eight-inch-deep cedar pack boxes to protect an outfit of mostly soft goods. The terrible road across the mountains would continue to be used until Thompson devised an excuse to abandon it.

11. Journal of the Rocky Mountain House Occurrences, 1806/07.

12. At some point before or after the peace council, McClallen entrusted a copy of his trade regulations to an obliging Nez Perce (*Nimi'ipuu*) whom he later called a chief of the Poltito Palton band. The courier returned by way of the present Kootenay River to meet McClallen at Lake Pend Oreille in September.

13. John McClallen is fishing for an admission that duties have not been paid, and possibly hoping to finance his western policing by extorting goods from the British trader.

14. Here is proof that McClallen was adapting his regulations to address the new situation on the upper river.

15. McClallen is making the first declaration of the extension of United States sovereignty.

16. Entry of November 10, 1807, "A Sketch of the principal Transactions and Occurrances on the Passage to and from Oxford House and during a Winter's residence at Edmonton House, Commencing July 19, 1807, Ending June 25 1808 by James Bird," HBCA B60/a/7, fols. 6–8d; published by J. B. Tyrrell, "Letter of Roseman and Perch, July 10th, 1807," *Oregon Historical Quarterly* 38, no. 4 (1937): 394–95.

17. Thompson wrote three versions of this day. One was copied into the daily journal, another repeated the same information in the narrative sent back to headquarters on September 23. The third version was a rewrite of events from May 10 to February 8, 1808 (AO20), which curiously omitted mention of the Americans. Because this fair copy was easier to read, the last was the version published by Belyea.

18. Thompson managed to keep up contact with the posts on the Saskatchewan. On the trip west he sent back letters on July 12 and again on June 19.

19. This is the "Narrative of the Establishment on the Sources of the Columbia, addressed to Mr. Duncan McGillivray, Director of the N. W. Coy, and the Gentlemen of the upper Fort des Prairies," manuscript (Cambridge: Royal Commonwealth Society Library, n.d.). Thompson's title was "Narrative of the Expedition to the Kootenae, Flat Bow Indian Countries, on the Sources of the Columbia River, Pacific Ocean, by D. Thompson on behalf of the N.w.Company 1807," which J. B. Tyrrell provided to his associate T. C. Elliott for publication in *Oregon Historical Quarterly* 26, no. 1 (March 1925): 43.

20. September 25, [1807], Journal 20, Archives of Ontario, Belyea, *Columbia Journals*, p. 69.

21. Ibid.

22. Thompson apparently misheard a rumor of the burning of the former post. See Glover, *Narrative*, p. 311; Coues, *New Light on the Early History of the Greater Northwest*, 2:566.

23. McDonald delivered eighty Made Beaver (an accounting term), in bear skins and swan skins, but few if any actual beaver skins.

24. James Bird was an auditor of North West Company operations on the upper Saskatchewan River. A more moderate competitor than his mentor, William Tomison, Bird got along with his neighbors while recording insights into rival operations. He drew upon his good relationship with Indian customers, whose travels extended his vision south beyond the Missouri and Yellowstone and west beyond the Rocky Mountains.

CHAPTER FIFTEEN:
FOLLOWING WESTERN WATERS

1. In their brief, imperfect exchanges, Lewis and Clark lumped the people they did not meet as Tushapaws. They knew themselves as *Kalispel*, Salish speakers living all along Clark's Fork.

2. They were following the present Jaco River, named later for Jacques Raphael Finlay, who led the North West Company expansion across the mountains.

3. This was Blackhorse Lake to the Salish (present Flathead Lake).

4. That was due to a rain shadow, and a town that grew up later was aptly named Paradise. From personal conversation with Bill Edleman and others familiar with Flathead Valley.

5. Carl W. Haywood, *Sometimes Only Horses to Eat: David Thompson, the Salish House Period 1807–1812* (Thompson's Falls, MT: Rockman's Trading Post, 2008), pp. 113–14.

6. "Specimen of the Flat Head Language," in Barry M. Gough, ed., *The Journal of Alexander Henry the Younger*, 2 vols. (Toronto: Champlain Society, 1992), 2:530.

7. The situation on the northern plains is described in the Edmonton House Journal 1806/07 HBCA B60/a/6, fols. 1, 2, and in Daniel William Harmon, *Sixteen Years in the Indian Country* (Toronto: Macmillan Company of Canada Limited, 1957), p. 100.

8. Alexander Henry estimated that there were three hundred fifty tents of *Piikani* compared to three hundred of the rest of the Slave tribes (generalized as Blackfeet). Elliott Coues, ed., *New Light on the Early History of the Greater Northwest: The Manuscript Journals of Alexander Henry and of David Thompson, 1799–1814*, 2 vols. (1897; reprint, Minneapolis: Ross & Haines, 1965), 2:530. McClallen probably met representatives of those later known as the Small Robes band.

9. Ibid., 2:537, 714–18.

10. "Narrative of the Expedition to the Kootenae & Flat Bow Indian Countries, on the Sources of the Columbia River, Pacific Ocean, by D. Thompson on behalf of the N.w.Company 1807," *Oregon Historical Quarterly* 26, no. 1 (March 1925): 42–43. This appears to be the same as "Narrative of the Establishment on the Sources of the Columbia addressed to Mr. Duncan McGillivray, Director of N. W. Coy, and gentlemen at Fort des Prairies, 1807," a manuscript now in the Royal Commonwealth Society Library, Cambridge. It represents a copy made from Thompson's field journal up to September 19, 1807, which was sent across the mountains with the Captain Perch letter.

11. McClallen appears to have used the term *Pilchenees* as a variation on Lewis and Clark's usage *Pahkees*, a Shoshone generalization for northern plainsmen. See Gary E. Moulton, ed., *The Journals of the Lewis and Clark Expedition*, 13 vols. (Lincoln: University of Nebraska Press, 1983–2001) [hereafter *Journals of L&C*], August 13, 1805, n. 11.

12. Based on Nez Perce descriptions, William Clark worked out a sketch

map showing the two branches of Clark's River (the present Bitterroot and Clark forks). Although he missed Flathead Lake, Clark grasped that the Flathead River joined the Clark Fork. *Journals of L&C*, Codex M, pp. 1–2, fig. 18. A nebulous Great Lake to the north that the Nez Perce described may have been Lake Coeur d'Alene rather than Lake Pend Oreille.

13. On July 4, 1806, Lewis wrote:

> It is worthy of remark that these people were about to return by the same pass by which they had conducted us through the difficult part of the Rocky Mountains, altho they were about to decend Clark's river several days journey in surch of the Shale's [Salish] their relations, a circumstance which to my mind furnishes sufficient evidence that there is not so near or so good a rout to the plains of Columbia by land along that river as that which we came. the several war routs of the Minetarees which fall into this vally of Clark's river concenter at traveller's rest beyond which point they have never yet dared to venture in pursuit of the nations beyond the mountains. all the nations also on the west side of the mountain with whom we are acquainted inhabiting the waters of Lewis's river & who visit the plains of the Missouri pass by this rout.

See Merle Wells, "Lewis & Clark's Water Route to the Northwest," *Columbia* (Winter 1994/95).

14. On June 30, 1806, Sergeant Gass heard a garbled description of Clark's Fork and believed that salmon did not ascend it because of a six-hundred- or seven-hundred-foot waterfall, where it emptied into the Columbia, perhaps Metaline Falls near the mouth or possibly an exaggeration of Thompson Falls, which was not a barrier. There is a hint that one of the corpsmen, Robert Fraser, recognized the potential of Clark's Fork when he had a map drawn to accompany the anticipated publication of his journal. That showed the Clark Fork River circling around to enter the Columbia well north of the Snake Fork. *Journals of L&C*, 1:Fraser's Map.

15. In fact the Corps of Discovery had failed to explore the Snake (Lewis's Fork) River above the mouth of the Clearwater, and Clark's Fork not at all.

16. William E. Farr, "Going to Buffalo: Indian Hunting Migrations across the Rocky Mountains," *Montana: The Magazine of Western History* (Winter 2003): 2–21.

17. Those winter pastures were later known as the Horse Plains.

18. This is based on an observation two years later that counted fifty-four Flathead lodges, twenty-three Pointed Hearts, and four Kutenais.

19. The first black was York, who came with Lewis and Clark, and the third, Joseph Lewis, would accompany Joseph Howse in 1810.

20. The words of Father De Smet in 1841 are taken from the highway marker at the site.

21. Thompson Falls: a military survey of that route was not completed for another fifty years when Lt. John Mullen surveyed a possible route for a wagon road from Fort Benton above the Great Falls of the Missouri to the Columbia and found it to be near water grade.

22. Two years later David Thompson called them Ilthkoyape Indians (*Sxoielpi* or *Skoyelpy*) but they are known as Kettle Falls Indians until the Hudson's Bay Company built Fort Colvile.

23. Barbara Belyea, ed., *Columbia Journals: David Thompson* (Montreal: Magill-Queens University Press, 1994; reprint, Seattle; University of Washington Press, 1998), p. 112.

24. The Pack River Trail connected to the Kootenay River.

25. Early tribal identification is complex. John McClallen revealed his limited understanding when he referred to the Poltito Palton, Cabanaws, and Pilchenee. He may have lumped Lewis and Clark's Ootlashshoots and Tushapaws as Flatheads. Alexander Henry had not met any of those peoples when he depended on Thompson's guesses in his 1810/11 ethnography. Henry named the Kootenae, Flat Bow or Lake Kootenae; Saleesh, Kullyspel (Kalispel); Ilthkoyape (Kettle Falls); Shawpatin [*sic*] or Green Wood Indians (Nez Perce); Simpoil (Sanpoil), Skeetsshoo (Coeur d'Alene); and Snake (Shoshone). The Sahaptan speakers or Green Wood Indians were Nez Perce. But the Blue Earth Indians probably referred to Kalispels living in the vicinity of the Pack River, where Thompson commented on finding blue clay to caulk log walls. Somehow McClallen confused them with the Poltito Palton band of Nez Perce who lived on the Clearwater River and gave the lake that name because of his Nez Perce courier. The French names: Tete Plattes, Nez Perce, Pend d'Oreille, and Coeur d' Alene have prevailed. See Gough, *Journal of Alexander Henry the Younger* (see note 6).

26. Thompson visited Lake Pend Oreille in 1809 about the same time of the season that McClallan had been there two years previous. Trader Thompson drew about a hundred Kutenais, Kalispels, Coeur d'Alenes, and others, an indication that the American found enough informants to gain a good idea of regional geography.

27. McClallen's impressions are reconstructed from Thompson's journal

318

when he visited the same area about the same time of the year in September 1809. Thompson's Journals 22 and 23, Belyea, *Columbia Journals*, 104–16; M. Catharine White, ed., *David Thompson's Journals Relating to Montana and Adjacent Regions 1808–1812* (Missoula: Montana State University Press, 1950), pp. 38–41, 43–58; T. C. Elliott, ed., "David Thompson's Journeys in Idaho," *Washington Historical Quarterly* 11 (1920): 99–103; "David Thompson's Journeys in the Pend Oreille Country," *Washington Historical Quarterly* 23 (1932): 19–24.

28. Alvin M. Josephy Jr. unraveled the derivation of the term *Pellate Paller* (*pello-ut pelu*) that Lewis and Clark applied to certain Nez Perce who lived on the Clearwater at a place where the river waters were greenish or murky. It may have designated the band living near present Kamiah, Idaho, where the snow-stalled corps spent time. Alvin M. Josephy Jr., *The Nez Perce Indians and the Opening of the Northwest* (New Haven, CT: Yale University Press, 1965), pp. 649–51n30. McClallen's usage descended from what he had heard from Lewis and Clark during the long evening he spent with them or from the two former corpsman now with him.

29. Lt. Jeremy Pinch to the British Merchant, Poltito Palton Lake, September 29, 1807, T. C. Elliott, "The Strange Case of David Thompson and Jeremy Pinch," *Oregon Historical Quarterly* (June 1939): 190–91. The difference in the name could be due to Thompson's handwriting or later misreading of copies.

CHAPTER SIXTEEN: "I COULD NOT ALTOGETHER INDIANIFY MY HEART"

1. Phillip Nolan to James Wilkinson, circa 1794, in John Edward Weems, *Men without Countries: Three Adventurers of the Early Southwest* (Boston: Houghton Mifflin, 1969), p. 58.

2. Donald Jackson, ed., *The Journals of Zebulon Montgomery Pike with Letters and Related Documents*, 2 vols. (Norman: University of Oklahoma Press, 1966) [hereafter *Pike Journals*], 2:128.

3. W. Raymond Wood and Thomas D. Thiessen, eds., *Early Fur Trade on the Northern Plains: Canadian Traders among the Mandan and Hidatsa Indians, 1738–1818* (Norman: University of Oklahoma Press, 1985), pp. 72, 270–71.

4. T. C. Elliott, "Thompson's Discoveries," *Oregon Historical Quarterly* (n.d.): 45.

5. Typing "smallpox infected blanket myth" into a search engine yields the full spectrum of politically correct opinion and argument on the validity of this erroneous folklore.

6. Barbara Belyea, ed., *Columbia Journals: David Thompson* (Montreal: Magill-Queens University Press, 1994; reprint, Seattle: University of Washington Press, 1998), p. 67. The disorder persisted at Rocky Mountain House until winter 1810 when Alexander Henry mentioned that two of the principal *Piikani*, Black Bear and White Buffalo Robe, were suffering from what he termed "bad colds." By the first of November Gros Blanc, the chief of the Siksika Cold band, died of the prevalent disease "… and all the Indians in the plains are affected with it." Elliott Coues, ed., *New Light on the Early History of the Greater Northwest: The Manuscript Journals of Alexander Henry and of David Thompson 1799–1814*, 2 vols. (1897; reprint, Minneapolis: Ross & Haines, 1965), 2:657–60.

7. This was recorded in bk. 18, p. 274, and also in "Narrative of the Establishment on the Sources of the Columbia, addressed to Mr. Duncan McGillivray, Director of the N. W. Coy, and the Gentleman of the upper Fort des Prairies" and also in the unpublished Royal Commonwealth Society Library manuscript. Curiously, it slipped out of bk. 20, which Belyea used to describe those events.

8. Belyea, *Columbia Journals*, p. 68.

9. Ibid., pp. 67, 227.

10. Elliott, "Thompson's Discoveries," p. 47.

11. His assurances to Duncan McGillivray survive as the almost-unreadable pencil draft he made as he descended the Saskatchewan, and there was no final draft after he learned of McGillivray's death.

12. The date would be April 20, 1808. He named the south-flowing river for the McGillivray brothers (the present Kootenay).

13. October 26, 1807, AO Journal 19, in Belyea, ed., *Columbia Journals*, p. 226.

14. Jack Nisbet, *Sources of the River: Tracking David Thompson across Western North America* (Seattle: Sasquatch Books, 1994), pp. 105–106.

15. Edmonton House Journal, November 10, 1807, HBCA B60/a/7, fols. 6–8d.

16. Donald Jackson, ed., *Letters of the Lewis and Clark Expedition, with Related Documents 1783–1854*, 2nd ed., 2 vols. (Urbana: University of Illinois Press, 1978) [hereafter *Letters of L&C*], 2:336–43.

17. Journal of Occurrences 1807, Archives of Ontario, no. 20, p. 291.

18. This was Thompson's entry for December 11, 1807, p. 291. See also Nisbet, *Sources of the River*, p. 106.

19. "David Thompson Journal," Vancouver Public Library manuscript. The letter was similar to two others written at the same time and reproduced in *Letters of L&C*, 2:336–43. However, this is the original in Thompson's hand.

20. Journal of Occurrences 1807, bk. 20, Archives of Ontario.

21. Lewis and Clark appear to use this name for a specific band, the Nez Perce with whom they spent a good deal of time. The two corpsmen must have passed it to McClallen. However, Thompson was using the term *Green Wood* or *Blue Earth Indians* by 1808, and Alexander Henry repeated it in his 1811 description of the Nez Perce.

22. Ibid. The entry was rediscovered by Robert Carlton Clark in 1927, enclosed in a letter dated February 26, 1846, from the Hudson's Bay Company to the British Foreign Office.

23. T. C. Elliott, "The Strange Case of David Thompson and Jeremy Pinch," *Oregon Historical Quarterly* 40, no. 2 (June 1939): 188–89. Thompson was trying to identify the Kalispels, whose tribal territory stretched from Lake Pend Oreille as far east as Flathead Lake. He later called them Blue Earth Indians in reference to the color of the clay near the northern lobe of the lake.

24. "Messrs McDonald, Hughes & McTavish" and a private letter to McTavish, HBCA A67/1, fols. 8–13d.

25. HBCA A67/1, 8–13d, preserves the two March 1808 letters from Thompson. They are office copies made years later with no apparent relationship in a bound collection of miscellaneous documents and trivia loosely organized by date.

26. It is likely that Iroquois trappers had already crossed the mountains as some freemen were doing, but this seems to be the first documentation of eastern Indians in the West.

27. Thompson Journal, bk. 19.

28. HBCA A67/1, fols. 8–11d; Nisbet, *Sources of the River*, p. 111.

29. HBCA A67/1, fols. 8–13d.

30. In what appears to be the original field journal, Thompson admitted that inconvenient presence and repeated pretty much the same information in the copy that he sent to his patron, Duncan McGillivray. Both records fail to mention the first letter from Captain Perch. Later versions of those overlapping journals censor out everything pertaining to the Americans. Forty years later, Thompson was even more circumspect in his much-rewritten *Narrative*. Finally, as an old man he lied that he had actually crossed the mountains many years before.

31. The trail by way of the Pack River came out at the west end of McClallen's Poltito Palton Lake (Lake Pend Oreille). Another trail from the Kootenai River passed Flathead Lake to the Salish winter camps on the Horse Plains.

32. Alexander Henry wrote, "Chastity is particularly attended among

them [Salish or Flat Head Indians], and their women will not barter their favors, even with Whites, for procuring reward. They may be easily prevailed upon to reside with our people, as man and Wife, after the custom of the Country." Barry Gough, ed., *The Journal of Alexander Henry the Younger, 1799–1814* (Toronto: Champlain Society, 1992), 2:525.

33. Belyea, *Columbia Journals*, p. 73; Nisbet, *Sources of the River*, p. 98.

34. As an example, the names that the tribes had for themselves or that others gave them were usually different.

CHAPTER SEVENTEEN: COKALARISHKIT, THE PROTEIN ROAD

1. In a May 8, 1808, journal entry, Thompson described another fight after forty-seven Peagans followed his men who were sent to teach the Kootanaes and Lake Indians how to work beaver. There was "a scuffle in which 1 Peagan was killed & another, his arm broken, on the Kootenae Side the old Chief was shot thro' the thigh & his Horse wounded B the Peagans hid themselves & shortly after stole 35 Horses." Thompson bk. 19, Archives of Ontario.

2. Edmonton House Journal, HBCA B60/a/7, fol. 12.

3. Ibid. That appointment had been set before the Salish/*Piikani* meeting was sabotaged by Bloods and other Blackfeet.

4. HBCA A67/1, fols. 8–13d; Thompson bk. 19.

5. HBCA B60/a/7, fol. 4d. Some freemen on the Saskatchewan were threatening to carry their packs all the way to Hudson's Bay to get fair prices.

6. Christina MacDonald Mckenzie Williams, "The Daughter of Angus MacDonald," *Washington Historical Quarterly* 8, no. 2 (April 1922): 107–17.

7. Joseph P. Donnelly, trans., *Wilderness Kingdom, Indian Life in the Rocky Mountains: 1840–1847: The Journals & Paintings of Nicolas Point* (New York: Holt, Rinehart and Winston, 1967), p. 43. The protein road continued in use through the first three quarters of the nineteenth century.

8. The evidence to support the speculation about John Colter and John B. Thompson is mostly circumstantial; a wisp of possibilities as thin as smoke, but an important implication that challenges a hoary legend of those times and, as will be seen, raises a larger question.

9. The men with McClallen were probably former boatmen who needed to return to St. Louis in order to collect two years' wages.

10. Gary E. Moulton, ed., *The Journals of the Lewis and Clark Expedition*, 13 vols. (Lincoln: University of Nebraska Press, 1983–2001), Lewis's entry, July 3, 1806.

11. Known to Thompson as Courtin's Defile because the trader/trapper was later killed there in an ambush, it is now called the Hellgate.

12. Seaman's Creek was later renamed for George Montour; the country son of one of the clerks who prepared the trail that Thompson used crossing the mountains.

13. This is the author's personal observation from riding into the adjacent Bob Marshall Wilderness.

14. The background of the Blackfoot expansion into the upper Missouri plains and piedmont is discussed in John C. Jackson, *The Piikani Blackfeet: A Culture Under Siege* (Missoula, MT: Mountain Press, 2000).

15. *Journals of L&C*, Lewis's entry, July 15, 1806. He concluded this had been the camp of a party of "Tushapaws" returning from the early hunt.

16. Horse capturing was a way of replenishing herds culled by hard winters.

17. John C. Jackson, "The Fight on Two Medicine River," *We Proceeded On* 23, no. 1 (February 2006): 14–23.

18. During the winter or the spring, the former corpsman George Drouillard made a sweep up the Big Horn Valley. Tradition holds that John Colter also traveled as far west as the Tetons and returned leading a combined party of Snakes and Salish. But that would have been unlikely if he had spent the winter west of the mountains with McClallen and Thompson.

19. Elliott Coues, ed., *New Light on the Early History of the Greater Northwest: The Manuscript Journals of Alexander Henry and of David Thompson 1799–1814*, 2 vols. (1897; reprint, Minneapolis: Ross & Haines, 1965), 2:539–40.

CHAPTER EIGHTEEN: A STEP INTO THE ABYSS

1. On October 22, 1807, Bird outfitted on credit one of "the Canadian freemen who are becoming numerous here. The N[orth]W[est]C[ompany] will not pay them in money unless they take their outfits from them. This man promises to cross the Rocky Mountains next summer and make a winter hunt in Cootenais lands where he has already wintered before and took 600 beaver." He was ready to take his furs to Edmonton or York to obtain a better price and Bird hoped this would set an example. Edmonton House Journal 1807/08, HBCA B60/a/7, fol. 4d. This must have been an inland reaction to the North West Company regulation of July 15, 1806, prohibiting men from bringing personal furs out of the country in the canoes, or money transactions inland. W. S. Wallace, ed., *Documents relating to the North West Company* (Toronto: Champlain, n.d.), p. 216.

2. Modern descriptions of the Pack River indicate that between November and June it can swell to a six- to ten-foot-deep torrent.

3. Entry for May 17, 1808, in Barbara Belyea, ed., *Columbia Journals: David Thompson* (Montreal: Magill-Queens University Press, 1994; reprint, Seattle; University of Washington Press, 1998), p. 88.

4. Thompson's Journal 21, Archives of Ontario, in Belyea, *Columbia Journals*, pp. 75–95.

5. Belyea, *Columbia Journals*, pp. 75, 86, 95. Because James Hughes had already descended the Saskatchewan before Thompson passed Fort Augustus, Thompson had no way on knowing more about the American officer.

6. Barry M. Gough, ed., *The Journal of Alexander Henry the Younger, 1799–1814*, 2 vols. (Toronto: Champlain Society, 1992) [hereafter *Henry Journal*], 2:434. Henry apparently obtained the copy when he returned to Fort William in the summer of 1809.

7. T. C. Elliott, "David Thompson's Discovery Source of the Columbia," *Oregon Historical Quarterly* 26, no. 1 (March 1925): 43. This is Tyrrell's reading of the "Narrative of the Establishment on the Sources of the Columbia, addressed to Mr. Duncan McGillivray" in the Royal Commonwealth Society Library, Cambridge.

8. The North West Company was trying to convince the Crown to alter the Hudson's Bay Company's chartered right to exclusive access through Hudson's Bay.

9. Pencil draft in Thompson's Journal 19, Ontario Archives microfilm, reel 2. Excerpts in Belyea, *Columbia Journals*, p. 236.

10. According to W. S. Wallace in his introduction to *Documents relating to the Northwest Company*, p. 19, Simon McGillivray sent his nephew to explore opening trade on the Pacific slope in 1800.

11. Arthur S. Morton, ed., *The Journal of Duncan McGillivray of the North West Company at Fort George on the Saskatchewan 1794–5, with Introduction, Notes and Appendix by Arthur S. Morton* (Toronto: Macmillan, 1929; reprint, Fairfax, Washington: Ye Galleon Press, 1989), appendix, 16–17, 23–24.

12. Elliott Coues, ed., *New Light on the Early History of the Greater Northwest: The Manuscript Journals of Alexander Henry and of David Thompson 1799–1814* (1897; reprint, Minneapolis: Ross & Haines, 1965), 1:253.

13. Henry to Cameron, February 1, 1809, National Archives of Canada, Selkirk Correspondence, MG19E1, pp. 8835–39. These letters must have contained Henry's observations on developments across the Mandan Connection or what to do to answer the threatening Captain Perch.

14. Coues, *New Light on the Early History of the Greater Northwest*, 1:195,239,

428, 436, 439–40. Note that Henry's orders to transfer to the Saskatchewan were started to him before Thompson arrived at Rainy Lake on August 2.

15. Gough, *Henry Journal*, 2.366–67, 395.

16. Ibid., 2:367. This and the prior Coues edition are both drawn from what is called the George Coventry copy of Henry's original journals, made about 1824. The originals have disappeared.

17. Ibid., 2:396–97.

18. Coues, *New Light on the Early History of the Greater Northwest*, 2:539–40. Henry might have had a twinge of guilt because he did not admit the transaction until the following year, after returning from the Fort William meeting.

19. Entries of October 2 and 12, 1808, Edmonton House Journal, HBCA B60/a/8, fol. 4.

20. Ibid., fols. 4–4d. This appears to have been a later incident in which John Colter and John Potts were intercepted near the Three Forks. The Atsiina believed that they had killed both men, but Colter had escaped in a race for his life. The heavy gun may have been the military rifle that he carried on the Lewis and Clark expedition and never turned in. A Model 1792 military rifle in the collection of Peyton C. (Bud) Clark depicted on p. 257 of Robert J. Moore and Michael Hayes, *Lewis & Clark: Tailor Made, Trail Worn*, is one of only five known to still exist out of 19,726 weapons made. But that model was brought into service for the War of 1812 and captured by a Canadian Indian who decorated it with silver tacks and could not be the heavy gun taken from Colter that Bloods carried to Edmonton House/Fort Augustus in 1808.

21. According to Henry, the North West Company *Piikani* trade at Fort Augustus up to December 23, 1808, amounted to 151 beaver skins, compared to the Falls Indian trade of only 17 large and 5 Small, or the Sarcee contribution of 19. Gough, *Henry Journal*, pp. 547–50.

22. "Appendage to John McDonald of Garth, Autobiographical Notes," Louis F. A. Masson, ed., *Les Bourgeois de la Companie du Nord-ouest: Recits de voyages, lettres et rapports inedits relatifs au Nord-ouest canadien*, 2 vols. (New York: Antiquarian Press, 1960), 2:41–42.

23. Lois McClellan Patrie and Gene McClellan, comps., *The Descendents of Michael and Jane (Henry) McClellan of Colrain, Mass.* (Bakersfield, CA: G. McClellan, 1997), p. 8. Like much genealogical material, this statement is misleading and seems to confuse a Maryland man of the same name who was appointed United State consul to that East Indian seaport about the time that John McClallen was in Baltimore completing the Santa Fe outfit.

24. W. Kaye Lamb, ed., *The Journals and Letters of Sir Alexander Mackenzie* (Cambridge: Hakluyt Society, 1970), pp. 516–18.

25. Henry to Cameron, February 1, 1809, National Archives of Canada, Selkirk Correspondence, MG19E1, pp. 8835–39.

26. The engagé, Boisverd, traded eighteen packs from the Flat Bow Indians. Jack Nisbet in *Sources of the River: Tracking David Thompson across Western North America* (Seattle: Sasquatch Books, 1994), p. 140, sets the total taken across the mountains in the spring of 1809 at fifty-four packs, but those must have been light field packs of seventy or eighty pounds.

27. John C. Jackson, "Old Rivet: The Surviving Member of the Corps of Discovery in the Northwest," *Columbia: The Magazine of Northwest History* 18, no. 2 (Summer 2004): 17–23.

28. Manuel Lisa vs. John B. Bouche, case no. 6, St. Louis Chancery Court, February 20, 1811, in L. R. Colter-Frick, *Courageous Colter and Companions* (Washington, MO: self-published, 1997), pp. 401–12.

29. Taken from notes on the Drouillard map.

30. The well-known yarn of John Colter's winter hike was not mentioned, which raises questions about the timing and circumstances. For reasoning, see John C. Jackson, "Revisiting the Colter Legend," *Rocky Mountain Fur Trade Journal* 3 (2009): 1–19.

31. After wintering at a camp above, the former corpsman John Potts came to Fort Remon on June 27 to settle a one-hundred-seventy-dollar debt to Lisa, rent two horses, and contract a joint outfit with Peter Weiser. Their note, witnessed by Jean Baptiste Champlain and Forest Handcock, suggests that Lisa and Drouillard were still there on July 7, 1808.

32. Pierre Chouteau to Secretary of War William Eustis, Mandan villages, December 14, 1809, Pierre Chouteau Letterbook, Missouri Historical Society, p. 144.

33. Account of George Drouillard, August 5, 1808, Joseph Philipson Business Account Book, M-73, St. Louis Mercantile Library at the University of Missouri–St. Louis. See also Stallo Vinton's additional note in Hiram Martin Chittenden, *The American Fur Trade of the Far West*, 2 vols. (New York: Press of the Pioneers, 1935; reprint, Lincoln: University of Nebraska Press, 1986), 1:125.

34. Donald Jackson, ed., *Letters of the Lewis and Clark Expedition, with Related Documents 1783–1854*, 2nd ed., 2 vols. (Urbana: University of Illinois Press, 1978), 2:697–719.

35. John B. Thompson to George Gibson, August 12, 1808, Deed Book B, p. 152, Recorder of Deeds, City Hall, City of St. Louis, St. Louis, Missouri. Gibson returned to the upper Missouri with the Pryor expedition and had been wounded in the fight with the Arikara.

CHAPTER NINETEEN:
POSTSCRIPT TO LOST LETTERS

1. In Wilkinson/Number 13's "Reflections on Louisiana," he suggested using Indians as a barrier to US expansion. Then the general appears to have changed his mind and ordered Pike to establish a positive relationship with the Comanche, who were now seen as the barrier.

2. Alencaster to Salcedo, Santa Fe, February 16, 1807, Donald Jackson, ed., *The Journals of Zebulon Montgomery Pike with Letters and Related Documents*, 2 vols. (Norman: University of Oklahoma Press, 1966) [hereafter *Pike Journals*], 2:166.

3. Ibid., 2:194, 204.

4. The Spanish charge d'affairs, the Marques de Casa Yrujo, erred in his interpretation of Pike's mission. He forwarded a copy of Wilkinson's August 6, 1806, warning to Pike about the intentions of Lisa and Clamorgan. That was not proof of ulterior motives, but it approximated what McClallen intended to do.

5. "Sibley's Council with the Comanche [August 18, 1807]," *Pike Journals*, 2:260–62.

6. Ibid., 2:228.

7. That connection may have survived the Burr scandal. One of the last acts of the Jefferson administration in January 1809 asked James Wilkinson "to feel the pulse of Cuba as to an estimate of the inducements to a incorporation of that island with the United States in comparison with those of an adherence to the Spanish Main." Wilkinson apparently mishandled that charge as President Madison later asked William Shaler, the special agent to Cuba, to renew the initiative. Robert A. Rutland et al., eds., *The Papers of James Madison: Presidential Series* (Charlottesville: University of Virginia Press, 1984–), 2:311.

8. Roger J. Spiller, ed., *Dictionary of American Military Biography* (Westport, CT: Greenwood Press, 1984), 3:1189–92.

9. Captain Zackery Perch's letter from the Yellow River, Columbia, was written on that same day.

10. Half of the twelve-thousand-dollar debt and interest ($6,459) was due in April 1808.

11. On July 26, 1809, the *Missouri Gazette* published a letter announcing Clamorgan's return from the Spanish provinces and the potential of trade there. Most of Lieutenant Pike's men were still held in Chihuahua until July 3, 1809, when Governor Salcedo ordered their release to Lt. Daniel Hughes. Next year, Clamorgan was still trying to collect from Lisa for his share of that debt. Richard Edward Oglesby, *Manuel Lisa and the Opening of the Missouri Fur Trade* (Norman: University of Oklahoma Press, 1984), p. 35n1.

12. Benjamin Wilkinson did not survive the trip. At the September 10, 1810, board meeting of the St. Louis Missouri Fur Company, Walter Wilkinson represented his brother's interest and later stood in for him when the company was dissolved in 1812. Nash had been an early settler in Spanish Louisiana in 1804, serving as a surveyor and obtaining a Spanish land grant in what became Boone County. He returned to start a farm in 1816.

13. "Robinson Printed Broadside," *Pike Journals*, 2:379–82n1, 387n.

14. *Pike Journals*, 2:379–82, 382–87, 392–93.

15. There are three versions of this map: a Library of Congress copy, another in the Beinecke Collection at Yale University, and the third referred to above, believed to have been a foldout of Abraham P. Nasatir, ed., *Before Lewis and Clark: Documents Illustrating the History of the Missouri 1785–1804* (St. Louis: St. Louis Historical Documents Foundation, 1952; reprint, Lincoln: University of Nebraska Press, 1990).

16. See William E. Lass, *Minnesota's Boundary with Canada: Its Evolution since 1783* (St. Paul: Minnesota Historical Society Press, 1980), pp. 28–31.

17. Madison to Monroe, Department of State, May 30, 1806, 10th Congress, 1st Session, in *American State Papers: Foreign Relations*, 3:126.

18. See appendix in Thomas C. Danisi and John C. Jackson, *Meriwether Lewis* (Amherst, NY: Prometheus Books, 2009), pp. 349–73.

19. M. Catharine White, ed., *David Thompson's Journals relating to Montana and Adjacent Regions 1808–12* (Missoula: Montana State University Press, 1950) [hereafter *Thompson's Montana Journals*], pp. 65, 67, 86.

20. Menard to Langlois, October 7, 1809, Kaskaskia Papers, Missouri Historical Society.

21. "The NWCo will not pay them in money unless they take their outfits from them." They wanted to pay trappers in high-priced, marked-up goods as a way of keeping them in the country. Edmonton House Journal, 1807/08, HBCA B60/a/7, fol. 4d.

22. White, *Thompson's Montana Journals*, pp. 88–89n62. Recall that Charles Courtin was a Detroit trader supplied by Hugh and Richard Patterson of Sandwich, upper Canada. Chouteau Papers, Missouri Historical Society.

23. Thompson named the place of the attack Courtin's Defile, but it was later known as the Hellgate.

24. White, *Thompson's Montana Journals*, p. 92. Thompson dates "Rivi's" arrival as March 3.

25. Ibid., pp. 92–93; Jack Nisbet, *Sources of the River: Tracking David Thompson across Western North America* (Seattle: Sasquatch Books, 1994), p. 159. Thompson traded about 500 beaver from Courtin's former associates and

other freemen. If the Salish had traded for 22 new guns, that could have added another 330 to 440 skins. About 2,000 pounds of beaver were hauled back to the Saskatchewan.

26. Thompson to Alexander Fraser, December 21, 1810, in Louis F. A. Masson, ed., *Les Bourgeois de la Companie du Nord-ouest: Recits de voyages, lettres et rapports inedits relatifs au Nord-ouest canadien*, 2 vols. (New York: Antiquarian Press, 1960), 2:41–42. Alexander Henry and James Bird also described the attacks on the St. Louis Missouri Fur Company in unmistakable detail. The officer whom Thompson reported killed was probably George Drouillard.

27. Richard Glover, ed. *David Thompsons Narrative, 1784–1813* (Toronto: Champlain Society, 1962), pp. 391–93. Actually, those who provided the production Thompson needed to establish a business survived and became a trapping cadre that would persist for many years.

28. HBCA, D5/8, fol. 102, Howse to George Simpson (GS), Cirencester, February 19, 1843.

29. HBCA D4/63, fol. 5. GS to Thompson, Lachine, September 27, 1843.

30. John Nicks, "David Thompson," *Dictionary of Canadian Biography*, 8:883.

31. HBCA D4/63, 174–75. GS to Barclay, Lachine, December 21, 1843.

32. D4/64, 107, GS to Rt. Hon. Richard Pakenham, Lachine, April 17, 1844.

33. "Thompson to Sir James Alexander, Royal Engineers Office, Montreal, May 9, 1845," from *Report of Archives of British Columbia 1913*, p. 123 in Gordon Charles Davidson, *The North West Company* (Berkeley: University of California Press, 1918), p. 97.

34. For recognition of this tendency to "willfully misrepresent facts," see *The Writings of David Thompson*, vol. 1, *The Travels, 1850 Version*, ed. William E. Moreau (Toronto: McGill-Queen's University Press, 2009), pp. xv–xvi, 280.

35. HBCA D5/16 [official letter March 26, 1846, in D4/67] private acknowledging. Letter January 28, 1846.

36. The problem has previously been treated in Frederick Merk, *The Oregon Question: Essays in Anglo-American Diplomacy and Politics* (Cambridge, MA: Harvard University Press, 1967).

37. Old Hoole was listed as a freeman in the "List of People on the Columbia for Winter 1813/14," Robert F. Jones, ed., *Annals of Astoria: The Headquarters Log of the Pacific Fur Company on the Columbia River, 1811–1813* (New York: Fordham University Press, 1999), p. 230; also see Ross Cox, *The Columbia River* (London: H. Colburn and R. Bentley), pp. 192–93.

38. Rivet founded a family that was active in the later fur trade and whose descendants still live on the Flathead Reservation.

BIBLIOGRAPHY

DOCUMENTS AND MANUSCRIPTS

Archives of Ontario
> David Thompson Rocky Mountain House Journal, notebook numbers 18 and 19

Boise State University Library
> J. Neilson Barry Collection

Chicago Historical Society
> James Wilkinson Letters, 1757–1825

Hudson's Bay Company Archives, Archives of Manitoba, Winnipeg, Manitoba, Canada

Indiana Historical Society
> John Armstrong Papers

Jefferson National Expansion Memorial Library, National Park Service, St. Louis, Missouri
> Grace Lewis Miller Collection

Library of Congress Manuscript Division
> Thomas Jefferson Papers

Minutes of the Albany Committee of Correspondence, 1775–1778. Albany: University of the State of New York, 1923

Missouri Historical Society, St. Louis, Missouri
> Auguste Chouteau Papers
> Captain Amos Stoddard Company Book
> Carr Family Papers
> E. G. Voorhis Memorial Collection
> Ludlow Field Maury Collection
> Pierre Chouteau Account Books
> Sibley Papers
> Tesson Collection

National Archives and Record Administration
> General James Wilkinson's Order Book, RG 94
> Records of the Accounting Officers of the Department of the Treasury, RG 217

Records of the War Department

United States Congress
> *American State Papers: Miscellaneous.* Washington: Gales & Seaton, 1834.
> *American State Papers: 10 Congress, 1 Session, Miscellaneous,* vol. 1, 571–77.
> *Report of the Committee Appointed to Inquire into the Conduct of General Wilkinson, Ezekiel Bacon, Chairman.* 582 pages, five tables. Washington: United States Congress, House of Representatives, 1811.
> "Report of Exploration of a Route for the Pacific Railroad near the 47th and 49th Parallels, from St. Paul to Puget Sound," by Isaac I. Stevens. *Senate Executive Document 129.* 12 vols. 33rd Cong, 1st Sess.
> "Report on the Exploration of the Yellowstone River." Captain W. F. Raynolds. *House Executive Document 77.* 40th Cong., 1st Sess.
> *Territorial Papers of the United States,* vols. 13–14, *The Territory of Louisiana-Missouri 1806–1814.* Edited by Clarence E. Carter. Washington: Government Printing Office, 1949.

United States Military Academy Collection, West Point, Papers of Ordinance Officer Samuel Hodgdon

St. Louis Recorded Archives

Vancouver Public Library, "David Thompson Journal"

BOOKS

Abel, Annie Heloise, ed. *Tabeau's Narrative of Loisel's Expedition to the Upper Missouri.* Norman: University of Oklahoma Press, 1939.

Abernethy, Thomas Perkins. *The Burr Conspiracy.* New York: Oxford University Press, 1954.

Allen, John Logan. *Passage through the Garden: Lewis and Clark and the Image of the American Northwest.* Urbana: University of Illinois Press, 1975.

Ambrose, Stephen E. *Undaunted Courage: Meriwether Lewis, Thomas Jefferson, and the Opening of the American West.* New York: Simon & Schuster, 1996.

Arima, Eugene Y. *Blackfeet and Palefaces: The Pikani and Rocky Mountain House: A Commemorative History from the Upper Saskatchewan and Missouri Fur Trade.* Ottawa: Golden Dog Press, 1995.

BIBLIOGRAPHY

Armour, David, ed. *Treason? At Michilimackinac: The Proceedings of a General Court Martial Held at Montreal in October 1768 for the Trail of Major Robert Rogers.* Mackinac Island: Mackinac Island State Park Commission, 1972.

Barry, Louise. *The Beginning of the West: Annals of the Kansas Gateway to the American West, 1540–1854.* Topeka: Kansas State Historical Society, 1972.

Belyea, Barbara, ed. *Columbia Journals: David Thompson.* Seattle: University of Washington Press, 1994.

Birkhimer, William E. *Historical Sketch of the Organization, Administration, Matériel and Tactics of the Artillery, United States Army.* 1884; New York: Greenwood Press, 1968.

Buchwald, Donald M. *Introduction to Chronological Listing of Significant Changes to Troop Units at West Point, New York, from 1775 to 1978.* West Point: United States Military Academy Library, 1978.

Chalfant, S. "Aboriginal Territories of the Flathead, Pend d'Oreille, and Kutenai Indians of Western Montana." In *Interior Salish and Eastern Washington Indians.* Vol. 2. New York: Garland, 1974.

Chandler, David Leon. *The Jefferson Conspiracies: A President's Role in the Assassination of Meriwether Lewis.* New York: William Morrow, 1994.

Chittenden, Hiram Martin. *The American Fur Trade of the Far West: A History of the Pioneer Trading Posts and Early Fur Companies of the Missouri Valley and the Rocky Mountains and of the Overland Commerce with Santa Fe.* 2 vols. 1902; Lincoln: University of Nebraska Press, 1986.

Clark, Robert Carlton. *History of the Willamette Valley.* Chicago, 1927.

Colter-Frick, L. R. *Courageous Colter and Companions.* Washington, MO: self-published, 1997.

Coues, Elliott, ed. *New Light on the Early History of the Greater Northwest: The Manuscript Journals of Alexander Henry and of David Thompson 1799–1814.* 1897; Minneapolis: Ross & Haines, 1965.

Cox, Ross. *The Columbia River; or, Scenes and Adventures during a Residence of Six Years on the Western Side of the Rocky Mountains among Various Tribes of Indians Hitherto Unknown; Together with "A Journey across the American Continent."* Edited by Edger I. Stewart and Jane R. Stewart. Norman: University of Oklahoma Press, 1957.

Crackel, Theodore J. *Mr. Jefferson's Army: Politics and Social Reform in the Military Establishment, 1801–1809.* New York: New York University Press, 1987.

Cunliffe, Marcus. *Soldiers & Civilians: The Martial Spirit in America, 1775–1865.* Boston: Little, Brown, 1968.

Danisi, Thomas C., and John C. Jackson. *Meriwether Lewis.* Amherst, NY: Prometheus Books, 2009.

Davidson, Gordon Charles. *The North West Company*. 1918; New York: Russell and Russell, 1967.

Donnelly, Joseph P. *Wilderness Kingdom: Indian Life in the Rocky Mountains: 1840–1847: The Journals & Paintings of Nicolas Point, S. J.* New York: Holt, Rinehart and Winston, 1967.

Fahey, William. *A History of Missouri*. Vol. 1. Columbia: University of Missouri Press, 1977.

Ferris, Robert G., series ed. *Lewis and Clark: Historical Places Associated with Their Transcontinental Exploration (1804–06)*. Washington, DC: United States Department of the Interior, National Park Service, 1975.

Ferris, Warren Angus. *Life in the Rocky Mountains 1830–1835*. Edited by Leroy R. Hafen. Denver: Old West Publishing, 1983.

Flannery, Regina. *The Gros Ventres of Montana, in Anthropological Series 15*. Washington, DC: Catholic University of America Press, 1953.

Flores, Dan L. *Jefferson & Southwestern Exploration: The Freeman & Custis Accounts of the Red River Expedition of 1806*. Norman: University of Oklahoma Press, 1984.

Foley, William E., and C. David Rice. *The First Chouteaus: River Barons of Early St. Louis*. Urbana and Chicago: University of Illinois Press, 1983.

Franchere, Hoyt C., trans. and ed. *The Overland Journal Diary of Wilson Price Hunt*. Ashland, OR: Oregon Book Society, 1973.

Gass, Patrick. *Gass's Journal of the Lewis and Clark Expedition*. 1904; Missoula: Mountain Press Publishing, 1995.

Glover, Richard, ed. *David Thompson's Narrative, 1784–1813*. Toronto: Champlain Society, 1962.

Gough, Barry M., ed. *The Journal of Alexander Henry the Younger, 1799–1814*. 2 vols. Toronto: Champlain Society, 1992.

Haig, Bruce, ed. *Journal of a Journey over Land from Buckingham House to the Rocky Mountains in 1792 & 3*. Lethbridge: Historical Research Centre, 1990.

Hamersly, Thomas H. S. *Complete Regular Army Register of the United States for One Hundred Years 1779–1879*. Washington: T. H. S. Hamersly, 1880.

Harris, Burton. *John Colter: His Years in the Rockies*. 1952; Lincoln and London: University of Nebraska Press, 1993.

Hay, Thomas Robson, and M. R. Werner. *The Admirable Trumpeter: A Biography of General James Wilkinson*. Garden City: Doubleday, Doran, 1941.

Haywood, Carl W. *Sometimes Only Horses to Eat: David Thompson, the Salish House Period 1807–1812*. Thompson's Falls: Rockman's Trading Post, 2008.

Heitman, Francis B. *Historical Register and Dictionary of the United States Army from Its Organization, September 29, 1789, to March 2, 1903*. 2 vols. Washington:

Government Printing Office, 1903; Urbana: University of Illinois Press, 1965.

Henry, Alexander. *Travels and Adventures in Canada and the Indian Territories, between the Years 1760 and 1776.* 1809; Ann Arbor: University Microfilms, 1966.

Horgan, Paul. *Great River: The Rio Grande in North American History.* New York: Rinehart, 1954.

Hoxie, Frederick, ed. *Encyclopedia of North American Indians.* Boston: Houghton Mifflin,1996.

Jackson, Donald, ed. *Among the Sleeping Giants: Occasional Pieces on Lewis and Clark.* Urbana: University of Illinois Press, 1987.

———. *The Journals of Zebulon Montgomery Pike with Letters and Related Documents.* 2 vols. Norman: University of Oklahoma Press, 1966.

———. *Letters of the Lewis and Clark Expedition, with Related Documents: 1783–1854.* 2 vols. Urbana: University of Illinois Press, 1978.

———. *Thomas Jefferson & the Stony Mountains: Exploring the West from Monticello.* Urbana: University of Illinois Press, 1981.

Jackson, John C. *Children of the Fur Trade: Forgotten Metis of the Pacific Northwest.* 1995; Corvallis: Oregon State University Press, 2007.

———. *The Piikani Blackfeet: A Culture under Siege.* Missoula: Mountain Press, 2000.

Jacobs, James Riley. *Tarnished Warrior: Major General James Wilkinson.* New York: Macmillan, 1938.

James, Thomas. *Three Years among the Indians and Mexicans.* Lincoln: University of Nebraska Press, 1984.

Johnson, Alice M., ed. *Saskatchewan Journals and Correspondence.* London: Hudson's Bay Record Society, 1967.

Jones, Robert F., ed. *Annals of Astoria: The Headquarters Log of the Pacific Fur Company on the Columbia River, 1811–1813.* New York: Fordham University Press, 1999.

Josephy, Alvin M., Jr. *The Nez Perce Indians and the Opening of the Northwest.* New Haven: Yale University Press, 1965.

Kline, Mary-Jo, ed. *Political Correspondence and Public Papers of Aaron Burr.* 2 vols. Princeton: Princeton University Press, 1983.

Kulka, Jon. *A Wilderness So Immense: The Louisiana Purchase and the Destiny of America.* New York: Anchor Books, 2004.

Lamb, W. Kaye, ed. *The Journals and Letters of Sir Alexander Mackenzie.* Cambridge: Hakluyt Society, 1970.

Lass, William E. *Minnesota's Boundary with Canada: Its Evolution since 1783.* St. Paul: Minnesota Historical Society Press, 1980.

Lavender. David. *The American Heritage History of the Great West.* New York: American Heritage, 1965.

———. *The Fist in the Wilderness.* 1964; Albuquerque: University of New Mexico Press, 1979.

MacGregor, Carol Lynn, ed. *The Journal of Patrick Gass: Member of the Lewis and Clark Expedition.* Missoula; Mountain Press Publishing, 1997.

Mair, Jackson Turner. *The Anti-Federalist: Critics of the Constitution 1781–1788.* Chapel Hill: University of North Carolina Press, 1961.

Marshall, Thomas Maitland, ed. *The Life and Papers of Frederick Bates.* 2 vols. St. Louis: Missouri Historical Society, 1926.

Masson, Louis F. A. *Les Bourgeois de la Companie du Nord-ouest: Recits de voyages, lettres et rapports inedits relatifs au Nord-ouest canadien.* New York: Antiquarian Press, 1960.

Mattes, Merrill J. *Colter's Hell & Jackson's Hole.* 1962; Yellowstone Library and Museum Association, 1980.

McDonald of Garth, John. "Autobiographical Notes." *Les Bourgeois de la Companie du Nord-ouest: Recits de voyages, lettres et rapports inedits relatifs au Nord-ouest canadien.* Vol. 2. Edited by Louis F. A. Masson. New York: Antiquarian Press, 1960.

Melton, Buckner F., Jr. *Aaron Burr: Conspiracy to Treason.* New York: John Wiley & Sons, 2002.

Merk, Frederick. *The Oregon Question: Essays in Anglo-American Diplomacy and Politics.* Cambridge: Harvard University Press, 1967.

Moreau, William E. *The Writings of David Thompson.* Vol. 1. *The Travels, 1850 Version.* Toronto: McGill-Queen's University Press, 2009.

Morris, Larry E. *The Fate of the Corps: What Became of the Lewis and Clark Explorers after the Expedition.* New Haven, CT: Yale University Press, 2004.

Morton, Arthur S., ed. *The Journal of Duncan M'Gillivray of the Northwest Company at Fort George on the Saskatchewan, 1794–1795.* 1929; Fairfield, WA: Ye Galleon Press, 1989.

Moulton, Gary F., series ed. *The Journals of the Lewis & Clark Expedition.* 13 vols. Lincoln: University of Nebraska Press, 1983–2001.

Munsel, Joel, comp. *The Annals of Albany.* 10 vols. Albany: Joel Munsell, 1871.

Nasatir, Abraham P., ed. *Before Lewis and Clark: Documents Illustrating the History of the Missouri 1785–1804.* 1952; Lincoln: University of Nebraska Press, 1990.

Nisbet, Jack. *Mapmaker's Eye: David Thompson on the Columbia Plateau.* Pullman: Washington State University, 2005.

———. *Sources of the River: Tracking David Thompson across Western North America.* Seattle: Sasquatch Books, 1994.

BIBLIOGRAPHY

Oglesby, Richard Edward. *Manuel Lisa and the Opening of the Missouri Fur Trade.* Norman: University of Oklahoma Press, 1984.

Patie, Lois McClellan, and Gene McClellan, comps. *The Descendents of Michael and Jane (Henry) McClellan of Colrain, Mass.* Bakersfield, CA: G. McClellan, 1997.

Payette, B., comp. *The Oregon Country under the Union Jack.* Montreal: Payette Radio Limited, 1962.

Powell, William H. *List of Officers of the Army of the United States from 1779 to 1900.* 1900; Detroit: Gale Research, 1967.

Quaif, Milo Milton, ed. *The Journals of Captain Meriwether Lewis and Sergeant John Ordway.* Madison: Publications of the State Historical Society of Wisconsin, 1916.

Robertson, James Alexander. *Louisiana under the Rule of Spain, France and the United States, 1785–1807.* Cleveland: Arthur H. Clark, 1911.

Rollins, Philip Ashton, ed. *The Discovery of the Oregon Trail: Robert Stuart's Narratives.* New York: Charles Scribner's Sons, 1935.

Ronda, James P. *Astoria and Empire.* Lincoln: University of Nebraska Press, 1990.

———. *Lewis and Clark among the Indians.* Lincoln and London: University of Nebraska Press, 1984.

Shreve, Royal Ornan. *The Finished Scoundrel: General James Wilkinson, Sometime Commander-in-Chief of the Army of the United States, Who Made Intrigue a Trade and Treason a Profession.* Indianapolis: Bobbs, 1933.

Smith, James Morton, ed. *The Republic of Letters: The Correspondence of Thomas Jefferson and James Madison 1776–1826.* 3 vols. New York: Norton, 1995.

Spaulding, Kenneth A., ed. *Alexander Ross: The Fur Hunters of the Far West.* 1855; Norman: University of Oklahoma Press, 1956.

Stewart, Edgar I., and James R. Stewart, eds. *The Columbia River . . . by Ross Cox.* Norman: University of Oklahoma Press, 1957.

Sullivan, James et al., eds. *Papers of Sir William Johnson.* 14 vols. Albany: University of the State of New York, 1921–1957.

Syrett, Harold C., ed. *The Papers of Alexander Hamilton.* 26 vols. New York: Columbia University Press, 1961–1975.

Teit, James. "Salishan Tribes of the Western Plateau." *45th Annual Report of the United States Bureau of Ethnology* (1930).

Thorne, Tanis C. *The Many Hands of My Relations: French and Indians on the Lower Missouri.* Columbia: University of Missouri Press, 1996.

Thwaites, Reuben Gold, ed. *The Original Journals of Lewis and Clark.* 1904–1905; New York: Antiquarian Press, 1959.

Tyrrell, J. B., ed. *David Thompson's Narrative of His Explorations in Western America, 1784–1813.* Toronto: Champlain Society, 1916.

Wallace, W. S., ed. *Documents relating to the North West Company.* Toronto: Champlain Society, 1934.

Weber, David J. *The Taos Trappers: The Fur Trade in the Far Southwest, 1540–1846.* Norman: University of Oklahoma Press, 1982.

Weems, John Edward. *Men without Countries: Three Adventurers of the Early Southwest.* Boston: Houghton Mifflin, 1969.

White, M. Catharine, ed. *David Thompson's Journals relating to Montana and Adjacent Regions 1808–12.* Missoula: Montana State University Press, 1950.

Wilkinson, James. *Memoirs of My Own Times.* 4 vols. Philadelphia: A. Small, 1816; New York: AMS Press, 1973.

Wood, W. Raymond, ed. "Journal of John Macdonnell, 1793–1795, Assinibones-River Qu'Appelle." In *Reprints in Anthropology* 28. Lincoln: J. & L. Reprint, 1984.

———. *Prologue to Lewis & Clark: The Mackay and Evans Expedition.* Norman: University of Oklahoma Press, 2003.

Wood, W. Raymond, and Thomas D. Thiessen, eds. *Early Fur Trade on the Northern Plains: Canadian Traders among the Mandans and Hidatsa Indians 1738–1818.* Norman: University of Oklahoma Press, 1985.

Zahniser, Marvin R. *Charles Cotesworth Pinckney: Founding Father.* Chapel Hill: University of North Carolina Press, 1967.

PERIODICALS

Barry, J. Neilson. "Lieutenant Jeremy Pinch." *Oregon Historical Quarterly* 38 (September 1937): 323–27.

Beattie, Judith Hudson. "Indian Maps in the Hudson's Bay Company Archives: A Comparison of Five Area Maps Recorded by Peter Fidler, 1801–1802." *Archivaria* 21 (Winter 1985–1986): 166–75.

Binnema, Theodore. "Old Swan, Big Man, and the Siksika Bands, 1794–1815." *Canadian Historical Review* 77, no. 1 (March 1996): 1–32.

Bradley, James H. "Affairs at Fort Benton, 1831–1869." *Contributions to the Historical Society of Montana* 3 (1900).

———. "Establishment of Ft. Piegan as Told to Me by James Kipp." *Contributions to the Historical Society of Montana* 8 (1917).

Chalfant, S. "Characteristics, Habits and Customs of the Blackfoot Indians." *Contributions to the Historical Society of Montana* 9 (1923).

Cox, Isaac Joslin. "General Wilkinson and His Later Intrigues with the Spanish." *American Historical Review* 19 (July 1914): 794–812.

———. "Opening the Santa Fe Trail." *Missouri Historical Review* 25 (October 1930).

Dickson, Frank H. "Hard on the Heel of Lewis and Clark." *Montana* 26 (January 1976).

Douglas, Jesse S. "Jeremy Pinch and the War Department." *Oregon Historical Quarterly* 39 (December 1938): 425–31.

Dunwiddie, Peter W. "The Nature of the Relationship between the Blackfeet Indians and the Men of the Fur Trade." *Annals of Wyoming* 46 (Spring 1974): 123–34.

Elliott, T. C. "David Thompson's Journeys in Idaho." *Washington Historical Quarterly* 11 (1920).

———. "David Thompson's Journeys in the Pend Oreille Country." *Washington Historical Quarterly* 23 (1932).

———. "The Discovery of the Source of the Columbia River, Narrative of the Expedition to the Kootenae & Flat Bow Indian Countries, on the Sources of the Columbia River, Pacific Ocean, by D. Thompson on behalf of the N. W. Company 1807." *Oregon Historical Quarterly* 26, no. 1 (March 1925).

———. "The Strange Case of David Thompson and Jeremy Pinch." *Oregon Historical Quarterly* 40 (June 1939): 188–91.

Farr, William E. "Going to Buffalo: Indian Hunting Migrations across the Rocky Mountains." *Montana: The Magazine of Western History* (Winter 2003): 2–21.

Flannery, Regina. "The Gros Ventres of Montana, Part 1." *Catholic University of America Anthropological Series* 15 (1953).

Ghent, W. J. "Jeremy Pinch Again." *Oregon Historical Quarterly* 40 (December 1939).

Giannettino, Susan. "The Middleman Role in the Fur Trade: Its Influence on Interethnic Relations on the Saskatchewan-Missouri Plains." *Western Canadian Journal of Anthropology* 7, no. 4 (1977): 22–33.

Jackson, Donald. "Jefferson, Meriwether Lewis, and the Reduction of the United States Army." *Proceedings of the American Philosophical Society* 125, no. 2 (April 1980).

Jackson, John C. "Brandon House and the Mandan Connection." *North Dakota History* 49, no. 1 (Winter 1982): 11–19.

———. "The Fight on Two Medicine River: Who Were Those Indians, and How Many Died." *We Proceeded On: Lewis and Clark Trail Heritage Foundation* 23, no. 1 (February 2006): 14–23.

———. "Old Rivet: The Surviving Member of the Corps of Discovery in the Northwest." *Columbia: The Magazine of Northwest History* 18, no. 2 (Summer 2004).

———. "Revisiting the Colter Legend." *Rocky Mountain Fur Trade Journal* 3 (2009).

Josephy, Alvin M., Jr. "A Man to Match the Mountains." *American Heritage* 11 (October 1960).

———. "The Naming of the Nez Perces." *Montana* 5 (October 1955).

Majors, Harry M. "John McClellan in the Montana Rockies 1807: The First American after Lewis and Clark." *Northwest Discovery: The Journal of Northwest History and Natural History* 2, no. 9 (November–December 1981).

Mattes, Merrill J. "Behind the Legend of Colter's Hell: The Early Exploration of Yellowstone National Park." *Mississippi Valley Historical Review* 36: 251–69.

Moodie, D. W., and Barry Kaye. "The Ac Ko Mok Ki Map." *Beaver* 307 (Spring 1977).

Nicks, John. "David Thompson." *Dictionary of Canadian Biography*: 8:883.

Ross, Frank E. "Early Fur Trade of the Great Northwest." *Oregon Historical Quarterly* 39 (1938): 389–409.

Tyrrell, J. B. "Letter of Roseman and Perch." *Oregon Historical Quarterly* 38 (December 1937): 391–97.

Wells, Merle. "Lewis & Clark's Water Route to the Northwest." *Columbia* (Winter 1994/1995).

Williams, Christina MacDonald Mckenzie. "The Daughter of Angus MacDonald." *Washington Historical Quarterly* 13, no. 2 (April 1922).

INDEX

1816, LOUISIANA PURCHASE AND NORTHWEST TERRITORIES